The Great Big (hunka hunka burnin') ^

CHEESE

Bathroom Reader Vol. 1

The Great Big (hunka hunka burnin') ^ CHEESE

Bathroom Reader Vol. 1

"Have cheese, will flush."
(The cheesiest trivia ever!)

Camille Smith Platt

CRANE HILL
PUBLISHERS

CRANE HILL
PUBLISHERS

The Great Big Cheese Bathroom Reader, Volume 1

Copyright © 2007 by Crane Hill Publishers

Book design by Miles G. Parsons
Illustrations by Tim Rocks, Miles G. Parsons, and Neal Cross

Printed in the United States of America

Library of Congress Cataloging-in-Publication Data

Platt, Camille Smith.
  The Great big cheese bathroom reader / Camille Smith Platt.
    p. cm.
  Vol. 1 is a compliation of four separately published works.
  Contents: p. 1. Real cheesy facts about TV & movies. Real cheesy facts about rock 'n' roll. Real cheesy facts about famous authors. Real cheesy facts about US Presidents
  ISBN-13: 978-1-57587-282-7 (v.1)
  ISBN-10: 1-57587-282-X (v.1)
  1. Curiosities and wonders. I. Title.

  AG105.P69 2007
  031--dc22

2007028236

TABLE OF CONTENTS

Making Good Use of Time

Most of us agree with singer Alicia Keys, who said, "If I want to be alone, some place I can write, I can read, I can pray, I can cry, I can do whatever I want—I go to the bathroom."

The bathroom is the one place where we can be sure we'll spend a few minutes every day, and, unless you have small children, the one place you can be alone. Your time there is your own. In today's fast-paced society, getting a few minutes alone anywhere is no small thing. Over the course of a year, it may even be a very big thing, adding up to as much as two weeks of time.

Now you can use that time productively, be enlightened, and even learn some fun facts with Volume 1 of *The Great Big Cheese Bathroom Reader*. Be entertained and be informed with this handy book that'll help you use your precious time wisely.

And it offers variety, from the purely want-to-know details of modern pop culture, to the need-to-know facts about men who have served in the country's highest office. Each section is divided so you can easily read little bits at a time, or more, depending on your schedule. No push to finish a chapter before you quit.

In "Real Cheesy Facts About: TV & Movies," you'll get all the scoop and back stories on your favorite stars and find out what really happened during the making of classic movies. Learn the real names of celebrities, as well as what happened to child stars of yesterday when their stars stopped shining.

If your interest is music, you'll enjoy the "Real Cheesy Facts About: Rock 'n' Roll." Find out the nitty-gritty about your favorite musician's brush with the law, famous firsts, and controversial moments that produced a sour note or two.

For a more academic topic, "Real Cheesy Facts About: Famous Authors" reveals what some of your favorite wordsmiths wouldn't want you to know about them. For instance, did you know that Ernst Hemingway's mother tried to pass him off as a girl during his early years, even referring to him as Ernestine? And did you know that Lewis Carroll of *Alice in Wonderland* fame was actually one of two men accused of being involved in the infamous Jack the Ripper serial killings?

Finally, "Real Cheesy Facts About: U.S. Presidents" will offer some insight into men who have been at the helm as our nation. Did you know that George Washington had to borrow money to attend his own inauguration? And speaking of the father of our country, did you know that some records indicate that he was not the first president at all?

Impress your friends, your family, and even yourself with the assortment of little-known facts you can learn in just a few minutes a day with this amusing volume.

Real Cheesy Facts About: TV & Movies

Chapter 1

★

Stories from the Set

Stories from the Set

★ ★ ★ ★ ★ ★ ★ ★ ★ ★ ★ ★ ★ ★ ★ ★ ★

Some pretty unusual things happen on the sets of movies and television shows—props get mixed up, and costars posing as lovers in a script can't stand each other in real life. Directors do their best to deal with prima donnas, and fans turn their backs on hosts for the sake of a big settlement. You haven't heard it all until you've heard these wacky tales from some of the most popular sets of all time.

On the classic TV series *I Love Lucy*, the Ricardos supposedly lived at 623 E. 68th Street in Manhattan. However, the real E. 68th Street ends at 600, meaning their building would be located in the East River.

★ ★ ★ ★ ★

LUCY, YOU'VE GOT SOME COMPLAINING TO DO

A veteran hypocrite of feel-good sitcoms, *I Love Lucy* may have been full of canned laughter in the 1950s—but **thanks to actress Vivian Vance, the moods on set weren't as chipper as one might imagine**. Before she was hired as Lucy's quick-witted neighbor, Ethel Mertz, Vance suffered a bout with depression and multiple psychosomatic diseases that led her to quit the popular show *The Voice of the Turtle*.

BEFORE SHE WAS A STAR...
VIVIAN VANCE

Born Vivian Roberta Jones in Cherryvale, Kansas, in 1909, she had dreams of being a star from a young age. Her strictly religious parents refused to let her pursue her passion, but at age sixteen she left home to be a stage actress regardless. After a stint of bad luck, she gave up and returned to Kansas—but the early retirement wouldn't last long. In her twenties, she changed her name to Vivian Vance and gave it another shot on Broadway alongside Jimmy Durante and Bob Hope.

Regardless, Desi Arnaz was a fan of her work and offered her the part. However, Lucy wasn't all that excited about her new costar.

Eager to be the only beauty with a major role, Ball had initially envisioned Ethel as a chunky housewife in smelly slippers. Vance was hot stuff—and just a few years older than she. In the end, Ball caved to her husband's vision for the comedy and agreed that Vance would have to do.

TIDBITS OF I LOVE LUCY TRIVIA

- The show was based on Lucille Ball and Richard Denning's popular radio program, *My Favorite Husband*. When it was turned into a sitcom, however, Ball dumped Denning for her real-life husband, Cuban-born Desi Arnaz. Although producers feared American audiences would not buy into a mixed marriage, Ball got her way.

- Ethel's middle name changed multiple times during the show's airing. It switched from Mae to Roberta to Louise.

- The kitchen at the Mertz's apartment was shown in only one episode.

- Lucille Ball liked to name new characters after people from her real life. Marion Strong, for example, was one of her friends from Jamestown, New York, and Carolyn Appleby was one of her old teachers. Ball also named places on the show after favorite locales from her personal life. Lucy and Ricky were married at Byram River Beagle Club in Greenwich, Connecticut—just like Ball and Arnaz.

If the tension between the two leading ladies wasn't enough, actor William Frawley (who played Ethel's husband, Fred Mertz) was just as much a grump offscreen as he was onscreen. He was chronically annoyed by the detailed practice Vance would put into perfecting her character. He also complained about their more than twenty year age difference. To Frawley, the spread was simply too great to pull off being her spouse.

Seems like Lucy may have some 'splaining to do about some things going on at her former home. Though she died during surgery on April 26, 1989, at the age of 77, some people say she's still living at 100 North Roxbury Drive. Current owners say that windows are broken by unseen forces, loud voices are heard from the attic, and furniture and other objects move around.

But Lucy's not the only one of her generation that's having a hard time leaving the spotlight. Here's a few of her fellow actors that have been seen still taking curtain calls:

- **Montgomery Cliff**—He's been seen at the Hollywood Roosevelt Hotel, particularly in room 928, where he paced the floor as he learned his lines for *A Place in the Sun* and *From Here to Eternity*.

- **Marilyn Monroe**—Also a frequent guest at the Hollywood Roosevelt, where she's seen reflected in a full-length mirror that used to be by her pool. She is sometimes seen at the home where she took a fatal dose of sleeping pills, where she reportedly told psychics that her death was an accident, not suicide.

- **Ozzie Nelson**—The spirit of this family patriarch has been seen at the home where he and Harriet lived for forty years. His spirit is not as well mannered as he was on his TV series *The Adventures of Ozzie and Harriet*. He's said to open and close doors, and to turn on faucets and lights.

★ ★ ★ ★ ★

LIGHTS, CAMERA, ABSENT

I Love Lucy wasn't the only set to struggle with tensions between cast members. While taping episodes of *The Honeymooners*, **actor Jackie Gleason refused to rehearse,** explaining that in order for his comedy to be off-the-wall, each performance needed to be fresh. He carried such power on set (he even got the nickname "The Great One") that he got his way, and everyone else had to rehearse their lines without him. The situation put so much stress on costar Audrey Meadows that she often cried out in frustration. Not knowing what to expect when Gleason took the stage, she had no way to fully prepare for each scene.

★ ★ ★ ★ ★

ADDING ALCOHOL TO INJURY

The Bourne Identity star **Matt Damon has come a long way** since his one-line debut in the 1988 film *Mystic Pizza* with fellow Hollywood fledgling Julia Roberts—and no one goes to extremes to prepare for time on the set like he does. On more than one occasion, Damon has submitted himself to injuries and desperate drunks to get his characters just right:

- He damaged most of the major organs in his body when he fasted—without being under a doctor's supervision—to lose nearly forty pounds for his role in *Courage Under Fire.*

19

- He separated a rib while practicing his golf swing for *The Legend of Bagger Vance*.

- He worked as a bartender in Knoxville, Tennessee, to study up on Southern accents and mixing drinks.

Actor Tom Hanks is another Hollywood superstar willing to go to extremes to prepare for roles. He has…

- Dislocated his shoulder falling through a rotten floor while helping Steven Spielberg pick out a location to tape the HBO show *Band of Brothers* in Germany.

- Gained thirty pounds eating ice cream to prepare for his role in *A League of Their Own* and lost thirty pounds to prepare for his role in *Philadelphia*.

- Got a staph infection in his leg that required emergency surgery while filming overseas.

- However daring Hanks may be, there is one thing he refused to do—he would not learn how to write with his left hand to accurately portray his character in *Apollo 13*.

★ ★ ★ ★ ★

I CRY WITH MY LITTLE EYE

Jay Leno has long been a leading funnyman of late night comedy. However, during one taping in 1998, unsuspecting *Tonight Show* audience member Stewart Gregory of Cincinnati, Ohio, was smacked in the face by a free

T-shirt the crew had fired into the crowd with an air gun. Instead of praising his prize like most guests, Gregory brought a lawsuit against Leno and NBC, claiming he had been "battered" and "forcefully struck." Just what did he need to get over the little incident? More than $25,000 in damages to cover his emotional distress, humiliation, and unending pain and suffering.

★ ★ ★ ★ ★

Like Pulling Teeth, Literally

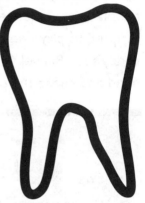

While preparing to hit the set to tape the 1984 war flick *Birdy*, **Nicolas Cage decided that the only way to research the true emotional condition of a maimed war veteran was to submit himself to something terribly painful.** In order to fully understand his character, he had several teeth pulled without novocaine. He later sacrificed his pucker (and his pride) for the sake of character development. In the late 1980s, he turned down a plastic prop bug and actually agreed to eat a live cockroach for *Vampire's Kiss*.

A KOOSH TO THE PUCKER

Rosie O'Donnell suffered a nasty $3 million lawsuit when a seventy-one-year-old widow complained of being hit in the mouth with a Koosh ball while attending a taping of Rosie's show in 2001. Not only did it cause her gums to bleed and swell, she contested, but the pain made her spend Christmas alone at home and put a damper on her relationship with her boyfriend.

★ ★ ★ ★ ★

COX'S IDENTITY CRISIS

They say first impressions are everything, but actress Courteney Cox would probably disagree. Few people know that she was originally scripted to play twenty-something daddy's girl Rachel Green on the sitcom *Friends*, but she changed her mind and chose the part of the obsessive-compulsive Monica Geller

TIDBITS OF FRIENDS TRIVIA

- The show was originally titled *The Six of Us*.

- Phoebe's porn star twin sister, Ursula, first appeared in a reoccurring role on the NBC sister sitcom *Mad About You*. Producers worried that viewers might be confused when they realized actress Lisa Kudrow was playing in two similar sitcoms at once, so they wrote Ursula into the Friends script to make light of the situation. They got even wittier when they had Helen Hunt make a cameo in a *Friends* episode mistaking Phoebe for Ursula.

- Gunther from Central Perk Coffee Shop, played by struggling actor James Michael Tyler, was just an extra during the first season of the show. He only had one line all year, but when producers realized he was the only extra who could actually work an espresso machine (in real life he had a part time job at a coffee shop), they made his part permanent.

instead. Cox says she just couldn't turn down Monica's sarcasm and strength. She told producers she related to Geller more, and the part was hers. As she settled into the new role in the early 1990s, Cox said that she and her cast mates had no clue how popular their sitcom was until they traveled to London to shoot the episode in which Ross and Emily get married. Paparazzi were everywhere, and they suddenly realized they were big stars.

★ ★ ★ ★ ★

I'VE GOT A GOLDEN DANCE NUMBER

When brainstorming choreography for the 1971 hit musical *Willy Wonka and the Chocolate Factory* starring Gene Wilder, Director Mel Stuart got a little nauseated when it came to coming up with the characters' dance moves for the song "I've Got a Golden Ticket." Because Charlie and Grandpa Joe had just found the fifth and final ticket for a

THE CANDY MAN CAN'T

Quaker Oats originally bought the rights to *Charlie and the Chocolate Factory* from author Roald Dahl and then agreed to fully finance the making of the film in exchange to use it as a marketing ploy for their new candy bar, the Wonka Bar. However, for various reasons, including a faulty formula, the chocolate bar never made it to the marketplace.

grand tour of the mysterious local candy factory, choreographer Howard Jeffery felt a little pressure to make the number a major production—but Stuart just couldn't imagine the entire town leaving work to sing and dance in the street in celebration of a little boy's candy bar. Instead, he opted for a simple tune… in a dilapidated shack with Charlie's four bedridden grandparents—who, according to the plotline, hadn't gotten up in the last twenty years. Not exactly what Hollywood would call an exciting Oscar-winning moment, but it fit the budget (and Stuart's idea of reality).

It's been rumored that Fred Astaire almost played Willy Wonka in the original *Willy Wonka and the Chocolate Factory*. Director Mel Stuart was looking for someone nutty, screwy and loony, and "someone who could sing." However, Astaire was never in the running for the part. The film's composer, Leslie Bricusse, was indeed a good friend of the famed dancer and apparently had lightheartedly discussed the opportunity with Astaire, but if he was interested, the news never got back to the film's producers or director.

Astaire was seventy-two at the time—too old—and they couldn't have afforded him anyway. They considered Joel Grey, who had recently acted in *Cabaret* on Broadway, but he was only 5'5"… the same height as some of the children.

Gene Wilder, who was finally chosen for the part, wasn't yet a comedic legend, but he was working on it. His persona was slowly gaining fame through his parts in *Bonnie and Clyde* and *The Producers*. Dave Wopler took one look at Wilder's wirey hair and sneaky grin and said, "That's a Willy Wonka."

★ ★ ★ ★ ★

GURU TO THE DUKE

The spitting image of a traditional cowboy, Wyatt Earp was quiet and stern-faced, but approachable. Living in Los Angeles, California, in the early 1900s, he often dropped by Hollywood movie sets to visit friends, and eventually befriended silent western film star William S. Hart. A sucker for butting in on rehearsals, Earp did what he could to teach Hart how to draw his gun with greater speed. By the time he was nearly eighty years old, Earp had such a traditional look of Western wisdom that he impressed prop man Marion Morrison on the set of yet another film. A young gun in the movie business, Morrison was affected by him forever—he changed his name to John Wayne and scored his first starring role in *The Big Trail*. Later, Wayne would tell friends that during his many years as a prop man, he had studied how to act like a true cowboy by simply watching Earp.

★ ★ ★ ★ ★

AN ELEPHANT NEVER REGRETS

When a cooky clown makes a cameo on a classic TV Land sitcom, viewers are usually in for a cheesy sight gag. One sidesplitting episode of **The Mary Tyler**

John Wayne is the record holder for the actor with the most leading parts in films. He starred in 142 movies during his lifetime.

***Moore Show* features the sad but laughable death of Chuckles the Clown,** who was crushed by an elephant while parading around in a peanut suit. When Moore first read the script, however, she didn't find the scene very funny. Regardless of her ploy to stop the merciless moment, the rest of the cast and crew got so tickled by the writers' creativity that they just couldn't stop laughing when they saw the trample take place on set. Moore lost her battle to change the scene, and Chuckles' fate was sealed.

★ ★ ★ ★ ★

A BAREFOOT BEAUTY

Not one to hide her cute personality and quirky sense of humor, *Live with Regis and Kelly* cohost **Kelly Ripa often hosts entire episodes of her bubbly morning show barefoot.** Viewers must not mind pondering her pedicured toes, because she was named one of *People* magazine's "25 Most Intriguing People" in 2001 and has been nominated for eight Daytime Emmy Awards.

BEFORE SHE WAS A STAR... KELLY RIPA

Kelly Ripa could be seen shaking her rump as a regular on the afternoon teen music program *Dance Party USA* in the late 1980s. Just a few years later, her first television role was as gothic teen Hayley Vaughan on the soap opera *All My Children.*

★ ★ ★ ★ ★

DRIVING MRS. BRADY

On the set of *The Brady Bunch*, during several seasons of taping, **Mike and Carol Brady sported a confusing, inconsistent array of autos**.

DOORS TO NOWHERE
On the set of *The Brady Bunch*, the door at the top of the stairs is never opened.

For the first two seasons, the family boasted a sporty blue 1969 Plymouth Fury convertible and a more practical, less-than-impressive 1969 Plymouth Satellite station wagon. The following year, however, the Plymouth Fury was replaced with a blue 1971 Plymouth Barracuda, and the station wagon was magically updated to a 1971 model.

While Carol's station wagon stuck around for a few more seasons, Mike Brady just couldn't keep a car. He may have been

A VERY BRADY TRESPASSING

Just inside the city limits of Los Angeles, California (11222 Dilling Street, to be exact), lies the split-level home that will forever be flocked with tourists hoping to peek through the blinds to catch a glimpse of any traces of the Bradys left inside. Regardless of remodeling projects done by previous owners to make the house less recognizable, unwelcome trespassers continue to poke around the yard. Unfortunately for the peeping toms, they may catch a glimpse of the current owner, but they will never spy any props from the show. The cast never actually filmed there. The house was used for exterior shots only.

leasing, but the plotline didn't give any hints to viewers who may have been confused by the mysterious upgrades.

The vehicles just kept switching on set without an explanation, which by 1972 were Chevrolets instead of Chryslers.

- 1972-1973—Mike Brady drives a 1972 Chevrolet Impala (blue).

- 1973-1974—Mike Brady drives a 1973 Chevrolet Caprice Classic convertible (maroon with white interior). Halfway through the season, the car is suddenly red with a sleek *black* interior.

- 1988—For the film *A Very Brady Christmas*, both the ever-upgrading Chevrolet and the family station wagon disappear in exchange for a 1988 Chrysler LeBaron.

- 1990—For the short-lived series *The Bradys*, Mike drives the same car as in *A Very Brady Christmas*, but the station wagon (now a 1990 Buick Estate) reappears as the car Marcia swerves about in when she has too much to drink.

★ ★ ★ ★ ★

WHERE EVERYBODY KNOWS YOU'RE LATE

Some say you can tell a man by the clothes he wears, but on the set of *Cheers,* actress **Shelley Long took the tip to the extreme.** She gave her costars a healthy dose of stress every time she headed back to her dressing room to update her duds. Always labeled as the black sheep among the bar buddies, Long was often blamed for delaying taping because she took so long to change from one outfit to another. Her tardiness got so bad that the crew built her a new dressing room closer to the set, hoping it would keep her from blaming her tardiness on the long walk. In the end, the writers just started keeping her scenes to one twenty-four-hour period so there wouldn't be a need to change clothes mid-taping.

★ ★ ★ ★ ★

PEE PEE RAYMOND REMINISCES

Directors have long discovered that not every laughable thing said on set is fictional. In one episode of the award-winning sitcom *Everybody Loves Raymond*, **Ray reminisces on his childhood nickname "Pee Pee Raymond,"** which credited him with using the bathroom on home base during a Little League baseball game. The tale is actually a true story from Romano's childhood. Carrying the joke over to the scriptwriters, the comedian even changed the

TIDBITS OF EVERYBODY LOVES RAYMOND TRIVIA

- The cereal that always appears on top of Ray and Debra Barone's refrigerator is a box of Flutie Flakes.

- Although Raymond's brother, Robert, is cast as four years older, he is actually three years younger in real life.

- The actress who plays Robert's wife, Amy, is the wife of the show's executive producer.

credits at the end of the episode to replace the usual "Ray Romano" with "Pee Pee Raymond."

A long-time comedian, Romano is also known to joke during filming about how jealous he is of fellow funnyman Jerry Seinfeld, who celebrated nine years of filming his own sitcom Seinfeld before it went off the air in 1998. Since then, *Everybody Loves Raymond* has celebrated the same success. Besides Seinfeld, however, Romano says comedy legend Bill Cosby is his greatest influence. In fact, Cosby once talked decision-makers at CBS into moving *Everybody Loves Raymond* from airing Friday nights to airing Mondays in order to help boost ratings. His generous suggestion was a hit, and Romano's sitcom became one of the network's most popular shows ever. Before the sitcom aired its final episode in 2005, Romano was reportedly the highest paid television actor in history. In 2001, alone he made $19 million.

> **BEFORE HE WAS A STAR...**
> **RAY ROMANO**
> Born December 21, 1957, in Queens, New York, Ray Romano had dreams of becoming an accountant before giving up number crunching in exchange for something more laughable—comedy. As his career blossomed, Romano was originally cast as Joe in the short-lived sitcom *NewsRadio*, but was fired when executives decided his dry humor didn't mesh with the rest of the cast.

> From his very first standup routine, comedian Ray Romano has been an avid supporter the New York Police Department, where his brother is a sergeant. In 2000, Romano won $125,000 for the NYPD's D.A.R.E. Program on, *Who Wants To Be A Millionaire*.

★ ★ ★ ★ ★

CROSS FOR GUN CONTROL

Rosie O'Donnell was once the queen of daytime television and K-Mart commercials across the globe. Publicly announcing her sexual orientation as a lesbian may have caused her days as a talk show host to hit the skids, but it was her love affair with gun control that took her off the set for good. After writing (and starring in) a handful of commercials for the one-stop shop K-Mart with friend Penny Marshall, O'Donnell called it quits when she realized the chain sold more guns than nearly any other store.

★ ★ ★ ★ ★

PINK SLIP FOR POSING NUDE

After sowing her wild oats posing for a nine-page spread in the December 1993 issue of *Playboy*, **actress Shannen Doherty was sent packing** from the set of the popular sitcom *Beverly Hills, 90210*. Executives were embarrassed, and she was so bitter for losing her job that when The Fox Network aired a one-hour reunion special years later, she refused to give them permission to show footage of her. To avoid breaking copyright laws,

DID YOU KNOW

Beverly Hills High School is actually zoned for the area code 90212.

the network had to blur out her face from every flashback. Five years later, Doherty pulled herself together to play the telekinesis big sister witch Prue on the WB sitcom *Charmed*. However, after costar Alyssa Milano began getting more press attention, a jealous Doherty tried to quit the show. Producers wouldn't let her out of the contract, but the animosity between the two stars became so unbearable that Doherty got her wish and got fired anyway. She would later go on to say that she regretted wasting three years of her life on a sitcom "for 12 year olds." Can anyone say "bitter?"

★ ★ ★ ★ ★

HARD LESSONS

Animal House (1978)
The Set: The University of Oregon

Because of his tight budget for the film, Universal Pictures director John Landis decided that instead of building a set, he would use an actual college campus. After being turned down by the

University of Missouri-Columbia's president when he read the script, the University of Oregon's dean agreed. He had previously been the president of a small California college, and had denied permission to film *The Graduate* at his school. He didn't make that mistake twice. The only off-campus building filmed

> The Motion Picture Production Code, self-imposed guidelines for the industry, were published in 1934, and continued to influence Hollywood until the 1950s.

was an old halfway house for criminals which was used for exterior shots of the Delta house. When it was torn down in 1986, the bricks were sold as souvenirs for $5 each.

★ ★ ★ ★ ★

Famous Set Locales

The Birds (1963)
The Set: Bodega Bay, California

One of Hitchcock's most classic horror flicks, *The Birds* was filmed just north of San Francisco. The haunting house still stands as a private home today.

The Bridges of Madison County (1995)
The Set: Winterset, Iowa

Located just thirty miles southwest of Des Moines, only six out of the nineteen bridges originally built in the town and shown in the film *The Bridges of Madison County* are still standing today. The farmhouse where Italian housewife Francesca (Meryl Streep) lived became a tourist attraction until a fire in 2003.

The Alamo (1960)
The Set: Mexico and Texas

Made for a jaw dropping $8 million, *The Alamo* was the most expensive movie ever made when it came out in 1960. In fact, filming got so costly that director John Wayne moved the set out of Mexico to a four hundred-acre ranch in Bracketville, Texas (about a hundred miles west of San Antonio). The original set still exists and is used for filming other movies.

Carrie (1976)
The Set: Hermosa Beach Community Center

The official backdrop for the fiery prom scene where high school reject Carrie lost her cool and wreaked havoc on her teasing classmates, the community center in Hermosa Beach, California, was home to one of the most chilling horror flicks of all time. Today, the gym looks nearly the same as it did during filming—minus the spilled bucket of pig's blood that fell from the sky onto the jaded prom queen played by Sissy Spacek.

Fast Times at Ridgemont High (1982)
The Set: Canoga Park High School in Canoga Park, California, and Van Nuys High School in Van Nuys, California

Written by Hollywood mogul Cameron Crowe, *Fast Times at Ridgemont High* used the two high schools for filming, and the set for mall scenes was Sherman Oaks Galleria in Sherman Oaks, California, which has since been renovated into an office complex.

Ghostbusters (1984)
The Set: New York and Los Angeles

While most of the scenes were shot in California, the exterior shots of the Ghostbuster headquarters were of a fire station located at 14 North Moore Street in New York City. The exterior shots of the apartment building where Dana Barrett (Sigourney Weaver) lived were on Central Park West.

DID YOU KNOW

Rumors have long suggested that the Ghostbusters logo was drawn based on the likeness of actor Jim Belushi.

Jurassic Park (1993)
The Set: Hawaiian islands of Oahu and Kauai

This daring dinosaur hit was filmed across the beautiful Garden Isles of Hawaii. The giant gates at the opening of Jurassic Park were off Blue Hole Canyon, and the electrical fence that T-Rex tore through was in Kauai's Olokele Valley. The "Badlands" scene at the beginning of the movie was not filmed in Utah, as implied, but at Red Rock Canyon in California's Mojave Desert.

Rocky (1976)
The Set:

- The gym where the film's opening fight scene takes place—Oscar de la Hoya Boxing Youth Center in Los Angeles, California

- The butchery where Rocky trained for his title fight punching hanging beef—Shamrock Meats, Inc. in Vernon, California

- The museum where Rocky ran to the top of the famous sixty-eight-step staircase pumping his arms in victory—Philadelphia Museum of Modern Art in Philadelphia, Pennsylvania

- Famous fight scenes with Apollo Creed—Olympic Auditorium in Los Angeles and Los Angeles Memorial Sports Arena

★ ★ ★ ★ ★

OTHER FAMOUS SETS

- **National Lampoon's Vacation**—Family vacation to Wally World was filmed at Six Flags Magic Mountain in Valencia, California.

- **Top Gun**—Eatery where Anthony Edwards pounds out "Great Balls of Fire" on the piano is the Kansas City Barbeque Restaurant in San Diego, California.

- **When Harry Met Sally**—The restaurant where Meg Ryan had her fake orgasm was filmed in Katz's Deli in East Village, New York City. Today a plaque in the deli reads, "You are sitting where Harry met Sally."

- **Raiders of the Lost Ark**—While most of the film was shot in Kauai, France, England, and Tunisia, the classroom where Indiana (actor Harrison Ford) teaches archaeology was located at the Conservatory of Music at the University of the Pacific in Stockton, California.

★ ★ ★ ★ ★

ACCIDENTS AND TRAGEDIES ON THE SET

- *Harrison Ford*—In January of 2003, this veteran actor was riding in a car driven by co-star Josh Hartnett during filming of his movie, *Hollywood Homicide*, when the vehicle went out of control and hit a wall. A source on the set admitted that the scenario should have been done by stuntmen, but "Harrison insists on doing all of his stunts, so his co-star Josh didn't want to be left out." The pair was lucky—they came through the incident with only a bump on the head and some pulled muscles between the two of them.

- *Brandon Lee*—An actor who earned acclaim in his own right, Lee was the son of legendary martial artist and actor Bruce Lee and Linda Emery. Bruce died suddenly from a cerebral edema when Brandon was eight. Young Brandon was often described as "a handful" by his mother, not to mention his teachers. At school, he was "either the teacher's pet, or the teacher's nightmare."

  Expelled from Chadwick School three months before graduating, Brandon followed his father into acting, and was part of the American New Theatre group founded by his friend John Lee Hancock. His first movie was *Legacy of Rage*, which also included Bolo Yeung, who had appeared in his father's last film.

Later, in Los Angeles, he was asked to audition for a role in *Kung Fu: The Movie*, a feature-length television movie. Lee got the role, due to the increasing posthumous fame of his father. He would become an important figure in not one, but two, sequels to the famous TV series.

Other acting assignments followed and Lee signed a multi-picture deal with 20th Century Fox. In 1992, he landed the role of Eric Draven, who returned from death to avenge his and his fiancée's murders, in the movie adaptation of *The Crow*, a popular underground comic book. Shooting began on February 1, 1993, Lee's twentieth birthday. It would be his last.

On March 31, 1993, the fifty-second day of a sixty-day shooting schedule, Lee's scene called for him to confront his fiancée's attacker, and subsequently be shot. Since production was slightly behind schedule, dummy cartridges would be made from real cartridges. The effects technician dismmantled them by removing the bullets, emptying out the gunpowder, detonating the primer, and reinserting the bullets. Some blanks were created by replacing gunpowder with firework powder, and not inserting the bullets. Though Lee was shot with a cartridge without its own bullet, there was a bullet in the gun from a previous shot, which was propelled out by the blank cartridge's explosion. Lee was shot and severely wounded, and the whole thing was caught on film at Carolco Studios in Wilmington, North Carolina. By the time the wound in Lee's abdomen was discovered, he was unconscious. Doctors fought for five hours to save his life, but he was pronounced dead at 1:04 p.m. His funeral was held several days later, and he was buried next to his father in Lake View Cemetery, Capitol Hill, in Seattle, Washington.

- **Eva Longoria**—This desperate housewife was rushed to the hospital when a piece of equipment fell on her head during filming of an episode of the hit series. She was taken to a nearby hospital, but released after treatment. Her spokesperson assured everyone, "She's just fine. It was a big jolt but she has a hard head. She's tough!"

- **Vic Morrow**—When Morrow died tragically in a helicopter accident during the filming of *Twilight Zone—the Movie*, Hollywood lost a veteran actor whose skills, honed over a lifetime of acting, would be sorely missed. But if that loss weren't enough, two children—Myca Dinh Le and Renee Shin-Yi Chen—were also killed.

  Morrow was not a fan of helicopters anyway. Oddly enough, earlier in his career, when he was filming *Dirty Mary Crazy Larry*, there was a scene where he was supposed to fly in a helicopter. He said, "I'm not getting up in the helicopter. . . I have a premonition that I'm going to get killed in a helicopter crash."

  That prophecy came true at 2:20 a.m. on July 23, 1982, as the final shot of a *Twilight* sequence was being recorded. Morrow was supposed to have the two children in his arms as he waded across a knee-deep river. A village under siege was in the background as the helicopter came to rescue them. Director John Landis ordered the helicopter increasingly lower, until it was finally a mere twenty-four feet above the water.

As explosions were going off all around, the pilot lost control of the helicopter, which came to rest on top of Renee, crushing her. Morrow and the other child, Myca Le, were decapitated by the forty-foot blades.

The announcement was immediately made, "Leave your equipment where it is. Everyone go home. Please, everyone go home!"

Vic Morrow's funeral took place two days later. John Landis gave a eulogy before Morrow's burial at Hillside Memorial Park. Landis also attended funerals held for the children on July 27. Renee is buried in Forest Lawn, Glendale, Myca Le in buried in Cerritos.

On a more positive note, the accident led to massive reforms in U.S. child labor laws and safety regulations on movie sets in California.

Chapter 2

Regret: Hollywood's Biggest Bombs

Regret: Hollywood's Biggest Bombs

★ ★ ★ ★ ★ ★ ★ ★ ★ ★ ★ ★ ★ ★ ★ ★ ★ ★

To quote German Chancellor Konrad Adenauer, "In view of the fact that God limited the intelligence of man, it seems unfair that he did not also limit his stupidity." There are easier ways of getting attention than by royally screwing up what should have been an amazing movie. But some directors just didn't get the memo. Love 'em or hate 'em, you just can't help but ask: How could so many good ideas go so wrong?

There were plans for big-name *M*A*S*H* stars like Alan Alda to make special guest appearances in the second season of *AfterMASH*, but the show was canceled before any such plans could be carried out.

★ ★ ★ ★ ★

BUTCHERING HISTORY: BIG SCREEN STORYTELLING GONE WRONG

History shmistory— who needs the truth when the embellished version sounds so much more romantic? Life is all too often too boring to make it to the big screen, so these films were beefed up a little… well… maybe more than a little.

- ***Edison the Man*** (1940)—In this classic historical tale, inventor Thomas Edison pops the question to his girlfriend in a whim of romanticism—he taps the big question in Morse code on a pipe for her to hear upstairs. Unfortunately, he never did such a thing. Edison did propose to his second wife in Morse code, but it wasn't tapped out on a pipe—he tapped it out on the palm of her hand.

- ***Ben-Hur*** (1959)—Jesus plays a big role in the underlying plot of this film, but the director forgot to do his math when penciling in his list of minor characters. When Pilate gives word of the upcoming chariot race, he drops a few names of contestants traveling from Corinth and Carthage. However, historically speaking, both of those cities were demolished in 146 BCE—before Jesus was ever born.

- **Braveheart** (1995)—William Wallace may have gone down in history for his famous "Freedom!" scream, but the film about his heroic efforts for the autonomy of Scotland tends to stretch the truth a bit. At the end of the movie, after brave Wallace has been martyred, the Scots rush out to battle the Brits right away. In reality, however, the battle didn't occur until nine years later.

- **Rudy** (1993)—Although the film was set in the mid-1970s, the director seemed to be too lazy to take out references to the 1980s and 1990s. Many of the cars that drive about on set are late model Toyota Corollas and Ford Explorers. In the opening scene, modern streetlights and floodlights line the road. Also, when Rudy goes outside to get his mail, Waddicks Café is in the background—a restaurant that wasn't named "Waddicks" until the 1990s.

★ ★ ★ ★ ★

SITCOMS THAT STUNK: TELEVISION'S WORST SPIN-OFFS

Seinfeld. M*A*S*H*. Cheers. The Brady Bunch. **Some sitcoms touch the American public** so deeply, or make them laugh so uncontrollably, that they go down in history as unforgettable. However, there can be too much of a good thing. These spin-off sitcoms proved that it's not always a good idea to go for Round Two.

AfterMASH
Spin-off of: M*A*S*H*

Why It Flopped: After a mere fourteen months on the air, every last clip of *AfterMash* hit the cutting room floor. Yep, they got canceled. So why didn't America care for the continuation of war, guns, and medical supplies? Maybe because the show was no longer about war, guns, and medical supplies. Following up from a hit show about a surgical hospital during the Korean War, it just didn't fly when the plotline was moved to the suburbia of Riverbend, Missouri. If that weren't enough, the show's original stars were nowhere to be found. The idea of a spin-off bored them, and three minor characters had to step up to be a part of the new show—Harry Morgan, who played Colonel Potter; William Christopher, who played Father Mulcahy; and Jamie Farr, who played Corporal Klinger. Aside from relocating to the bland deserts of America, *AfterMash* just didn't have the same appeal when Corporal Klinger lost his fetish for dressing in women's clothing. The show's entire plotline conflict had disappeared, and nothing that happens in Missouri could possibly be as exciting as the front lines.

The Bradys
Spin-off of: *The Brady Bunch*

Why It Flopped: Kicked off the air in only one month, *The Bradys* wasn't nearly as captivating as the original sitcom. Maybe the new theme song was getting a little too annoying for veteran viewers, but with the Brady kids grown, the storylines got grim. Instead of chuckling at how cute little Cindy was when she got jealous of her sisters, now the Bradys were juggling alcoholism, HIV, and infertility. Makes being in trouble for breaking the family lamp (and breaking your sister's nose with a football) sound like a trip to the beach. To make things worse, network executives thought they would brighten the gloomy show with canned laughter. It just didn't mesh.

The Ropers
Spin-off of: *Three's Company*
Why It Flopped: Off the air in only one year, *The Ropers* centered around the lives of the landlords of the original show. Mr. Roper was a stubborn, grumpy old man who never seemed to leave the house. Mrs. Roper was a horny woman who, too, never seemed to leave the house. Despite producers trying to spice up interest in their show by tossing in a new female boarder, it just didn't do the trick.

That '80s Show
Spin-off of: *That '70s Show*
Why It Flopped: Almost immediately after its pilot episode, the show's new viewers called in to producers complaining that they didn't get their '80s jokes right. It was one stereotype after another—overkill on clunky shoes, huge telephones, etc. *That '80s Show* was cut after just one season, and unfortunately, most people didn't even notice it was pulled.

★ ★ ★ ★ ★

HOLLYWOOD'S BIGGEST MOVIE BLOOPERS: EDITING GONE WRONG

With all the details that go into making a movie, it's no surprise that every now and then, an oversight leaves room for a few flops in consistency. Check out the following most ridiculous bloopers popular movies have to offer.

- In the animated film *Emperor's New Groove* (2000), Yzma plays on the emperor's throne while her eyelashes magically multiply and disappear. In some shots there are three lashes per eye, in others there are four, five, or six.

- In *King Kong* (1933), Kong trashes the village after Ann escapes from his lair while villagers run for their lives. One villager trips over a chicken cage, and viewers can see his wig falling off his head.

- In *As Good As It Gets* (1997), Carol takes a bus to visit Melvin. As the camera pans out from the scene, however, a sign on the bus reads "Not In Service."

- In *Armageddon* (1998), Harry loses his cool at the oil rig and slams A.J.'s door after pounding it with a golf club, causing a fan to fall to the floor. In the very next shot, however, the fan is back up on the shelf.

- In *Mary Poppins* (1964), Mary powders her nose with black soot before going to explore London's rooftops, but seconds later, her nose is clean again.

- In *10 Things I Hate About You* (1999), Michael has trouble deciding whether he wants the goggles on his helmet up or down. When he visits Kat at her car in the parking lot, they are over his eyes. In the very next shot, they are up on his forehead.

- In *Smokey and the Bandit* (1977), the Bandit sees Carrie and skids, leaving marks on the road that are gone moments later when Cledus's truck passes by.

- In the first two *Austin Powers* flicks, Dr. Evil has brown eyes, but in *Goldmember,* they changed to blue in several scenes.

- In *Dirty Dancing* (1987), as Patrick Swayze's character fights Robbie, his belt switches from being perfectly fastened to broken and dangling—then back to fastened again.

- In *Catch Me If You Can* (2002), the skyline at the LaGuardia Airport shows the Twin Towers. However, the movie is set in 1969, and the Towers weren't built until 1973.

- In *Indiana Jones and the Temple of Doom* (1984), an elephant sprays Indie and Willie with water. Actor Harrison Ford knew it was coming—viewers can see him flinch right before he gets hit.

- In *The Lost World: Jurassic Park* (1997), Jeff Goldblum's character looks through his binoculars backwards at the helicopters, but when the camera cuts to the view, it is zoomed in as if he had looked through them correctly.

- In one of the opening scenes of *A Few Good Men* (1992), the buttons on Tom Cruise's shirt keep appearing as buttoned then unbuttoned. Additionally, a small stain on his shirt appears and disappears more than once.

- In *Save the Last Dance* (2001), Derek (played by actor Sean Patrick Thomas) walks into a restaurant just as one of his buddies says, "What up, Sean!"

★ ★ ★ ★ ★

MOMENTS OF SHAME: AWARD CEREMONIES GONE WRONG

The Academy Award and Golden Globe ceremonies are a time for schmoozing on the red carpet, sashaying around in skimpy skirts, and rubbing Vaseline on your teeth to help fake that perfect paparazzi smile. One would think such an evening would lead to glitz and glamour, but these stars weren't thinking straight when they suddenly embarrassed themselves on their big night.

- In her 2002 Academy Award acceptance speech, actress Halle Berry had to thank just about everyone—her mother, her manager, her husband, and … her lawyer. "I gotta thank my lawyer Neil

Meyer for making this deal!" she squealed. No one in the audience could believe their ears.

- When Tom Hanks won the Best Actor Academy Award for his work in *Philadelphia*, barely beating costar Denzel Washington for the prize, he sang the praises of Bruce Springsteen and Neil Young

STEAL FROM THE RICH AND GIVE TO THE RICHER

At the 2003 Academy Awards, an expensive goodie basket was handed off to performers, nominees, and presenters at the award show. It included:

- A $1,500 gift card to Morton's Steakhouse
- A $350 cashmere halter top
- A $250 Omas blue pen
- A $3,000 vanity makeup kit
- A $1,000 sampler of Revlon makeup
- A $475 sheet
- A $500 evening bag
- A $15,000 spa package from Estee Lauder

That's just some of the loot. The following year, the estimated total value of the goodie bag jumped to at least $110,000, including tickets to see Celine Dion in Las Vegas, an espresso machine, a seven-day cruise, and a wide-screen television. That's the good news. The bad news is that the freebies qualify as taxable income and must be reported on tax returns.

AWARD-WINNING TRIVIA

- The first Academy Awards ceremony to be telecast was the 25th, in 1953.

- The 1st Academy Awards were presented in 1927.

- Between 1931 and 1969, Walt Disney collected thirty-five Oscars.

- In 1969, *Midnight Cowboy* became the first and only X-rated production to win the Academy Award for Best Picture. Its rating has since been changed to R.

for their work on the film's title track, "Streets of Philadelphia." Referencing his wife, Rita Wilson, and then fellow cast mate Antonio Banderas, Hanks got a little out of control when he referred to Banderas as "second to my lover, is the only person I would trade for." So his wife is not all that bad, but Banderas is a tempting person to cheat with? Hanks should have thought twice.

- In 1999, when actress Sharon Stone was nominated for Best Actress for her work in *The Muse*, USA Films delivered a handful of complimentary Coach watches to the Hollywood Foreign Press Association voters responsible for the outcome of the upcoming Golden Globe Awards. However, once the press caught wind of the apparent bribery (the watches were sent as a gift from Stone), the voters returned the watches. Stone lost the award to *Tumbleweeds* star Janet McTeer.

★ ★ ★ ★ ★

CENSOR ME THIS: SCRIPT SELECTIONS GONE WRONG

CENSOR

Directors will go a long way to make a movie that pushes the envelope or makes people think about a social issue in a new light. However, if it's going to be a shock fest that results in the best parts getting censored, is it really worth the headache? Here are the top four films ever screened by associations and governments worldwide and why they just had to be altered.

Amistad (1997)
Director—Steven Spielberg
Awards—1998 Broadcast Film Critics Association Awards for Best Supporting Actor (Anthony Hopkins)
Cast—Morgan Freeman, Nigel Hawthorne, Anthony Hopkins, Matthew McConaughey, Djimon Hounsou
Summary—The shocking story of the Spanish slave ship *La Amistad*, the film chronicles the painful journey of fifty-three kidnapped native Africans being kept in the cargo hold until they decided to break their shackles and fight for freedom.
Why It Was Censored—Brigham Young University (a Mormon school) probably banned the film because of its excessive nudity. Jamaica's governmental Cinematographic Authority had a sinking feeling *Amistad* was simply too graphic for the locals—especially the scene where the slaves kill the slave traders with machetes. A large percentage of Jamaicans were descendants of West African

slaves at the time, and the government just didn't want the film to pose as an insult to their heritage. They had the bloodiest scenes removed.

The Birth of a Nation (1915, originally titled *The Clansmen*)
Director—D.W. Griffith
Awards—NONE
Cast—Lillian Gish, Mae Marsh, Henry B. Walthall, Miriam Cooper
Summary—Griffith adapted his tale of racism and riots during the Reconstruction of the South from two novels that were all the rage in the early 1900s—*The Clansmen* and *The Leopard's Spots*. One of the books' authors was a Southern preacher whose uncle was a bigwig in the Ku Klux Klan. Needless to say, the plotline, which highlighted a Northern family (the Stonemans) and a Southern family (the Camerons), involved a lot of racial slurs.
Why It Was Censored—The film opens with "A Plea for the Art of the Motion Picture" stating that some viewers may be offended by content, but filmmakers wanted to "show the dark side of wrong, that we may illuminate the bright side of virtue." Initially released in the most popular movie theaters in large cities, *The Birth of a Nation* made big bucks. However, it was highly criticized by the National Association for the Advancement of Colored People, who had previously asked the National Board of Censorship of Motion Pictures to shut down production. After a handful of marches on the state capitol, the governor of Ohio banned the film from his state, as did officials in cities like Denver, Pittsburgh, St. Louis, and Minneapolis. Regardless, an estimated 825,000 people paid to see the flick in 1915 alone.

Pressure for censorship in the movies began in the 1920s, when as many as twenty-two state legislatures considered bills to impose state and local censorship. Hollywood responded in 1922 by establishing the Motion Picture Producers and Distributors of America as an agency to regulate from within what they didn't want regulated from without. The group published its list of "The Don'ts and Be Carefuls" in 1927, which asked them to be careful of such things as those listed below:

- Profanity that included the name of God in any form
- Licentious or suggestive nudity
- Illegal drugs
- Any implication of sexual perversion
- White slavery
- Intimate relationships between races
- Venereal diseases
- Depictions of actual childbirth
- Children's private parts
- Ridicule of the clergy
- Deliberate offense to any race or creed

In addition, special care was directed in such matters as the treatment of the flag, international relations, violent crimes, graphic surgical scenes, cruelty to children and animals, and sympathy for criminals.

La Dolce Vita (1959)

Director—Federico Fellini

Cast—Marcello Mastroianni, Anita Ekberg, Anouk Aimee, Yvonne Furneaux, and Magali Noel

Awards—1961 Academy Award for Best Costume Design, 1961 Cannes Film Festival Golden Palm Award, 1961 New York Film Critics Circle Award for Best Foreign Language Film

Summary—This feisty film follows the life of journalist Marcello Rubini, a man unsatisfied with both his work and his women. Looking for true fulfillment, he explores the life of Roman nightclubs, hookers, and B-list movie stars, hoping for love and a good lead on a story. Although it is credited with coining the word "paparazzi," to some *La Dolce Vita* was nothing more than an exploration of sex and religion.

Why It Was Censored—The Roman Catholic Church banned the flick in most predominantly Catholic parts of the world not because of its sexual prowess but because of the way it criticized its traditional belief system when the main character doubted two girls who claimed to have seen visions of the Virgin Mary. In the U.S., the nudity was written off as art (foreign films always get off the hook for showing skin), but the Catholic Legion of Decency immediately deemed it was only for adults.

Spartacus (1960)

Director—Stanley Kubrick

Cast—Kirk Douglas, Laurence Olivier, Jean Simmons, and Charles Laughton

Awards—1960 Academy Award for Best Art Direction and Set Decoration as well as Best Cinematography and Best Costume Design

Summary—Based on the social condition of Rome before the birth of Christ, *Spartacus* explores a historical slave as he fights as a gladiator for the amusement of the upper class. As Spartacus studies how to be a fighter and an entertainer, he leads an uprising among his fellow slaves, and they fight for their rights as men, husbands, and fathers.

Why It Was Censored—Before the film was even released, some movie critics were in an uproar because *Spartacus* vaguely suggested that protagonist Marcus Crassus was a little light on his feet (he was bisexual). The Production Code Administration had the story line changed and warned that the loincloth costumes better not show too much skin.

Chapter 3

★

Rags to Riches: How Big Stars Earned Their Keep

Rags to Riches: How Big Stars Earned Their Keep

★ ★ ★ ★ ★ ★ ★ ★ ★ ★ ★ ★ ★ ★ ★ ★ ★

Before they were draped in Chanel petticoats and Louis Vuitton handbags, these A-list celebrities were shacking up in trailers and sleeping on the couches at California comedy clubs. A few million bucks later, now people are paying them to wear the most expensive jewels miners have to offer. These lucky actors have left their former dumpster-diving selves in the dust and are ready to splurge.

CHEESY MOMENTS WITH... JIM CARREY

When he was ten years old, he mailed his resume to *The Carol Burnett Show* to try and get some publicity.

He also wrote letters to rapper Tupac Shakur to cheer him up while he was in jail.

★ ★ ★ ★ ★

JIM CARREY

Best Known For: *In Living Color, Dumb and Dumber,* and *Ace Ventura: Pet Detective*

Humble Beginnings: As a teenager, Carrey's entire family had to take jobs as security officers and janitors at the Titan Wheels Factory just outside of Toronto, Canada. While they lived out of a camper, sixteen-year-old Carrey dropped out of high school to work on his rubber-faced celebrity impersonations and eventually left home to try his hand at the Comedy Store. He worked every night from 1983-1984 in Los Angeles, sleeping on a couch there while he worked on his routine.

Big Break: In 1990, Carrey met comedian Damon Wayans and ended up on the sketch show *In Living Color,* where his eccentric Fire Marshal Bill character would humor some and disturb others who thought his "safety tips" might actually be taken seriously by viewers.

Rollin' in the Dough: As his reputation continued to rise, Carrey wrote himself a $20 million check and set it aside until he made enough to actually cash it. After getting paid for his work in the *The Cable Guy,* he had his dough. Today, Carrey relaxes in a $4.5 million Los Angeles home, a luxurious holiday hotspot in Malibu, and a multimillion-dollar jet. He now requires a cool $25 million per movie.

Little Known Fact: His first wife, Melissa, took him to court because she believed the $10,000 a month he was sending her in child support simply wasn't enough.

★ ★ ★ ★ ★

HILARY SWANK

Best Known For: *The Next Karate Kid* and *Million Dollar Baby*

Humble Beginnings: Swank may have been a high school dropout with a traditional trailer park upbringing, but a hometown role as Mowgli in the play *The Jungle Book* changed everything. Producer and talent scout Suzy Sachs coached her in more small-town roles, but at first, Swank preferred to shine as a local swimmer and gymnast instead. After swimming at the Junior Olympics and ranking fifth in the state for gymnastics, she was ready to focus on acting and moved to L.A., with her mother, where they lived out of their car and never looked back.

Big Break: As a teenager, Swank landed cameo roles in the syndicated series *Harry and the Hendersons* and *Growing Pains*, but it was her breakout role as a young judo prodigy in *The Next Karate Kid* that would allow her to use her limber, ex-gymnast ways to climb to fame. After cutting her hair and dressing up as a guy for *Boys Don't Cry* won her an Oscar in 1999, she took her $75/day salary to the mall and broke the bank.

Rollin' in the Dough: In 2002, Swank and husband Chad Lowe—brother of acclaimed actor Rob Lowe—bought a $4 million four-story mansion in Greenwich Village, New York City. In 2004, she signed an exclusive contract with Calvin Klein to pose in the company's classic underwear ads. Today, Swank lives on the edge, often taking time out for skiing, skydiving, and water rafting.

Little Known Fact: On January 15, 2005, Swank was fined $142 plus court costs of $21 for carrying fruit that she didn't declare in customs into New Zealand. She wrote in a letter to the court that "After my twenty-hour flight, I simply forgot I had one orange and one apple. I do apologize sincerely."

★ ★ ★ ★ ★

 LINDSAY LOHAN

Best Known For: *The Parent Trap* and *Mean Girls*

Humble Beginnings: Her family may not have had much money in their early years, but at three years old, she helped pay the bills as she supported the family, making more than sixty commercials, including spots for Jell-O, The Gap, and Pizza Hut.

Big Break: Although she was first recognized in Hollywood as Hallie Parker/Annie James in *The Parent Trap*, when Lohan first moved to Los Angeles as a teenager, she shared an apartment with fellow child star Raven Simon. The

two single girls were making plenty of money and had a private maid and chef service in their apartment complex.

Rollin' in the Dough: Lohan has made so much cash between her days as a young, freckle-faced commercial kid and a star-power pop diva-turned-actress that her estranged father has engaged in lengthy court battles to try and get his fair share. Lohan has wrecked her Mercedes-Benz convertible multiple times while trying to escape nosy paparazzi.

Little Known Fact: She is allergic to blueberries, and she used to collect Beanie Babies.

★ ★ ★ ★ ★

Martin Lawrence

Best Known For: *Bad Boys* and *House Party*

Humble Beginnings: The Lawrence family was wanting when it came to cash. Martin's mother worked multiple retail jobs just to pay the bills, and, in hopes of cheering her up at the end of a long day, Lawrence started telling jokes. At school, it was well known among students and teachers that he had a knack for comedy, but he interrupted so many classroom lectures with smart-aleck remarks that one teacher started helping him get gigs at local clubs, so he would direct his jokes away from the blackboard and toward the proper audience. The early days of stand-up involved some tough crowds who weren't used to his crude humor and language, though— so Lawrence had to supplement his income by cleaning the floors at Sears alongside aspiring rappers Salt-N-Pepa and Kid 'N Play.

Big Break: Like many stars, Lawrence was discovered on *Star Search*, although he was initially afraid that his foul mouth would put off Ed McMahon. Luckily, the host laughed and let him on the show. Lawrence may have headed back to Sears after losing in the last round, but the five minutes of fame got him work:

- 1988—Had a small role on the final season of the sitcom *What's Happening Now!!*

- 1989—Played Cee in the Spike Lee film *Do the Right Thing*

- 1990—Played deejay Bilal in *House Party*

- 1992—Made phrases like "wassup" and "talk to the hand" famous on Fox's *Martin*

Rollin' in the Dough: In 1997, Lawrence made $6 million for his part in *Nothing To Lose*. Six years later, his rate had risen significantly—he made a whopping $20 million for *Bad Boys II*.

Little Known Fact: As a child, Lawrence was so sure that his comedy was funny that one of his teachers agreed to reserve the last five minutes of class for his stand-up routine in exchange for his promise to stop disrupting class with his humor.

★ ★ ★ ★ ★

OPRAH WINFREY

Best Known For: *The Oprah Winfrey Show*

Humble Beginnings: Born in a small farm house in rural Mississippi, Winfrey couldn't get a break from her very first breath—her name was spelled wrong on her birth certificate. She would end up being called Oprah instead of Orpah (from the Bible), as her parents intended, and she spent much of her childhood working her grandparents' farm with no television, no radio, and no bathroom. She owned two pairs of shoes. Rebellious in her youth, she was a lover of all things naughty and got in loads of trouble until her father laid down the law and, as she says, saved her life.

Big Break: Within months of getting the host spot on *A.M. Chicago*, the show went from last place in ratings to over taking *Donahue* as the highest rated talk show in Chicago. He encouraged her to leave to further her career, and they are still friends. Her show was then renamed *The Oprah Winfrey Show*—and Winfrey got her riches.

Rollin' In The Dough: A 2005 *Forbes Magazine* report listed Winfrey as worth $1.3 billion. She lives on a 42-acre Oceanside estate in Montecito, California. When she met the original owners at a party early in her career, she reportedly wrote them a check for $50 million on the spot. The house was not for sale, but Winfrey was convincing.

Little Known Fact: Oprah really got her start interviewing her corncob doll and the crows on the fence of her family's property. Her grandmother said she was "on stage" from the minute she could talk.

★ ★ ★ ★ ★

HALLE BERRY

Best Known For:
Monster's Ball and
Catwoman

Humble Beginnings:
Because her parents
divorced when she was
just four years old, Halle Berry was raised by a single mother who
worked as a nurse in the psych unit of a hospital. But the lack of cash
didn't hurt her reputation as might be expected. A prom queen since
high school, Berry won the Miss Teen All-American Pageant in 1985,
and was first runner-up in the Miss
USA Pageant the following year.

Big Break: After trying her hand at
modeling, Berry first hit the big
screen playing an aspiring catwalker
in the 1989 sitcom *Living Dolls*. It
bombed and was soon off the air. It
was her next role as a drug addict in
Jungle Fever that truly put her on the
map.

Rollin' In The Dough: In 2004, she
made $14 million for her work in
Catwoman, and pocketed an extra tip of $500,000 to do her first
topless love scene in the film *Swordfish.*

A CHEESY MOMENT
WITH... HALLE BERRY
Christy Fichtner, the
contestant who
beat Berry for the
Miss USA title in
1986, competed on
the 2003 reality
show *Who Wants to
Marry My Dad?*

Little Known Fact: In 2005, Berry became the first actress to actually attend and accept an insulting Razzie Award for her alleged terrible acting in *Catwoman*. Her speech: "When I was a kid, my mother told me that if you could not be a good loser, then there's no way you could be a good winner. Thank you, and I hope to God I never see you guys again."

★ ★ ★ ★ ★

 Johnny Depp

Best Known For: *Edward Scissorhands* and *Pirates of the Caribbean*

Humble Beginnings: Born in Kentucky, Depp moved more than thirty times with his parents (sometimes to the house next door) before he was a teenager. His mom, who is part Cherokee, bought him a guitar when he was thirteen years old, and two years later, desperate to be a rock and roll star, he dropped out of school to make it big with his band, The Kids. They thought they had hit the big time when they opened for Iggy Pop, but the band broke up after tensions mounted when Depp married one of his bandmate's little

A CHEESY MOMENT WITH... JOHNNY DEPP

Johnny Depp wanted to cap some of his teeth in gold for his role as the comical pirate Captain Jack Sparrow in *Pirates of the Caribbean: The Curse of the Black Pearl*, but he had a sneaking suspicion that his director and producers would disagree. To make room for a compromise, he had most of his teeth capped then agreed to get rid of some of them (but not all) before taping began.

sisters. Desperate for cash, Depp worked as a telemarketer (selling pens); his wife, Lori Anne Allison, was a makeup artist.

Big Break: Heeding some hardy advice he got from actor Nicolas Cage, whom he met on a trip to Los Angeles, Depp decided to support his family with Hollywood dollars and made it big when he landed a role as an undercover cop on *21 Jump Street*.

Rollin' In The Dough: He spent $350,000 revamping a Los Angeles nightclub and dubbed it the Viper Room, beating out similar bids made by Arnold Schwarzenegger, who also had hoped to make the buy. Depp also bought his very own tropical island in 2004.

Little Known Fact: Depp is an underground musician and has recorded with British band Oasis on more than one occasion. He plays the slide guitar on the 1997 album *Be Here Now*.

★ ★ ★ ★ ★

MARY TYLER MOORE

Best Known For: *The Mary Tyler Moore Show*

Humble Beginnings: The humble winner of seven Emmy Awards, life wasn't always so sweet for actress Mary Tyler Moore. She started out in Hollywood as an elf that danced around appliances in a General Electric commercial that aired during the 1955 *Ozzie and Harriet* show. Moore's first reoccurring role was a small part on *Richard Diamond, Private Detective*, but producers never showed her face. Moore's life would later include a series of personal tragedies— her son accidentally shot and killed himself, her sister committed suicide, and her last living sibling died of cancer.

Big Break: Moore's major breakout role was as Laura Petrie, the wife of a New York comedy writer, in *The Dick Van Dyke Show*. Although struggling with a drinking problem like costar Van Dyke, she sobered up and went on to win an Academy Award nomination for her work in the film *Ordinary People*, which was the first time she stepped away from her lighthearted persona as an actress.

Rollin' in the Dough: In 1970, Moore and her then husband formed MTM Enterprises. This production company produced many hit TV series, including *The Mary Tyler Moore Show, Rhoda, The Bob Newhart Show, WKRP in Cincinnati,* and *Hill Street Blues*. Moore maintains a ritzy apartment on the Upper East Side of Manhattan.

Little Known Fact: Today, a statue of Moore sits in downtown Minneapolis near the Nicollet Mall in honor of her role as the quirky thirty-something news reporter from *The Mary Tyler Moore Show*.

★ ★ ★ ★ ★

RICHARD GERE

Best Known For: *Pretty Woman* and *An Officer and a Gentleman*

Humble Beginnings: Richard Gere grew up with his extended family on a demure dairy farm and stuck around small-town settings while he studied at the University of Massachusetts Amherst on a gymnastics scholarship. A few back handsprings later, he decided to

A CHEESY MOMENT WITH...
RICHARD GERE
Richard Gere's middle name is Tiffany.

71

leave the gym and instead pursue two new careers—acting and playing the trumpet.

Big Break: After wowing British crowds as hot rod racer Danny Zuko in the 1973 play *Grease*, he landed a role as a male prostitute in *American Gigolo* (1980), in which he made designer Armani famous with his dashing good looks. Gere hasn't stopped wooing women onscreen since, earning him a coveted 1999 election as *People* magazine's sexiest man alive.

Rollin' In The Dough: The winner of multiple Golden Globe Awards over the years, Gere's talent and good looks are so well known that he was actually stalked in 2002 by a crazed fan who called him more than a thousand times. She would leave him haunting voicemails saying, "I will follow you" and "I want to be with you and share your life."

Little Known Fact: Gere was the first man ever to have his picture on the cover of *Vogue* magazine (with wife Cindy Crawford in the early 1990s). Since then, George Clooney has been the only other actor to have that honor.

★ ★ ★ ★ ★

KIM BASINGER

Famous Flicks: *Batman*

Humble Beginnings: Basinger's family may not have had much money in their early years, but after she won the Junior Miss competition in her Georgia hometown, she signed a contract with Ford Models and posed for hundreds of print advertisements. When she left to pursue her acting dreams (and more cash) in the fall of

1971, her father wished her well with some cash and a locket that read, "Today a Star, Tomorrow a Superstar."

Big Break: Although her first sitcom, *Dog and Cat*, was canceled without even completing its first season, Basinger demanded the attention of every man in America when in 1982 she became one of the first actresses to pose in *Playboy*. She went on to become the legendary Bond girl Domino in *Never Say Never Again*, and she hasn't stopped bringing in the riches since.

Rollin' in the Dough: In 1989, Basinger paid $20 million for the town of Braselton, Georgia, in hopes of making it a tourist attraction with a popular new film festival. Unfortunately, she had to sell it when business went bad in 1993.

Little Known Fact: She once wrote a letter to the U.S. Agriculture Secretary insisting that the mistreatment of circus animals in America has got to stop. The actress had heard a story about a baby elephant in the  Ringling Bros. and Barnum & Bailey Circus who was forced to perform while it was sick. The elephant died, and Basinger got on her soapbox.

★ ★ ★ ★ ★

ROSIE O'DONNELL

Famous Flicks: *Sleepless in Seattle* and *A League of Their Own*

Humble Beginnings: As a high school student in Long Island, Rosie wasn't the richest kid at school—but she sure was popular. Her peers voted her class president, homecoming queen, and prom queen. Increasingly popular for her boyish looks and her heavyset midriff, she started piecing together a living doing stand-up along the East Coast.

> **A CHEESY MOMENT WITH…**
> **ROSIE O'DONNELL**
> Rosie O'Donnell was such a fan of the hit show *Who Wants to Be a Millionaire?* that she got on a fan's lifeline list and helped brainstorm the correct answer to the $32,000 question.

Big Break: O'Donnell's comedy act was discovered by Claudia McMahon (the daughter of popular *Star Search* host Ed McMahon), who convinced her to audition for the show. Rosie held the voters' top spot for five weeks and made $20,000 off the project. Later, she hosted VH1's comedy series *Stand-Up Spotlight* and never looked back.

Rollin' In The Dough: O'Donnell recently put her money where her mouth is and paired up with partner Kelli Carpenter to start R Family Vacations, a cruise line to the Bahamas specifically for gay families. The highlight of the trip—discussion groups on artificial insemination, surrogacy, and adoption.

Little Known Fact: She shares a birthday with Matthew Broderick, collects Happy Meal toys, and loves the band Savage Garden.

O'Donnell also refuses to sign autographs for anyone older than a teenager.

★ ★ ★ ★ ★

BEFORE THEY WERE STARS... EARLY NOT-SO-GLAMOUROUS JOBS

- Ashton Kutcher worked at a Cheerios factory in Iowa.

- Shemp Howard of *The Three Stooges* was an apprentice to a plumber.

- *Saturday Night Live's* Phil Hartman was a graphic designer.

- Brad Pitt dressed up in a giant chicken suit to advertise outside Mexican restaurant El Pollo Loco when he first moved to Los Angeles. He made just over $3 an hour.

- Funnyman Andy Dick worked as a tour guide and directed commercials for the Utah Transit Authority before making his big screen debut in *In the Army Now* with Pauly Shore.

- Comedian Bob Hope was a boxer.

- After high school, Ellen Degeneres worked shucking oysters, painting houses, and bartending.

- *Gilligan's Island* star Bob Denver got a degree in political science from Los Angeles Loyola University and was a teacher in California in the 1950s.

- *Home Improvement's* Richard Karn (Al Borland) was the superintendent of an apartment complex.

- Edgy comedian Chris Rock worked at Red Lobster.

- Keanu Reeves sharpened ice skates.

- Whoopi Goldberg worked as a beautician at a funeral home—putting makeup on dead bodies.

★ ★ ★ ★ ★

BEFORE THEY WERE STARS... EARLY GIGS

- Denzel Washington played a nervous doctor on *St. Elsewhere*, an award-winning 1980s medical drama.

- *60 Minutes* interviewer Mike Wallace was a game show host for *The Big Surprise, Who's The Boss?*, and *Guess Again* in the 1950s.

- In the early 1980s, George Clooney shot pilots for fifteen different failed sitcoms and had small roles in six other sitcoms, including *The Facts of Life*.

- Leonardo DiCaprio played a homeless boy taken in for the holidays by the Seaver family on *Growing Pains*.

- Jim Carrey was a cartoonist for the 1984 sitcom *The Duck Factory*, but it went off the air after just a few months.

- In 1982 Demi Moore played a reporter on *General Hospital*.

- Jennifer Lopez got her start dancing as a Fly Girl on *In Living Color*.

- Salma Hayek's first American gig was a recurring role on *The Sinbad Show* in 1993.

- Ryan Phillippe played the first openly gay adolescent daytime TV had ever seen on *One Life to Live*.

★ ★ ★ ★ ★

Don't Quit Your Day Job: Actors Who Tried Their Hand at Singing

These leading Hollywood men may have been desperate to make a buck before they landed roles in blockbuster flicks, but they should have never passed time behind the microphone.

- Keanu Reeves: Played bass in a grunge band called Dogstar that put out two albums.

- Russell Crowe: Sang in the group 30 Odd Foot of Grunts.

- William Shatner: Put out several spoken-word songs including a cover of "Lucy in the Sky with Diamonds" and the single "Common People," which, despite its terrible lyrics and melody, have gained a cult following similar to that of *American Idol* wannabe William Hung.

- David Hasselhoff: A huge pop star in Germany, he has put out seven solo albums since the 1980s.

- Billy Bob Thornton: Singer and drummer who played countless covers of Creedence Clearwater Revival songs with his buddies in high school and released his first album, *Private Radio*, in 2001.

- Bruce Willis: Wasted two decades putting out his version of classics, which sold millions.

Chapter 4

✫

Embarrassing Celebrity Scandals

Embarrassing Celebrity Scandals

★ ★ ★ ★ ★ ★ ★ ★ ★ ★ ★ ★ ★ ★ ★

There's something fishy going on amidst the Hollywood red carpet, and mum's been the word for too long. Here are the secrets behind the greatest stories your favorite celebrity mischief-makers have to offer. From a talk show host hooking up with his stripper guest to a drunken actor passing out in a stranger's bed, these superstars are nothing but trouble.

TIDBITS OF GARY COLEMAN TRIVIA

He sued his parents for "misappropriating" $8.3 million while he was a child actor, and in 1993 won a $1.28 million settlement.

In 1999, after his entrepreneurship for a California video game arcade flopped, he filed for bankruptcy and got a job as a security guard at the mall.

He was a candidate for governor in the 2003 California election and was voted as the eighth most likely winner (out of 135 possible candidates).

★ ★ ★ ★ ★

COOKIE MONSTER MISBEHAVES

When a theme park brings in the cast of *Sesame Street* for the week, business is bound to be good. **But when the characters start roughing up the children**, you know it's going to be a long day. One such park in Langhorne, Pennsylvania, suffered this sad fate when a pushy father asked Cookie Monster to pose for a photo with his daughter. The character allegedly put his "big blue paw" on the little girl's head and gave her a shove. Whether it was an act of aggression or simply an encouraging pat gone wrong, the girl's father got rowdy and assaulted the monster in return, kicking and shoving him repeatedly. Needless to say, he was arrested, and hundreds of children—who had just helplessly watched their furry blue friend get tackled to the ground—had a good cry.

★ ★ ★ ★ ★

SNUB ME UP, SCOTTY

William Shatner has long been known for his brave façade—he narrated hundreds of life-saving moments on *Rescue 911* and demonstrated stern-faced leadership on *Star Trek*, didn't he? Regardless of his heroic reputation, Shatner was in for a shock when he found out that many of his costars thought he was a total snob. While contacting the old cast of *Star Trek* to interview them for his memoir, *Star Trek Memories*, he uncovered the fact that everyone who worked with him on the set thought he was rude, distant, and disinterested. Upset that he had come across so uncouth, Shatner tried to organize a reunion to patch up old wounds and reminisce on good times, but one famous face—James Doohan, who played "Scotty"—refused to attend.

★ ★ ★ ★ ★

DIRTY LAUNDRY: THE SECRET LIFE OF TALK SHOW HOSTS

DID YOU KNOW

In 2003, William Shatner's version of "Lucy in the Sky with Diamonds" was voted one of the worst "massacres" of a Beatles single ever.

The world of daytime talk shows is a circus of crude confessions and scandalous paternity tests, but the lives of those mysterious men behind the microphone have a few trashy secrets of their own.

- **Montel Williams**

    Montel graduated from the United States Naval Academy in Annapolis, Maryland, with a degree in General Engineering. Sounds like an intelligent, respectable man, right? Not so fast. A few weeks after the breakout of his new talk show *Montel,* he actually "fell in love" with one of the guests from the shocking "Mother-Daughter Strippers" episode. The two ended up getting married, and Grace, known as Bambi Jr. on the job at several hot Las Vegas hotels, consulted a psychic to see if the two were really compatible. The relationship didn't last.

- **Geraldo**

    Whether it's a glimpse into his personal life or the many places he takes the camera, controversy has always seemed to follow Geraldo Rivera. In high school, he joined a gang and got busted stealing a car. In college, he got married to postpone his chances of getting drafted into the Vietnam War. It was during an early job at WABC in New York, however, that would seal his boldness (and stupidity) as a journalist in history—while taping a story about how easy it is to obtain heroin on the street, he bought a bump (which is a felony). After a brief suspension, no charges were formally filed.

- **Dr. Phil**

    Texas television psychologist Phil McGraw was in hot water after a few former fans accused his "Shape Up!" diet and exercise plan of being completely useless. McGraw's book, they said, instructed them to take twenty-two herbal supplements and vitamins that have put a damper on their monthly budget. The weight didn't come off as expected, so they sought out for cash in court instead.

★ ★ ★ ★ ★

WHATCHOO ANGRY ABOUT, GARY?

Ever the master of wisdom with wit, Gary Coleman—the short-but-feisty star of *Diff'rent Strokes*—went a little overboard when a woman asked for his autograph while he was working as a security guard at the mall. She accused him of throwing a punch, and he was arrested under misdemeanor assault and battery charges. Coleman told the jury that he thought he was in danger—the woman was taller than him and had been spouting off insults about his talent (or lack thereof). In the end, however, he pleaded "no contest," spent ninety days in jail and paid a measly small fine. After a few rounds of anger-management classes, he shelled out more cash to pay off the woman's hospital bills and continued with his struggle to keep his name out of the headlines.

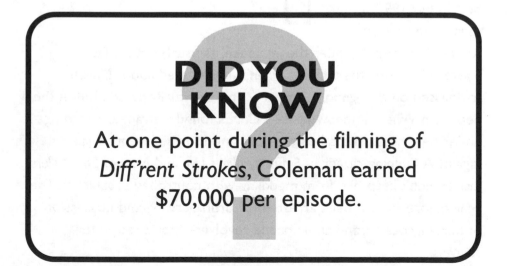

DID YOU KNOW

At one point during the filming of *Diff'rent Strokes*, Coleman earned $70,000 per episode.

Since then, Coleman has been known to frequently lose his cool. While filming a cameo appearance on the celebrity has-been reality show *The Surreal Life*, he lost it again when rapper Vanilla Ice got nearly everyone in a restaurant to beg him to spout off his famous lines "Whatchoo talkin' 'bout, Willis?" He lashed out in embarrassment, quit the show, and called a cab. Talk about good reality TV.

★ ★ ★ ★ ★

NAPPING WITH NARCOTICS

You know tomorrow is going to be a bad day when the paparazzi catch you snoozing in a stranger's bed. In July 1997, a thirty-one-year-old Robert Downey Jr. (under the influence, as usual) got his face plastered all over the tabloids when he wandered about Malibu, trespassed on a neighbor's property, and eventually passed out in the bedroom. When homeowner Lisa Curtis found a stranger snoozing under her sheets, she called the cops and Downey went to jail (again). A budding career in *Saturday Night Live* and *Natural Born Killers* just couldn't keep him from meddling with controlled substances. The year before, he had been arrested for drunk driving and possession of heroin, cocaine, and an unloaded revolver—not a recipe for success.

★ ★ ★ ★ ★

IN LIVING TROUBLE

Always known as one of the edgiest potty-mouth comedians to step on stage, Martin Lawrence was in true form in 1996 when police chased him down for running into a busy Los Angeles intersection and waving a gun at passing cars. It turns out he was suffering from a serious case of anxiety. Cops (and doctors) decided he was depressed, dehydrated, and in need of a good night's sleep. Just a few months later, Lawrence was in trouble again after authorities found a pistol on him at Burbank Airport. This time he couldn't get off by saying he was in desperate need of a nap. In fact, Lawrence has spent the rest of his career explaining away similar shady "incidents":

- His wife accused him of being verbally abusive, took out a restraining order, hired a bodyguard, and then divorced him in 1996.

- *Martin* costar Tisha Campbell filed a sexual harassment lawsuit against him and threatened to quit the show unless producers promised she would never have to tape a scene with him again.

- He was questioned and arrested after a fight broke out in a nightclub in 1997.

★ ★ ★ ★ ★

SWIMMIN' POOLS... MOVIE STARS... GET A LAWYER...

Originally scripted as *The Hillbillies of Beverly Hills*, CBS's **The Beverly Hillbillies had legal woes right out of the gate.** As soon as the show became popular, a four-man musical group who called themselves The Beverly Hillbillies filed a $2 million suit against Filmways Pictures for copying their namesake. Not long after they settled out of court, writer Hamilton Morgan accused the show's writers of plagiarism and filed a $15 million suit explaining that he had previously been turned down by CBS for his script titled *Country Cousins*, which was remarkably similar to *The Beverly Hillbillies*. A hung jury led to the charges being dismissed, but even after the show went off the air, producers suffered another headache when even more people filed a suit—this time claiming they owned the 1921 Hillbilly flatbed truck and wanted it back. The allegations were proved false, and the beloved truck was shipped to be on permanent display in a museum at the Missouri School of the Ozarks.

DID YOU KNOW

A former back-up singer for Gene Autry and Bing Crosby, Jerry Scoggins sang the theme song for *The Beverly Hillbillies*.

HILLBILLY LINGO

Because it may have been hard to understand exactly what the Clampett family was a-sayin' on their weekly program *The Beverly Hillbillies,* here are their most popular phrases revealed:

- Slippery as a hog on ice
- Feelin' lower than a well digger's heel
- Fine as a frog's hair
- It ain't hern, it's hisn

★ ★ ★ ★ ★

OPRAH GETS OSTRACIZED

The staff at *Ladies Home Journal* isn't much of a fan of Oprah Winfrey and her liberal counseling ways. In fact, the magazine's ex-editor-in-chief, Myrna Blyth, dissed the talk show queen for touting off what she calls feminism and bad advice in the book *Spin Sisters: How the Women of the Media Sell Unhappiness—and Liberalism—to the Women of America.* For example, Blyth believes Winfrey's shows about marital problems focus on cheating men and their poor, pitiful wives rather than noting that oftentimes women are the ones who taint their relationships. She isn't alone in her criticism—others believe that the show's book club is a joke. While it oftentimes brings up big names like Hemingway and Faulkner, other highlights have little literary value. Just ask author Jonathan Franzen, who wished that Winfrey had not chosen his book, *The Corrections,* because he thought her womanpower ways would doom the chances of a man ever picking it up again. There's also that unfortunate James

Frey situation. His popular novel, *A Million Little Pieces,* was lavishly praised on her show until it was revealed that the work was largely fiction, instead of autobiographical as he had insisted.

★ ★ ★ ★ ★

SHE'S DARING DARLING

Known for her love of short-lived marriages, snappy wit, and calling just about everyone "darling," Hungarian-born actress Zsa Zsa Gabor doesn't always use common sense when it comes to complying with the law. In June 1989, cops flagged her down for speeding in Beverly Hills—but instead of hitting the curb, she panicked and sped off. When she finally obliged and pulled over three blocks away, Gabor was shocked that the policeman actually had the audacity to write her (a rich snob) a ticket. To make sure she clearly communicated her disgust, she smacked him across the face. The speeding ticket cost Gabor a hefty fine, and the slap cost her jail time.

THE MANY HUSBANDS OF ZSA ZSA GABOR

Burhan Belge	1937-1941	Writer, diplomat, and press director for Turkey's foreign ministry
Conrad Hilton	1942-1946	Hilton Hotel mogul
George Sanders	1949-1954	Actor who later married Gabor's sister, Magda.
Herbert Hutner	1964-1966	Financial consultant
Joshua S. Cosden Jr.	1966-1967	Oil heir
Jack Ryan	1975-1976	Inventor of the Chatty Cathy doll
Michael O'Hara	1977-1982	Attorney
Felipe de Alba	1982-1982	Actor, however, the ceremony wasn't valid because she was still married to O'Hara at the time.
Frederick Prinz von Anhalt	1986	German who claims to be a prince because as an adult, he was adopted by a princess.

★ ★ ★ ★ ★

THE WORD OF THE DAY: FREAK!

When Pee Wee Herman (actor Paul Reubens) was visiting his folks in Sarasota, Florida, in the summer of 1991, he decided to go out for a late-night flick—an X-rated flick, that is. A few hours later, he was arrested for "exposing himself" in the theater (which has since been replaced with a restaurant). In no time, every gray-suited Pee Wee doll was pulled from the shelves of toy stores across the nation, and CBS dropped the five remaining episodes of his children's program, *Pee Wee's Playhouse*. Surprisingly, Herman's fellow actors weren't offended—they were supportive. The following September, he got a standing ovation at the MTV Video Music Awards when he acted ignorant of the fact that he had been the butt of Hollywood's jokes. He simply asked the crowd, "Heard any good jokes lately?" They thought he was hilarious.

★ ★ ★ ★ ★

PLAYING NICE WITH NATURE

Leonardo DiCaprio and crew found themselves in a sticky situation in 1999 while filming the tropical flick *The Beach* in Thailand. Apparently, they had a bit of a problem playing nice with nature. The entire time the cast was filming, the set was bombarded by protestors claiming that they had destroyed Phi Phi Leh island's Maya Beach. Native plants had been ripped up, the beach had been plowed, and new palm trees and colorful foliage had been brought in

instead. Local environmentalists called the makeover "sinful," but producers said they were simply doing what was necessary to make their flick as accurate as possible.

★ ★ ★ ★ ★

RATHER'S NASTY RUN-IN

In 1986, two mysterious men made headlines when they attacked CBS anchorman Dan Rather on New York City's Park Avenue and asked him one question over and over—"Kenneth, what's the frequency?" Confused and intimidated, Rather had no clue what they were talking about and didn't know what to say in return. Because of his silence, however, he got the crap beat out of him. When the story broke, many people didn't know whether or not to believe it. Rock band R.E.M. even released a hit song based on the event, titled "What's the Frequency, Kenneth?"

★ ★ ★ ★ ★

BRENDA'S BAD HUMOR

Beverly Hills, 90210 star **Shannen Doherty has long criticized her fans for not being able to separate her real personality with the irritable**, controlling Brenda she embodied for several years on the show. In fact, fans of *90210* even circulated an *I HATE BRENDA* newsletter across the country. However, Doherty's track record with the law reveals that she just might have a problem with keeping her cool.

- August 1992—She lost much of her sitcom earnings and two of her cars when she was sued by California United Bank for writing bad checks. She ended up so broke that she agreed to appear in a Slaughter music video to make some extra cash.

- December 1992—She was charged with battery after getting into a fist fight with another young actress at Hollywood's Roxbury club.

- 1993—Her landlord filed a lawsuit saying she owed him $14,000 in unpaid rent and $100,000 for the damage done to the apartment during a violent fight with her boyfriend.

- August 1996—She threw a bottle through the windshield of a college student's car and was charged with assault with a deadly weapon.

- December 2000—She was arrested for drunken driving, had to pay a $1,500 fine, and agreed to speak to teens about the dangers of alcohol as a community service project.

★ ★ ★ ★ ★

BERRY'S BIG BUMP

On February 23, 2000, **Hollywood bombshell Halle Berry was accused of running a red light** in a rental car, hitting another vehicle, then speeding off in a panic. Though the incident was clearly a hit and run, someone must have felt sorry about the twenty stitches she had to endure at the hospital after she fled. In the end, Berry pleaded "no contest," paid $14,000 in fines, and did two hundred hours of community service.

★ ★ ★ ★ ★

BACHELOR BOB'S BIG BREAK MISTAKE

The chubby comedian from *The Bachelorette*, **Bob Guiney, found himself in a bit of trouble** when he broke contract and tried to launch his music career right after his big moment on the reality show aired on ABC. He had allegedly signed an exclusivity clause with the network that prevented him from promoting other products without an OK from producers. Guiney used his newfound fame to push his new album, *3 Sides*, anyway and wound up in court.

★ ★ ★ ★ ★

THE REAL PASSION OF MEL GIBSON

In a story that stunned those who had seen Mel Gibson's *Passion of the Christ* as a return to religion and traditional values, **the actor was arrested on July 28, 2006, in Malibu,**

California, on suspicion of driving under the influence of alcohol.

A press release from the Los Angeles County Sheriff's Department indicated that Gibson was pulled over after "deputies were alerted by their radar that his speed was above the posted limit." Approaching deputies noted the strong odor of alcohol, and a subsequent Breathalyzer test showed that his blood-alcohol level to be 0.12; the California legal limit is 0.08.

When taken to the station, Gibson launched into an anti-Semitic tirade laced heavily with profanity and sexist remarks for good measure. Although he was not officially charged with DUI—that call will be made by the district attorney—Gibson faced an avalanche of ill will, not the least of which came from Jewish groups that claimed he had expressed his true feelings during the rant.

Gibson admitted that "I disgraced myself," and offered numerous apologies and confessions of guilt to everyone from religious groups to the deputies who arrested him. Then he entered a rehab center for the drinking problem that had plagued him even since the early years of his career.

★ ★ ★ ★ ★

Just Picking Up a Few Things

Actress Winona Ryder was shopping in the Saks Fifth Avenue store in the upscale shopping district of Wilshire Boulevard in December of

COUPON
5 FINGER DISCOUNT

2001 when something unexpected happened: **she was arrested for stealing** after security guards suspected her of taking clothing and hair accessories.

Through her attorney, Ms. Ryder said there had been a misunderstanding – she had simply been carrying clothes between departments within the store. But police felt sure of their suspicions, since they based them on a surveillance tape in which the actress was seen removing tags from the store items. Beverly Hills police also said she was carrying drugs for which she did not have a prescription.

She was later acquitted of burglary, but convicted of grand theft and vandalism for stealing $5,560.40 worth of designer merchandise. She was sentenced to three years probation and 480 hours of community service. At the completion of the latter, she was praised by the judge for her behavior during probation.

★ ★ ★ ★ ★

HUGH'S DEVINE ENCOUNTER

There's an old saying that it doesn't matter what they print about you as long as they spell your name right. That certainly turned out to be the case for Hugh Grant, British star of movies like *Nine Months* and *Two Weeks Notice*.

On June 27, 1995, **Grant was arrested for being found in his car, engaged in a sex act with a Hollywood prostitute** named Devine Brown. He was charged with lewd conduct, and was later fined $1,180 and placed on two years' probation.

People wondered why Hugh would have been involved in such action since his long-standing girlfriend was the beautiful Elizabeth

Hurley. Other than that, the most amazing thing about the incident was the way Hugh faced up to it. Within just days of the arrest, he spoke publicly about the whole thing, telling Jay Leno, "I think you know in life what's a good thing to do and what's a bad thing, and I did a bag thing…and there you have it."

Chapter 5

⭐

The Antics of Acting Animals

The Antics of Acting Animals

★ ★ ★ ★ ★ ★ ★ ★ ★ ★ ★ ★ ★ ★ ★ ★

French writer Romain Rolland once said, "I know at last what distinguishes man from animals: financial worries." He was right on the money. When it comes to bringing in big bucks for doing things like napping and trotting across screen, these pampered pets have made it big in Hollywood. But don't be too impressed. You may be surprised at some of their untold stories from the set.

DID YOU KNOW

The Benji dog from the latest film, *Off the Leash!*, was "discovered" at an animal shelter in Gulfport, Mississippi.

★ ★ ★ ★ ★

Boars That Won't Get Lost

When the cast of the sci-fi goes-tropical television series *Lost* filmed the Season One episode "Walkabout," **the plan was for a pack of boars to get chased out of the airplane wreckage** when bad-boy Sawyer found them feeding on the rotten corpses. To manage the rowdy animals, producers brought in a real boar wrangler, but things went awry when the animals refused to cooperate. The wrangler had planned to coax the boars into running across the set by jogging ahead of them with food. However, the extras on set had fed them so many snacks that day that their bellies were full, and they had no interest in the jog at all.

Not So Special Effects

To prepare for a camera shot of a giant white polar bear attacking castaways in one of the first episodes of *Lost*, the crew skipped out on handling a real animal, and instead attached a giant stuffed bear to a wire and swung it past the camera. For shots of the bear running through the jungle, a crewman put on some white furry pants and ran through the trees himself.

★ ★ ★ ★ ★

THE DOG WHO COULDN'T DIE (UNTIL HE DID)

Boasting a loveable pooch with the courage of a lion, **the 1974 blockbuster *Benji* was never expected to be a hit**. However, the brave little dog that rescued kidnapped children in between naps made a whopping $40 million in the United States alone. Two sequels and four prime-time television specials later, few viewers realized that Benji was not one talented pup, but four. After watching *Lady and the Tramp*, writer Joe Camp, the mastermind behind the series, came up with his idea for the family-friendly doggie flick and embarked on a seemingly endless search for a cute little puppy to play the lead role. He searched animal shelters across the country, and finally found the perfect Benji.

★ ★ ★ ★ ★

ANOTHER DOG WHO BIT THE DUST

Unfortunately for the cast and crew of *The Brady Bunch*, **fluffy family dog Tiger was hit by a car and killed early in the taping of the show's first season**. When a replacement dog wouldn't cooperate on set, producers decided to write the pooch out of the script and only bring him in for an occasional cameo. This worked for a while, but it wasn't long before the replacement Tiger got tossed a pink slip in lieu of a Frisbee. Regardless of the fact that a dog would never again grace the Brady home, the doghouse remained throughout every season because it covered holes in the artificial backyard.

★ ★ ★ ★ ★

FROM THE GARBAGE PAIL TO GREEN PAL

With an official celebrated birthday (May 9, 1955) and an honorary doctorate of "Amphibious Letters" from Southampton College (he gave the commencement speech the same day he gave his acceptance speech), **Kermit the Frog is one of the most famous amphibians of all time.** One of puppeteer Jim Henson's most famed figures, Kermit hasn't always been so glamorous and pampered. In fact, the original vision for Kermit's design came from a bunch of garbage—a dirty green jacket Henson found in the trash and two eyes made out of old Ping-Pong balls. Not only was Kermit once ratty and in need of a serious dry cleaning, he was also supposed to be a lizard. He didn't appear as a frog until the 1969 television special *Hey, Cinderella!*, but Kermit's extreme makeover was a hit, and Henson hasn't turned back since. So just how did a stuffed amphibian rise above the likes of Miss Piggy and Fozzie Bear to steal the show as Henson's premier puppet? He was simply the lightest, making him easier to operate for long periods of taping.

WHAT'S WITH THE NAME?

It was once rumored that Kermit the Frog was named after Sesame Street Muppet designer Kermit Love; however, Henson named Kermit while drawing sketches of the character at just eight years old—long before he ever met Love. Others say the frog gets its name from Theodore Kermit Scott, one of Henson's boyhood friends.

COWABUNGA, DUDE!

Kermit's not the only famous green friend. In fact, here's a quartet of them, the Teenage Mutant Ninja Turtles. The story behind them goes like this: In 1984, Kevin Eastman was a college kid dying to impress his roommate with his cartoons of turtles with mighty cool headbands. A comic book junkie, Eastman and his friend Peter Laird put out a black and white version of their drawings, which soon morphed into a hit television show and three movies. Eastman took his fortune and decided to stay in the comic book biz. He bought the rights to *Heavy Metal*, an adult comic book magazine famed for its big-busted drawings of women wearing little clothing. In 1993, he married *Penthouse* hottie Julie Strain and partnered with her to make the film *Heavy Metal 2000*, based on his comics.

★ ★ ★ ★ ★

THE WOOKIE'S WHEEDLE

An overwhelming amount of problems plagued director George Lucas and his colleagues as they worked on creating a "galaxy far, far away" for the film *Star Wars* in the 1970s—they were running out of money, their robots kept breaking down on the set, and there were rumors around Hollywood that the film would turn out to be a children's flick instead of a sci-fi blockbuster. However, one thing bugged producers more than anything—the Wookie wasn't wearing any pants. Along with actors Mark Hamill and Harrison Ford, Lucas could not believe they were wasting their time arguing over such a "bare" issue.

★ ★ ★ ★ ★

WHAT'S WITH THE VOICE? THE MANY MOUTHS OF MICKEY

No male can hit his falsetto like the famed cartoon Mickey Mouse. In fact, Mickey's high-pitch, friendly voice is part of what makes him so approachable and appealing to children. Walt Disney prided himself on personally recording the voice of Mickey for 19 years, but by 1946, his voice had become so raspy from chain-smoking cigarettes that he could no longer do the part. After one last taping for *Mickey and the Beanstalk*, he passed the torch to fellow animation specialist Jim MacDonald. Today, Wayne Allwine serves as Mickey's pipes, and his wife, voiceover specialist Russi Taylor, is the voice of Mickey's first love, Minnie.

WHY THE GLOVES?

Walt Disney decided to add white gloves to Mickey Mouse's hands so audiences could distinguish his fingers—and so his arms and hands did not disappear when they laid flat against his body in early black and white versions of the cartoon.

WHY THE BIG FUSS?

Mickey Mouse has stirred up quite a bit of trouble outside the United States in his day. In 1935, Romanian authorities insisted that children would be scared of the giant mouse and banned the videos from being played in movie theaters across their country. The following year, Nazi Germany's Adolf Hitler declared Mickey an official "enemy of the state."

★ ★ ★ ★ ★

BIG BIRD'S TALL TALES

A giant, golden-feathered puppet who promotes goodwill through sharing and saying please and thank you, Big Bird has caused quite a stir in children's television for his long list of lies. First, young viewers everywhere were confused when Big Bird

DID YOU KNOW

Although Big Bird (played by actress Caroll Spinney) could roller skate, ice skate, write poetry, and ride a unicycle, producers at Sesame Street deemed him only six years old.

made a special appearance in the *Mister Rogers' Neighborhood* Land of Make Believe and proceeded to tell X the Owl that he was a golden condor. However, for years, the bird (by the prompting of his producers) had been describing himself as a giant canary. Next, there was an issue about Mr. Snuffleupagus, whom most of the other characters believed to be imaginary because he only came along when Big Bird was alone. The elusive friend was modeled in part on imaginary

WHAT'S IN THE NEST?

The children's book *Sesame Street Unpaved* reveals that Big Bird keeps the following trinkets in his nest:

- A feather duster
- A record player
- A photo of friend Mr. Hooper
- A bubble gum dispenser
- An umbrella
- A mailbox
- A pair of snowshoes
- A lava lamp
- A football helmet
- A clock (with no hands)
- A watering can
- A tricycle wheel
- A golf bag (with only one club in it)
- A megaphone
- A Roman bust

friends that many of the show's viewers created. Many adults believed that Big Bird used "Snuffy" as a scapegoat to excuse unexplainable mishaps, which tapped into the issue of believing sometimes incredible truths that children say. Creators of the show considered all of these factors against a backdrop of stories where children had not been believed when they reported incidents of abuse and assault that only they had witnessed. In the end, Snuffy was proven to be real, the other characters apologized for their unbelief, and all was well on Sesame Street.

★ ★ ★ ★ ★

FROM SHELL SHOCK TO SPOILED

If there ever was a pampered pup, Rin Tin Tin was it. He dined on choice cut steak to the soothing tunes of classical music. He died in the arms of actress Jean Harlow (or so legend says). His remains are buried in a Paris suburb in a renowned pet cemetery called Cimetiere des Chiens.

A sharp German shepherd with a knack for barking on cue, the original Rin Tin Tin was found with his tail between his legs in a bombed-out animal shelter in France near the end of World War I. Not long after the dog's rescue, American

WHAT'S WITH THE NAME?
Rin Tin Tin was named after a puppet called Rintintin, which a French child gave to American soldier Lee Duncan during World War I for good luck.

serviceman Lee Duncan flew him home to Los Angeles, taught him a few tricks (he had a thirteen-foot long jump), and nicknamed him "Rinty." While leaping for a Frisbee at a California dog show, Rinty caught the eye of producer Darryl F. Zanuck, who recruited him to take the place of the stubborn wolf he had been trying to film in *The Man from Hell's River* (1922). His popularity took off as he became one of the first animals to launch a highly successful movie career. He filmed *Where the North Begins* (1923), *Shadows of the North* (1923), and an array of other doggie rescue flicks. After "hosting" a short-lived 1930 radio program called *The Wonder Dog* (he did his own barking), brave Rin Tin Tin earned his right to Hollywood stardom and became the hero of ABC's *The Adventures of Rin Tin Tin*—but what most people do not know is that the original star of the show was only one of three dogs in front of the camera. In fact, the other German shepherds (Rin Tin Tin II and Rin Tin Tin Jr.) were of no blood relation to the original at all.

★ ★ ★ ★ ★

COME HERE, GIRL! I MEAN ... BOY!

Known around the world for playing friend to a curious little boy named Timmy, **Lassie was played by a young collie named Pal** and a number of his (yes, his) offspring by the same name. Although Timmy referred to his animal pal as a girl, most dogs who played the role were male because their coats were fuller and shinier. Male dogs were also stronger and able to complete the difficult stunts on set.

THREE THINGS YOU NEVER KNEW ABOUT... MR. ED

- The horse's real name was Bamboo Harvester, but a second horse was often used as a stand-in for publicity work.

- In the 1990s, a rumor circulated that Mr. Ed had been a zebra painted solid white, which viewers never figured out because of black and white television. The story was a hoax.

- The horse is buried near Tahlequah, Oklahoma.

★ ★ ★ ★ ★

THEY CALL HIM FLIPPER...

The role of Flipper, the famous bottlenose dolphin, was actually filled by several different dolphins. The first was Mitzi, a female who was the first pupil of famed dolphin trainer Milton Santini. Mitzi did all her stunts except for the famous tail walking, which was done by a male dolphin named Mr. Gipper. Mitzi died of a heart attack when she was fourteen, and is buried at the Dolphin Research Center. Her grace is the first stop on a tour for visitors, where they read a simple plaque in Mitzi's honor. It reads:

Dedicated to the Memory of Mitzi

The original Flipper

1958 – 1972

The last dolphin to serve in the famous role was Bebe, who specialized in high-jumping tricks, and was the longest survivor following the series. She was born at the Seaquarium, where she lived for forty years, giving birth to a calf just months before her death.

Chapter 6

Hollywood Aliases from A to Z

Hollywood Aliases from A to Z

★ ★ ★ ★ ★ ★ ★ ★ ★ ★ ★ ★ ★ ★ ★

Rip Torn is without a doubt a cooler name than "Elmore Rual Torn," and Michael Caine flows off the tongue much more smoothly than "Maurice Joseph Micklewhite." Hollywood has been fooling you for years with romantic, ear-catching names that make aspiring actors and actresses sound like superstars before you even see them on screen, but many of them are hiding from the wacky names their parents dared to dub them.

The Estevez family is well known in Hollywood. Father Ramon (Martin Sheen) created his stage name using Rev. Fulton J. Sheen's last name. He and his son Charlie are very close, often playing father-son roles, leading Charlie to use the Sheen name himself. Oldest son Ramon has been known to use both Sheen and Estevez, while the other Estevez children, Emilio and Renée, chose to keep the family name.

★ ★ ★ ★ ★

"A"

Alias: Alan Alda, played Hawkeye in *M*A*S*H**
Actual Name: Alphonso Joseph D'Abruzzo

Alias: Jason Alexander, played George on *Seinfeld*
Actual Name: Jason Scott Greenspan

Alias: Tim Allen, played Tim on *Home Improvement*
Actual Name: Tim Allen Dick

Alias: Woody Allen, writer and director
Actual Name: Allen Stewart Konigsberg

Alias: Kirstie Alley, played Rebecca Howe on *Cheers*
Actual Name: Gladys Leeman

Alias: Julie Andrews, starred in *The Sound of Music*
Actual Name: Julia Elizabeth Wells

Alias: Jennifer Aniston, played Rachel on *Friends*
Actual Name: Jennifer Linn Anastassakis

Alias: Desi Arnaz, co-star of *I Love Lucy*
Actual Name: Desiderio Alberto Arnaz y de Acha III

Alias: Rosanna Arquette, starred in *Desperately Seeking Susan* and *Pulp Fiction*
Actual Name: Rosanna Lauren

Alias: Bea Arthur, played Maude on *The Golden Girls*
Actual Name: Bernice Frankel

Alias: Fred Astaire, actor and dancer
Actual Name: Frederick Austerlitz

★ ★ ★ ★ ★

"B"

Alias: Lauren Bacall, played Hannah in *The Mirror Has Two Faces*
Actual Name: Betty Joan Perske

Alias: Catherine Bach, played Daisy Duke in *The Dukes of Hazzard*
Actual Name: Catherine Bachman

Alias: Lucille Ball, star of *I Love Lucy*
Actual Name: Diane Belmont

Alias: Anne Bancroft, played Mrs. Robinson in *The Graduate*
Actual Name: Anna Maria Luisa Italiano

Alias: Warren Beatty, played in *Bonnie and Clyde* and *Dick Tracy*
Actual Name: Henry Warren Beatty

Alias: Bonnie Bedelia, played Holly McClane in *Die Hard*
Actual Name: Bonnie Culkin

IT'S ALL RELATIVE
Warren Beatty's sister is Shirley MacLaine. He is also the godfather of Melanie Griffith's son Alexander and uncle of Sachi Parker.

Alias: Tom Berenger, played Butch Cassidy in *Butch and Sundance: The Early Days*
Actual Name: Thomas Michael Moore

Alias: Milton Berle, comedian
Actual Name: Milton Berlinger

Alias: Ernest Borgnine, played Ted Denslow in *BASEketball*
Actual Name: Ermes Effron Borgino

Alias: Charles Bronson, played Danny Velinski in *The Great Escape*
Actual Name: Charles Buchinsky

Alias: Mel Brooks, directed *Blazing Saddles*
Actual Name: Melvin Kaminsky

Mel Brooks is one of the few people to have won an Oscar, an Emmy, a Grammy, and a Tony. In fact, he has 3 Emmys, 3 Tonys, and 3 Grammys. Now if he could just get two more Oscars, he'd be set.

Alias: George Burns, played in *Oh God!*
Actual Name: Nathanial Birnbaum

Alias: Richard Burton, played in *Who's Afraid of Virginia Woolf?*
Actual Name: Richard Walter Jenkins Jr.

★ ★ ★ ★ ★

"C"

Alias: Nicolas Cage, played Castor Troy in *Face Off*
Actual Name: Nicolas Coppola

Alias: Michael Caine, played Alfred in *Batman Begins*
Actual Name: Maurice Joseph Micklewhite

DID YOU KNOW?

Michael Caine was formally knighted in November 2000 for his contributions to the performing arts. Although knighted under his real name, he is known professionally as Sir Michael Caine.

Alias: Kate Capshaw, played Willie in *Indiana Jones and the Temple of Doom*
Actual Name: Kathleen Sue Nail

Alias: Captain Kangaroo
Actual Name: Robert Keeshan

Alias: Tia Carrere, played Cassandra Wong in *Wayne's World*
Actual Name: Althea Janairo

Alias: Phoebe Cates, played Linda in *Fast Times at Ridgemont High*
Actual Name: Phoebe Katz

Alias: Kim Cattrall, played Samantha Jones on *Sex and the City*
Actual Name: Clare Woodgate

Kim Cattrall once said that she realized fans didn't like the ending of *Sex and the City* because they figured her character, Samantha Jones, would have left her younger boyfriend within a few weeks.

Alias: Cedric the Entertainer, played in *Barbershop*
Actual Name: Cedric Kyles

Alias: Jackie Chan, famous for martial arts movies
Actual Name: Chan Kong-Sang

Alias: Chevy Chase, played Ty Webb in *Caddyshack*
Actual Name: Cornelius Crane Chase

Alias: Gary Cooper, starred in *High Noon* and *Sergeant York*
Actual Name: Frank James Cooper

Alias: David Copperfield, magician
Actual Name: David Kotkin

Alias: Joan Crawford, starred in *What Ever Happened to Baby Jane?*
Actual Name: Lucille Le Sueur

Alias: Bing Crosby, actor and singer
Actual Name: Harry Lillis
Crosby

Alias: Tom Cruise, played Joel in
Risky Business
Actual Name: Thomas Cruise
Mapother IV

Tom Cruise was the first actor to star in the films that won the Academy Award for Best Picture (*Rain Man*) and the Razzie for Worst Picture (*Cocktail*) in the same year.

★ ★ ★ ★ ★

"D"

Alias: Ted Danson, played Sam Malone on *Cheers*
Actual Name: Edward Bridge Danson III

Alias: Tony Danza, played Anthony on *Who's The Boss*
Actual Name: Anthonio Ladanza

Alias: James Dean, starred in *Rebel Without a Cause*
Actual Name: James Byron

Alias: Rebecca DeMornay, played Lana in *Risky Business*
Actual Name: Rebecca George

Alias: Catherine Deneuve, French actress
Actual Name: Catherine Dorleac

Alias: Bo Derek, starred in *10*
Actual Name: Mary Cathleen Collins

Alias: Susan Dey, played Laurie Partridge on *The Partridge Family*
Actual Name: Susan Smith

Alias: Angie Dickinson, star of TV series *Police Woman*
Actual Name: Angeline Brown

Alias: Vin Diesel, played Dominic in *The Fast and the Furious*
Actual Name: Mark Vincent

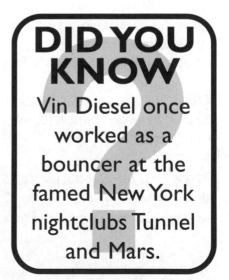

DID YOU KNOW

Vin Diesel once worked as a bouncer at the famed New York nightclubs Tunnel and Mars.

CHEESY MOMENTS WITH KIRK DOUGLAS

Kirk Douglas celebrated his bar mitzvah twice—once at age 13 and later at age 83.

He wore lifts in many of his movies, making him appear 5'11" or 6' instead of his actual height—5'9".

Alias: Phyllis Diller, comedian and actress
Actual Name: Phyllis Driver

Alias: Kirk Douglas, played Ned Land in *20,000 Leagues Under The Sea*
Actual Name: Issur Danielovitch Demsky

★ ★ ★ ★ ★

"E"

Alias: Barbara Eden, played the genie on *I Dream of Jeannie*
Actual Name: Barbara Huffman

Alias: Blake Edwards, director
Actual Name: William Blake McEdwards

Alias: Carmen Electra, played Lani McKenzie on *Baywatch*
Actual Name: Tara Leigh Patrick

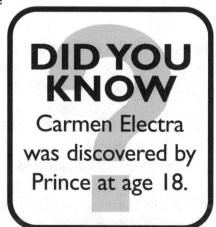

DID YOU KNOW
Carmen Electra was discovered by Prince at age 18.

Alias: Elvira, a.k.a. Mistress of the Dark
Actual Name: Cassandra Peterson

Alias: Linda Evans, played Krystle Grant Jennings Carrington on *Dynasty*
Actual Name: Linda Evanstad

★ ★ ★ ★ ★

"F"

Alias: Jamie Farr, played Klinger in M*A*S*H*
Actual Name: Jameel Joseph Farah

Alias: Douglas Fairbanks, played the Earl of Huntingdon in *Robin Hood*
Actual Name: Douglas Elton Ulman

Alias: Morgan Fairchild, played in *Falcon Crest*
Actual Name: Patsy Ann McClenny

Alias: Sally Field, played Mrs. Gump in *Forrest Gump*
Actual Name: Sally Mahoney

Alias: Glenn Ford, played in *Blackboard Jungle* and *Cimarron*
Actual Name: Gwyilyn Ford

Alias: Jodie Foster, played Clarice Sterling in *Silence of the Lambs*
Actual Name: Alicia Christian Foster

Alias: Michael J. Fox, played in *Family Ties*, *Back to the Future*, and *Spin City*
Actual Name: Michael Andrew Fox

Michael J. Fox was chosen to play Alex P. Keaton on *Family Ties* only after Matthew Broderick turned down the role.

Alias: Jamie Foxx, played Max in *Collateral*
Actual Name: Eric Bishop

Alias: Redd Foxx, played Fred G. Sanford (named after his brother) in *Sanford and Son*
Actual Name: John Elroy Sanford

★ ★ ★ ★ ★

"G"

Alias: Zsa Zsa Gabor, played Jane Avril in *Moulin Rouge* (1952)
Actual Name: Sari Gabor

Alias: Greta Garbo, actress
Actual Name: Greta Lovisa Gustafsson

Alias: Andy Garcia, played Vincent in *The Godfather III*
Actual Name: Andres Arturo Garci-Menendez

Alias: Judy Garland, played Dorothy in *The Wizard of Oz*
Actual Name: Frances Ethel Gumm

Alias: James Garner, played Marshal Zane Cooper in *Maverick*
Actual Name: James Scott Baumgarner

Alias: Mel Gibson, played Rev. Graham Hess in *Signs*
Actual Name: Mel Columcille Gerard Gibson

DID YOU KNOW Mel Gibson's name means "honey" in Portuguese.

Alias: Whoopi Goldberg, played Oda Mae Brown in *Ghost*
Actual Name: Caryn Johnson

Alias: Elliott Gould, played Ross and Monica's dad on *Friends*
Actual Name: Elliott Goldstein

Alias: Cary Grant, actor
Actual Name: Archibald Leach

Alias: Peter Graves, played Captain Clarence Oveur in *Airplane!*
Actual Name: Peter Aurness

Alias: Joel Grey, played in *Cabaret*
Actual Name: Joel Katz

Alias: Robert Guillaume, played in *Benson* and TV series *Soap*
Actual Name: Robert Peter Williams

★ ★ ★ ★ ★

"H"

Alias: Arsenio Hall, played Winston in *The Real Ghostbusters*
Actual Name: Chuckton Arthur Hall

Alias: Rex Harrison, played in *My Fair Lady*
Actual Name: Reginald Carey

Alias: Mary Hart, host of *Entertainment Tonight*
Actual Name: Mary Johanna Harum

Alias: Rita Hayworth, played Gilda in *Gilda*
Actual Name: Margarita Carmen Cansino

Alias: Pee Wee Herman of *Pee Wee's Play House*
Actual Name: Paul Rubenfeld, aka Paul Reubens

Alias: Charlton Heston, played Henry Hooker in *Tombstone*
Actual Name: John Charles Carter

Alias: Hulk Hogan, television wrestler
Actual Name: Terry Bollea

Alias: William Holden, played in *The Wild Bunch*
Actual Name: William Beedle

Alias: Bob Hope, comedian
Actual Name: Leslie Townes Hope

Alias: Harry Houdini, magician, escape artist
Actual Name: Erich Weiss

Alias: Rock Hudson, actor
Actual Name: Roy Scherer Jr.

★ ★ ★ ★ ★

"J"

Alias: Angelina Jolie, played Lara Croft in *Tomb Raider*
Actual Name: Angelina Jolie Voight

> Angelina Jolie has appeared in music videos for Meatloaf, Lenny Kravitz, Antonello Venditti, and The Lemonheads.

Alias: Grace Jones, played May in *A View To Kill*
Actual Name: Grace Mendoza

Alias: James Earl Jones, voice of Darth Vader in *Star Wars*
Actual Name: Todd Jones

Alias: Spike Jonze, director
Actual Name: Adam Spiegel

★ ★ ★ ★ ★

"K"

Alias: Madeline Kahn, played Lili Von Shtupp in *Blazing Saddles*
Actual Name: Madeline Gail Wolfson

Alias: Casey Kasem, Shaggy's voice on *Scooby-Doo* cartoons
Actual Name: Kemal Amin Kasem

Alias: Diane Keaton, played Annie in *Annie Hall*
Actual Name: Diane Hall

Alias: Michael Keaton, played Batman in *Batman*
Actual Name: Michael Douglas

127

Alias: Larry King, TV personality
Actual Name: Larry Zieger

Alias: Ben Kingsley, played Itzhak Stern in *Schindler's List*
Actual Name: Krishna Banji

★ ★ ★ ★ ★

"L"

Alias: Michael Landon, played Pa on *Little House on the Prairie*
Actual Name: Eugene Maurice Orowitz

Alias: Nathan Lane, played Albert Goldman in *The Bird Cage*
Actual Name: Joseph Lane

> Nathan Lane chose his stage name after the character Nathan Detroit from the musical *Guys and Dolls*.

Alias: Larry from *The Three Stooges*
Actual Name: Louis Fienberg

Alias: Piper Laurie, played Sarah Packard in *The Hustler*
Actual Name: Rosetta Jacobs

Alias: Bruce Lee, actor in martial arts movies.
Actual Name: Lee Yuan Kam (also spelled Lee Jun Fan)

Alias: Vivien Leigh, played Scarlett in *Gone With The Wind*
Actual Name: Vivien Mary Hartley

Alias: Bela Lugosi, played Count Dracula in *Dracula*
Actual Name: Be'la Ferenc Dezso Blasko

★ ★ ★ ★ ★

"M"

Alias: Elle MacPherson, played Blanche Ingram in *Jane Eyre*
Actual Name: Eleanor Gow

Alias: Jayne Mansfield, played Jerri Jordan in *The Girl Can't Help It*
Actual Name: Vera Jane Palmer

Alias: Dean Martin, played Matt Helm in *Murderers' Row*
Actual Name: Dino Crocetti

Alias: Harpo Marx, comedian
Actual Name: Adolph Marx

Alias: Walter Matthau, played in
The Odd Couple
Actual Name: Walter
Matuschanskayasky

Alias: Groucho Marx
Actual Name: Julius
Henry Marx

Alias: Marilyn Monroe,
played Sugar Kane in *Some
Like It Hot*
Actual Name: Norma
Jeane Mortenson

Alias: Demi Moore, played Erin Grant
in *Striptease*
Actual Name: Demetria Gene Guynes

129

★ ★ ★ ★ ★

"P"

Alias: Lou Diamond Phillips, played Jose Chavez y Chavez in *Young Guns*
Actual Name: Lou Upchurch

Alias: Natalie Portman, played Padme in *Star Wars*
Actual Name: Natalie Hershlag

Alias: Roman Polanski, director
Actual Name: Raimund Liebling

Roman Polanski fled to Europe after he was accused of raping a thirteen-year-old girl.

Alias: Stefanie Powers, played in TV series *Hart to Hart*
Actual Name: Stafdnia Zofija Federkiewicz

★ ★ ★ ★ ★

"R"

Alias: Tony Randall, played Felix Unger on *The Odd Couple*
Actual Name: Leonard Rosenberg

Alias: Della Reese, played Tess on *Touched by an Angel*
Actual Name: Delloreese Patricia Early

Alias: Debbie Reynolds, played in *Singin' in the Rain*
Actual Name: Mary Frances Reynolds

Alias: Joan Rivers, TV personality
Actual Name: Joan Alexandra Molinsky

Alias: The Rock, played Mathayus in *The Scorpion King*
Actual Name: Dwayne Douglas Johnson

Alias: Ginger Rogers, actress and dancer
Actual Name: Virginia Katherine McMath

Alias: Mickey Rooney, played Mr. Yunioshi in *Breakfast at Tiffany's*
Actual Name: Mickey McGuire

Alias: Meg Ryan, played Sally Albright in *When Harry Met Sally*
Actual Name: Margaret Mary Emily Anne Hyra

WORK AND LOVE DON'T MIX

Shortly after Meg Ryan met Anthony Edwards on the set of *Top Gun*, the two actors began dating and moved in together. A short while later, she met Dennis Quaid while filming *Innerspace*. and dumped Edwards for Quaid, whom she eventually married. Before the two divorced, Ryan was linked romantically to Russell Crowe, whom she met while working on *Proof of Life*.

Alias: Winona Ryder, played Lydia in *Beetlejuice*
Actual Name: Winona Laura Horowitz

★ ★ ★ ★ ★

"S"

Alias: Susan Sarandon, played Louise in *Thelma and Louise*
Actual Name: Susan Abigail Tomalin

Alias: Dick Sargent, played Darrin #2 on *Bewitched*
Actual Name: Richard Cox

Alias: Peter Sellers, played in Pink Panther movies
Actual Name: Richard Henry Sellers

Alias: Jane Seymour, played Dr. Quinn on *Dr. Quinn, Medicine Woman*
Actual Name: Joyce Penelope Wilhelmina Frankenburg

Alias:: Charlie Sheen, played Dep. Mayor Charlie Crawford on *Spin City*
Actual Name: Carlos Irwin Estevez

Alias: Martin Sheen, played President Bartlet on *West Wing*
Actual Name: Ramon Estevez

Alias: Christian Slater, played Daniel in *The Good Shepherd*
Actual Name: Christian Michael Leonard Hawkins

Alias: Anna Nicole Smith, actress
Actual Name: Vickie Lynn Hogan

Anna Nicole Smith met her oil-tycoon husband while she was working as a topless dancer in Houston.

Alias: Kevin Spacey, played Detective Wallace in *Edison*
Actual Name: Kevin Spacey Fowler

Alias: Sylvester Stallone, starred in *Rocky* and *Rambo* movies
Actual Name: Michael Sylvester Enzio Stallone

Alias: Meryl Streep, played in *Sophie's Choice* and *Bridges of Madison County*
Actual Name: Mary Louise Streep

★ ★ ★ ★ ★

"T"

Alias: Mr. T, played Clubber Lang in *Rocky III*
Actual Name: Lawrence Tureaud

Alias: Robert Taylor, played Armand in *Camille*
Actual Name: Spangler Arlington Brugh

Alias: Jonathan Taylor Thomas, played Randy on *Home Improvement*
Actual Name: Jonathan Taylor Weiss

Alias: Rip Torn, played Agent Zed in *Men in Black*
Actual Name: Elmore Rual Torn Jr.

Alias: Lana Turner, played in *Peyton Place*
Actual Name: Julia Jean Mildred Frances Turner

★ ★ ★ ★ ★

"V"

Alias: Jean Claude van Damme,
played Jacques Kristoff in
Derailed
Actual Name: Jean-Claude
Camille Francois van Varenberg

> Jean-Claude van
> Damme says he learned
> English from watching
> *The Flintstones*.

★ ★ ★ ★ ★

"W"

Alias: Lindsay Wagner, played Jaime on *The Bionic Woman*
Actual Name: Lindsay Jean Ball

Alias: Christopher Walken, played Frank Abagnale Sr. in *Catch Me If You Can*
Actual Name: Ronald Walken

Alias: Burt Ward, played Robin in *Batman* (1960s series)
Actual Name: Bert John Gervis Jr.

Alias: John Wayne
Actual Name: Marion Michael Morrison

Alias: Sigourney Weaver, played Ellen Ripley
in *Alien*
Actual Name: Susan Weaver

Alias: Adam West, played Batman in
Batman (1960s series)
Actual Name: William West Anderson

Alias: Vanna White from *Wheel of Fortune*
Actual Name: Vanna Marie Rosich

Alias: Gene Wilder, played The Waco Kid in *Blazing Saddles*
Actual Name: Jerome Silberman

Chapter 7

⭐

Where Are They Now? The Skinny on Child Stars

Where Are They Now?
The Skinny on Child Stars

★ ★ ★ ★ ★ ★ ★ ★ ★ ★ ★ ★ ★ ★ ★

From getting busted for drug possession and dodging rumors of their deaths, to fighting for animal rights and sharing their faith, here's the scoop on what your favorite child stars have been doing since the spotlights faded.

DID YOU KNOW

Malcom-Jamal Warner was named after Malcolm X and jazz pianist Ahmed Jamal. Warner won *Celebrity Poker Showdown* in 2003 in record time. The regular two-hour show only had enough material to fill one hour.

★ ★ ★ ★ ★

THE BUSTED BUD: BILLY GRAY

Nominated for an Emmy Award at just twenty-one years old for his portrayal of Bud Anderson on the 1950s sitcom *Father Knows Best*, **Billy Gray became known as one of the first child stars to be busted for possession of drugs** when his stash of marijuana earned him more than a month behind bars in 1962. Since then, he has insisted that the arrest ruined his career, and he has been dodging accusations of addiction ever since. In 1998, Gray settled a libel suit with popular movie critic Leonard Maltin, who mistakenly called him a drug addict while reviewing the 1974 movie *Dusty and Sweets McGee* in one of his film guides. Today, Gray is an inventor—he created the F-1 Guitar Pick—and an avid Speedway motorcycle racer. His bike, the Orange Blossom Special, was named by a clever announcer at California's Irwindale Speedway in honor of its shiny orange rims.

★ ★ ★ ★ ★

THE BABY BRADY: SUSAN OLSEN

She may have missed the filming of the popular Brady 1988 reunion show, *A Very Brady Christmas,* because she was busy living it up on her Jamaican honeymoon, but Susan Olsen's years of training at the American Academy of Dramatic Arts was time well spent. Although she has dodged rumors of tarnishing her innocent image in pornographic films (she did not) since her role as Cindy Brady on *The Brady Bunch*, Olsen has worked as a graphic designer, a radio talk-show host, and a spokesperson for Migraine Awareness Month. Her final attempt to shed the annoying reputation that she is still the perky baby Brady—she had surgery to correct that pesky lisp.

★ ★ ★ ★ ★

THE ALIEN'S BEST FRIEND: HENRY THOMAS

In the early 1980s, a shy nine-year-old Thomas walked onto the set of the blockbuster hit *ET: Extra Terrestrial* with almost no experience to try out for the part of the loveable, curious Elliott. Regardless of his green ways, director Steven Spielberg gave him a shot and cast him in the part of a lifetime. After the media attention for his performance died down, however, Thomas did a few more small films and at just thirteen years old left Hollywood for a sales job behind the counter at a video store. He took some time to recover from his short-lived fame while studying at Blinn College in College Station, Texas.

Although a little embarrassed of his namesake, Thomas wouldn't be gone from show biz for long. In 1994, he left his childhood reputation behind and reappeared on screen as Brad Pitt's brother Samuel in *Legends of the Fall* and the sinister Johnny Sirocco in *Gangs of New York*.

★ ★ ★ ★ ★

THE HOTHEAD HUXTABLE: MALCOLM-JAMAL WARNER

After starring as the charming big brother Theo Huxtable on *The Cosby Show*, Malcolm-Jamal Warner moved on from acting and stepped behind the camera to produce shows like *Malcolm & Eddie* and *Fresh Prince of Bel Air*. Today, he rocks out on the electric guitar and upright bass in his popular jazz band, Miles Long. He says fans are surprised to see him in dreadlocks behind the microphone, and if they slip up and call him Theo, he is quick to correct them with his real name.

★ ★ ★ ★ ★

THE STRAIGHT-LACED SIBLINGS: CANDACE AND KIRK CAMERON

Known as a straight-A student and the best friend to nosy neighbor Kimmie Gibbler, actress Candace Cameron played big sister D.J. Tanner on the family-friendly ABC series *Full House* from 1987-1995. The real-life sister of *Growing Pains* star Kirk Cameron, she spent her teenage years mingling among other Hollywood youngsters. While filming the eight-year series, she studied at California's Chatsworth High School with fellow young actresses Lori Beth Denberg (of Nickelodeon's *All That*) and Lindsay Sloane (of USA's *Sabrina the Teenage Witch*). After *Full House* came to a close and Cameron taped a stint of cheesy Lifetime movies, she married pro hockey player Valeri Bure and today stays at home with her three children, Natasha, Lev, and Maksim.

As for Kirk, he has taken his religious ways to the street as the cofounder of Living Water Ministries and The Way of the Master Ministries, which chronicles street evangelism in a Christian television series. He also started Camp Firefly, a refuge for children suffering from terminal illnesses. When he's not witnessing for Jesus, Cameron is playing parent to six children with wife and fellow *Growing Pains* star Chelsea Noble, whom he married in 1991.

Both Candace and Kirk have announced that because of their commitment to the Christian faith, they will no longer accept roles that compromise their values (that means no nude scenes).

★ ★ ★ ★ ★

THE MORAL MAKER: JERRY MATHERS

Known as Theodore "Beaver" Cleaver in the wholesome 1950s and '60s classic *Leave It to Beaver*, Jerry Mathers is known as one of the first childhood actors to ever receive a percentage of a sitcom's merchandise revenue. To this day, he makes money off his boyhood gig, which first went on air October 4, 1957. After the show's producers called it quits after seven years, Mathers finished high school and got a degree in  philosophy from the University of California, Berkeley. Before giving in to the daily grind of adulthood as a banker and real estate developer, he tried his hand at fame and fortune one last time in a band named Beaver and The Trappers. After a few summers of cutting records, he entered the real world and today is a motivational speaker, traveling the country shaming the moral decline of America with all the lessons *Leave It to Beaver* has to offer.

THREE THINGS YOU NEVER KNEW ABOUT... JERRY MATHERS

- The Associated Press released reports that he had died while serving in the Air Force National Guard during the Vietnam War, but it was a mix-up with a soldier who had a similar name.

- He sells autographed photos of himself for $50 online.

- He was once a spokesman for the National Psoriasis Foundation.

★ ★ ★ ★ ★

THE SPOILED RICH GIRL: LISA WHELCHEL

Blair Warner from *The Facts of Life* was known to worship herself every now and then, but offscreen actress Lisa Whelchel was a humbled-hearted Christian. In fact, her faith caused trouble with the cast when scriptwriters wrote an episode about Blair having sex with her crush. Strongly believing in the need for teens to wait until marriage before jumping between the sheets, Whelchel refused to do the part. Today, she is a mother and the author of several books on homeschooling and parenting. She recently came under fire for her "hot sauce on the tongue" suggestion in one of her books, which recommends parents discipline their children with a little drop of the burning condiment.

★ ★ ★ ★ ★

THE TWO COREYS: COREY FELDMAN AND COREY HAIM

Famous for their onscreen duos in the 1980s, Feldman and Haim first made their mark on the film industry when they played Edgar Frog and Sam Emerson in cult classic vampire flick *The Lost Boys.* Afterwards, they became so popular as best pals that they made seven more movies together. However, as they got older, the two heartthrobs got burnt out on being on the set so often. They had a falling out, took a break to regain their individual identities, and never looked back. The son of famous songwriter/producer Bob Feldman, who wrote 1950s hits like "My Boyfriend's Back," today Feldman is spicing up his career with an array of cheesy appearances on reality television shows like VH1's *The Surreal Life,* and is working on a music career with his first solo album, *Former Child Actor.* Haim recently kicked a long-time drug addiction that caused him to have a minor stroke in 2001, and now works in a Toronto record store while still pursuing a career in acting.

★ ★ ★ ★ ★

THE VOICE OF SIMBA: JONATHAN TAYLOR THOMAS

Known as the voice of young Simba on the popular Disney flick *The Lion King,* and as the heartthrob middle child, Randy, on *Home Improvement,* JTT lured a whole new audience to the ABC tool-man show in the 1990s—an audience interested in anything but hot rods and Binford saws. After seven seasons, Thomas quit the show to go to college—It was a toss-up between a handful of Ivy League academies. He picked Harvard (and spent some time at the University of Saint Andrews in Scotland) and today is known for speaking out against abortion, and for doing a lot of cartoon voiceover work.

★ ★ ★ ★ ★

THE POSSESSED PRETTY GIRL: LINDA BLAIR

She may have been nominated for the 1973 Best Supporting Actress Academy Award at the ripe age of fifteen for her work spitting pea soup in the legendary horror flick *The Exorcist*, but today Linda Blair spends her time praising pleather and defending the rights of animals with PETA. She owns her own clothing line (Linda Blair's Wild West Collection) and is the author of a book about her animal-friendly eating habits called *Going Vegan!*

THREE THINGS YOU NEVER KNEW ABOUT... LINDA BLAIR

- In 1985, she was mocked with a Razzie Award for Worst Career Achievement as the queen of scream.

- After *The Exorcist* premiered in 1973, she had to hire policemen to stay at her family home because of all the death threats she received from frightened fans.

- To the surprise of many Hollywood veterans, Blair did not have a body double in the 1979 disco flick *Roller Boogie*. She did all of her own skating.

★ ★ ★ ★ ★

THE MUNSTER MAN: BUTCH PATRICK

Since sporting a widow's peak and playing with his famous woof-woof doll on *The Munsters* in 1964, child actor Butch Patrick has made friends with the rival family—he dated actress Lisa Loring, who played Wednesday Addams on *The Addams Family*. In the 1980s, Patrick formed the one-hit wonder band Eddie and the Monsters, best associated with the little known single "Whatever Happened to Eddie?" Although they were featured on *Basement Tapes*, a short-lived MTV show for unsigned bands, they never made it big as musicians. Today, Patrick spends every October dressing up as Eddie Munster for Halloween parties and sells woof-woof replicas on www.Munsters.com.

★ ★ ★ ★ ★

THE STARLET TURNED RECLUSE: DEANNA DURBIN

The Shirley Temple of the 1930s who grew famous alongside fellow singing actress Judy Garland, Deanna Durbin was the highest paid actress of her time. She won a juvenile Oscar for her work in the 1936 flick *Three Smart Girls* the same year Garland won for *The Wizard of Oz*, but in 1948, at 27 years old, she left Hollywood for a little peace and quiet. Today, she is a widow and protects her right to privacy in Paris, where she continues to refuse all requests for interviews.

THREE THINGS YOU NEVER KNEW ABOUT... DEANNA DURBIN

- She was considered to play Dorothy in *The Wizard of Oz* (1939).

- In 1980, she sent a photo of herself to *Life* magazine to squash rumors among her fans that she had gained weight.

- She was a favorite actress of Winston Churchill and Holocaust victim Anne Frank. Frank allegedly kept photos of Durbin in her secret Amsterdam annex, and Churchill used to request private screenings of her films before they were released in Great Britain.

★ ★ ★ ★ ★

ONE OF THE GANG: ROBERT BLAKE

Although he is more recently known for his acquittal of murder charges, child star Robert Blake (or Mickey Gubitosi, as he was known as a boy) got his start at just five years old in the series *Our Gang*. One of the more popular members of the rowdy gang, his career continued to blossom when he won parts in a number of films, including the coveted role of Little Beaver in the

Red Ryder Western series. Today, he still hasn't lost his passion for cowboy ways, and after he was let off the hook for the murder of his wife in 2005, he told several journalists that he was going to get a van and head out west. However innocent he may be, Blake has inspired many fellow actors in the art of playing the bad guy. His performances in *Baretta* and *In Cold Blood* were a help to Anthony Hopkins as he prepared for his creepy role as Hannibal Lecter.

★ ★ ★ ★ ★

THE ORIGINAL MOUSEKETEER: ANNETTE FUNICELLO

The Mickey Mouse Club has served as a launching pad for countless child stars, and Annette Funicello is no exception. Her roles sporting a one-piece in the sand led her to an adulthood full of beach flicks with Italian-American teen idol Frankie Avalon and chart-topping pop singles like "Tall Paul" and "Pineapple Princess." Unfortunately, while filming *Back to the*

THREE THINGS YOU NEVER KNEW ABOUT... ANNETTE FUNICELLO

- When Walt Disney cast her in her first beach movie, he asked her to avoid the temptation to show off her slim body in a bikini because a one-piece swimsuit would better uphold her wholesome image.

- Her son, Jason Gilardi, is in the rock band Caroline's Spine and played himself in her biographical movie, *A Dream Is a Wish Your Heart Makes*.

- Singer/songwriter Paul Anka wrote his hit single "Puppy Love" about how he had a crush on her.

Beach in 1987, Funicello was diagnosed with multiple sclerosis and has since set up the Annette Funicello Fund for Neurological Disorders. She announced her battle with the disorder in 1992, and in 1995, told her story in the biographical made-for-TV-movie, *A Dream Is a Wish Your Heart Makes: The Annette Funicello Story*.

★ ★ ★ ★ ★

THE STINGY PEN PAL: STANLEY LIVINGSTON

Stanley Livingston's portrayal of Chip Douglas may have made him one of the least loved personas on *My Three Sons* in the 1960s (he was known to throw away his fan mail without reading it), but he has since lived down the poor reputation. Livingston continued his youthful fame in a other TV and movie roles, but today he has left the spotlight for good. Instead of pursuing fame for himself, he serves the stars as an artist—his popular stained glass has been purchased by the likes of Tom Hanks and Hugh Hefner.

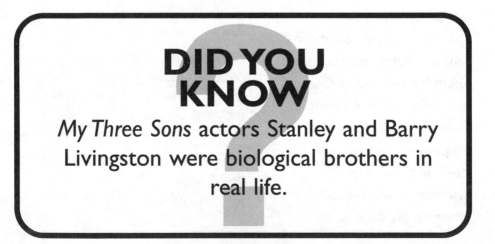

DID YOU KNOW

My Three Sons actors Stanley and Barry Livingston were biological brothers in real life.

★ ★ ★ ★ ★

THE SHORT-LIVED PARTRIDGE: JEREMY GELBWAKS

Known around the world as Chris Partridge number one on *The Partridge Family*—he was replaced when his father got an out-of-state job transfer in 1971—today, Gelbwaks is a product manager for a computer company in New Orleans. Ironically, New Orleans is also the hometown of drummer Susan Cowsill of The Cowsills, the band upon which *The Partridge Family* story was based.

★ ★ ★ ★ ★

THE STEREOTYPE SMASHER: MARY BADHAM

Famous for her portrayal of the innocent Scout Finch in *To Kill A Mockingbird*, today Badham restores aged art for a living and helps coordinate college testing on the side. She also travels around the world speaking about the importance of tolerance and kindness, messages from her hit childhood movie role. In

THREE THINGS YOU NEVER KNEW ABOUT... MARY BADHAM

- For years after filming *To Kill A Mockingbird*, she kept in touch with actor Gregory Peck and continued to call him Atticus until his death in 2003.

- She is the sister of *Saturday Night Fever* director John Badham.

- In 1963 at just ten years old, she was the youngest ever Academy Award nominee for Best Supporting Actress. She has since lost the record to Tatum O'Neal for the 1973 film *Paper Moon*.

2005, she appeared onscreen for the first time in thirty-eight years in the Cameron Watson film *Our Very Own,* and has since agreed to come out of retirement and consider future roles if the script fits.

★ ★ ★ ★ ★

THE BOLD BRADY: CHRISTOPHER KNIGHT

Since playing curious middle child Peter on *The Brady Bunch*, Christopher Knight has joined a cast of other Hollywood has-beens like Charo on a host of VH1 reality television shows, where he makes a fool of himself for all of America to see. His most recent project, *My Fair Brady*, portrays his relationship with *America's Next Top Model*'s Adrienne Curry, who is half his age. When he's not making jokes about his girlfriend's sexuality on camera, Knight works as a computer nerd (he was once the executive vice president at Eskape Labs) and occasionally makes appearances as his former Peter Brady self in cast reunion flicks like *The Brady Brides* (1981) and *A Very Brady Christmas* (1988).

★ ★ ★ ★ ★

THE BLOSSOMING BRAINIAC: MAYIM BIALIK

Despite rumors that she had died of alcohol poisoning in 1997, the child star who portrayed the brainy babe Blossom Russo in the hit sitcom *Blossom* is alive and well, living the posh life of a smarty-pants

UCLA graduate working toward a Ph.D. in neuroscience. She will still admit, however, that while filming the show during her teenage years, she had a huge crush on TV brother Anthony, played by Michael Stoyanov.

★ ★ ★ ★ ★

AN UPDATE ON OTHER CHILD STARS:

- **Peter Ostrum**, who played the lead role in *Charlie and the Chocolate Factory*, was offered a contract for three more films by Warner Brothers but declined and quit acting altogether. Today he is a veterinarian in upstate New York.

- **Mindy Cohn**, who played Natalie Green on *The Facts of Life*, graduated from Loyola-Marymount University in 1995 and has since served as the voice of Velma in the cartoon series *What's New Scooby-Doo?* She is also an avid member of weSPARK, a cancer support group.

- **Valerie Bertinelli**, who was known for perfect hair and perky smiles as Barbara Royer on the sitcom *One Day At A Time*, married rocker Eddie Van Halen and joined the cast of a slew of Lifetime movies in the 1980s and 1990s. Things must not have been all smiles, though; the couple divorced in 2005.

- **Ron Howard**, otherwise known as Opie Taylor from *The Andy Griffith Show*, has become a very successful director/producer. He won two Academy Awards and a Directors Guild of America Award for producing and directing *A Beautiful Mind*.

Chapter 8

✩

The Ultimate Television/Movies Quiz

The Ultimate Television/Movies Quiz

★ ★ ★ ★ ★ ★ ★ ★ ★ ★ ★ ★ ★ ★ ★ ★

So you think you know everything there is to know about the hottest television series and box office movies. Try your hand at the ultimate test of trivia about the best moments 1950-2005 had to offer:

★ ★ ★ ★ ★

WHAT'S IN A NAME: PART 1

1. Mouth and Chunk were the nicknames of what characters in *The Goonies?*

   _____

2. In *Dirty Dancing*, what was Baby's real name?

   _____

3. Bill and Ted introduced several historical figures to Missy in *Bill and Ted's Excellent Adventures.* Who were they?

   _____

4. Name all four Ghostbusters.

    _____

5. In *Labyrinth*, Sarah is trying to save her baby brother. What was his name?

    _____

6. In *Aliens*, what was Newt's real name?

    _____

7. Name the robot from the *Short Circuit* flicks.

    _____

8. In *Ferris Bueller's Day Off*, what is the principal's name? His assistant?

    _____

9. In the 1980s cult classic film *Sixteen Candles*, what was the name of the exchange student kept by Sam's grandparents?

    _____

10. In *Tootsie*, what was the name of the woman played by Dustin Hoffmann?

    _____

★ ★ ★ ★ ★

CAMEO CHARACTERS: TRIVIA ABOUT SPECIAL APPEARANCES

Who was the actor/actress who played...

1. the pretty blond girl Elliot danced with in *ET: The Extra-Terrestrial*?

   _____

2. the burnout at the police station Ferris's sister, Jeanie, kisses in *Ferris Beuller's Day Off*?

   _____

3. Sarah Jessica Parker's best friend in *Girls Just Wanna Have Fun*?

   _____

4. Julie's best friend in *I Still Know What You Did Last Summer*?

   _____

5. Jodie Dallas, the first openly gay character on network television, in the sitcom *Soap*?

   _____

6. Spicolli's sidekicks in *Fast Times at Ridgemont High*?

   _____

7. Karen's divorce lawyer on *Will & Grace*?

   _____

8. the spaceship's voice in *Flight of the Navigator*?

   _____

9. an ambulance driver on the 2005 season of *ER*?

    _____

10. an ambulance driver on the 2004 season of *Scrubs*?

    _____

★ ★ ★ ★ ★

OTHER CAMEO TRIVIA

1. What was Judge Smales's grandson's name in *Caddyshack*?

    _____

2. What *Cheers* actor appeared in *Star Wars: The Empire Strikes Back*?

    _____

3. What famous director makes an appearance at the end of *Blues Brothers*?

    _____

4. What famous director often scripted himself into small background roles in his own films?

    _____

★ ★ ★ ★ ★

THE DAILY GRIND: TRIVIA ABOUT WORK

1. In *Say Anything*, what did John Cusack say he would never do for a living? What career did he want?

    _____

    _____

2. In *Office Space*, what was Milton's prized possession that Peter pulled from the rubble after Intitech burned to the ground?

    _____

3. What job does Tom Hanks's character have in *Bachelor Party*?

    _____

4. On *The Jeffersons*, what business does George Jefferson own?

    _____

5. On *24*, what agency employs Jack Bauer?

    _____

6. In the movie *Notting Hill,* what magazine does Hugh Grant's character say he works for in an attempt to get an "interview" with the movie star played by Julia Roberts?

    _____

7. What was Adam Sandler's occupation in *Big Daddy*?

    _____

8. In *Midnight Run*, what agency does Walsh (Robert De Niro) work for?

    _____

9. On *Friends*, what were the names of the restaurants where Monica was head chef?

   _____

10. In *Beverly Hills Cop*, Axel Foley enters the hotel and uses an alias. Who does he say he works for, and who is he allegedly going to interview?

    _____

11. What does Michelle say she invented in *Romy and Michelle's High School Reunion*?

    _____

12. Who was the sponsor for *Wayne's World*?

    _____

13. In *The Karate Kid*, what color did Mr. Miagi make Daniel paint his house as part of his training?

    _____

★ ★ ★ ★ ★

MAN'S BEST FRIEND: TRIVIA ABOUT ANIMALS

1. In *Next Friday*, what name is given to the ferocious dog?

   _____

2. What is the donkey's name in *Shrek*?

   _____

3. In the film *Jumanji*, what is the last animal to stomp through the room after the stampede?

   _____

4. In *Splash,* what does the mermaid choose to name herself after?

   _____

5. What is the name of the animal star whose theme song describes him as "faster than lightning?"

   _____

6. In *The Little Mermaid*, what did the seagull Scuttle name a fork?

   _____

7. By what name is Mickey Mouse known in Italy?

   _____

8. In *Star Trek*, what name does Captain Jean-Luc Picard give his fish?

   _____

9. What kind of a bird kept Robert Blake company on *Baretta?* What was his name?

   _____

★ ★ ★ ★ ★

ON THE ROAD AGAIN: TRIVIA ABOUT TRAVELING

1. In *National Lampoon's Vacation*, what did the legendary Griswald family call their green station wagon?

   _____

2. What kind of car was made famous by *The Dukes of Hazzard?*

   _____

3. In *Spaceballs*, what does the bumper sticker say on the back of Lonestar's ship?

    _____

4. In *Innerspace*, what did Igoe's license plate say?

    _____

5. What was on the license plate of the Ghostbusters' car?

    _____

★ ★ ★ ★ ★

NUMBER CRUNCHERS: TRIVIA ABOUT DIGITS

1. How many days were the castaways on the mysterious island during the first season of *Lost*?

    _____

2. How many gigawatts of electricity did Doc Brown need to power the Delorion in *Back to the Future*?

    _____

3. What was the hottest possible temperature on the Klopek's furnace in *The 'Burbs*?

    _____

4. What was Dirty Harry's badge number?

    _____

5. Above what speed did the bus in the movie *Speed* need to go in order to keep from blowing up?

    _____

6. In *National Lampoon's Animal House,* what is Blutarski's grade-point average?

   _____

7. In *Stripes,* how much money does Ox (John Candy) pay to mud wrestle with women?

   _____

8. In *Monty Python and the Holy Grail,* what number must you count to before throwing the Holy Hand Grenade?

   _____

9. On *The Brady Bunch,* at what address did Mike and Carol Brady live?

   _____

★ ★ ★ ★ ★

WHAT'S IN A NAME: PART II

1. Who ordered the Code Red in *A Few Good Men?*

   _____

2. What big-hearted, underprivileged character did Leonardo DiCaprio play in *Titanic?*

   _____

3. What was the name of Milla Jovovich's character in *The Fifth Element?*

   _____

4. In *Jerry McGuire,* what was the name of Jerry's stepson?

   _____

5. In *Matilda*, what was the name of Matilda's teacher?

   _____

6. In *Fantasia*, what is the name of the Sorcerer?

   _____

7. On *I Love Lucy*, what was Lucy Ricardo's maiden name?

   _____

8. On *Friends*, to what person was Chandler's *TV Guide* delivered?

   _____

★ ★ ★ ★ ★

SHE LOVES ME, SHE LOVES ME NOT: TRIVIA ABOUT RELATIONSHIPS

1. Where did Ronald take Cindy for their final date in the movie *Can't Buy Me Love*?

   _____

2. On *Friends*, why did Phoebe and Mike break up?

   _____

3. In *Weird Science*, what don't Gary and Wyatt do when they take a shower with Lisa?

   _____

4. What was the real name of Carrie's lover (Mr. Big) on *Sex and the City*?

   _____

5. Which onscreen lover did Gene Kelly make cry by telling her she couldn't dance in *Singin' in the Rain*?

    _____

6. Because the movie *Ghost* was so romantic, what was handed out to women at showings in Mexico?

    _____

★ ★ ★ ★ ★

FAMOUS FIRSTS: TRIVIA ABOUT GROUNDBREAKING HISTORY

Do you know these famous firsts?

1. First feature-length animated film

    _____

2. First (and only) silent film to win an Academy Award

    _____

3. First PG-rated Disney picture

    _____

4. First film with audible dialogue

    _____

5. First black woman to win an Oscar

    _____

6. First person to make $1 million for a single picture

    _____

7. First name Bugs Bunny appeared under in his early 1930s cartoons

   _____

8. First interracial sitcom kiss

   _____

   _____

9. Winner of the first televised Miss America pageant in 1954

   _____

10. First U.S. company to make a commercial featuring lingerie models

    _____

11. First character to speak in the original *Star Wars*

    _____

12. First film in which Pierce Brosnan appeared as James Bond

    _____

13. First woman director to bring in more than $100 million at the box office

    _____

★ ★ ★ ★ ★

GASP! TRIVIA ABOUT SCANDALS

1. Which *Survivor* contestant lied about his grandmother's death to gain sympathy on the show?

    _____

2. Which of President Bartlet's children was kidnapped on *The West Wing?*

    _____

3. What did Livia try to arrange for her son, Tony, on the first season of *The Sopranos?*

    _____

4. What childhood trauma constantly haunted Fox Mulder on *The X Files?*

    _____

5. In *The Breakfast Club*, what was found in Brian's locker that he was going to try to kill himself with?

    _____

6. What was used as blood for the famous shower scene in Alfred Hitchcock's *Psycho?*

    _____

7. On a finale of *Desperate Housewives*, what secret did Mary Alice die to protect?

    _____

8. What was everyone on set of *The Alamo* (2004) told to do to passing news helicopters to keep them from being able to use their footage on television?

    _____

Answers

★ ★ ★ ★ ★

WHAT'S IN A NAME: PART 1

1. Clark and Lawrence

2. Frances

3. Socrates, Billy the Kid, Joan of Arc, Sigmund Freud, Genghis Khan, Beethoven, and Abraham Lincoln

4. Peter Venkman, Egon Spengler, Ray Stantz, and Winston Zedmore

5. Toby

6. Rebecca Jorden

7. Johnny

8. Ed Rooney and Grace

9. Long Duk Dong

10. Dorothy Michaels

★ ★ ★ ★ ★

CAMEO CHARACTERS: TRIVIA ABOUT SPECIAL APPEARANCES

Name the actor/actress who played...

1. Erika Eleniak

2. Charlie Sheen

3. Helen Hunt

4. Brandy

5. Billy Crystal

6. Eric Stolz and Anthony Edwards

7. Macaulay Culkin

8. Pee Wee Herman

9. John Stamos

10. Molly Shannon

★ ★ ★ ★ ★

OTHER CAMEO TRIVIA

1. Spaulding

2. John Ratzenberg

3. Steven Spielberg

4. Alfred Hitchcock

★ ★ ★ ★ ★

THE DAILY GRIND: TRIVIA ABOUT WORK

1. He said he would never buy anything, sell anything, or process anything. He wanted to be a kickboxer.

2. The red stapler

3. He is a school bus driver.

4. Dry cleaning

5. CTU

6. *Horse and Hound*

7. Tollbooth worker

8. Mosconi Bail Bonds

9. Alesandro's and Javu

10. *Rolling Stone*, Michael Jackson

11. Post-its

12. Noah's arcade

13. Green

★ ★ ★ ★ ★

MAN'S BEST FRIEND: TRIVIA ABOUT ANIMALS

1. Chico

2. Donkey

3. A rhinoceros

4. Madison Avenue

5. Flipper

6. Dinglehopper

7. Topolino

8. Livingston

9. Cockatoo, Fred

★ ★ ★ ★ ★

ON THE ROAD AGAIN: TRIVIA ABOUT TRAVELING

1. The Family Truckster

2. 1968 Charger

3. I Love Uranus

4. SNAPON

5. ECTO-1

★ ★ ★ ★ ★

NUMBER CRUNCHERS: TRIVIA ABOUT DIGITS

1. 44

2. 1.21 gigawatts

3. 5,000 degrees

4. 2211

5. 50 mph

6. 0.0

7. $413.58

8. Three… no more, no less

9. 4222 Clinton Way. No city was ever specified.

★ ★ ★ ★ ★

WHAT'S IN A NAME: PART II

1. Colonel Nathan P. Jessup

2. Jack Dawson

3. Lelu

4. Ray

5. Jennifer Honey

6. Yensid (Disney spelled backward)

7. McGillicuddy

8. Miss Chanandler Bong

★ ★ ★ ★ ★

SHE LOVES ME, SHE LOVES ME NOT: TRIVIA ABOUT RELATIONSHIPS

1. An airplane junkyard

2. He never wanted to get married.

3. Take off their pants

4. John

5. Debbie Reynolds

6. Envelopes of tissues

★ ★ ★ ★ ★

FAMOUS FIRSTS: TRIVIA ABOUT GROUNDBREAKING HISTORY

1. *Snow White and the Seven Dwarfs* (1937)

2. *Wings* (1927)

3. *The Black Hole* (1979)

4. *The Jazz Singer* (1927)

5. Hattie McDaniel

6. Elizabeth Taylor, *Cleopatra*

7. Happy Rabbit

8. *Star Trek* stars Captain James T. Kirk (William Shatner) and Lt. Uhura (Nichelle Nichols) on November 22, 1968

9. Miss California, Lee Ann Meriwether

10. Playtex in 1987

11. C-3P0

12. *Golden Eye* (1995)

13. Penny Marshall for *Big*

★ ★ ★ ★ ★

GASP! TRIVIA ABOUT SCANDALS

1. Jon Dalton

2. Zoey

3. His death.

4. His sister was kidnapped by aliens.

5. A flare gun

6. Chocolate syrup

7. She murdered her son's biological mother.

8. Show them their middle fingers

Real Cheesy Facts About: Rock 'n' Roll

Chapter 1

✰

Divas: Rock Stars' Wacky Habits and Demands

BERRY

Divas: Rock Stars' Wacky Habits and Demands

★ ★ ★ ★ ★ ★ ★ ★ ★ ★ ★ ★ ★ ★ ★ ★

Just what is it that brings out the wild side in rockers on tour? Is it the lyrics and the screaming groupies, or is it simply boredom from so many weeks on the road? Or maybe their crazy antics are publicity ploys, as they try anything to maintain their stardom. Whether it's going nuts onstage, shooting off their mouths on late-night talk shows, or making wacky demands to the people trying to please them, these artists are nothing short of divas.

Prince demands to have a physician inject him with Vitamin B12 before each of his shows. He also requires all food located backstage remain covered with cellophane until he can uncover each item.

★ ★ ★ ★ ★

Break Stuff—Bad Backstage Behavior

When it came to finding innovative ways to look badass on tour, The Who was unbeatable. The first band to make smashing instruments onstage cool, they were infamous for their mess-making ways. Drummer Keith Moon first tossed his drums around during his audition with fellow band mates. The trend stuck, and the adrenaline rush of destroying something so expensive, in front of a crowd so loud, was contagious. Guitarist Pete Townshend quickly caught on, and front man Roger Daltrey started swinging his microphone over his head. Townshend, however, claims his first guitar-busting incident was actually an accident when it was smacked by a low ceiling fan at an indoor club. Regardless, the rocker legend of shattering pricey gear lives on.

Other Rock Stars Who Smashed Their Stuff

Kurt Cobain—Grunge bands like Pearl Jam often took after Nirvana's Kurt Cobain and vented their frustration by smashing their guitars.

Jimi Hendrix—The king of playing guitar in the most terribly uncomfortable positions (with his teeth and between his legs), Hendrix first got violent onstage when he smashed his guitar to bits at the Monterey International Pop Festival in 1967.

★ ★ ★ ★ ★

CRAZY (AND INTOXICATED)

Smashing stuff onstage may be a rush to some famous rockers, but others prefer to keep it in the privacy of their own hotel rooms. **An infamous pair often nicknamed the "Toxic Twins," Steven Tyler and Joe Perry of Aerosmith, had their fair share of drug problems** in the 1970s, and thanks to cabin fever brought on by being on the road for months at a time, they quickly developed a fetish for destruction. To keep them busy in their hotel rooms after concerts, Tyler and Perry always took two staples on tour with them: chainsaws and extra-long extension cords. Why? Because they wanted to do as much damage as possible. The chainsaws were used to slice up the hotel room. The cords were used when they tossed the television out of the hotel window, so they could watch their favorite shows all the way down.

> ### GUITARIST WHO ROCKS
>
> Joe Perry
>
> Band: Aerosmith
>
> Guitar of Choice: All kinds
>
> Best Known For: "Walk This Way" on the album *Toys in the Attic*

Aerosmith wasn't the only band to trash its temporary living quarters while on tour. While in Germany in 1984, **Mötley Crüe tossed mattresses out of their windows** because they thought the mattresses would look cool bouncing off the cars below. The government didn't put up with such antics for long, though—the band was tossed out of the country within the week. Keith Moon of

185

The Who, nicknamed "Moon the Loon," was also infamous for making a mess. When a hotel manager asked him to turn down his noisy tunes one afternoon (which happened to be a cassette of his own music), Moon tore his room to shreds and said, "That was noise." Restarting his tape, he continued, "This is The Who."

★ ★ ★ ★ ★

THIS USED TO BE MY PLAYGROUND

A shock-value pop idol who loves to push the envelope with her edgy lyrics and constant reinvention of image, Madonna was a little star-struck (and jealous) when Anaheim skater chick Gwen Stefani emerged in Hollywood from the ska music scene. Since opening for industry veterans Red Hot Chili Peppers and rock reggae star Ziggy Marley in the early 1990s, No Doubt had struggled to earn their fame. As the band continued to push for recognition and their first hits, "Just

CELEBRITY ALIAS
Alias: Ziggy Marley
Actual Name: David Marley

186

A Girl" and "Spiderwebs," climbed the charts, Stefani stole the spotlight from the Material Girl and became increasingly popular for her rock-hard midriff and eastern bindi jewel. Taking a bit of a backseat to the newbie, Madonna was rumored to have called Stefani a poser for copying Madonna's signature dance moves and hairstyles.

"Just A Girl" was not the first music video No Doubt ever made for MTV. As the band struggled for recognition in the early 1990s, they sent producers a low-budget video for the single "Trapped in the Box," but MTV didn't air it once.

Soon after the comment, Madonna's long-time friend Rosie O'Donnell canceled Stefani's upcoming appearance on her talk show. O'Donnell claimed it was because of "scheduling differences," but No Doubt fans suspected it was a friendly favor.

★ ★ ★ ★ ★

AIN'T TOO PROUD TO BEG (FOR FORGIVENESS)

DID YOU KNOW

Madonna is distantly related to both Gwen Stefani and Celine Dion.

A rock and roll legend dating back to hits such as "Roll Over Beethoven" (1956) and "Johnny B. Goode" (1958), **Chuck Berry is used to getting what he wants**. Known for never sharing the spotlight, Berry always toured by himself and required venues to provide a backup band at each concert. His demanding ways embarrassed him at the Hollywood Palladium Theatre in 1972, however. The concert was rockin' until his lead guitarist suddenly let someone else take his place on stage. Confused about the switch, Berry stopped in the middle of a song to complain that the replacement was playing too loud and drowning out his vocals. Later, he blushed when he realized that the swap was a surprise appearance by Rolling Stones legend Keith Richards.

★ ★ ★ ★ ★

THIS IS A REBEL CHICK

More famous for her buzz cut than for her actual talent as an artist, Irish pop singer **Sinead O'Connor was the queen of attitude and anti-patriotism**. In 1990, she turned down an offer to play a gig in New Jersey because she didn't want to support any event where the national anthem would be played. Later that year, while shopping at a health food store in California, she allegedly had an employee fired for playing the tune overhead to get on her nerves.

O'Connor's most famous anti-everything escapade was, of course, when she finally agreed to appear on Saturday Night Live in 1992. (She had refused the first offer in 1990 because she did not want to appear with comedian Andrew Clay, who she said was too edgy.) As O'Connor began her opening monologue, however, producers quickly regretted the second offer. Instead of spouting off the expected one-liners, O'Connor sang the Bob Marley song "War" and tore up a photo of Pope John Paul II.

★ ★ ★ ★ ★

IF YOU WANNA BE MY PRODUCER—YOU'VE GOTTA GET WITH MY DEMANDS

When Posh Spice Victoria Adams and soccer hunk hubby, David Beckham, got the news that a British television station wanted to film a documentary about their ultra-extravagant lives, they did what any star would do—they got picky and took over. Not only did the couple want complete control over censoring private or potentially embarrassing video segments they might want deleted from the documentary, they also demanded the right to fire anyone they didn't like during the filming. Program producers decided Adams and Beckham were a little too demanding and soon canceled the project. A documentary was made, and a DVD version of *The Real Beckhams* was released in 2003.

★ ★ ★ ★ ★

PSYCHED FOR PSEUDONYMS

Changing their name is something bored rock stars have always been delighted to do, so long as their fans comply. Hoping to reinvent himself (over and over again), **David Jones of Brixton, England, thought his name was too dorky**—and too similar to cheesy heartthrob Davy Jones of the Monkees. So he changed his name to Lou. Then he changed it to Calvin. Then, after being inspired by a very sharp (and very manly) Bowie knife, he changed it once and for all to David Bowie. No stranger to identity crisis, Bowie has since been known by an assortment of other alter egos, including Ziggy Stardust, Aladdin Sane, and Thin White Duke.

More famous for changing his name (and his funky purple outfits) than anyone, however, is the wacky artist formerly known as Prince. While his weirdest (and most unpronounceable) change was back in 1993 with the perplexing squiggle—which looked something like the overlapped symbols for

CELEBRITY ALIAS

Alias: Prince
Actual Name: Prince Rogers Nelson

male and female—he has a history of silly pseudonyms that include Joey Coco, Jamie Starr, Alexander Nevermind, and, who could forget, His Royal Badness (because he likes to think that he is "bad" in the same way that Michael Jackson was "Bad," meaning good).

★ ★ ★ ★ ★

BOTTOMS UP

Friends and musicians **Gibby Haynes and Paul Leary had trouble deciding what to call themselves** before landing on this ingenious name The Butthole Surfers. In their early years, the band gave themselves a new name for every show they played—Abe Lincoln's Bush, the Dave Clark Five, the Vodka Family Winstons, and a long list of other ridiculous monikers.

Students at Trinity University in Texas, Haynes and Leary started their own business selling pillowcases and T-shirts decorated with pictures of Lee Harvey Oswald.

While many bands made the bad move of converting their stardom to the small screen as video game protagonists, Gary Garcia and Jerry Buckner paid tribute to classics such as *Pac-Man*, *Donkey Kong*, and *Centipede* through music. After their first single, "Pac-Man Fever," climbed the Billboard Top 40 in the early 1980s, they decided to create a whole album based on video games. Its most memorable songs include "Do the Donkey Kong" and "Ode to a Centipede."

★ ★ ★ ★ ★

WHO'S BAD?

When KISS kicked onto the music scene in the 1970s, they were instantly famous for their heavy metal pyrotechnics and outrageous makeup. A symbol of all things rebellious (and sometimes satanic), the band's live shows and albums were a huge success. Longing for even more fame and fortune, they asked themselves, "Could we make fans out of video gamers?" Not quite.

> CELEBRITY ALIAS
> Alias: Gene Simmons
> Actual Name: Chaim Witz

During the band's comeback tour in the 1990s, they noticed that vintage KISS pinball machines had become a collectible in high demand, and decided to market the game for home computers and Nintendo systems. The idea bombed, but the band didn't lose heart—they released a *second* video game even more horrible than the first called *Psycho Circus*, which also bombed just as miserably.

Gene Simmons wasn't the only rock legend to flop when he tried to take his tunes to the gaming realm. **Featuring cheesy musical synthesizer versions of "Beat It" and "Billie Jean,"** Michael Jackson's *Moonwalker* game for Sega Genesis hit stores in 1989. The premise: defeat kidnappers and drug dealers and rescue children around the world while wearing a stylin' zoot suit and holding funky dance-offs in graveyards and dark closets.

★ ★ ★ ★ ★

PROVOKING THE PISTOLS

The Sex Pistols never set out to fire off a round of curse words on an evening talk show in the U.K. in 1976, but after the band was provoked by interviewer Bill Grundy to "step outside," every British kiddie up past their bedtime had several crude new additions to their vocabulary. Initially brought on to tell late-night viewers about the underground punk movement, the Pistols' interview was quite peaceful at first. They were actually charming (if a little over-dressed). Possibly disappointed that he couldn't reveal the rockers as talentless metal heads, Grundy laid on the vague insults and finally snapped, "You've got another ten seconds, say something outrageous." Guitarist Steve Jones gave him what he asked for. A few f-bombs later, England had a taste of what punk rock was all about.

CELEBRITY ALIASES

Alias: Johnny Rotten
Actual Name: John Lydon

Alias: Sid Vicious
Actual Name: John Simon Ritchie

GUITARIST WHO ROCKS

Steve Jones

Band: The Sex Pistols

Guitar of Choice: Les Paul Custom

Best Known For: "Anarchy in the U.K." from the album *Never Mind the Bollocks, Here's the Sex Pistols* (1977)

★ ★ ★ ★ ★

FIGHT FOR YOUR RIGHT TO RIOT

Right-wing daddies, fearing the sexual rebellion of their innocent teenage daughters, reared their ugly heads when the Beastie Boys set out to tour Great Britain in the spring of 1987. Rumor had it that the band's stage show was obscene, and that their fans were known to riot. Although exaggerated, the trepidation materialized when the rockers played their gig at the Liverpool Royal Court. Thanks to a steady rain of beer cans and tear gas lobbed into the crowd by drunken fans, the show was stopped after only ten minutes. Beastie Ad-Rock allegedly joined the madness to spite those who had predicted the trouble—he was charged with throwing a beer car in a fan's face.

★ ★ ★ ★ ★

YOU GIVE STRIPPERS A BAD NAME

After ditching his high school R&B cover band, Atlantic City Expressway, rocker **Jon Bon Jovi formed a hot New Jersey band** called Jon Bon Jovi and the Wild Ones, and hit the town with his tunes. While still too young to get into the clubs where he played every weekend, he recorded his first record at age nineteen, but it wasn't all that glamorous. His first big hit was "R2-D2, We Wish You a Merry Christmas," which he recorded for a holiday Star Wars album. The humble, cheesy beginnings would soon change.

Bon Jovi's band began acting like true rock divas when their third album rolled around, and they chose singles like "Wanted Dead or

Alive" for the album they eloquently titled *Slippery When Wet*. While the front man says they chose the title based on signs they saw on the highway, David Bryan disagreed. Bryan openly spread the rumor that the title was a tribute to striptease clubs where women would pour soapy water all over each other.

CELEBRITY ALIAS

Alias: Jon Bon Jovi
Actual Name: John Bongiovi

195

★ ★ ★ ★ ★

NICE GUYS LIGHT UP LAST

Billie Joe Armstrong and Mike Dirnt of Green Day had a slow start to fame, but like any hopeful rock star, persevered through the rough years of being no-namers. While in high school, the boys were scheduled to play a gig with the Lookouts in California. But when they got there, the power didn't work, the bathrooms were out of order, and only about five people had shown up for the party. Unscathed by the disappointment, Sweet Children—which was the name of their band at the time—plugged into a generator, lit a few candles, and rocked out. Lookouts guitarist Larry Livermore, who also ran an independent music label, offered them a record deal on the spot.

As a sixteen-year-old artist new to the punk music scene, Billie Joe Armstrong earned the nickname "Two-Dollar Bill" for selling joints for $2 each. He changed his band's name to Green Day, which is slang for spending an entire day smoking pot. His mother must have been proud.

★ ★ ★ ★ ★

REACH OUT AND TOUCH SOMEONE

Diana Ross was called Diane by friends and family until her early twenties.

When a security guard frisked soul diva Diana Ross at London's Heathrow Airport in the late 1990s, she flipped out. Upset that she had been needlessly fondled and that her complaint had not been taken seriously, Ross walked back over to the smirking guard and gave her a taste of her own medicine. Ross felt the guard's body in the same way, saying, "There, how do you like it?" Ross continued to explain that she was wearing a tight bodysuit that would have made any hidden weapon obvious—there was no need to feel her breasts and in between her legs. Ross was arrested for her retaliation. Since then, she has been no stranger to run-ins with the police. In 2002, she failed a sobriety test and was arrested for drunk driving in Arizona.

When Ross tried to organize a reunion tour with the other original members of The Supremes in the 2000s, her plea fell on deaf ears when Mary Wilson and Cindy Birdsong were only offered $3 million and $1 million, respectively. They simply could not support a tour where their ultra-famous third wheel would make so much more money than they. Ross had been offered a whopping $15 million.

★ ★ ★ ★ ★

PLAYING WITH FIRE

The Rolling Stones had no idea that they could have a party so full of booze, drugs, and women that they would actually set a New York hotel on fire during the

blackout of 1965. Hotel officials had provided candles to all of their residents, and when the bed caught on fire, no one seemed to notice until the blaze was out of control. How did the groupies handle the flames? They threw ice buckets at it, of course.

CELEBRITY ALIAS

Alias: Bill Wyman (The Rolling Stones)
Actual Name: William Perks

GUITARIST WHO ROCKS

Keith Richards
Band: The Rolling Stones
Guitar of Choice: Fender Telecaster
Best Known For: "Honkey Tonk Women" on the album *Hot Rocks 1964-1971*

★ ★ ★ ★ ★

OPPORTUNITIES LOST

A rock star just wouldn't be a rock star if she didn't turn down major movie roles. All jealousy (and touring schedules) aside, Britney Spears did just that when she missed out on the opportunity to star in not one, but

five big-screen productions. *Chicago* producer Harvey Weinstein had allegedly hoped the pop queen would play the part of Kitty Baxter, which later went to actress Lucy Liu. Britney was also considered for the part of Allie in the award-winning film *The Notebook*, but newcomer Rachel McAdams won the part instead. Spears turned down small roles in *Scary Movie* and *Buffy the Vampire Slayer* because of scheduling conflicts, but her biggest loss was when Jessica Simpson beat her out in the race to play Daisy Duke in the 2005 remake of *The Dukes of Hazzard*.

Madonna has also had her fair share of roles thrown her way. She was offered roles in *Showgirls* and *Casino,* as well as Michelle Pfeiffer's part in *Batman Returns*, Jada Pinkett Smith's part in *Madagascar,* and Renee Zellwegger's part in *Chicago*.

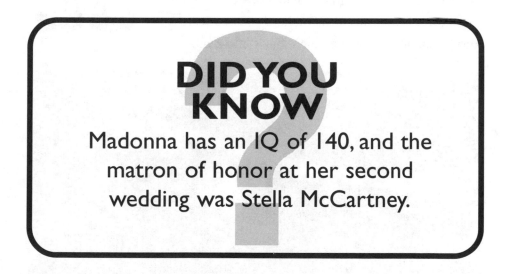

DID YOU KNOW

Madonna has an IQ of 140, and the matron of honor at her second wedding was Stella McCartney.

★ ★ ★ ★ ★

YOU CAN'T ALWAYS GET WHAT YOU WANT

When it comes to rock stars and the things they "need," the sky is the limit for wacky demands. What does every head banger crave backstage? Australians INXS say a Ping-Pong table. Pop-R&B crossover diva Mariah Carey cannot do without a box of bendy straws. From these strange demands to others— everything from a personal masseuse to an endless supply of Captain Crunch cereal—these rock stars aren't afraid to make their requests known to all who are at their beck and call.

That's not fair! I WANT IT!

Aerosmith—Famous for their post-concert rendezvous with promiscuous women, Aerosmith frequently requested that a dozen clean bath towels and a massive pasta pit await them

> Aerosmith lead vocalist Steven Tyler hates it when friends call him "Steve."

after gigs (and no, it was not for eating). Band members would take turns hopping into the slimy pit and wrestling with their young female fans. The boys of summer made sure they got their snacks, too. On the first night of their first Japanese tour, they reportedly freaked out and destroyed their room backstage when the concert promoter put turkey rolls on their complimentary private buffet (the nerve!).

Van Halen—Known for one specific (and annoying) request in every concert contract, Van Halen always asks for a backstage bowl of M&Ms—with the brown ones removed, of course. If this crucial

DID YOU KNOW

Songwriter Janis Ian received hundreds of Valentine's Day cards on February 14, 1977, after releasing the Billboard No. 3 hit "At Seventeen," in which she sang about how she never received Valentines as a teenager.

detail is overlooked, the band stresses that the paperwork should have been read more carefully. Their picky appeals have turned them into sloppy businessmen, though. Van Halen actually canceled a Colorado concert in 1981 because when they showed up for rehearsal, brown M&Ms were still in the bowl. Well, that and when they set up their heavy equipment, the faulty stage sank to the ground. Frustrated, they reboarded the tour bus and went home.

Def Leppard—Most famous for the 1980s hit single "Pour Some Sugar on Me," these rockers were techno savvy. At concerts, they wanted a list of the radio frequencies used by every local police, ambulance, and fire station, so they could make sure the signals wouldn't interfere with their state-of-the-art wireless guitars. Just to be sure nothing else would ruin the show with feedback, they also

In 2005, Def Leppard held an online trivia contest and awarded the winner a candy blue Jackson JS1 Dinky guitar autographed by band members. The three "not-so-easy" questions were:

- When Vivian joined the band in 1992 after Steve Clark passed away, he was not the only ex-Whitesnake guitarist who was considered to join the band. Who was the other one? (Answer: John Sykes)

- During the recordings of "Let's Get Rocked," at what time did the band eat? (Answer: 6:00 p.m.)

- Which guitarist, who used to play with David Bowie, was the original inspiration for Joe and Phil to start their Cybernauts project? (Answer: Mick Ronson)

demanded that all stadium police and security turn off their cell phones, pagers, and walkie-talkies.

Christina Aguilera—A superstar at just seventeen years old with the hit pop song "Genie in a Bottle," and the epitome of *Girls Gone Wild* just three years later, Christina Aguilera learned early that what a girl wants backstage, she can have—organic foods, Flintstone chewable vitamins, herbal tea, chewing gum, and breath mints. She wasn't all health nut, though. Aguilera also made sure she had Oreos, chocolate chip cookies, and white bread for her pre-concert sandwiches.

Mariah Carey—If you aren't going to take a picture of the right side of Mariah Carey's face, you'd better not take one at all. When the pop diva is on a photo shoot, she's a bit picky about photographers paying attention to her "good side." Carey is known for whipping her head around or pulling hair over her left eye to hide her shortcomings when paparazzi are in view. And as for her live shows, Carey demands a healthy supply of Captain Crunch cereal *and* hires a personal towel-handler to pass her warm, dry towels as needed.

Korn—When it comes to describing the ideal backstage haven, urban heavy metal band Korn can think of only one word—it should have "vibe." They need a homey hangout that resembles a small, well-decorated apartment. And if the decorator

DID YOU KNOW

Paul Simon may have sung that there were officially fifty ways to leave your lover, but for fans he only listed five:

Slip out the back, Jack

Make a new plan, Stan

You don't need to be coy, Roy, just set yourself free

Hop on the bus, Gus

Drop off the key, Lee

(yes, decorator) plans on using fabric to "soften" the look of the walls and windows, the band kindly requests it be a fabric with some sort of pattern (nothing bland).

Britney Spears—Before the busy days of motherhood set in, Spears matured from the innocent-but-alluring Catholic schoolgirl in "Hit Me Baby One More Time" to the sexpot sound of the electronica-enhanced "Toxic." Just what did this million-dollar superstar want waiting for her backstage? A clean (and smell-free) carpet or rug, a telephone, and a massive fine slapped on anyone who made an incoming call that interrupted her pre-concert preparations.

★ ★ ★ ★ ★

MORE STRANGE BACKSTAGE DEMANDS...

Foo Fighters—White tube socks (U.S. size 10-13) and twelve cans of cranberry juice

Moby—Ten pairs of white socks and ten pairs of cotton boxers

Limp Bizkit—Dimmable lamps

Fiona Apple—Four red Fiji apples, one kiwi, and one ripe papaya

Nine Inch Nails—Two boxes of cornstarch

Axl Rose of Guns N' Roses—White bread and Dom Perignon champagne

Jennifer Lopez—A white room with white flowers, white couches, white candles, white curtains, and white tables (with white tablecloths, of course)

Jennifer Lopez moved to Manhattan from the Bronx to learn how to dance and used to sleep in the studio where she practiced.

DID YOU KNOW

Nine Inch Nail's entire 2005 U.S. Club tour sold out in less than 10 minutes. Some tickets sold for more than $200 on eBay.

★ ★ ★ ★ ★

OTHER ROCKERS WITH BAD FORM:

Axl Rose of Guns N' Roses once beat up a man having a drink in a hotel bar for telling him he looked like Jon Bon Jovi.

Donnie Wahlberg of New Kids on the Block dumped vodka in the hallway of a Louisville, Kentucky, hotel and lit it on fire.

Keith Moon once trampled his neighbor's manicured tree garden with his motorcycle.

At **Madonna's** wedding to actor Sean Penn, Penn got so upset with the noise and invasion of privacy from press helicopters flying overhead that he shot at them.

GUITARIST WHO ROCKS

Slash
Band: Guns N Roses
Guitar of Choice: '85 Gibson Les Paul standard with a Crybaby wah-wah
Best Known For: "Sweet Child O' Mine" on the album *Appetite for Destruction*

New Kids on the Block was originally called Nynunk. Inspired by a rap song Donnie Wahlberg wrote for their debut album, they changed it and eventually shortened it to just NKOTB.

WHAT BIG STARS NAME THEIR BABIES:
IT'S A GIRL!

- August (Garth Brooks)
- Calico (Alice Cooper)
- Carmella (Munky from Korn)
- Chastity (Cher)
- Dandelion (Keith Richards)
- Diva Muffin and Moon Unit (Frank Zappa)
- Dusty Rain (Vanilla Ice)
- Fly (Erykah Badu)
- Fuchsia (Sting)
- Lourdes (Madonna and Guy Ritchie)
- Memphis Eve (Bono from U2)
- Paris Michael Katherine (Michael Jackson)
- Phoenix Chi (Melanie "Scary Spice" Brown)
- Zoe Moon (Lenny Kravitz)

Chapter 2

★

I Fought the Law (and the Law Won): Famous Lawsuits

I Fought the Law (and the Law Won): Famous Lawsuits

★ ★ ★ ★ ★ ★ ★ ★ ★ ★ ★ ★ ★ ★ ★ ★

It's not surprising that artists as famous as Metallica, The Beatles, and The Doors get tangled up in a confusing web of accusations and court battles from time to time. When you're a genius, everyone thinks they had the right to your brilliance before you did. When a song like "How Deep Is Your Love?" became a major hit, every struggling songwriter who ever attempted to write a song with the word "love" in it got a little upset that they didn't get any props from the Bee Gees. But when rock halls start accusing sub-par websites of stealing logos, and entire cities catch stars dumping their toilets into public waterways, you know things have gotten a little out of hand. Here is a synopsis of the most cheesy, and most popular, rock-star lawsuits of all time.

LIKE A BAT OUT OF HELL

Meat Loaf sued his former writing partner, Jim Steinman, for using the phrase "Bat out of Hell," from his 1977 album. Meat Loaf claims he owns the phrase in a musical context, even though he didn't actually write the song.

★ ★ ★ ★ ★

DON'T DRINK THE WATER—DAVE MATTHEWS BAND VS. THE CHICAGO RIVER

When the Chicago River spat out a raunchy smell in August 2004, **the state of Illinois pointed a finger at the Dave Matthews Band**. No, it wasn't the fact that the annoying guitar-picking single "Satellite" had just been released on yet another live album—the DMB tour bus had just dumped 80 to 100 gallons of "liquid human waste" off a bridge, showering tourists on a boat passing

below. The band said they had no memory of the event, but thanks to a truth-telling surveillance video, they were taken to court. Despite their lack of recollection, however, two months later, the band made several $50,000 contributions to environmental groups like Friends of the Chicago River and The Chicago Park District. While the city manned the investigation, owners of Mercury Skyline Yacht Charters filed a suit of their own, claiming that since their passengers had been dumped on (literally and figuratively),

Chicago city officials canceled a free Smashing Pumpkins concert celebrating the band's tenth anniversary because they feared as many as one hundred thousand people might show up to celebrate. The facility could only hold sixty thousand.

business had gone bad. They wanted damages between $50,000 and $5 million. Luckily for Matthews and band, it was proven that the bus driver, Stefan Wohl, was the only one around when the illegal disposal took place. Generous donations may have gotten DMB off the hook, but Wohl faced criminal charges of reckless conduct and discharging contaminates to pollute the water. He pleaded guilty and took on a few years of probation, community service, and a pretty hefty fine.

★ ★ ★ ★ ★

AN APPLE A DAY—THE BEATLES VS. APPLE COMPUTERS

When The Beatles formed their own recording company to handle their business affairs in the 1960s, they thought they would be original and call the organization Apple Corps. Nearly ten years later, Steve Wozniak and Steve Jobs founded the first Apple computer (and along with it, the multi-million dollar industry Apple Computers). George Harrison didn't think much of the similarity until he spotted a magazine ad for the new fruit on the block and noticed the trademark was remarkably similar to his own. Jobs admitted he had named his company as a "tribute" to the Beatles, and the two mega-companies have been fighting over the copyright ever since. At first, a 1981 agreement outlined that Apple Corps could be the only "Apple" in the world of entertainment, and Apple Computers would stick to the computer industry. However, when Apple Computers launched its iPod and iTunes music store in 2003, they crossed over into the music and entertainment realm. Apple Corps representatives say their rival company breached the contract even further when they began to campaign their new product with the term AppleMusic. The Beatles took them back to court, and Apple Computers settled with them for a cool $27 million. The two Apples seem to have gotten along since then, as John Lennon has been featured in more than one advertisement for the iMac.

After his death in 2001, Harrison's estate sued his oncologist for pressuring him to sign autographs while ill at home. Dr. Gilbert Lederman was taken to court for showing up at the former Beatles star's home uninvited and using his position as a doctor to obtain "unique collectors' items of enormous value."

★ ★ ★ ★ ★

Sue Me, Sue You Blues—George Harrison vs. The Chiffons

The battle between Apple Corps and Apple Computers wasn't George Harrison's only headache in court. A single off his first solo LP in 1970, "My Sweet Lord," became a worldwide hit in no time. Not long after the song's release, however, Harrison was harshly criticized when listeners noticed that a bit of its melody and chords resembled those of The Chiffons' hit "He's So Fine" from just seven years earlier. Bright Tunes, the original publishers of "He's So Fine," took Harrison for a ride in court to the tune of $587,000. Harrison stressed repeatedly that any plagiarism was unintentional.

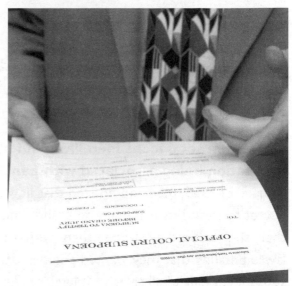

Subconscious or not, the court sided with The Chiffons, and Harrison had to pay up. Ironically, not long after he settled with his accuser, Beatles' manager Allen Klein purchased the publishing rights to all of Bright Tunes' music.

Three years later, reminiscing on his copyright woes, Harrison made light of his legal problems and entertained supporters with the song "Sue Me, Sue You Blues." He took another stab at

George Harrison's "My Sweet Lord" made him the first Beatle to have a No. 1 hit after the band's break-up.

Bright Tunes in 1976 when he wrote "This Song," in which he sings "This tune has nothing bright about it." Hoping for the last laugh, Harrison shot a video to promote the new melody set in a courtroom with images of a bailiff hauling him off to jail.

★ ★ ★ ★ ★

NOTHING ELSE MATTERS [BUT GETTING OUR NAME OFF GIRLY STUFF]—METALLICA VS. VICTORIA'S SECRET

Heavy metal icons Metallica couldn't stand their kick-ass reputation being associated with panties and lipsticks. In January of 1999, the band noticed that lingerie mogul Victoria's Secret had used its namesake to brand a new shimmering lipstick on their shelves. So they slapped them with a copyright infringement lawsuit stating that they wanted punitive damages and the subsequent halt of all sales of "Metallica" lip pencils. They also requested that any catalogues listing the products be destroyed so as not to confuse bra and makeup shoppers with songs like "Unforgiven." The alleged deception came to an end when the band's attorney settled the suit. The back-to-manly days weren't gone for long, however. Just a few years later, they filed a second lawsuit—this time against a French perfume manufacturer who had released a limited-edition vanilla scent called Metallica.

★ ★ ★ ★ ★

BLAME IT ON THE FAME—MILLI VANILLI VS. EVERYBODY

When **Rob Pilatus and Fab Morvan were denied modeling contracts** in the 1980s, they were so desperate for fame that they decided to put their looks behind a microphone and form the

German hip-hop group Milli Vanilli. The artists could hardly even speak English, but they hoped to use their hard bodies and baby faces to mask the fact that their accents were missing from their music. Milli Vanilli was instantly embraced by pop enthusiasts around the world and was honored as "Best New Artist of the Year" at the 1990 Grammy Awards. After enjoying an ample amount of fame with the singles "Girl You Know It's True" and

THREE THINGS YOU NEVER KNEW ABOUT ... MILLI VANILLI

- The singers whose voices are actually heard on their hit album *Girl You Know It's True* are Johnny Davis, Charles Shaw, and Brad Howell.

- They are the only group to ever have their Grammy Award stripped from them.

- The word "milli" means "national" in Turkish.

"Blame It on the Rain," however, a live performance gone wrong exposed Pilatus and Morvan for the fakes they really were. The tape they were lip-synching to at an MTV concert in Connecticut looped the same line over and over again, and their careers were over in an

After Milli Vanilli was busted for not singing a single lyric on their first album, other artists faced accusations of lip-synching. One of Paula Abdul's former back-up singers claimed the pop diva's voice could rarely be heard on several of the songs on the album *Forever Your Girl*. Mariah Carey was also pressured to schedule a series of live performances to prove that her top-notch notes were not studio tricks but her own.

instant. The band's manager fought for his clients, claiming they weren't doing anything that hadn't been done before. Plenty of producers had taken someone who could barely hum a tune and beefed up vocals with background singers and digital technology. The public didn't buy his ploy.

Although they had sold ten million albums and had three No. 1 hits, fans and radio stations fought back with a class action lawsuit for racketeering and breach of consumer protection laws. The court ruled that anyone who had purchased a Milli Vanilli album could get a refund if they so desired. Desperate for money and the public attention they had long lost, the duo made a Carefree Sugarless Gum commercial in which they poked fun at themselves by lip-synching the jingle. When self-mockery didn't work, they tried actually singing. Insisting that they were, in fact, talented, Pilatus and Morvan tried making music again in 1993 with the self-titled album Rob and Fab, but only three thousand copies were produced. They were never released outside the United States.

★ ★ ★ ★ ★

What Makes You Think You're the One (Who Wrote That Song)–Stevie Nicks vs. Carol Hinton

Fleetwood Mac's Stevie Nicks was thrown into a copyright battle when she was sued for allegedly stealing the lyrics to "Sara," one of the most widely played singles from her hit album *Tusk*, released in 1979. Two years after it hit the shelves, the album perked the ears of a stressed-out songwriter named Carol Hinton of Rockford, Michigan. Having struggled for years without much success in the music industry, Hinton was furious when she heard "Sara," claiming she had written and submitted the song in a demo tape to Warner Brothers (Fleetwood Mac's recording company) in 1978. She put her accusation against Nicks and her folk-rock band mates on paper, but it simply couldn't hold up in court. Nicks quickly proved that she had sent her own work-in-progress tape of "Sara" to the same recording company in July of 1978, and Hinton's hopes for the credit were crushed.

★ ★ ★ ★ ★

ROCK THE DREIDEL OF LOVE— THE ROCK AND ROLL HALL OF FAME VS. WWW.JEWSROCK.ORG

Journalists David Segal and Jeffery Goldberg and XM Satellite Radio executive Allen Goldberg decided to honor Jewish contributions to rock music with a new website called the Jewish Rock and Roll Hall of Fame, but the original Cleveland-based Rock Hall flexed its mega-museum muscles and took them to court. Worried that the title would infringe on their trademark, representatives of the original Rock and Roll Hall of Fame and Museum complained that the website had stolen their namesake to simply boost popularity. They also thought the online articles would confuse the public. A former music critic for *The Washington Post*, Segal laughed at the accusation and said he highly doubted an amateur, non-profit website made by "two Jewish guys" would be confused with a museum that has attracted more than 5.5 million tourists since it opened in 1995. The suit was filed regardless, claiming that Cleveland's Rock Hall had "suffered" from the new site (which hadn't even been uploaded to the Internet yet) and wanted damages exceeding $100,000.

In the end, Segal and Goldberg were instructed to remove similar logos and the words "Jewish Rock and Roll Hall of Fame" from their site altogether. Today the website is headlined with the simple title www.JewsRock.org.

★ ★ ★ ★ ★

I Said I Was Original, But I Lied—Michael Bolton vs. The Isley Brothers

Coupled with his long, wavy hair, **Michael Bolton's adult contemporary remakes made him an instant success** when his first single came out in 1991. With a new album of gold nugget R&B hits of the past, it came as a surprise to everyone when Bolton was sued for allegedly ripping off the song "Love Is A Wonderful

Thing" from rock and soul band The Isley Brothers. His fate lay in the hands of a jury, who ruled that he had indeed lifted five elements of the original song. Despite the fact that the two songs in question were remarkably similar in both lyrics and sound, Bolton assured fans that he had never heard another version in his life. He appealed the case to the U.S. Supreme Court, but was denied a second chance. In the end, three representatives had to pay up to compensate for the error—Bolton, Sony Music, and the apparent co-author of Bolton's version of "Love Is A Wonderful Thing." They shelled out a total of $5.4 million, which included much of the profits Bolton had made selling albums with that song on it. However, The Isley Brothers failed to ever make a successful comeback, and by 2000, the band was nearly $5 million in debt.

THREE THINGS YOU NEVER KNEW ABOUT ... MICHAEL BOLTON

- He signed his first record deal at age fifteen, and was belting out power ballads with bar bands long before he was old enough to drink.

- As a child, he idolized R&B greats like Otis Redding, Ray Charles, and Marvin Gaye.

- Since his first album, *Time, Love and Tenderness*, debuted in 1991, Bolton has sold fifty-two million albums and has been awarded six American Music Awards and two Grammy Awards.

★ ★ ★ ★ ★

COME ON BABY, CANCEL MY TOUR-THE DOORS VS. THE DOORS OF THE 21ST CENTURY

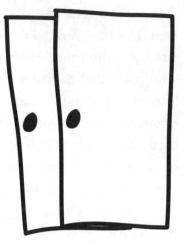

Drummer John Densmore of The Doors was not a happy camper when he found out that guitarist Robby Krieger and keyboardist Ray Manzarek had set out on a new tour without him. He was even more upset when he found out they were playing old favorites under the name The Doors of the 21st Century, marketing their upcoming tour on late-night talk shows as a reunion for hardcore Doors fans from the 1960s. Upset that he (and the late Jim Morrison) had been left out of the deal, Densmore declared that they could call themselves the Hinges, but they could not play under the original band name.

Afraid that The Door's legacy was being flawed by its rebirth as an "oldies act," Densmore teamed up with Jim Morrison's parents and took Krieger and Manzarek to court. A 1971 agreement had outlined that all three surviving band members (along with the

> While touring as The Doors of the 21st Century, guitarist Robby Krieger and keyboardist Ray Manzarek played with former Police drummer Stewart Copeland and a British singer named Ian Astbury (taking the place of the late Jim Morrison).

Morrison estate) had to agree on any future use of The Doors name and logo. In the end, the Los Angeles Superior Court ordered that any cash the two non-retired rockers had earned by themselves be shared with Densmore.

★ ★ ★ ★ ★

Jim Morrison's epitaph is written in Greek. Located in the Cimitière du Père Lachaise in Paris, his gravestone reads James Douglas Morrison, 1943-1971, KATA TON ØAIMONA EAYTOY, which means, "He did his own thing."

HOW DEEP IS YOUR WALLET FOR ME?–THE BEE GEES VS. RON SELLE

With a slew of songs hitting No. 1 on the Billboard music charts in 1971, **British-Australian pop-turned-funk group The Bee Gees seemed unstoppable**—but their fame and fortune would come into question in 1983, when Chicago antique dealer and songwriter Ron Selle stepped into the picture. Selle accused the band of lifting "How Deep Is Your Love?," made famous by the 1997 best-selling soundtrack for the movie Saturday Night Fever, from his song "Let It End." The song did indeed resemble The Bee Gees' cut-in melody, but that was about it. Regardless, Selle was persistent in his accusations and insisted that he originally recorded the song as a demo from his home, then sent it to a handful of recording companies to consider, none with ties to The Bee Gees, he says. Brothers Barry, Robin, and Maurice Gibb claimed they have always had a policy never to listen to unsolicited songs—and they hardly ever record songs they did not write themselves (with the exception of a few Beatles tunes).

Although Selle's attorneys couldn't prove that the Gibb brothers had ever heard "Let It End," they did manage to convince the jury that the musical bars in the very beginning and the very end of the two songs were strikingly similar. The jury awarded the pitiful lounge singer his damages, but later a sympathetic judge overturned the verdict—Selle simply hadn't proven his case.

★ ★ ★ ★ ★

WHY DON'T YOU BE MY GIRLFRIEND—JUSTIN TIMBERLAKE VS. FIFTEEN-YEAR-OLD FAN

When former 'NSync hottie Justin Timberlake got on his beat box at the group's concerts, he welcomed the endless screams of teenage girls—but  when fifteen-year-old Danielle McGuire smarted off to him after a show that band mate J.C. Chasez was cuter, Timberlake allegedly flipped his lid. In a lawsuit filed by McGuire in December of 2000, the former boyfriend of pop queen Britney Spears was accused of verbally abusing Danielle at a hotel for her smart-aleck comment. Apparently, McGuire and friends had crashed the lobby where the singers were staying, hoping for a handshake or an autograph. When Timberlake walked by without obliging, McGuire shouted out that she didn't care about the snub—she liked J.C. better. After being escorted to an upstairs hallway by a security guard for a few "fighting words" from the singer, McGuire says she was let off the hook when an NBC news affiliate walked in and Timberlake shut his mouth. McGuire, now considering herself a "former" fan, filed suit, but dropped it in 2001 because of heavy publicity.

★ ★ ★ ★ ★

OTHER STARS WHO GOT SUED:

Rap mogul Puff Daddy (or P. Diddy) was doing an interview to promote his tour for the album *Forever* in 1999 when radio deejay Roger Mills asked him the unthinkable—was he involved in the murder of the late rapper Notorious B.I.G.? Diddy's bodyguards retaliated and tried to take the interview tape. Mills allegedly filed suit against Diddy, who was let off the hook by a jury in Detroit.

When punk band Blink 182 first hit the music scene in 1992, they originally called themselves *blink*. After being threatened with a lawsuit from an Irish techno band with the same name, band members Tom Delonge, Mark Hoppus, and Scott Raynor added the 182. Despite rumors that the number represents the number of times actor Al Pacino says the f-word in the movie *Scarface*, the band says the number was chosen at random and means absolutely nothing.

DID YOU KNOW

Travis Barker, who started playing drums when he was four, replaced Scott Raynor in 1998.

Cleveland-based disc jockey Alan Freed pushed urban-blues records on an evening radio show, calling himself the Moondog, and keeping his mic turned on while music played so he could drum out the beat on the table and ad-lib shout-outs such as, "Yeah, daddy! Let's rock and roll!" He even had a theme song that he lifted from a blind New York street musician whose name was also Moondog. Unfortunately, as Freed became more and more famous, the original Moondog threatened to sue, so he changed his show's name to The Rock and Roll Show.

Whitney Houston's father, John, filed a breach of contract lawsuit against her for allegedly not paying him for two years of managing her as an artist. He wanted $100 million but died in February 2003 before settling.

DID YOU KNOW

During the summer of 2005, record industry bigwigs estimated that there were still about 28 billion songs being downloaded illegally every year.

WHAT BIG STARS NAME THEIR BABIES:
IT'S A BOY!

- Brooklyn (Victoria Beckham)
- Diezel Ky and Denim (Toni Braxton)
- Eja (Shania Twain and Mutt Lange)
- Elijah Blue (Cher)
- Maile (Wayne Brady)
- Maison (Rob Thomas)
- Prince (Michael Jackson)
- Rocco (Madonna and Guy Ritchie)
- Romeo (Victoria and David Beckham)
- Seven (Erykah Badu)
- Speck Wildhorse (John Cougar Mellencamp)
- Wolfgang (Eddie Van Halen)
- Zyon (Lauryn Hill)

Chapter 3

Losing My Religion

Losing My Religion

★ ★ ★ ★ ★ ★ ★ ★ ★ ★ ★ ★ ★ ★ ★

Let's face it—being a saint just doesn't sound cool when being a sinner is so much fun. Depravity is what gives most rockers their it-factor, right? You might be surprised. When it comes to being down with religion, some stars hit their knees, some get out their checkbooks, and others simply take a hit of LSD and call their drummer Krishna. Whether they pay their dues to Allah, Jesus, or the devil himself, you might be surprised at the interesting tales of how these artists attempt (yes, attempt) to stick to their faith.

Dee Snider and J.J. French of Twisted Sister, Scott Ian of Anthrax, and Leslie West of Mountain discussed being Jewish and their lives in the music industry on the VH1 special *Matzo and Metal: A Very Classic Passover.*

231

★ ★ ★ ★ ★

LIKE A PRAYER

Hollywood's self-proclaimed expert on spirituality, Madonna dove headfirst into the Kabbalah, an ancient Jewish mysticism, and has since donated more than $30 million to its headquarters around the world. She has such faith in the religion's sacred book of the law, the Zohar, that she insists it is the foundation for all spiritual beliefs. In fact, in 2004, Madonna gave another $21 million to fund New York's new Kabbalist Grammar School for Children, or K-School, as the kids call it. Regardless of how dedicated the Material Girl is to her belief system, however, most traditional Jewish rabbis would say the mystic way is off base from what The Torah would preach.

Besides the complaints of a few religious leaders, Kabbalah has even more controversy surrounding its New Age push of a special "dynamic living water" to heal body and soul. CultNews.com reported that they had busted the New York

When Madonna and her husband, Guy Ritchie, visited Israel for the Jewish New Year, they spent $2,000 per night shacking up in the largest suite of David's Inter-Continental Hotel.

Center's claims about the product when an unnamed source reported having seen the water bottles being delivered to the center with "product of Canada" stamped on the packaging. Coincidence? Maybe it's blessed beyond the border. On another note, the IRS may even be looking into whether it is an official religion at all, as some reports suggest they are re-evaluating the group's tax-exempt status.

★ ★ ★ ★ ★

RIDIN' THE NOT SO PEACEFUL TRAIN

When Cat Stevens tired of selling forty million albums and paying Great Britain taxes in the mid-70s, he packed up his things and moved to Brazil, where he explored his spirituality like never before. After nearly drowning off the coast of California and begging God to

THREE THINGS YOU NEVER KNEW ABOUT … KABBALAH

- It teaches that everything in the world is on different levels, and the closer to God you are, the more you can see His godliness.

- It also teaches that the soul is made up of three elements— Nefesh, or the "animal part" everyone gets at birth; Ruach, or the "spirit" of moral virtues; and Neshamah, or the "super-soul" that makes man different from other forms of life.

- Many traditional, organized Jewish groups have complained that the Los Angeles Kabbalah Center popular among celebrities is off base with what they believe to be religious truth.

save him, Stevens committed his life to charity work, joined the Muslim faith, and changed his name to Yusef Islam. He left his former rock legend identity behind, even requesting that the recording industry stop selling his music. They didn't listen.

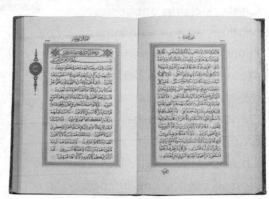

It wasn't long before government officials suspected Islam was an extremist, and accused him of taking his religious loyalties too far, allegedly supporting the "fatwa" order to kill others in the name of Allah. The former rocker lost his respect among fellow Americans and artists around the globe. In fact, the band 10,000 Maniacs took their remake of his single "Peace Train" off future copies of their albums, and the United States government put his name on a do-not-fly list. While traveling from London to Washington in 2004, Islam's flight was diverted to Maine, and he was detained and deported back to England due to rumors that he was linked to terrorist activities.

At a 1985 Life Aid concert benefiting famine-plagued Ethiopia, Yusef Islam (Cat Stevens) was supposed to make his first live appearance in years singing a song he had written as a tribute for the evening. His performance was cut, however, when the artist before him—Elton John—sang for longer than expected.

★ ★ ★ ★ ★

SLIPPIN' AND A SLIDIN' FOR JESUS

Raised a Seventh-Day Adventist by his parents, Little Richard (Richard Penniman) spent much of his childhood developing his wild gospel roots, and the nonsense babbles and screams of "Tutti Frutti" reveal that he loved to mimic what he saw at church. However, the days of hollerin' for Jesus were over in no time. After proclaiming himself a homosexual and diving into the outlawed abyss of rock and roll, Penniman called it quits as a religious man. His wayward ways as a self-proclaimed sinner wouldn't last long, though. While in Australia for a tour in the 1950s, a scare with a turbulent airplane ride

LITTLE RICHARD

In 1955, Little Richard was recording a demo in New Orleans when he shouted out an off-color, impromptu version of "Tutti Frutti," which was slang for a gay male. Afraid the song would be offensive to just about everyone who heard it, producers changed the lyrics from "Tutti frutti loose booty" to "Tutti frutti all rooty."

235

changed him for good. When the plane landed, Penniman threw out the flashy jewelry, kissed the ground, and ran back to Jesus. He immediately retired but, true to his form, returned to rock and roll in the 1960s, once he felt he could indeed marry his love for God and music. Since then, Little Richard has worked as a Bible salesman and an evangelist for the Universal Remnant Church of God, where he continues to flip flop between denouncing the demons of secular music and, of course, making secular records.

★ ★ ★ ★ ★

STAIRWAY TO HELL

　　While he never spit blood onstage like KISS, **Led Zeppelin guitarist Jimmy Page was the ultimate artist of spiritual black magic.** His offstage façade is painted with dark rumors of robes, tarot cards, and even pacts with the devil. In 1970, Page became the proud homeowner of a mansion just off Scotland's Loch Ness. Its appeal? The house faced just the right direction for him to perform specific magic rituals. He even hired a Satanist to paint murals on the walls that would suit his "religious" tastes. In his personal records of his dark practices, Page wrote about how he had summoned so many demons in his day that most of his house help had either gone mad or quit.

DID YOU KNOW

Led Zeppelin's "Stairway to Heaven" was broadcast more than three million times on American airwaves by the end of the 1990s. That adds up to forty-four years of nonstop playtime.

★ ★ ★ ★ ★

GOODBYE BLACK MAGIC WOMAN

Famous for their unique blend of salsa and jazz, Santana flew to the forefront of American rock in the 1970s, but legendary guitarist Carlos felt fatigued by the pressure to maintain a fresh, successful band. Luckily for him, friend (and former guitarist for Miles Davis) John McLaughlin had the answer—a retro-chic following of a Bengalese Hindu philosopher and mystic named Sri Chinmoy. Intrigued by his British pal's dedication to such an interesting theology, Santana jumped on the bandwagon and looked into the faith himself. Later officially converting to the belief system, Santana changed

> Santana's first album hit U.S. charts in 1969 with "Evil Ways," "Jingo," and "Soul Sacrifice."

THREE THINGS YOU NEVER KNEW ABOUT ... SRI CHIMNOY

- At just twelve years old, both of his parents died, and he spent the next twenty years in a "spiritual community" called Sri Aurobindo ashram in India.

- He teaches ultra-fitness, celibacy, and meditation, though many religious leaders worldwide call his following a cult.

- Ashrita Furman, who once held the world record for the most number of world records, told editors at *Hinduism Today* that Sri Chinmoy inspired him to enter a state of transcendence to accomplish feats such as resting a nine-pound brick on his hand for sixty-four miles.

his name to Devadip and recorded his next album, *Love Devotion Surrender*, with McLaughlin in 1974. The new spiritual commitments must have worked because a drug- and stress-free Santana sailed to consistent success all the way up to his Grammy Award-winning *Supernatural* a few years ago.

★ ★ ★ ★ ★

THAT'LL BE THE DAY WHEN I DIE

Known as one of the early influences of the 1950s rock and roll revolution, Buddy Holly may have been known as a religious man, but he certainly

THE EARLY YEARS

Buddy Holly's last name is actually spelled "Holley," but a spelling error in an early contract caused it to be changed in the public eye forever. It wasn't corrected until it was placed on his headstone in 1959.

wasn't restrained by his beliefs. He grew up a young bluegrass musician at Tabernacle Baptist Church in the sleepy hometown of Lubbock, Texas. He made a public profession of faith and was baptized at age fourteen, but barely a teen, the devil wasn't through tempting him yet. At a time when pastors saw rocking and rolling as anything but kin to Jesus Christ, Holly was a religious outlaw. In his

biography, *Buddy Holly*, author Ellis Amburn describes the singer's rebellious days of shoplifting, smoking, drinking, gambling, and "carousing with women." Holly even reportedly told friends that regardless of what he told the churchgoers about having Jesus in his heart, he had little intention of letting go of the sin in his life. According to Amburn, Holly's brother, Larry (who is still a member at Tabernacle Baptist today), believes the Lord took Buddy's life at such a young age because he was too rebellious. Holly died in a plane crash in 1959 at just twenty-three years old.

★ ★ ★ ★ ★

EVERYBODY'S GOT SOMETHING TO HIDE EXCEPT ME AND MY MONK-Y

In the 1960s, eastern spiritual guru Swami Prabhupada was commissioned to evangelize the West with his Hindu know-all and establish the International Society for Krishna Consciousness (ISKCON) in New York City and San Francisco. A fan of "spiritual highs" himself, he related to rock lovers by comparing religious freedoms to being tripped out on LSD, which most Deadheads associated with being close to God (or in fact being God) anyway.

Inspired with a vision for reaching "spiritual" citizens through music, Prabhupada organized a Mantra-Rock Dance concert with acid-rock bands such as the Grateful Dead, Jefferson Airplane, and the Holding Company to raise money to build a temple on the coast. Five thousand people showed up, and Prabhupada welcomed them with an hour-long chant before the music began.

> Often referred to as "the quiet one" of The Beatles, George Harrison was obsessed with the music and religious aspects of India. He once abstained from sex because his Hindu guru urged him to... but he ended up having an affair with Ringo Starr's wife, Maureen Cox.

Prabhupada had his hopes set higher than a silly psychedelic rock concert, though. His next goal was to play on the eastern interests of George Harrison and turn The Beatles into walking billboards for the Krishna Conscious cause. Members of ISKCON started sending little messages to the band at their Apple Corps headquarters in London—an apple pie with the Hare Krishna mantra spelled out on top and a record of mantra chantings. When the Fab Four ignored their hints, a devout follower paid Harrison a visit and eventually became his friend. The ploy must have worked because Canadian ISKCON devotees chanted in the background of John Lennon's "Give Peace a Chance." Harrison later took a group from the temple to record a single of the "Hare Krishna Mantra," which became a Top 20 hit in 1969.

★ ★ ★ ★ ★

Dancin' with the Devil

As a boy, Roy Orbison just couldn't get a break when it came to wanting to, as rappers Outkast would say, shake it like a Polaroid picture. As devout members of a Church of Christ congregation in Wink, Texas, Orbison's parents thought dancing was the root of all evil. Naturally, the family had conflicts when Orbison announced that to further the early years of his musical career, he needed to play gigs at local dances. Despite their son's dream to play a few instruments, the Orbisons couldn't bear the thought of Roy giving aid to those sinful rump-bumpers. He resented his parents' pleas, and since he had always felt uncomfortable in the sanctuary, he simply skipped out on Sunday services. Even without Jesus, however, he managed to walk the straight and narrow to some degree—he never struggled with drug or alcohol abuse. In spite of his righteous ways, he would suffer a

241

tragic future. His wife, Claudette, died in a motorcycle accident, and two of his three sons died when the family's Hendersonville, Tennessee, home caught fire in 1968. Orbison's sorrow drove him back to church in the 1970s, and he eventually ended up at a Baptist church with the likes of Johnny Cash and Skeeter Davis.

★ ★ ★ ★ ★

CHURCH-HOUSE ROCK

Ask Reverend James E. Hamill of Memphis, Tennessee, how pretty Elvis's voice was in the choir, and he will quickly debunk the myth—though Elvis attended with his parents for several years, Presley never sang in his church once. In fact, he never even became an official member of the church. In the late 1950s, Presley sought redemption with the old pastor and visited him after one Sunday evening service to talk about his misery. Hamill, who wasn't very happy that anyone who used to hear his preaching could ever lead a life of such sinful "entertaining," listened to him moan about how his money, his fame, and his rebellion had brought him no joy.

Near the end of his life while performing in Las Vegas several years later, Presley asked again whether he should turn his talents back to God— he met with evangelist Rex Humbard and talked to him about whether he should quit the rock scene and start singing only gospel music. Humbard said no.

★ ★ ★ ★ ★

SMOKE GANJA, NO CRY

Dating back to the 1914 founding of the Universal Negro Improvement and Conservation Association, Rastafari was key to the rapid-spreading rumor that Ethiopia was the supreme and black people were superior to all others. After the "Negro Bible" came out, insisting that the God and all of his messengers described in Christian Scriptures were

fabulous firsts
Elvis Presley made his first appearance on national television singing "Blue Suede Shoes" and "Heartbreak Hotel" on The Dorsey Brothers Show in 1956.

dark-skinned, the Rastafari dream caught the ears of Bob Marley. The official founder of the religion, Leonard Howell, spread the word that eventually all blacks who were exiled from their "homeland" would one day return. Marley liked what he heard and put the message to a rockin' reggae beat to let the world know it wasn't just the Caribbean that supported this new belief system.

Bob Marley grew up in a Pentecostal church that incorporated African pagan traditions of chanting, dancing, and warding off evil with "good" magic. The family had hoped he would become a white witch like his grandfather—but instead he chose music.

Using reggae as a way to socially respond to the poverty around him, Marley sold more than $250 million worth of records and was considered by his religion as a prophet and a priest. He found some inspiration in the Bible, relating to the Psalms and the plight of the Old Testament Israelites who were living in captivity. Rastafari's most well known practice of escaping captivity and creating harmony among the peoples is smokin' the ganja, a "spiritual herb" used to purify the soul and reveal wickedness. Marley and friends believed the devil hated ganja and that certain verses in Genesis supported it, such as Genesis 1:29 (KJV), which reads, "Behold, I have given you every herb bearing seed."

★ ★ ★ ★ ★

MxPx

While most Christian bands assign themselves obvious names of faith, such as Point of Grace and Casting Crowns, religious rockers MxPx have no such pretense. In fact, the name of their band is an inside joke between friends, poking fun at someone's "magnification plaid" shirt. They don't play in sanctuaries. In fact, they don't play in churches at all. Lead singer Mike Herrera says his band has never been out to preach—they just want to play good music. But they do pray before shows and take opportunities to influence other punk bands on the music scene.

Not long after MxPx went mainstream, other rockers were asking the band questions about the Bible and asking them to pray for their families. Hoping to change the pretense that Christianity is a weird minority, MxPx isn't afraid to announce their beliefs when asked. In all, the band just sticks to their punk sound and lets the lyrics do the witnessing. In "Party, My House, Be There," the band purposefully leaves out the usual punk references to drug and alcohol use. In "Tomorrow's Another Day," they sing about how God is faithful even when hope is lost.

★ ★ ★ ★ ★

OTHER ARTISTS OF FAITH:

- Rapper Kanye West paid $350,000 to have a painter recreate the Sistine Chapel ceiling in his home.

- The lead singer of Disturbed grew up in an Orthodox Jewish family and almost became a rabbi.

- Black Sabbath's Ozzy Osbourne got his start playing R&B in a church basement.

- Alice Cooper once claimed to be born-again, but after hearing the rumor that he ripped the head off a live chicken at a concert, clergymen beg to differ.

- As a child, Michael Jackson went door-to-door as a missionary, passing out copies of *Watchtower* magazine.

- Phish sometimes performs a version of the High Holiday prayer in Hebrew.

- Prince was born into a Seventh-Day Adventist family, but later converted to Jehovah's Witness.

★ ★ ★ ★ ★

ROCKERS' WACKY THOUGHTS ON RELIGION

- "My experience of God came from acid. It's the most important thing that ever happened to me." —Brian Wilson, the Beach Boys

- "God isn't a pill, but LSD explained the mystery of life. It was a religious experience." —Paul McCartney

- "As God has been losing his percentage, the devil has been picking up." —John Phillips, the Mamas and the Papas

- "There are black musicians who think we are acting as unknown agents of Lucifer and others who think we are Lucifer. Everybody's Lucifer." —Keith Richards, the Rolling Stones

- "I feel so close to the Lord when I'm that aroused. Never closer." —Prince

DID YOU KNOW

"Joy To the World" by Three Dog Night was originally written by Hoyt Axton for a new animated children's television show (*The Happy Song*) that was never produced nor aired.

Chapter 4

✩

Controversial Moments in
Rock History

LENNON

Controversial Moments in Rock History

★ ★ ★ ★ ★ ★ ★ ★ ★ ★ ★ ★ ★ ★ ★

Think of the word "scandal," and one of two arenas probably come to mind: politics and sports. But what about celebrities in the music industry? With loads of cash and something to prove to competitors, most rock stars are itching to make their opinions known through controversial songs and music videos. From the very first time Elvis swung his hips on live television, to the shocking moment when AC/DC realized their band name was gay, America has loved every minute. Scandals sell, and if it has to be through wild reputations, cheesy band lyrics, shady business deals, or ridiculous racial tensions, some stars say, "So be it."

Drummer Keith Moon was involved in an accident that left his driver, Neil Boland, dead. Moon was invited to a disco opening in Hatfield, but the scene was not what he thought it would be. Boland was trying to drive away when a group of young people began attacking their car. Boland got out of the Bentley, trying to protect it, but the car continued to roll forward. Moon and another passenger tried to stop it, grabbing the wheel, but were unsuccessful. Boland was run over and killed.

★ ★ ★ ★ ★

(HE) SHOOK ME ALL NIGHT LONG (MOST CONTROVERSIAL BAND TITLE)

When Angus and Malcolm Young first formed their power-chord group AC/DC at just fourteen and nineteen years old (respectively), it was initially just an innocent ploy to spite their brother, who had just joined a successful new band himself. However, when it came to beating their rivals with a rockin' band name, the Young Brothers flopped. They were psyched when they came up with AC/DC, an acronym they had read off the front of a sewing machine, but they didn't quite catch on to the fact that it suggested something a little more than electric currents— in some parts of the country, AC/DC was slang for being bisexual. A few awkward moments later (*and* after dodging the rumor that their name stood for "Anti-Christ Devil's Children"), the band decided to make the most of a queer situation and make some money off their slip-up. Just starting out and desperate for gigs, they were hired to play at a handful of gay clubs and parties.

YOUNG AND DUMB

AC/DC front man Angus Young was a little confused when it came to fashion. First, he wore a gorilla suit on stage. When that didn't elicit just the right rocker façade, he tried a Zorro outfit. Nope, still not outrageous enough. In one last attempt to be original, Young tried an Australian schoolboy get-up recommended by his sister. It stuck.

★ ★ ★ ★ ★

DON'T STAND SO CLOSE TO ME (MOST CONTROVERSIAL CLASH OF BAND MEMBERS)

Drummer Stewart Copeland may have been the glue that initially bound and sustained The Police through its early days, but when Sting came along, the newbie became the poster child for everything pop. A jealous Copeland turned sour, and the two international stars quickly became known for their prideful clashes when one seemed to have more groupies than the other. The two fame-hungry stars were rumored to be at each other's throats at all times. When Sting would write a hit, Copeland would rewrite it as his own. When Copeland would get the band together for a recording session, Sting would get him his own "private" studio to keep him out of the way.

> The Police released their first single, "Fall Out," in February 1977.

★ ★ ★ ★ ★

STRANGE FRUIT (MOST CONTROVERSIAL SONG)

At the fragile beginning of the Civil Rights Movement in the late 1930s, Jewish poet, schoolteacher, and passionate Communist Abel Meeropol caught a gruesome glimpse of a photograph that changed his life forever. A candid shot of a black man being lynched in the racist South, the photo disturbed him to such an extent that he took on a pen name (Lewis Allan) and wrote the emotional poem "Strange Fruit." His words were candid and descriptive with the lines "Southern trees bear a strange fruit / Blood on the leaves and blood at the root / Black body swinging in the southern breeze / Strange fruit hanging from the poplar trees." The honesty of the poem caught the ears and heart of a twenty-four-year-old Billie Holiday, who begged her recording company to let her remake it to music. When denied, she went to another label and finally released the tune in 1939. However, her persistence nearly led to her downfall as an artist. Civil rights activists quickly adopted "Strange Fruit" as an inspirational anthem, and Holiday's white fans were disappointed in her social and political outspokenness. When she performed the song onstage, she suffered verbal and sometimes physical abuse at the hands of her own admirers. Radio stations refused to play it, and *Time* magazine called it nothing more than propaganda. "Strange Fruit" practically disappeared from airwaves until a U.S. congressman got hold of a copy and spread it across the nation as a statement against Southerners' brutal treatment of blacks.

CELEBRITY ALIAS

Alias: Billie Holiday
Actual Name: Eleanora Fagan

★ ★ ★ ★ ★

I JUST CALLED TO SAY I'M SORRY (MOST CONTROVERSIAL APOLOGIES)

When it comes to blurting out the unthinkable (and subsequently having to put a foot in their mouths), many rock stars have spouted off comments or gestures to fans and journalists they wish they could take back. All convictions (and bad habits) aside, these rockers had to bite their lips and say they were sorry, whether they meant it or not.

John Lennon—John Lennon's lyrics in songs like "God" and "Imagine" revealed to fans that he often struggled with questions about religion. It may have been acceptable to explore his questions in song, but when he told a reporter at the *London Evening Standard* that Christianity would eventually disappear and that The Beatles were "more popular than Jesus" in 1966, he had to apologize to praying people around the world. While Londoners seemed to have no problem with Lennon's metaphor,

LENNON

Americans were furious and burnt their albums in protest when the interview was reprinted in the teenybopper magazine *DATEbook*. The artist wasn't very happy about having to apologize for what he said was a quote taken out of context. Regardless, conservative parents everywhere finally had the confirmation they needed to label the longhaired Fab Four as nothing more than the epitome of rock and roll evil.

David Bowie—Controversy came knocking on David Bowie's door when he gave the Nazi salute to people cheering at him in public. Combined with his comments in a *Playboy* magazine interview suggesting Hitler was respectable and Great Britain could "benefit from a fascist leader," Bowie didn't impress fans much. Later, he humbled himself and admitted he had probably shot off the phrase in the middle of a cocaine high. Bowie left the country in shame and made his new home in Berlin.

Janet Jackson—The term "wardrobe malfunction" took on a whole new meaning when, thanks to the sticky hands of 'NSync dreamboat Justin Timberlake, Janet Jackson flashed a breast to 140 million people watching the live Super Bowl halftime show in 2004. Despite the fact that an MTV posting the week before the game read "Janet Jackson's Super Bowl show promises shocking moments," Jackson claims the channel knew nothing about the last-minute plan for Timberlake to rip off a piece of her corset. The Monday immediately after the event, the Federal Communications Commission issued an investigation, and CBS ended up with a record-breaking $550,000 fine—the largest fine ever issued to a television broadcaster.

Bono—While partying with California rockers The Red Hot Chili Peppers in the Dublin Clarence Hotel, U2 front man Bono was caught lighting up a cigarette and violating Ireland's new

ban on smoking. After staff and friends reminded him of the new law, he put it out and penned a formal apology to the country's outraged health fanatics. The ironic thing—Bono co-owns the Clarence Hotel with his band mates.

THE ART OF [APPARENT] SELF-DESTRUCTION (MOST CONTROVERSIAL MUSIC VIDEO)

When industrial rock group Nine Inch Nails was brainstorming for cool effects to put in their new music video for the song "Down In It," they thought it would be

pretty awesome if lead vocalist and keyboarder Trent Reznor were portrayed as dead. After a heavy dose of pale makeup, Reznor lay on the ground while his band mates tied the camera to a helium balloon for a cool angle shot from above. However, the balloon-cam drifted away and landed in a nearby field. NIN never recovered the video, but the farmer who found it was so freaked out that he gave the tape to the Federal Bureau of Investigation.

★ ★ ★ ★ ★

TALK THIS WAY (MOST CONTROVERSIAL LYRICS)

In 1963, one of the most famous rock songs of all time, "Louie Louie," caused a panic among parents and preachers looking to keep their teenagers pure when it was initially thought to be the most filthy song to ever hit the airwaves. Rumors of its unthinkable (and incomprehensible) lyrics quickly spread to Washington, D.C., and the FBI stepped in to examine whether the song violated federal obscenity laws or was simply one of the dumbest, most meaningless pieces ever written. The investigation, which lasted nearly three years, concluded that there was

DID YOU KNOW

With the exception of Paul McCartney's "Yesterday," "Louie Louie" has been covered more times than any other pop song.

no "dirty" version of "Louie Louie" floating through the radio frequencies. In fact, some say the only reason the lyrics turned out so dang hard to understand was that lead singer Jack Ely was hoarse from singing a ninety-minute jam session the night before (not to mention the fact that he was wearing braces). Others say the studio's boom microphone wasn't set up correctly. Regardless, the day he recorded the new song, Ely had no idea that he was actually working on the final cut—he simply thought it was a rehearsal. In the end, the band liked what they heard and decided to keep it—mumbles and all.

I Stole Your Lyrics (Most Controversial Plagiarism)

Fire-breathing vocalist and bassist Gene Simmons and guitarist Paul Stanley wrote the line "The bigger the cushion, the better the pushin'" in the single "Spit," from their 1992 album *Revenge*. However clever the metaphor seemed at the time, though, fans were quick to notice that the lyrics were almost identical to a song by Spinal Tap called "Big Bottom," which read "the bigger the cushion, the sweeter the pushin'." Simmons and Stanley, in spite of any apparent copycat conundrum, insisted they did not plagiarize the line.

THREE THINGS YOU NEVER KNEW ABOUT... KISS

- Ever the master thespian, Gene Simmons made a cameo in the little-known film *Red Surf* in 1990.
- The band's first big gig was at The Coventry in Queens, New York.
- "God Gave Rock 'N' Roll to You II" was originally recorded by Argent, a group who once opened for KISS, for the film soundtrack of *Bill & Ted's Bogus Journey*.

★ ★ ★ ★ ★

UNDER THE TABLE AND DEALING (MOST CONTROVERSIAL DISC JOCKEY)

Broadcast live from New York at the height of its popularity in the late 1950s,

> GUITARIST WHO ROCKS
> Ace Frehley
> Band: Kiss
> Guitar of Choice: Gibson Les Paul
> Best Known For: "Shock Me" on the album *Love Gun*

American Bandstand had twenty million fans and was being carried on at least sixty-four television stations. However, some music industry veterans were suspicious of how selective host Dick Clark was when it came to choosing bands to showcase on the air. He seemed to give artists represented by Philadelphia recording companies more airtime than the rest. Clark also owned partial copyrights to 150 songs and was accused of playing those specific songs over and over again to boost record sales and, in turn, his own profits. In the end, a 1959 U.S. Senate committee investigated the case, and Clark admitted to one of the allegations—he had accepted a lavish gift (a fur stole and some jewelry) from the president of a well-known

> B.B. King is the only performer who did *not* lip-sync on *American Bandstand*.

recording company. Other than that, investigators could not find anything worth trying him for, so Clark agreed to behave and give up the extracurricular business deals to focus on *Bandstand* instead.

★ ★ ★ ★ ★

THE HIGH COST OF LOW LIVIN' (MOST CONTROVERSIAL FAN)

The Allman Brothers made a name for themselves when they blended smooth southern soul with psychedelic rock and country in the 1970s, but with a drug-induced wild side, their concerts sometimes got a little out of control. A roadie with a passion for rock, Twiggs Lyndon did not appreciate it when a Buffalo, New York, club owner refused to pay The Allman Brothers for their performance because they showed up late. Standing up for his favorite band and venting his frustration, Lyndon whipped out a fishing knife and stabbed the owner multiple times. Shocked at what its self-proclaimed No. 1 fan had just done, the band returned to its tour and let the cops take care of Lyndon, who was arrested for first-degree murder.

Lyndon's defense in trial seemed ridiculous at first—he claimed to have been temporarily insane from spending too much time on the road with The Allman Brothers. In the end, his assertion was not as unbelievable as it initially sounded. When drummer Berry Oakley was called to testify, he spent so

> ### THE EARLY YEARS
> Duane and Gregg Allman played in a band called the Allman Joys before forming the Allman Brothers Band in 1969.

much time running back and forth to throw up in the bathroom that everyone began to wonder if Lyndon's insanity ploy was actually true. The dominance drugs had over Oakley (and his bandmates) became so obvious that Lyndon was found not guilty.

ASHES TO ASHES (MOST CONTROVERSIAL DEATHS)

Rolling Stone Rocker Brian Jones: On July 2, 1969, Brian Jones was found dead in the swimming pool at his home. While the

coroner suggested he had drowned while swimming under the influence of drugs and alcohol, his friends and family have disputed the theory for the last thirty-five years. His girlfriend, Anna, even wrote a book about the incident, titled *The Murder of Brian Jones*, which claimed that Jones had not drowned on his own but that someone had held his head underwater until he lost consciousness.

Seattle Grunge Gal Mia Zapata: A twenty-seven-year-old up-and-coming star of the Seattle grunge band the Gits, Mia Zapata was last seen alive hanging out with friends at her favorite bar. A few hours later, her father got a call from the coroner asking him to come and identify her body, which had been found on the side of the road. With their victim being so young and so locally famous, police felt pressure to solve the case—but it took more than a decade to even match DNA found on her body to a Cuban-born fisherman who was living in the Florida Keys. He was sentenced to thirty-seven years in prison.

R&B Diva Aaliyah: On August 25, 2001, twenty-two-year-old Aaliyah was flying to Miami from a trip to the Bahamas when her plane, weighed down with too much luggage (and the singer's beefy bodyguards), crashed into a marsh just after lift off. Her pilot had allegedly been convicted of possessing crack cocaine just weeks before and was not even licensed to fly in those skies.

DID YOU KNOW

Jimi Hendrix, Janis Joplin, and Jim Morrison were all twenty-seven years old when they died.

Chicago Lead Guitarist Terry Kath: On January 23, 1978, Terry Kath was cleaning his guns at a party in his home when a friend told him to put them away before somebody got hurt. Joking that there weren't even bullets in the barrels, Kath put one to his head and pulled the trigger. He was killed instantly.

★ ★ ★ ★ ★

TABOO TUNES (MOST CONTROVERSIAL CENSORSHIP)

After the ashes fell and New York began cleaning up Ground Zero in the fall of 2001, Americans were a little hesitant when it came to any potential signs of future terrorist attacks on U.S. soil. The emotional aftermath of those grieving lost loved ones even led executives at Clear Channel Communications to reevaluate what was playing on their airwaves. Were there songs insensitive to the families affected or suggestive of celebrating such a tragic day? In turn, Clear Channel made a controversial move that would upset some listeners and comfort others—the company temporarily blacklisted songs with "questionable lyrics" from their stations' play lists. The tunes frowned upon included:

- AC/DC—"Highway to Hell"
- The Bangles—"Walk Like an Egyptian"
- Beastie Boys—"Sabotage"
- Dave Matthews Band—"Crash into Me"
- Led Zeppelin—"Stairway to Heaven"
- Red Hot Chili Peppers—"Aeroplane"
- U2—"Sunday Bloody Sunday"
- Queen—"Another One Bites the Dust"
- Foo Fighters—"Learn to Fly"
- Cat Stevens—"Morning Has Broken"

- Black Sabbath—"War Pigs"

- Paul McCartney and Wings—"Live And Let Die"

- Simon and Garfunkel—"Bridge Over Troubled Water"

★ ★ ★ ★ ★

CONCERTS GONE WRONG (MOST CONTROVERSIAL CONCERTS)

Thanks to the thousands of concerts of old, all rockers know that mosh pits plus alcohol (plus pyrotechnics) equals serious problems. But unfortunately for these Deadheads, they didn't listen and paid the price as they hosted the most controversial concerts in history.

At a 1969 Altamont rock concert in northern California, featuring The Rolling Stones, Jefferson Airplane, and The Grateful Dead, eighteen-year-old Meredith Hunter was parting with friends when she was allegedly beaten and stabbed to death by the security, Hell's Angels. Three other people were also reported to have died at the concert—two from a hit-and-run accident and another from an alleged drowning in a drainage ditch. The violence of the drug-induced rioting crowds became so bad that many of the bands refused to take stage.

At a 1970s show featuring Frank Zappa and The Mothers of Invention at the Montreux Casino in Switzerland, one idiotic fan fired a flare gun at the ceiling and burnt the place to the ground. The band Deep Purple memorialized both the casino and the accident when they sang about it in the song "Smoke on the Water," which included the lyrics, "Frank Zappa & the Mothers were at the best place around / But some stupid with a flare gun burned the place to the ground / Smoke on the water, fire in the sky." The casino was rebuilt, and reopened in 1975.

In a poor attempt to emulate the historical success of the first Woodstock Festival in 1969, MTV hosted the infamous Woodstock 1999 in upstate New York. Attended by more than two hundred thousand people, the event was plagued with violence, riots, and reports of rape allegations. At least five hundred policemen had been hired as security, and a twelve-foot fence made of wood and steel was built to keep out the inevitable party crashers, but in the end the fence came down, ATMs were broken into, and vendor booths were set on fire. MTV pulled its crews out quickly. All they could do was watch the angry mob destroy the place.

In 2003, a whopping ninety-seven people died in a Rhode Island nightclub called The Station, where rockers Great White were performing. The club manager said he had no idea the band would be bringing fireworks, and a pyrotechnics error set the place on fire, trapping many concert-goers inside a blazing inferno. Because the building was built before 1979, it did not have a sprinkler system, which firefighters said would have put out the fire immediately. It burnt to the ground.

DIE HARD FANS DO THE DUMBEST THINGS

- The President of the Worldwide Elvis Fan Club, Henry Newinn of Houston, Texas, once announced that he had discovered a patch of bark on a tree with a striking resemblance to the King's profile. The tree was in his own backyard.

- When six hundred thousand people crowded to hear the Allman Brothers play in New York in 1973, one super fan decided to make a grand entrance with fireworks and a parachute. As he jumped out of the plane, he lit and threw a stick of dynamite into the air, forgetting that it would fall at the same rate as he. The dynamite exploded mid-air and killed him before he ever reached the ground.

- Bob Dylan once noticed one of his most enthusiastic (and most nosy) neighborhood fans, A. J. Weberman, regularly nosed through his garbage for scraps of poetry and personal items. Dylan got so upset that he met Weberman on a New York City street and beat him up.

★ ★ ★ ★ ★

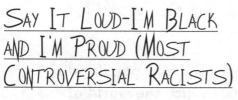

SAY IT LOUD—I'M BLACK AND I'M PROUD (MOST CONTROVERSIAL RACISTS)

During the 1940s, rock and roll was just taking root across America as a rebellious teenage phenomenon. Parents weren't happy with the sexual references in the new songs popping up across the charts or with the term "rock and roll" itself, which traditionally referred to sex in popular blues tunes. To try and skirt the negative connotations associated with rhythm and blues, major recording companies fueling album sales and recruiting new stars decided to abandon black artists and audiences altogether. Their talent scouts were predominately white and had such little knowledge of black tastes that they often completely overlooked the demographic. Most admitted that they felt that blacks had such a sparse income that they would never buy enough records to influence the music industry anyway. Overall, racial bias ruled the airwaves—with the exception of a few catchy tunes by Nat King Cole, The Mills Brothers, and The Ink Spots, which were in high demand by white audiences. In the end, smaller independent music companies popped up around the country to fill in the void and push talented black artists back to the top of mainstream music: Atlantic Records of New York, Chess Records of Chicago, King Records of Cincinnati, Specialty Records of Los Angeles, and Sun Records of Memphis.

★ ★ ★ ★ ★

COLOR ME BAD (MOST CONTROVERSIAL ANTI-RACIST)

Famous for coining the term "rock and roll," **popular disc jockey Alan Freed carried his fame into the world of television** in 1957 with a show not too different from *American Bandstand.* A self-proclaimed "racially color-blind" host, he had no problem showing white and black teens sharing the stage. But when African-American Frankie Lymon of the band Teenagers danced on air with a white woman, viewers were outraged that Freed would dare to promote such racial tolerance. Southern affiliates could not ignore the uproar and shut down the show.

Freed moved on to broadcast locally, sticking to a more open-minded New York crowd, but the racial tension wasn't over yet. Now it was the black community's turn to take a punch at his impartiality. Why, they asked, should a white producer make so much money off the success of talented black artists? When Freed's bosses at

Crossing his fingers for a good turnout, disc jockey Alan Freed once rented out a facility that could hold ten thousand for his Moondog Coronation Ball in 1952. He underestimated, though, and twenty thousand people showed up. Due to overcrowding, the show had to be canceled, but Freed went on to plan other events that would have an attendance of up to one hundred thousand.

his radio station, WIN, heard rumors of controversy, they didn't have enough public relations propaganda to defend themselves and simply let the issue lie. The turmoil continued, however, and riots broke out at local concerts Freed organized. To prevent continued trouble the following year, WIN chose not to renew his contract.

In the end, however, it would be financial woes rather than racial strain that would end Freed's career. On March 15, 1964, he was indicted by a federal grand jury for alleged tax evasion, claiming he had never paid the IRS taxes on a large sum of his income. He may have been living in Palm Springs, California, but he was no aristocrat. Freed was poor, out of a job, and being pressured to shell out more than $30,000 to the U.S. government. He fell ill and died at age forty-three before he could even think about coming up with the cash.

MO' MONEY, MO' PROBLEMS (MOST CONTROVERSIAL MONEY-MAKING SCHEME)

Long before Napster and iTunes, the American Society of Composers and Publishers (ASCAP) found a tricky way to make as much money as possible off radio producers on the cutting edge of new technologies.

With complete ownership over the artists whose songs were appearing on air for the first time, they charged radio stations to rent sheet music, band programs, and variety shows to fill up the airtime in each market. They also charged stations for each time they featured one of its artists. The ASCAP made a fortune, but producers thought the policy was crap and soon rebelled, arguing that they should not have to pay for the music. Each time a song played was free advertising for the artist, wasn't it? It generated album sales, didn't it? Disc jockeys had the power to make or break an artist's career based on how many times they played a song on the air, so they took their power to the bank and formed Broadcast Music Incorporated (BMI) to skirt the sky-high fees. New artists caught on to the free publicity and the demand for the BMI genius went through the roof.

★ ★ ★ ★ ★

WHO IS THE FIFTH BEATLE? (MOST CONTROVERSIAL CLAIM)

Over the years, many Beatles fans have tried to put a finger on which fifth wheel associated with the Fab Four has the right to be called the fifth and final Beatle. While many groupies, managers, and buddies came and went throughout the years, only these guys make the running. Who will it be? You be the judge.

Pete Best—A drummer for the Beatles from August 1960 to August 1962, Best played with the Fab Four during their famous tour

DID YOU KNOW

Even though they broke up twenty-five years ago, The Beatles continue to sell more records each year than the Rolling Stones.

of Germany and on the renowned *Anthology I* collection. With a little help from his mommy, who bragged on her son's new endeavor, the band slowly became famous. However, Best's bandmates admitted he wasn't the greatest drummer they had ever heard. When the longhaired boys signed their first record deal, producer George Martin broke the news

that he wanted to replace Best with someone, well, better. Ringo Starr stepped in, but fans weren't comfortable with him right away. At first the Beatles were harassed at concerts by Best fans who missed their old friend. Best's career would never quite recover. He spent the rest of the sixties poor and bouncing between B-list bands before he retired to work at a bakery and later as a civil servant in Liverpool.

> CELEBRITY ALIAS
> Alias: Ringo Starr
> Actual Name: Richard Starkey

Brian Epstein—The Beatles' manager from 1961-1967, Epstein was a theater student and a manager at a family-owned North End Music Store when he first met the band while chillin' at a nightclub. He had never managed before, but he went nuts when he heard The Beatles perform at Liverpool's Cavern Club in 1961 and promised he could make them superstars. Ever the fashion guru, it was Epstein who gave the Fab Four their matching suits and haircuts, and in less than six months, he had gotten them a recording contract. His loyalty to The Beatles didn't go unnoticed by his other clients, though. They regularly complained of not getting the marketing they deserved as they took a backseat to Epstein's "Yesterday" pretty boy project.

George Martin—A bigwig at Parlophone Records, Martin was the producer of most Beatles albums, including the original recording of "Let It Be." He was the first to let the band experiment with their sound and write their own music. Even when Martin's instincts told him the guys should stick to work from outside writers, he let them try some original songs and overdubs that helped mold their sound. Hungry for a bigger paycheck, Martin was denied a raise and quit Parlophone in 1965 to form his own company but continued to work with The Beatles. Even after the band broke up, he produced records for Ringo Starr and Paul McCartney. Since then, he has worked with the likes of industry veterans Celine Dion and Elton John.

Neil Aspinall—A classic fifth wheel who befriended the band while renting a room in Pete Best's house, Aspinall became The Beatles' road manager. He had originally considered going to school to be an accountant but soon found his alternate calling driving the band back and forth from gigs. He ditched the college dream and decided to stick around. When his drummer roomie was fired in 1962, Aspinall had plans to quit the project ... but Best told him not to be stupid. It was a good move because he ended up doing an array of odd jobs for the band, and was even invited to play instruments on the original recordings of "Within You Without You" and "Being Mr. Kite." Later, he became the managing director of Apple Corps, The Beatles' personal record company.

Mal Evans—An engineer in Liverpool, Evans spent a lot of free time at the Cavern Club and eventually earned enough respect to be hired on as a bouncer. While he was throwing out the drunks and breaking up bar fights, Evans befriended The Beatles and their manager, Brian Epstein. He was a charmer and eventually was brought on as a roadie to help set up the equipment at gig sites.

DID YOU KNOW

In 1970, The Beatles' released the No. 1 hit "The Long and Winding Road," but George Harrison and Ringo Starr don't play on the track at all. It is just Paul McCartney playing the piano and John Lennon playing bass.

Chapter 5

★

Papa's Got a Brand New Bag: How Big Stars Blow Their Dough

JAGGER

Papa's Got a Brand New Bag: How Big Stars Blow Their Dough

★ ★ ★ ★ ★ ★ ★ ★ ★ ★ ★ ★ ★ ★ ★

In their younger days, money didn't come so easy to the filthy rich stars of today. Madonna worked behind the counter at Dunkin' Donuts. David Lee Roth changed bedpans and bed sheets as a hospital orderly. Vince Neil was an electrician, Rod Stewart was a gravedigger, and Jon Bon Jovi flipped hamburger patties at Burger King. These rockers may have searched their car for quarters years ago, but these days they follow the golden rule of riches—if you've got it, flaunt it.

In 1999, Mariah Carey bought Marilyn Monroe's white baby grand piano for $662,500.

★ ★ ★ ★ ★

Ruby Tuesday

When it comes to showing off their hard-earned bread, no one does it like rappers. But long before *their* platinum grills hit the red carpet, **Mick Jagger of The Rolling Stones flashed his cash when he implanted an emerald into one of his teeth** on

the upper right side of his mouth. Unfortunately, from a distance it looked more like a bit of broccoli than a precious jewel. When friends kept telling him he had food in his teeth, Jagger swapped it for a ruby. When they started handing him tissues to wipe the spot of "blood" off his mouth, he learned that red, too, wasn't quite his color. Refusing to give up so easy on something so dang cool, he swapped once more—this time for a diamond.

★ ★ ★ ★ ★

Don't Stop Spending Til You Get Enough

Dropping dollars on jewelry and expensive toys is a signature pastime of rockers worldwide, but nothing compares to how they blow millions to shine on MTV and VH1. Hoping to shock viewers (and sell more records) with state-of-the-art special effects, producers will break the bank

when it comes to constructing the hottest music videos of all time. And no one does it like pop king Michael Jackson. In 1983, the groundbreaking thirteen-minute "Thriller" was the most expensive music video ever made at $1 million (which translates to nearly double that amount today). However, Jackson has since one-upped

The longest amount of time it ever took Elton John to write a song was three-and-a-half hours for "Paris." In an interview with a reporter from CNN, he said that the duration drove him nuts and that he thought he was going to have a "mental breakdown."

himself with the video for "Scream," a futuristic duo with sister Janet Jackson that cost a jaw-dropping $7 million. The pair spent at least $11,000 a day on makeup alone. Was it worth the big bucks? Also boasting the theme song for kiddie flick *Free Willy 2*, Jackson's album at the time, *HIStory*, only sold 3.5 million copies.

★ ★ ★ ★ ★

LUCY IN THE SKY WITH ALBUMS

What kind of morning shopping ritual would a colorful male diva sporting thousands of pairs of designer glasses and fifteen hit singles have? Every Tuesday morning at 9:30 a.m., Elton John swings by Tower Records in Atlanta, Georgia, to flip through new album releases. Because he's, well, Elton John, employees let him slip in before the store opens to sip coffee and take a gander at hundreds of CDs alphabetized on carts waiting to be distributed throughout the store. Elton simply buys the ones he wants and sneaks out before the store is packed with shoppers.

★ ★ ★ ★ ★

EXPRESS YOURSELF (WITH INK)

Taboo in many parts of the world, tattoos have been the ultimate (and most permanent) means of self-expression since prehistoric times. In East Asian countries, most people with body art keep it covered because tattoos are so closely associated with criminal activity. In Japan, businesses and recreational facilities ban those with visible tatoos. It's this outlaw image that

OOPS ... I DID IT AGAIN

When Britney Spears had a Hebrew tattoo put on the back of her neck in 2004, she thought it stood for "new era," in honor of her dedication to Kabbalah. However, Spears had two things wrong—the symbol actually stood for "protection," and she failed to realize that in Judaism, the very act of getting a tattoo is a sinful taboo. What makes the situation even more ironic is that it was not the first time she was duped by a tattoo artist. In 2003, a friend told her that the tattoo on her hip, which she thought meant "mysterious," actually was more literally translated to "strange."

makes spending money on getting inked so popular among rock and roll greats looking to stain their skin with a symbol of a rockin' memory or subculture. Some of the most outrageous rocker tattoos include:

Billie Joe Armstrong (Green Day)—Circled number 27, two angels, a rose, a small cross, a vine, a baby smoking a cigar, and a tiny black heart on his right arm, as well as a baby, a clown bracelet, Jacob, a flower, and the acronym P.U.N.X. on his left arm.

Travis Barker (Blink 182)—Checkered design on both sides of his neck, "Can I Say" across his collarbone, nude women outlines on his upper chest, a radio on his stomach, and both arms sleeved with designs.

David Bowie—Lizard on his ankle.

Fatboy Slim—Smiley face with crossbones on his arm.

Kid Rock—Detroit Tigers' "D" on right arm, the name "Paul" on left bicep, a bald eagle, and the phrase "American Bad Ass."

Kurt Cobain (Nirvana)—K Records logo on his arm.

Jonathan Davis (Korn)—Korn logo on his back and a bishop ripping his skin off to reveal Jesus on his right bicep.

> ### CELEBRITY ALIAS
> Alias: Fatboy Slim
> Actual Name: Quentin Cook, later Norman Cook

★ ★ ★ ★ ★

WAKE ME UP BEFORE YOU BID

At a transatlantic auction held at the New York and London Hard Rock Cafés, **George Michael wrote a check for a staggering $2.1 million** to take home the Steinway piano John Lennon played while writing the hit single "Imagine" in the early 1970s. British tabloids reported that brothers Liam and Noel Gallagher of Oasis made bids on the historical instrument as well but quit before the bids hit a million pounds.

★ ★ ★ ★ ★

IF I WAS A RICH GIRL—HOLLYWOOD GETAWAYS

When it's time for big stars to take a break from the Hollywood buzz, it's not a question of whether they have a vacation home to run off to— it's a question of how many and

---

CELEBRITY ALIAS

Alias: George Michael
Actual Name: Georgios Panayioutou

In 2005, Lennon's handwritten sheet music and lyrics for "All You Need is Love" were bought for a whopping 600,000 pounds at a London auction.

how lavish. With nine different sandy white beaches to choose from, some stars sunbathe at the exclusive Mustique Caribbean Island—by invitation only. Who has to review and approve their application for a little R&R? Rolling Stones legend Mick Jagger. Flash a few platinum records, and he *might* let you rent the place for a cool $15 million per week. Jagger may be known for his skinny figure, but there's nothing small about his private piece of land. Tip him enough and get an over-the-top getaway getting sporty on his tennis courts and, yes, sleeping in his bed.

OTHER STARS WITH BIG BUNGALOWS

- Sting—A cozy cottage in Malibu just thirty minutes from his Hollywood mansion.

- Jennifer Lopez—A five-bedroom $5 million mansion complete with tennis courts and an infinity pool in Los Angeles.

- Shania Twain—A twenty-six-room chateau in Switzerland.

★ ★ ★ ★ ★

PSYCHO CARTOON CIRCUS

It's career day at a local elementary school, and while most kids are caught up bragging about how their parents work at hospitals and beauty salons, Nick Simmons (son of KISS star Gene Simmons) is holding up a poster of his dad breathing fire and drooling blood on stage. The humor in the situation gave rocker Gene a fabulous new idea for how to spend his loads of cash—why not make a cartoon exploring the wild life of a kid whose dad is a superstar? In 2003, Simmons made the vision a reality when he created and produced *My Dad the Rock Star* for Nickelodeon. The show follows the life of twelve-year-old Willy Zilla, who has just settled down in a new hometown after touring with his dad's wild band. Complete with life lessons learned through guitar solos and a wacky New Age mother figure, the show aired alongside the likes of *Rugrats*, *Sponge Bog Square Pants*, and *Jimmy Neutron*. Simmons says the main character may look strikingly similar to his made-up psycho stage self, but insists that *most* of the show's storylines are strictly fiction.

MOMENT OF STUPIDITY

When KISS had its first big performance alongside Iggy Pop in 1974, Gene Simmons thought it would be cool to impress the audience by breathing fire. Instead, he set his hair on fire.

★ ★ ★ ★ ★

DON'T PASS ON GRASS

Just what does the multi-platinum selling Dave Matthews Band buy after hosting a rockin' concert in their hometown of Charlottesville, Virginia? A whole lot of grass. Held at the University of Virginia's stadium, the concert was packed and the damage done to the turf was so irreversible that the band had to pitch in and pay up for some new green. Before the show, the band had allegedly offered to install a special tile over the grass for protection. However, the athletic department requested the band save their dollars and just replace what they ruined after the fact.

LITTLE RED CORVETTE: WHAT THE STARS ARE DRIVING

Roland Gift—Saab

Mick Fleetwood—Jeep

Paula Abdul—Jaguar

Madonna—Mercedes, Thunderbird

Elvis Presley—Cadillac, Mercedes

Bono—Mercedes

Mike Mills—Thunderbird

★ ★ ★ ★ ★

WON'T GET CAUGHT AGAIN

British rocker Pete Townshend of The Who turned a little red when he admitted to the media that he used his credit card to enter a Web site advertising child pornography to simply "see what was there." Luckily for his reputation, the confession was in the middle of a statement he was making against the horrendous crime of exploiting children. Townshend, who was writing his autobiography about how he was sexually abused as a child, said that explicit Web sites were abhorrent and any of his further "compulsions in this area" would be to fight for child rights and ban all similar sites from the Web.

★ ★ ★ ★ ★

AND AFTER ALL, YOU'RE MY WONDER MALL

Oasis front man Noel Gallagher was all about girls, drugs, and fancy digs when his band first went mainstream with the single "Supersonic" in 1994. He even bought a whole convoy of cars, despite the fact that he has *never* had a driver's license. There is one thing, however, that Gallagher is proud to say he was never tempted to purchase—leather pants.

★ ★ ★ ★ ★

STINGY STAR

Frank Zappa never bought a wedding ring for his wife, Adelaide Gail. The couple got married just a few days before Zappa left for his first European tour, and his nine-month pregnant fiancée

GUITARIST WHO ROCKS

Pete Townshend
Band: The Who
Guitar of Choice: Gibson SG Special with Hiwatt 100-watt heads
Best Known For: "Won't Get Fooled Again" on the album *Who's Next*

Oasis drummer Zak Starkey is Ringo Starr's son.

was in a bit of a hurry to shotgun the ceremony and move on with her life. Possibly the least lavish wedding of any rock star, Zappa bought a pen out of a New York City Hall vending machine (which read, "Congratulations from Mayor Lindsay"), filled out the marriage license, and headed off to Europe. In his autobiography, *The Real Frank Zappa Book*, he admits that to this day, Gail has no bling on her finger.

MOMENT OF STUPIDITY

When Frank Zappa was in the hospital for the birth of his son, the nurse hated his first choice for his new baby's name so much (Dweezil) that Zappa rattled off a long list of common male names to make her happy. The birth certificate reads "Ian Donald Calvin Euclid Zappa."

★ ★ ★ ★ ★

CAN'T SLEEP, SNAKE WILL EAT ME

When Alice Cooper went on tour, his right-hand gal was none other than a pet boa constrictor named Veronica, who measured at about fifteen feet long. He had originally purchased the snake to take onstage as a prop, but eventually decided to let the animal accompany him in his hotel room after concerts. One day, he left Veronica lounging in his Knoxville, Tennessee, Marriott suite when she decided to take a gander down the toilet. Cooper notified management, but the snake didn't reappear for two weeks—when it crawled out and terrified singer Charlie Pride during his stay at the same hotel.

CELEBRITY ALIAS

Alias: Alice Cooper
Actual Name: Vincent Furnier

MOMENT OF STUPIDITY

Once when rehearsing for an upcoming performance with his pet boa constrictor, Evan Marie Snake, Alice Cooper was choked by it. It would not stop, and Cooper's bodyguard had to cut off its head with his pocketknife.

★ ★ ★ ★ ★

REAL ESTATE REALITY CHECK

Rap icon Nelly was test-driving a truck in Missouri in 2002 when he saw a for-sale sign and actually considered adding to his long list of riches by purchasing his own town. With hopes for his very own place to hunt and fish, he almost made the buy—but after considering it more realistically for a few minutes, he declined. For the next several weeks, however, Nelly couldn't help but daydream of how he would have called his little town Nellyville. With that fantasy in mind, Nelly made it the name of his next album.

★ ★ ★ ★ ★

ROCKERS WHO GOT RIPPED OFF

It is difficult for musicians to break into the rock and roll A-list and finally make some cash. But once they sashay down the red carpet a few times, the pressures of dropping dollars on flashy toys are tough to resist. Besides trying to keep the cash from burning a hole in their pockets, however, if stars aren't careful they can get scammed by nasty thieves looking to con a celebrity unaware. These rockers were shocked when they found out they had been duped by the best.

• Nine Inch Nails front man Trent Reznor sued ex-manager John Malm for allegedly taking millions of dollars from him after he had him sign a five-year management contract in the late 1980s. What Reznor failed to notice was that the paperwork guaranteed the managing company 20 percent of all his earnings for the rest of his career—regardless of whether they were still working together. This star should have read his contract more closely.

- When Lil' Kim lugged her luggage into New York's JFK Airport in 2003, she just couldn't keep track of the one bag full of bling. Although she intended to take her sack full of $250,000 worth of jewels on the plane with her for safekeeping, the Louis Vuitton carry-on accidentally got checked with the rest. Panicked that her diamonds had just gotten lifted, Kim had the airline hold the plane. By the time the bag was recovered, however, the jewels were long gone. One airline worker who had heard about the stolen jewels tried to cash in when he phoned and offered to give the jewelry back (which he didn't even have) for a whopping $25,000. Lucky for Kim, the idiot left her a message with his name and phone number, so that when she gave in she could give him a ring. The cops took the message instead, and he was arrested. The real jewels were later found wrapped in some rags in an airport locker.

- When a Pittsburgh identity thief charged credit cards in Will Smith's name to the tune of nearly $33,000, the star got jiggy with his lawyers and hunted down forty-two-year-old Carlos Lomax. The tip-off—Lomax had gone on a shopping spree at Sears. Assuming that Smith (or Willard C. Smith, as the credit cards read) wouldn't be caught dead at a department store, his business manager called the cops. How did the police track down the imposter? They simply looked up where he was having the goods shipped to his home.

- Young pop artist Aaron Carter fired his manager of ten years, his mother, Jane, when he was led to believe that she had taken

GUITARISTS WHO ROCK

Scotty Moore
Band: Elvis Presley's band
Guitar of Choice: Gibson ES-295 and Gibson Super 400
Best Known For: "Mystery Train" from Elvis's *The Complete Sun Sessions* (1976)

Johnny Ramone
Band: The Ramones
Guitar of Choice: Mosrite Ventures II
Best Known For: "Blitzkrieg Bop" from album *The Ramones*

David Gilmore
Band: Pink Floyd
Guitar of Choice: Fender Stratocaster
Best Known For: "Comfortably Numb" from the album *The Wall*

Steve Howe
Band: Yes
Guitar of Choice: Gibson ES-175 and a Fender Telecaster
Best Known For: "Roundabout" from the album *Fragile (1972)*

BB King
Guitar of Choice: Gibson ES-355
Best Known For: "The Thrill is Gone" from the album *Anthology*

Albert King
Guitar of Choice: Gibson Flying V
Best Known For: "Born Under a Bad Sign" from the album of the same name

$100,000 out of his bank account without his knowing about it. Feeling a little guilty, he rehired her just one month later.

DID YOU KNOW

Guitarist Bernie Leadon of The Eagles, most famous for "Take it Easy" (1972) and "Hotel California" (1976), once dated Patti Davis, the daughter of former President Ronald Reagan. He even convinced his bandmates to sing one of the songs she had written ("I Wish You Peace").

Chapter 6

Four Faces That
Shaped Rock

BO DIDDLEY

Four Faces That Shaped Rock

★ ★ ★ ★ ★ ★ ★ ★ ★ ★ ★ ★ ★ ★ ★ ★ ★

Some early rock personalities made such an impact on the music business that it would never be the same again. They weren't all musicians, but they all had a vision for a hipper, more united rock subculture. One may not have guessed they would become such significant role models early in their lives—none came from wealthy families, and some had very little ambition. But when these early geniuses got their big break, they influenced the music industry like no one had ever done before. These are their legacies.

The American Music Awards, one of four major music award shows in the U.S., were created by Dick Clark in 1973 to compete with the Grammys.

★ ★ ★ ★ ★

THE SELF-MADE COWBOY: BILL HALEY

Getting Started—The son of a hard-working high school dropout who had taught himself to master the banjo and the mandolin, Bill Haley was kin to a small-town country music legacy. At thirteen years old, he followed in his father's self-made footsteps and learned basic chords on the guitar. The very moment he mastered it, he developed a lifelong dream to become a singing cowboy—just like in the movies. Despite his family's bleak financial situation, Haley practiced diligently and joined a handful of local country and western bands, releasing his first record, "Candy Kisses," at just eighteen years old. He went on tour with a band of high school buddies called the Down Homers Haley, but after releasing a few unsuccessful singles in the 1940s, they went broke so quickly that Haley came crawling home, begging his mother to keep his failure a secret. Not even his fiancée, Dorothy, knew that her love had given up on fame and was sleeping off the disappointment at his parents' house.

> ## fabulous firsts
> Bill Haley and his Comets were the first American rock and roll stars to visit Great Britain.

The Turning Point—Leaving behind the dream of becoming a "singing cowboy" like Gene Autry, Haley married Dorothy, his childhood sweetheart, and became a radio show host in Chester, Pennsylvania. Bored by his twelve to sixteen-hour shifts nearly seven days a week, he decided to spice up the programming by putting together his own band to perform on the show. They were a hit, and

BILL HALEY

Date of Birth: July 6, 1925

Hometown: Highland Park, Michigan

Little Known Fact: Haley's father worked as a mechanic while his mother made 25 cents an hour giving piano lessons from home. The family was so poor that Haley's dream of becoming a singer nearly fizzled when at fifteen years old, he left school to work at a local plant bottling spring water for 35 cents an hour.

Greatest Accomplishment: In 1954, Haley's cover of Joe Turner's "Shake, Rattle, and Roll" became the first rock and roll record to sell one million copies. His next hit, "See You Later Alligator," repeated the feat—in only four weeks.

in 1950, Bill Haley and His Saddlemen cut a record of old cowboy tunes. For their next album, the band decided to change their image and put a new twist on western swing music. Their ingenuity changed the music industry forever, but the name "Saddlemen" didn't  quite capture their newfound energy and popularity. Haley remembered a cheesy nickname from a friend and applied it to the group—Bill Haley and His Comets were ready for the world.

DID YOU KNOW ?

The 1956 movie *Rock Around the Clock* featured nine onscreen lip-synched performances by new artist Bill Haley, making him famous around the world.

Leaving a Legacy—Combining key elements of classic country, swing, and rhythm and blues, Bill Haley and His Comets fabricated some of the earliest rock and roll hits, including "Rock the Joint," which sold an impressive seventy-five thousand copies. Haley's next hit single, "Crazy, Man Crazy," became the first rock and roll record to make the *Billboard* pop charts, shooting to the Top 20 within weeks. It would be "Rock Around the Clock," however, that would make history and set their fame in stone. Only a partial hit at first, the song's popularity went through the roof when it was used as the title track in the cult-classic film *The Blackboard Jungle*, becoming an anthem for the nation's rebel youth. The song held *Billboard*'s No. 1 spot for eight weeks and sold 22 million copies worldwide. Haley continued to score hit singles throughout the 1950s and later starred in early rock and roll musical movies. Although his fame and fortune in the United States was eventually surpassed by a controversial young Elvis, Haley continued to be a major star in Latin America and in Europe. He died on February 9, 1981.

STUDIOS THAT SHAPED ROCK:
Abbey Road

Made famous by the unforgettable Beatles album cover snapshot of Paul, Ringo, George, and John strutting their stuff down the crosswalk in 1969, Abbey Road is one of the world's most

legendary streets. One of its most famed buildings of musical history is, of course, Abbey Road Studios. Originally designed for recording classical music, Abbey Road was opened in 1931 by The Gramophone Company, or EMI Records. In the beginning, though, it wasn't the swanky hangout that it is today. The first person to ever record there was the English composer Sir Edward Elgar, who sang "The Land of Hope And Glory" with the British National Symphony Orchestra. (Snore.) Regardless of the sleepy start, however, the studio slowly acquired a host of famous connections with rock artists. When The Glen Miller Orchestra recorded its final album at Abbey Road, the studio's reputation for coolness reached the ears of Cliff Richards and the Drifters, who dropped in to cut the track for "Move It," followed by the likes of Gene Pitney, Gerry and The Pacemakers, and others. The Beatles got their start at Abbey Road Studio in 1963 with "Love Me Do" and spent the next seven years recording there. Since then, the studio has served as a recording hotspot for popular rock artists like Eric Clapton, Pink Floyd, Sting, and Oasis. It has also hosted famed composers and their orchestras recording scores for box office films including *Raiders of the Lost Ark, Braveheart,* and the *Lord of the Rings* trilogy.

★ ★ ★ ★ ★

THE SUBSTITUTE-TURNED-TV TALENT: DICK CLARK

Getting Started—Born Richard Wagstaff Clark in 1929, Dick Clark was infamous for his poor grades in high school—that is, until he discovered radio. A tenth grader with big dreams, Clark set his sights on broadcasting and got a job at WRUN-AM in Rome, New York, just after graduation. He was a lowly office boy without much responsibility until his boss asked him to fill in for a vacationing weatherman. Shocked to take on such an important role, he jumped at the chance for practice behind the microphone. He graduated from Syracuse University with a major in advertising and a minor in radio, then worked an array of jobs in broadcasting. In 1952, he joined WFIL radio in Philadelphia, Pennsylvania, to try his hand at an interesting new trend—deejays playing records for their listening audiences.

The Turning Point—As Clark learned how to spin records at the station, fellow deejay Bob Horn experimented with a hot new television music show called *Bandstand*. After a few episodes, Horn invited local high school students to

> ### DICK CLARK
> Date of Birth: November 30, 1929
>
> Hometown: Mount Vernon, New York

dance while he played music. The show was a huge success, but Horn blew it when he took a vacation and left Clark at the wheel as substitute. At just twenty-six years old, Clark was so in tune with teenagers that he quickly developed a repertoire among them, discussing the latest dance fads and clothing trends. It wasn't long before he took Horn's spot permanently. After returning from his time off, Horn was arrested for driving under the influence of alcohol and *Bandstand* producers had the confirmation they needed to pass the torch.

Leaving a Legacy—On August 5, 1957, *Bandstand* changed its name to *American Bandstand* for its first-ever national airing from 3:00 to 4:30 p.m. each day on ABC. (It later moved to Saturday.) A good balance of partying with limitations, the show had after-school entertainment value for teens and class for parents. Its famous dress code denied girls the right to wear tight clothes or slacks, and boys were asked to don a coat and tie. Calming parents' fears that rock and roll would corrupt their children, *American Bandstand* made Dick Clark and new artists like Chuck Berry, Buddy Holly, and Jerry Lee Lewis stars among the whole family. Clark stuck with the show for several decades, and when he said goodbye in 1989, it had become the longest-running program of its kind.

★ ★ ★ ★ ★

The Pioneer Music Journalist: Paul Williams

Getting Started—In the mid-1960s, those who weren't actually making music stepped up as critics to separate the good from the bad, speaking out about which stars were hot and which stars were not. The best way to share their opinions was to write about them, but where could the praises and rantings be publicly read? Trade magazines like *Billboard* and *Cashbox* had long been popular, predicting which bands would flop and which would sell, but they were more known for their charts than for solid critiques. There was a hole in journalism just waiting for music critic and college student Paul Williams to step in. A freshman at Swarthmore College, just outside of Philadelphia, Williams was a science-fiction junkie familiar with the sci-fi fanzine following. He wrote a column for a local folk magazine and hosted blues programs for his college radio station.

The Turning Point—On a whim, Williams decided to start his own magazine and name it after a British club where the Rolling Stones made it big—the *Crawdaddy!* He hoped the weekly publication would provide readers with substantial musical reviews—not fluff. It was not much to look at in the beginning, though. The magazine was held together with staples, and he sold it for a quarter at record shops and bookstores from Philadelphia to New York City to Boston. *Crawdaddy!* became so popular in the northeast that he hired a handful of writers and moved the operation to an office in New York.

PAUL WILLIAMS
Birthday: May 19, 1948

Hometown: Boston, Massachusetts

Little Known Fact: Although *Crawdaddy!* stopped printing in 1979, Williams revived it once again for a brief twenty-eight issues in 1993. Unfortunately, financial problems forced him to put it to rest for good in 2003.

Leaving a Legacy—*Crawdaddy!* gained steam as an influence in the music industry when critical New York newspaper *The Village Voice* called it the most fascinating magazine covering the rock scene for people who "dig rock 'n' roll as an art form." It went on to influence the early years of *Rolling Stone*, a similar publication out of San Francisco. Williams quit and the magazine stopped printing for a few years, but in 1970, it returned—without its signature exclamation point and with a broader, more pop-culture approach to its articles. Sadly, the new *Crawdaddy* didn't sell as well as its former self, and shut down by 1979.

★ ★ ★ ★ ★

THE MUSICAL GENIUS: BO DIDDLEY

Getting Started—
Often described as one of the most original musical geniuses of the 1950s, Bo Diddley was born in McComb, Mississippi, in 1928. Originally named Ellas Bates, Diddley was raised by distant relatives who took him to Chicago when he was just nine years old. He took violin lessons from Ebenezer Missionary Baptist Church for twelve years, even composing two of his own concertos. The following year, his sister gave him a guitar for Christmas, and he hasn't stopped playing since. Diddley formed his own band in high school called The Hipsters

Some people believe Ellas Bates changed his name to Bo Diddley as a tribute to a slang phrase that meant "nothing," while others believe it was his nickname in the boxing ring.

(later known as The Langley Avenue Jive Cats) and began making cash landing regular gigs at the 708 Club in downtown Chicago. After graduation, he continued to play music but had to pay the bills, so he took odd jobs including truck driving and boxing.

The Turning Point—At twenty-seven years old in 1955, Diddley signed a record deal and put out his first singles, "Uncle John" and "I'm A Man." As he grew in fame with fellow artists like Chuck Berry, he became famous for influencing a rhythmic style called hambone, slapping your hands on your legs and chest while singing simple songs. Diddley became a regular at Harlem's Apollo Theatre. He was larger than life.

Leaving a Legacy—As he rose in fame, Diddley invented rock's most foundational rhythm, the "Bo Diddley beat." The popular bass line has

BO DIDDLEY

Birthday: December 30, 1928

Hometown: McComb, Mississippi

Little Known Fact: Bo Diddley was the first African American to be a guest on *The Ed Sullivan Show* on November 20, 1955. However, he and Sullivan didn't get along when he decided to sing his No. 1 hit "Bo Diddley" instead of "Sixteen Tons," as requested. He was banned from ever performing on the show again.

been picked up by decades of artists since then, including The Who, U2, and Bruce Springsteen. Diddley also gained steam as a respected artist when he designed the square-bodied cigar box guitar, one he designed for himself while at school in 1945. To this day, it is his trademark instrument. In 2005, he celebrated his fiftieth anniversary of playing music with a worldwide tour.

BO DIDDLEY SONGS COVERED BY OTHER ARTISTS:

"Who Do You Love" —The Doors and George Thorogood

"Hey Hey" —Eric Clapton

"The Story of Bo Diddley" —The Animals

"I'm a Man"—The Yardbirds

THREE THINGS YOU NEVER KNEW ABOUT "HAPPY BIRTHDAY"

- It was written in 1893 by two teachers in Louisville, Kentucky, originally intended as a song to greet students titled "Good Morning to All."

- The copyright is owned by Warner Communications, who purchased it for $28 million in 1985. The copyright will expire at the earliest in 2030.

- Astronauts on the Apollo IX sang "Happy Birthday" on March 8, 1969, making it the first song sung in outer space.

STUDIOS THAT SHAPED ROCK:
The Brill Building

Named after the Brill brothers, who originally built the space for their clothing store in 1931, The Brill Building is located at 1619 Broadway in the heart of New York's unique music district. When the Great Depression hit their business hard, the Brills were forced to rent out space to some of the only people still working—music publishers. Thirty years later, the department store was long gone and 165 music businesses bustled through the halls. Shoppers passing by outside could hear the smooth sounds flowing from the building onto the streets below.

In the early 1960s, The Brill Building became a one-stop-shop for anyone in the music business. There, you could write a song, then knock on a handful of doors until a publisher decided to buy it. Once you signed a contract, you could step upstairs to get your song arranged, hire a singer to record a demo, and have copies made to distribute to artists and their managers. Convince someone to make it a hit, and marketing agents were hanging around to put the record on the radio and push it to young audiences across the nation.

Chapter 7

I Heard It Through the Grapevine: Classic Rock Rumors

I Heard It Through the Grapevine: Classic Rock Rumors

★ ★ ★ ★ ★ ★ ★ ★ ★ ★ ★ ★ ★ ★ ★ ★

Mama Cass never died choking on a ham sandwich (blame it on heart failure), and Robert Johnson never made a pact with the devil. (He was actually tutored by a blues guitarist named Ike Zimmerman.) It's tough to admit, but you have been duped. For much of your life, you have been taken for a ride by your friends, the media, and the many mistakes of oral tradition. These are just a few countless myths that have haunted the reputation of big-name celebrities for years—and it's time to face the facts. It may be tough to admit you've been wrong all this time, and let's face it, some rumors are fun to spread around. But the following tabloid treasures are just plain false.

Roy Orbison was not albino, nor was he nearly blind. His trademark glasses were simply to correct a regular vision impairment.

★ ★ ★ ★ ★

MYTH #1—PAUL MCCARTNEY IS DEAD.

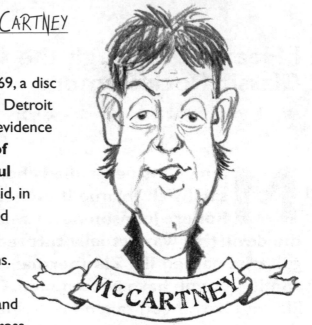

On October 12, 1969, a disc jockey at WKNR-FM in Detroit broke "the news." The evidence of **the secret death of legendary Beatle Paul McCartney** was, he said, in the many clues sprinkled throughout the band's songs, artwork, and films. While dedicated fans sobbed their eyes out and lit memorial candles across the globe, the announcement was proven a hoax. However, to this day many Beatles junkies believe that the real McCartney died in a 1966 car accident while driving home from Abbey Road Studios—and that the man who claims to be him today is just a look-alike. Here's a list of why fanatics think the remaining of the Fab Four have left behind clues in their music about the fate of their beloved band mate:

- In the single "Yesterday," McCartney sings that there is a shadow hanging over him.

- In "And Your Bird Can Sing," McCartney sings, "You can't see me... You can't hear me."

- On the cover of the album *Yesterday and Today*, McCartney is sitting inside a trunk that resembles a coffin.

- On the cover for *The Yellow Submarine*, McCartney is sitting in a "sea of green," signifying being underneath the grass.

- On the cover of *Sergeant Pepper's Lonely Hearts Club Band*, a figurine of the Hindu god Shiva, also known as The Destroyer, seems to be pointing at Paul (who himself is holding a black instrument).

- On the *Abbey Road* cover, a barefoot Paul represents a dead man, John represents an angel (he is wearing white), Ringo represents the leader of a memorial service (he is wearing black), and George represents a gravedigger (he is wearing denim).

- In the song "A Day In The Life," John sings, "He blew his mind out in a car. He didn't notice that the lights had changed." Could the lyrics be a description of his friend and former band mate's death?

Regardless of how passionate believers of this popular myth may be, the band continues to stress that they are, in fact, false. Props for the creativity, though.

DID YOU KNOW
Phil Collins was an extra in The Beatles' film *A Hard Day's Night*.

★ ★ ★ ★ ★

MYTH #2—JOAN JETT WROTE "I LOVE ROCK N' ROLL"

A rebel anthem of everything hip about rock, the song "I Love Rock N' Roll" has been recorded by a long list of musical wannabes and greats including Dragon Ash, Five, The Sex Pistols, Weird Al Yankovic, Hit Crew, and Britney Spears. The greatest myth surrounding this ever-re-recorded hit, however, is that it was originally recorded by punk guitarist Joan Jett. The song's true authors: Alan Merrill and Jake Hooker of The Arrows. After releasing two singles that raced to the top of the charts in Great Britain ("Touch Too Much" and "My Last Night With You"), The Arrows were looking to follow up their newfound fame with another big hit. Although producer Mickie Most wasn't a huge fan of the original recording and initially pushed the band to release ballad "Broken Down Heart" instead, "I

Music enthusiasts are often confused by the songwriting credits listed on the many cover versions of "I Love Rock N' Roll"— some list Alan Merrill and Jake Hooker of The Arrows as the original songwriters, while others list Allan Sachs and Jerry Mamberg. Why? Because Allan Sachs is Alan Merrill's legal name, and Jerry Mamberg is Jake Hooker's legal name.

Love Rock N' Roll" was an instant favorite after the band was invited to play it on Muriel Young's show *45* in 1975. On tour in England with her band The Runaways at the

---

CELEBRITY ALIAS
Alias: Joan Jett
Actual Name: Joan Larkin

---

time, Joan Jett saw The Arrows' television performance and fell in love with the raw sound.

Jett released the first cover version of "I Love Rock N' Roll" in 1979, but her adaptation wouldn't go multi-platinum until 1982—after guitarist Steve Jones and drummer Paul Cook of The Sex Pistols released *their* version of the single. In fact, despite the fact that pop-diva Britney Spears's cover has an uncanny resemblance to Jett's, representatives at Jive Records claim that while gearing up for her 2002 release, she listened to the The Arrows' original cut—not Jett's rewrite. In Great Britain, Britney's version ended up a bigger hit than Jett's—she made it to the No. 2 spot, while back in 1982, Jett just couldn't budge past No. 3.

★ ★ ★ ★ ★

MYTH #3—DIANA ROSS WAS IN THE ORIGINAL SUPREMES.

Diana Ross and soulful sidekicks Florence Ballard and Mary Wilson were not the first group to call themselves The Supremes during the early rock and roll

In 1993, Diana Ross was listed in *The Guinness Book of World Records* as the most successful female artist ever.

313

era of the 1950s and 1960s. In 1957, a group from Columbus, Ohio, released a single called "Just You and I" under the band name The Supremes. The 1963 hit "Our Day Will Come" was sung by a second group of the same name that was originally Ruby and the Romantics.

★ ★ ★ ★ ★

MYTH #4—MARILYN MANSON ACTED ON THE WONDER YEARS.

From 1988-1993, every little girl with a crush on Kevin Arnold would have given anything to be his beautiful sidekick (and first kiss) Winnie Cooper on sitcom *The Wonder Years*. The same girls got nauseous, however, when they heard the unthinkable rumor that Marilyn Manson (or Brian Warner, as his parents called him) starred as the geeky, allergy-ridden Paul Pfeiffer on the same show. How could such a loyal friend and nerd turn out to be someone as rebellious and sickly satanic as Manson? When confronted with the nasty myth his cult-fans were spreading across the nation, the mysterious rocker left them without much of an answer, saying it was "irrelevant" as to whether or not the rumor was true.

However, fans can breathe a sigh of relief because Paul Pfeiffer was not played by Marilyn Manson but instead by Josh Saviano, a young actor who also made frequent appearances on children's shows like *Reading Rainbow* and *Fun House*. A graduate of Yale University, today Saviano is a lawyer. Manson has also dodged rumors that he played the innocent, good-hearted Charlie Bucket in the quirky film *Willy Wonka and the Chocolate Factory* with Gene Wilder—that, too, is not true.

★ ★ ★ ★ ★

MYTH #5—CREED IS A CHRISTIAN BAND.

As a teenager, **Scott Stapp wanted to prove to his parents so badly that rock music wasn't the antithesis of religion** that he eventually ran away from home. Years later as a student at Lee University, a Christian liberal-arts college, he was kicked out for smoking marijuana. A rocker raised on faith and his own love for rock and roll, Stapp was so inspired by the tunes of Led Zeppelin that he got together with some high school buddies from Tallahassee, Florida, and put together the band Creed and its premier album *My Own Prison*. At first they were criticized for their predictably Christian lyrics in singles like "My Sacrifice" and "With Arms Wide Open," but none of the band members ever openly admitted any kind of personal religious commitment. Similar to U2, the guys denied being a "Christian band" but still wanted to sing about their religious thoughts and questions in their music.

What many of the band's anti-religion enemies do not know, however, is that Stapp wrote those seemingly Christian lyrics while questioning the very faith he was raised on—in fact, in more than one interview, he admitted that *My Own Prison* wasn't referencing a specific God at all. He didn't want to directly support a Christian God or a Muslim God or a Buddhist God. His God was just the God he "saw in nature," he said. At the height of making music in the 1990s, Stapp refused to even call himself a Christian because of all the theological problems he had with the faith. USA Today may have called Creed "Bible thumping rockers," but they would claim otherwise. Whether Stapp denies or openly admits any form of faith today, his music has had a positive effect on fans, driving them toward the possibility of hope and heaven.

Myth #6-"American Pie" is Named After Buddy Holly's Fallen Plane.

On February 3, 1959, Buddy Holly, Ritchie Valens, and J.P. Richardson drew straws with their road crew to see who had to ride in the steamy, un-air-conditioned tour bus and who got to hitch a ride on the airplane. The three young stars won, but their fate would change when their four-passenger Beechcraft Bonanza crashed into a snowy Iowa cornfield at 1:05 a.m.

CELEBRITY ALIAS

Alias: Buddy Holly
Actual Name: Charles Hardin Holley

Twelve years later, Don McLean wrote the ballad "American Pie" as a tribute to the ill-fated rock heroes, making February 3rd the unofficial "day the music died." However, some music lovers took the tribute too far when they spread the rumor that "American Pie" was actually the name of the fallen airplane. The claim is simply not true.

★ ★ ★ ★ ★

MYTH #7-JACK AND MEG WHITE ARE SIBLINGS.

Although they had been playing together since 1999, when punk garage band White Stripes first became widely noticed with the single "Fell in Love With a Girl" in 2001, they had fooled music lovers with the legend that they were brother and sister. Claiming to be the youngest of a family of ten, the duo did share pasty white skin and jet-black hair. However, they were not blood relatives—they were married. In 2001, a reporter revealed the fact that Megan White and John (Jack) Gillis had actually been wed from 1996-2001. Today copies of their divorce papers circle the Web, telling the true tale of their relationship.

★ ★ ★ ★ ★

MYTH #8-BLACK SABBATH IS NAMED AFTER A WITCHES' GATHERING.

Rumors of gothic references to the occult in band names and lyrics are nothing new to the rock scene. In fact, some bands like the mystery

and controversy that comes with such confusion. With dark onstage performances by the wild and questionable Ozzy Osbourne, it was easy for Black Sabbath fans to believe the myth that their favorite rockers were a tribute to witchcraft. However, the band's name actually comes from their love of horror flicks—one in particular, the 1963 *Black Sabbath* starring Boris Karloff. Since retiring, Ozzy has appeared on a number of

talk shows explaining that the band's act was not satanic but mere theater.

★ ★ ★ ★ ★

Myth #9—Michael Jackson Does ... Just About Everything.

The King of Pop has pulled off quite a few cheesy stunts in his day. He performed at the 1996 BRIT Awards dressed as the Messiah, surrounded by kids and a mock rabbi. He outbid a good friend (Paul McCartney) for ownership of The Beatles' catalog of songs. As a grown man, he purchased a California ranch, filled it with amusement park rides and zoo animals, and named it Neverland.

Despite his addiction to utterly weird ways, Jackson is a misunderstood man surrounded by countless rumors, including:

- He sleeps in a pressure chamber to prevent aging. Anyone who paid attention to his 2005 lawsuit and trial knows Jackson clearly sleeps in a bed. It should be whether he has company that is up for question.

- He purposefully lightened his skin because he hates being black. Jackson actually has a condition called vitiligo, which causes pigment to fade away, leaving behind white splotches.

fabulous firsts
"Billie Jean" by Michael Jackson was the first video by a black artist to air on MTV.

• He purchased the remains of "Elephant Man" Joseph Merrick. The actual organs were destroyed during World War II. Jackson may have visited the Royal London Hospital to view casts of Merrick's head and appendages, but he certainly never took them home.

DID YOU KNOW ?

After staying in a hospital incubator for fifty-two days after his birth, Stevie Wonder was blinded from receiving too much oxygen.

Chapter 8

Famous Firsts
and Origins

Famous Firsts and Origins

★ ★ ★ ★ ★ ★ ★ ★ ★ ★ ★ ★ ★ ★ ★ ★

J ust what inspired ingenious songwriters to pen their famous lyrics, and how did bands like The Ramones and 10,000 Maniacs come up with their stage names? Take an inside look into these origins, as well as famous firsts, such as the first music video and first model of the electric guitar. You might be surprised at the stories behind these classic rock origins.

fabulous firsts

The first *Billboard* chart, introduced in 1936 as Chart Line, listed the most-played songs on three radio networks.

★ ★ ★ ★ ★

THE ORIGIN OF ... ROCK AND ROLL'S MOST FAMOUS LYRICS

The Song: "Tutti Frutti"

The Artist: Little Richard

The Story: Richard coined the phrase "a-wop-bop-a-loo-bop-a-lop-bam-boom" while working as a dishwasher.

The Song: "My Boyfriend's Back"

The Artist: The Angels

The Story: While working as a songwriter for April-Blackwood music in 1963, Bob Feldman caught word that his favorite Brooklyn Sweet Shoppe (located across the street from his old high school) was going to be torn down. While paying it one last visit, Feldman overheard a young girl arguing with a hoodlum-looking young man outside. "My boyfriend's back in town, and you're gonna be in trouble," she screamed. Laughing at the episode with friends later that night, Feldman penned the No. 1 song "My Boyfriend's Back" for The Angels.

The Song: "You Ain't Seen Nothin' Yet"

The Artist: Bachman-Turner Overdrive

The Story: When Randy Bachman first practiced the "b-b-b-baby" in the single "You Ain't Seen Nothin' Yet," he was making fun of his brother, Gary, who had a problem with stuttering. The band laughed at the mockery at first but later realized it was a golden idea for the chorus.

The Song: "I Saw the Light"
The Artist: Todd Rundgren
The Story: The lyrics to the 1972 single "I Saw the Light" came so quickly to Todd Rundgren that he vowed to never write that rapidly again—if it only takes fifteen minutes, it will end up as nothing more than a string of stupid clichés. To this day, Rundgren thinks the song is rubbish.

The Song: "Sweet Home Alabama"
The Artist: Lynyrd Skynyrd
The Story: Guitarist Gary Rossington had a bone to pick with Neil Young in the 1970s for dissing the South in his single "Southern Man." As a joke to retaliate and fix the damage done to the South's surly reputation, Lynyrd Skynyrd wrote "Sweet Home Alabama," *never* expecting it to be a hit or even a single.

DID YOU KNOW

Stevie Wonder, born Steveland Morris, wrote "Isn't She Lovely" in honor of his daughter Aisha Zakia, whose name means "strength" and "intelligence" in a native African language.

DID YOU KNOW

Gladys Knight's hit song "Midnight Train to Georgia" was originally written as "Midnight Plane to Houston."

The Song: "Running on Empty"
The Artist: Jackson Browne
The Story: Singer/songwriter Jackson Browne drove back and forth from his home to the recording studio so often that he really didn't feel like changing his

route to find a gas station when the tank flirted with "E." Praying that the car would get him home from work one day, Browne randomly started humming the tune that would later become the melody for the new song titled "Running on Empty."

The Song: "Proud Mary"
The Artist: Credence Clearwater Revival
The Story: John Fogerty wrote the song "Proud Mary" in the midst of a joyful celebration after he opened a letter that said he had been discharged from the army.

The Song: "That'll Be the Day"
The Artist: Buddy Holly
The Story: Sang by Buddy Holly and Jerry Allison in their hip new band The Crickets, "That'll Be The Day" was inspired by a John Wayne film called *The Searchers* in which a loner cowboy sneers the phrase, "That'll be the day."

The Song: "You're in My Heart"
The Artist: Rod Stewart
The Story: Stewart says many women may think he wrote "You're in My Heart" as a tribute to them, but in reality, it's a reflection on all the loves of his

life—soccer, football, Scotland, his parents, and maybe two or three different women he has swooned over the years.

MOMENT OF STUPIDITY

When Rod Stewart first performed at the Filmore East in New York in 1968, he was so nervous that he sang his first song from backstage.

The Song: "Aqualung"
The Artist: Jethro Tull
The Story: After mulling over some photographs his wife had taken of a homeless man, front man Ian Anderson came up with "Aqualung" as a tribute to spiritual equality. Regardless of how low the man in the photograph may be labeled, he says, there is still a piece of God inside him.

The Song: "Daniel"

The Artist: Elton John

The Story: Songwriter Bernie Taupin read a story in a national newsmagazine about a wounded soldier from Vietnam who wanted to settle back into his average life but was treated like such a hero that he had to leave the U.S. to get some peace and quiet. It was that article that inspired him to write "Daniel" for Elton John, who recorded it the very same day.

The Song: "Heartbreak Hotel"

The Artist: Elvis

The Story: When the *Miami Herald* printed a suicide note for the public to read in conjunction with one of their top news stories, Elvis took one look at it and was inspired enough to pen the lyrics to "Heartbreak Hotel."

CELEBRITY ALIAS

Alias: Elton John

Actual Name: Reginald Dwight

MOMENTS OF STUPIDITY

Elton John has appeared in concert dressed as:

Donald Duck
Prince Charming
Mozart
Ronald McDonald
Uncle Sam
Santa Claus

THREE THINGS YOU NEVER KNEW ABOUT … ELVIS

- He had an identical twin brother named Garon who died at birth. Elvis honored him with the middle name Aron.

- He loved to visit the morgues in Memphis to "check out the corpses."

- He was not the first artist to record "Blue Suede Shoes"—Carl Perkins recorded it for Sun Records.

The Song: "Brand New Key"
The Artist: Melanie
The Story: Songwriter Melanie Safka was a hopeless vegetarian until she gave into temptation and downed a McDonald's hamburger one day in the early 1970s. All stomachaches aside, the meal was a good move, because just after she ate, she came up with the hit song "Brand New Key."

The Song: "Layla"
The Artist: Eric Clapton
The Story: When Clapton wrote "Layla," he was lusting after Beatle George Harrison's wife, Patti, whom he had met when she was just nineteen years old on the set of *A Hard Day's Night*. Desperately in love with a woman who refused to leave her husband, Clapton wrote the Top 10 single as a tribute to his broken heart.

DID YOU KNOW?

While a young musician struggling to make it big, Billy Joel recorded a pretzel commercial with Chubby Checker.

★ ★ ★ ★ ★

THE DAY THE MUSIC DIED (AND ROSE AGAIN): THE ORIGIN OF ... THE ROCK ERA

When WWII peaked as a major conflict, the swingin' Big Band era came to a halting end. Musicians enrolled in the armed forces, the American Federation of Music went on strike, and clubs dishing out their dues to wartime taxes had to shut their doors for good. For those who did stick it out in the music business, touring was hardly an option, thanks to the rationing of tires, gas, and other materials. By the time fighting came to an end, teenagers took life pretty seriously. Straight-laced with nothing to look forward to but a forty-hour workweek, they were too busy with the daily grind to mess around with music—but not for long.

Enter the 1950s—the economy is booming and parents, who were bored to tears during their own childhoods, are suddenly eager to live vicariously through their

> In the 1950s, "cats" became a nickname for white teens who listened to traditionally black jazz tunes.

kids by pushing them to the party scene. Spending more time out with friends than ever before, youngsters finally started making decisions for themselves. With their newfound freedom (and newfound allowances), they had the power and the cash to make an impact on the music biz. In the October 13, 1958, edition of *Billboard* magazine, singer Jo Strafford commented on the turnaround. "Today's 9- to 14-year-old group is the first generation with enough money

THE EARLY YEARS

- When Paul Anka was fifteen years old, he wrote the 1957 No. 1 hit "Diana" as a poetic tribute to his younger sibling's babysitter, who was older than he and had no romantic interest in him whatsoever.

- Malcolm Angus of AC/DC once worked as a maintenance man in a bra factory. A mechanic, he fixed sewing machines when they broke down.

- Before they were famous, Sonny and Cher were known as Cleo and Caesar.

- Eddie Van Halen played guitar on Michael Jackson's hit single "Beat It."

- Guns N Roses' Axl Rose (aka Billy Bailey and William Bruce Rose) was infamous with the police as a teenager in Indiana. He was put in jail more than twenty times. He must have held a grudge, because when he returned to his home state to play a concert in 1991, he compared his hometown to Auschwitz.

- When auditioning for a record deal in England in 1967, The Bee Gees sang a set of three songs that included "Puff the Magic Dragon." Executive Robert Stigwood was appalled and left the room, but later reconsidered and signed them to his label.

- At twenty-two years old, Barry Manilow, born Barry Alan Pinkus, had a letter printed in *Playboy* magazine asking editors for advice on how to start a successful music career. Their reply: "Go sow your wild musical notes." It doesn't get any wilder than "Copacabana."

given to them by their parents to buy records in sufficient quantities," he said. "In my youth, if I asked my father for 45 cents to buy a record, he'd have thought seriously about having me committed."

The freedom for teens to party hard would come at a price—they would all end up grounded. A lot. The more they dropped dollars on records and dance clubs, the more they clashed with their parents about music—which (according to the media and to most adults) was the ultimate road to eternal damnation and juvenile delinquency. In the end, teens bought their own radios, ran off to a random field (think *Footloose*), and joined the rockabilly, swivel-hip dancing of Elvis Presley and Jerry Lee Lewis.

★ ★ ★ ★ ★

THE ORIGIN OF ... THE TERM "ROCK AND ROLL"

History buffs often disagree on who first coined the term "rock and roll" (and from what song the phrase got its inspiration). While most accounts credit Cleveland disc jockey Alan Freed, who certainly gave America's population its first taste of the expression, others insist the term had been around for decades before. But what did it insinuate before it classified a type of music? Originally, the term was a bit of a blues double entendre, referencing both saints and sinners—religion and sex. Some of its earliest uses date back to nautical phrases used by sailors in

Alan Freed may have introduced the term "rock and roll" to listening audiences across America, but most rock historians dispute what song first inspired him to do so. Some say "Sixty Minute Man" by The Dominoes, while others say "My Baby Rocks Me with a Steady Roll" by Rumba Caliente.

the 1600s (referring to the sway of a ship, or possibly the sway of a woman's hips). African Americans often referred to rocking as a euphoric religious experience accompanied by powerful music, so the word "rock" made its way into spiritual music and gospel lyrics like "rock my soul in the bosom of Abraham," "rock me Jesus" and "rock me in the cradle of Thy love."

★ ★ ★ ★ ★

THE ORIGIN OF … THE FIRST CROSSOVER ALBUM

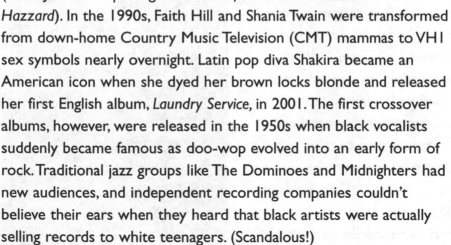

When it comes to boosting record sales, nothing is more effective than tapping into the tastes of multiple fan bases (think Jessica Simpson goes *Dukes of Hazzard*). In the 1990s, Faith Hill and Shania Twain were transformed from down-home Country Music Television (CMT) mammas to VH1 sex symbols nearly overnight. Latin pop diva Shakira became an American icon when she dyed her brown locks blonde and released her first English album, *Laundry Service,* in 2001. The first crossover albums, however, were released in the 1950s when black vocalists suddenly became famous as doo-wop evolved into an early form of rock. Traditional jazz groups like The Dominoes and Midnighters had new audiences, and independent recording companies couldn't believe their ears when they heard that black artists were actually selling records to white teenagers. (Scandalous!)

★ ★ ★ ★ ★

ORIGIN OF ... THE PHONOGRAPH

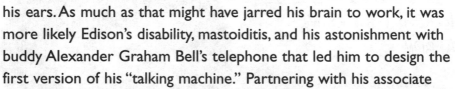

Folklore tells the story of how Thomas Edison first had his idea for the phonograph when a train conductor yanked him onto a locomotive by his ears. As much as that might have jarred his brain to work, it was more likely Edison's disability, mastoiditis, and his astonishment with buddy Alexander Graham Bell's telephone that led him to design the first version of his "talking machine." Partnering with his associate Charles Batchelor and machinist John Kruesi, in less than a year Edison was wowing the staff of *Scientific American* with the first gadget to ever record sounds/speech. Initially more of a business tool than a form of entertainment, the Talking Machine ended up costing way too much for the average citizen to afford. Plus, the little strip of tinfoil that taped the speeches wore out after just one or two uses (and took a ridiculous amount of

fabulous firsts

The first annual Grammy Awards were awarded in 1959. The Record of the Year was *Volare* by Domenico Modugno, the Album of the Year went to Peter Gunn by Henry Mancini, and the winner of the best R&B performance was "Tequila" by Champs.

work to replace). One headache after another, the original phonograph flopped—it was one of Edison's worst-selling inventions.

★ ★ ★ ★ ★

THE ORIGIN OF ... THE JUKEBOX

Edison's original phonograph company may have been a nightmare, but at least one of his employees hit the big time after the fact. **Louis Glass, who had once worked for Edison, had a genius idea for how to jazz up his former boss's invention.** Why not record a handful of hits on the (new and improved) phonograph and stick a coin box on the side to make money every time someone wanted to play a song? Glass put the new creation in San Francisco's Palais Royal Saloon, and the jukebox was born. Two things that made it a huge success:

The jukebox got its name from two sources. The word Jook is an old African-American term meaning to dance (or to dance sexually). The word Juke, on the other hand, is a spoof on lower-class bars called juke joints that were frequented by Southern jute field workers at the end of a long, hot harvest.

- **Alcohol.** When the Automatic Music Instrument Company created the world's first "electrically amplified multi-selection phonograph," or jukebox, in 1927, it was Prohibition that caused initial sales to skyrocket. Underground speakeasy joints loved the product because they needed music to keep their guests around, but could never afford to pay a live band to play in such a dank place.

- **Racists.** The jukebox was considered "color blind in a segregated world." When black clientele at local bars heard the popular tunes of Bill Black, Carl Perkins, and Steve Cropper, they assumed they were black artists and showed them great respect. Similarly, whites more easily accepted and enjoyed black musicians' music when they could listen to it without seeing the live performance.

THREE THINGS YOU NEVER KNEW ABOUT... THE JUKEBOX

- While some people believed jukebox-manufacturing company Rock-Ola was named after the rise of rock and roll, it was actually named after the company's founder, Canadian David Rockola.

- The Wurlitzer 1946 model 1015 jukebox was the most popular of the 1940s era. It toted the slogan, "Wurlitzer Is Jukebox."

- From 1942-1946, the United States government called off jukebox production to preserve labor and materials for the war effort.

★ ★ ★ ★ ★

The Origin of ... The Electric Guitar

Some say Nat King Cole was among the first to start the rock and roll phenomenon with his 1942 *Jazz at the Philharmonic* single titled "Blues Part 2." Others would say it was the later works of Chuck Berry, Carl Perkins, and Big Joe Turner. Regardless, the invention of the solid-body electric guitar changed the future of rock as we know it.

Les Paul (formerly known as Lester Polfus in his hometown of Waukesha, Wisconsin) knew the value of a guitar—he had been playing since he was a boy, starting out on a Sears and Roebuck Gene Autry model that cost him $5. Hungry for a little extra cash, Paul performed in drive-in hamburger joints but realized that his music was too muffled for everyone making out in the back row to hear. So he turned his radio into a PA system to help amplification. When that wasn't enough, he decided to simply build a louder guitar.

PACK RAT FEVER
Les Paul kept all his memorabilia from the early days of designing guitars. He still has his first amplifier and PA system (an Atwater Kent radio).

Paul's first version of the solid-body electric guitar was a needle and a cartridge attached to his original acoustic. To keep the feedback down, he stuffed it with rags and plaster of Paris. A few versions later, the final product was the renowned commercial version of the Les Paul electric guitar. Since then, Paul's work has been so respected that he has designed models for industry suppliers such as Gibson.

★ ★ ★ ★ ★

ORIGIN OF ... COOL BAND NAMES

- Wild Cherry, the band that sang the disco hit "Play that Funky Music," is named after a box of cough drops.

- Duran Duran took its band name from the 1968 film *Barbarella*.

- Rocker Adam Ant came up with his pseudonym after laughing at the British sitcom *Adam Adamant Lives!*

- Bo Diddley, born Utha Ellas Bates McDaniel, is rumored to have named himself after a unique African guitar.

- Elvis Costello, whose real name is declan Patrick Aloysius McManus, put together his stage name to honor the famed Elvis Presley and his mother (whose maiden name was Costello).

MOMENT OF STUPIDITY

The Ramones had the cops called on them by a Rhode Island club owner for walking out after only playing for twenty minutes. The band argued that they had played a full set of twenty-two songs; they just did it more quickly than usual.

- The Ramones renamed themselves in honor of Paul McCartney's former alias, Paul Ramon. Their real names are Douglas Colvin (Dee Dee), Jeffrey Hyman (Joey), John Cummings (Johnny), Richard Beau (Richie), Marc Bell (Marky), and Thomas Erdelyi (Tommy).

- Moby named himself after his relative Herman Melville's acclaimed novel *Moby Dick*.

- Conway Twitty coined his name after a couple of small towns in Arkansas.

- 10,000 Maniacs were inspired by the horror flick *2000 Maniacs*.

MOMENT OF STUPIDITY

British rockers Depeche Mode took their name from the French phrase that translates to "fast fashion." Those who didn't like the band often teased them with the nickname Depede Mode, which means "dirty pedophiles."

- The Black Crowes were originally Uncle Crowe's Garden, a tribute to a fairy tale.

- ABBA is an acronym for the band members' first names: Agnetha, Bjorn, Benny, and Anni-Frid.

- Radiohead came up with its name after listening to a Talking Heads song called "Radio Head."

- Despite rumors that Eddie Vedder's delicious jam-making grandmother was named Pearl, rockers Pearl Jam got their name from the natural process by which wastes from the ocean are made into beautiful jewels.

★ ★ ★ ★ ★

MORE CELEBRITY ALIASES FROM A TO Z

Alias: Tori Amos
Actual Name: Myra Ellen Amos

Alias: Andre 3000 of Outkast
Actual Name: Benjamin Andre

Alias: Babyface
Actual Name: Kenneth Brian Edmonds

Alias: Bobby Day
Actual Name: Robert Byrd

Alias: Mickey Dolenz
Actual Name: George Michael Braddock

Alias: Gloria Estefan
Actual Name: Gloria Fajardo

Alias: Enya
Actual Name: Eithne ni Bhraonain

Alias: Fish
Actual Name: Derek William Dick

Alias: Leif Garrett
Actual Name: Leif Per Narvik

Alias: Boy George
Actual Name: George O'Dowd

Alias: Richard Hell
Actual Name: Richard Meyers

Alias: Billy Idol
Actual Name: William Board

Alias: Iggy Pop
Actual Name: James Jewel Osterberg Jr.

Alias: Rick James
Actual Name: James Ambrose Johnson

Alias: Alicia Keys
Actual Name: Alicia Augello Cook

Alias: Chaka Khan
Actual Name: Yvette Marie Stevens

Alias: Huey Lewis
Actual Name: Hugh Cregg

Alias: Courtney Love
Actual Name: Love Michelle Harrison

Alias: Meatloaf
Actual Name: Marvin Lee Aday

Alias: Freddie Mercury
Actual Name: Farrokh Bulsara

Alias: Billy Ocean
Actual Name: Leslie Sebastian Charles

Alias: Pink
Actual Name: Alecia Moore

Alias: Queen Latifah
Actual Name: Dana Owens

Alias: Terminator X (Public Enemy)
Actual Name: Norman Lee Rogers

Alias: Tina Turner
Actual Name: Annie Mae Bullock

Alias: Vanilla Ice
Actual Name: Robert van Winkle

★ ★ ★ ★ ★

THE ORIGIN OF ... THE MONKEES

When record company executives were looking for a couple of wacky, longhaired musicians to play in a new television show called *The Monkees* in 1965, they put an ad in two American newspapers that read: "Madness! Folk and Roll Musicians- Singers for acting roles in new TV series. Running parts for four insane boys, age 17 to 21." The new sitcom band was considered so dreamy among young teenage girls that the boys were invited to choose a few songs to record for a real record. They may have been

HAIR TODAY, GONE TOMORROW

In several second-season episodes of *The Monkees* television series, Micky's hairstyle switches back and forth from straight to curly because half of the episodes were filmed in the spring of 1967 and the rest were filmed later that fall.

one of the most popular groups of their time, but they didn't have much savvy when it came to song selection—they turned down "Knock Three Times," which later became a huge hit for Tony Orlando and Dawn in 1970, and "Love Will Keep Us Together," which sold more than a million records for The Captain and Tennille in 1975.

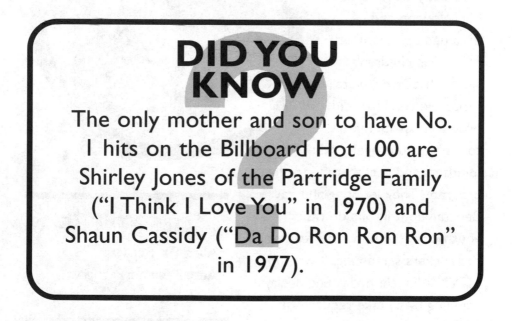

DID YOU KNOW

The only mother and son to have No. 1 hits on the Billboard Hot 100 are Shirley Jones of the Partridge Family ("I Think I Love You" in 1970) and Shaun Cassidy ("Da Do Ron Ron Ron" in 1977).

★ ★ ★ ★ ★

VIDEO KILLED THE RADIO STAR: THE ORIGIN OF ... MTV...

On August 1, 1981, every ugly singer's stomach sank when the Music Television Network aired its first flick, "Video Killed the Radio Star," by the Buggles. What was once a form of audio entertainment now required a new element—hotness. MTV was the brainchild of James Lack and Bob Pittman, who had previously worked with Nickelodeon and dreamed up a number of musical children's series that never quite made the cut. How did producers switch gears to tap into teenager's rebel mindsets and reel them in to the program? They let Sting and Pat Benatar do it in bits on other youth-oriented networks featuring the rockers screaming, "I want my MTV!" With six hot young deejays standing by to take requests, the ploy did well—and the videos did

CELEBRITY ALIAS

Alias: Pat Benatar
Actual Name: Patricia Andrejewski

even better as they managed to keep the attention of impatient young teens with remote controls. After two years, MTV had increased the number of cable companies carrying its channel by 600 percent. Sixteen million homes were tuning in.

As groundbreaking as MTV was during its first few years of syndication, the early music videos weren't what they are today. They were sort of like choppy commercials for upcoming record releases. In fact, before the term "music video" came out, the three-to-four minute clips of singing and dancing were often called "promotional clips." MTV did one thing for American music lovers in the end—they proved that a good video could make a terrible song a huge hit.

fabulous firsts

MTV's five original veejays were Martha Quinn, Mark Goodman, Alan Hunter, Nina Blackwood, and J.J. Jackson.

MOMENT OF STUPIDITY

Dionne Warwick's birth name was actually Marie Dionne Warrick—but a spelling error on her first album in 1962 forced her to get used to the alternate spelling. Ever the psychic, she added an "e" to the end after being advised to do so by a numerologist, but it never stuck.

Real Cheesy Facts About: Famous Authors

Chapter 1

✩

Best-kept Secrets:
The Details They Never
Wanted You to Know

Best-kept Secrets: The Details They Never Wanted You to Know

★ ★ ★ ★ ★ ★ ★ ★ ★ ★ ★ ★ ★ ★ ★ ★ ★ ★

Everyone has little secrets. You know, covert details about their lives that they would really rather remain unpublished. Unfortunately for these authors, their most hush-hush mysteries have now been let out of the bag. Here is the dirty laundry they hoped you would never find out.

THREE THINGS YOU NEVER KNEW ABOUT ... F. SCOTT FITZGERALD

- He was named after Francis Scott Key, a distant relative famous for penning *The Star-Spangled Banner*.

- His wife, Zelda, developed schizophrenia and was permanently hospitalized in 1932. She died when a fire broke out at the Highland Mental Institution in Asheville, North Carolina, in 1948.

- An avid drinker, Fitzgerald died of a heart attack while visiting a friend. He was only forty-four years old.

★ ★ ★ ★ ★

My Lips Are Sealed: Maya Angelou

Her Big Secret: Before she hit the books, she hit the brothel.

The Juicy Details Unveiled: When literature lovers envision the beautiful imagery in the classic poem "I Know Why the Caged Bird Sings," thoughts of brothels and rowdy nightclubs hardly come to mind. But those who spent time with author Maya Angelou in her younger years know she sowed some wild oats in her day. A single mother struggling to support her young son, Angelou was once a San Diego madam. She also earned some extra cash by cooking at a Creole café, scraping paint off of old cars at a body shop, and running cable cars. It's hard to believe respected historic figures such as Dr. Martin Luther King Jr. could overlook such a shady past—he appointed Angelou as a coordinator of the Southern Christian Leadership Conference in the 1960s.

THREE THINGS YOU NEVER KNEW ABOUT … MAYA ANGELOU

- She was born Marguerite Johnson.
- She was once kicked out of school for being afraid to speak in front of the class.
- She took a pilgrimage to Ghana in the 1960s so her son could attend the University of Ghanato and get in touch with his African roots.

★ ★ ★ ★ ★

MY LIPS ARE SEALED: BRAM STOKER

His Big Secret: The initial plans for his vampire were thrown in the trash.

The Juicy Details Unveiled: Bram Stoker's Count Dracula was originally supposed to be named Count Vampyre, but while researching the historic details for his book, he came across the new name, which meant "son of the dragon" or "son of the devil." It was the actual name of a fifteenth-century Romanian nobleman who became a hero when he fought off Turkish invaders. Dracula became tainted, however, by his reputation for brutally executing his prisoners. It was a perfect past for a monster, and Stoker had his protagonist.

LOVE'S LITTLE SURPRISES
Bram Stoker married one of author Oscar Wilde's ex-girlfriends in 1878.

★ ★ ★ ★ ★

MY LIPS ARE SEALED: THOMAS HARDY

His Big Secret: He hid the shady details of how hundreds of women cheated on their husbands.

The Juicy Details Unveiled: After Hardy published *Tess of the*

d'Urbervilles, a controversial novel about a woman who becomes pregnant by a man who is believed to be her relative, he received scores of letters from women with similar dark pasts. The women poured out their private stories, revealing their guilt and asking Hardy what he thought they should do. Surprised that so many people would sign their names to such confidential, scandalous stories and send them to a stranger, Hardy didn't quite know what to do. A friend advised him not to reply (or call, as some women requested), so instead, he burned each letter. He was forever careful not to mention any of their names to his peers or interviewers for fear their identities would become publicly revealed.

★ ★ ★ ★ ★

MY LIPS ARE SEALED: CHARLES DICKENS

His Big Secret: He was nearly caught vacationing with his mistress.

The Juicy Details Unveiled:

Desperately trying to hide the fact that he was traveling with actress Ellen Ternan—who was rumored to have broken up his marriage—Charles Dickens told few people that he was involved in a serious train wreck. On June 9, 1865, six train cars plunged off a faulty bridge between London and Dover. Dickens was in the only first-class section that didn't jump the track. At first he rushed to aid the wounded, but when he realized the press would soon arrive and discover him with Ellen, he grabbed the manuscript he was working on (the novel *Our Mutual Friend*) and left the scene of the accident. Possibly due to the wreck, he struggled with swelling in his left foot for the rest of his life.

★ ★ ★ ★ ★

MY LIPS ARE SEALED: F. SCOTT FITZGERALD

His Big Secret: His wife caught him plagiarizing.

The Juicy Details Unveiled:

The mastermind behind popular classics such as *The Great Gatsby*, F. Scott Fitzgerald was once accused of having trouble keeping his work original—his wife, Zelda, claimed he plagiarized things he found around the house. In a tongue-in-cheek review in the *New York Tribune* in 1922, she joked that on more than one occasion she recognized pieces of her husband's work as fragments from her old diaries and letters from friends. Call it secondhand inspiration, call it a temporary solution to writer's block—but some editors would call it theft.

★ ★ ★ ★ ★

MY LIPS ARE SEALED: L. FRANK BAUM

His Big Secret: He sank like a brick.

The Juicy Details Unveiled: He may have been the creative inventor of Toto, the Tin Man, and those pesky singing munchkins, but author L. Frank Baum had quite a problem when it came to kicking back on a hot summer day. While his buddies were playing "beach bum" in the pool, he stayed on shore. Though Baum couldn't swim, he wasn't entirely afraid. To keep track of whether or not he was

L. Frank Baum wasn't the only writer who had a troubled relationship with water. *Lolita* author Vladimir Nabokov once said, "I dislike immersing myself in a swimming pool. It is, after all, only a big tub where other people join you — makes one think of those horrible Japanese communal baths, full of a floating family, or a shoal of businessmen."

getting into too-deep water, he would smoke a cigar while wading. If the water got high enough to put out his puffs, he would head for dry ground.

★ ★ ★ ★ ★

My Lips Are Sealed: James Thurber

His Big Secret: He could barely see.

The Juicy Details Unveiled: Best known for his 1950s short stories and sketches published in *The New Yorker*, James Thurber was nearly blind. He lost one eye in an accident with a bow and arrow at just six years old. Because the first eye wasn't removed immediately, the second became infected and grew weaker as he got older. Over time, the disability required Thurber to write and draw on large sheets of white paper with chunky black crayons, or on black paper with thick sticks of white chalk. Neuroscientists later proposed that he had Charles Bonnet syndrome, which causes people with visual impairments to hallucinate. It's no wonder his handwriting and sketches seemed so eerie.

★ ★ ★ ★ ★

MY LIPS ARE SEALED: E.E. CUMMINGS

His Big Secret: He hated it when people wrote his name using all lowercase letters.

The Juicy Details Unveiled: Born Edward Estlin Cummings, poet and playwright E.E. Cummings was duped when his publishers went behind his back and started publishing his name in a modern-looking lowercase form: e. e. cummings. Despite stories that circulated during the nineteenth century, Cummings never legally changed his name to the lowercase version—in fact, he hated it. While famous for his unorthodox use of punctuation and capitalization in his poetry, he said it belonged nowhere in his byline, and he never endorsed the change.

> **THE SPY WHO TAGGED ME**
> While serving in an ambulance unit during the First World War, E.E. Cummings and friend William Slater Brown were arrested under suspicion of espionage. They may have been pacifists, but they were not spies. After a few weeks in a Normandy detention center, Cummings was released and later drafted into the army.

★ ★ ★ ★ ★

MY LIPS ARE SEALED: EDGAR ALLAN POE

His Big Secret: He's not buried where you think he is.

The Juicy Details Unveiled: Relatives of renowned poet Edgar Allan Poe aren't quite sure if the body buried at Poe's gravesite is actually his. Poe was originally buried in 1849 amid other lesser-known people at Baltimore's Westminister Hall and Burying Ground, which has since been annexed by the University of Maryland School of Law. In 1875, a group of ambitious schoolchildren raised the cash to erect a memorial and move Poe's remains to a more prestigious spot near the front gate. However, no one thought to tell the crew in charge of digging up Poe's body that all of the headstones had been rotated to the west in 1864—

positioning the bodies behind the stones instead of in front. They most likely dug in the wrong spot, and today many speculate the reburied remains are actually of a teenager from the Maryland Militia named Private Philip Mosher Jr.

THE MYSTERY OF THE POE TOASTER

Every January 19 since 1949, an unnamed man with a black hood and a silver-tipped cane has visited Edgar Allan Poe's grave. He toasts the deceased author with a glass of Martel cognac, then departs while it is still dark, leaving behind the half-full liquor bottle and three red roses—one for Poe, one for Poe's mother, and one for Poe's wife.

★ ★ ★ ★ ★

My Lips Are Sealed: Fyodor Dostoevsky

His Big Secret: He made lofty wagers.

The Juicy Details Unveiled: *Crime and Punishment* may be remembered as one of Dostoevsky's most ingenious works, but few know that he wrote the book in a hurry—he was in desperate need of a gambling fix. Having lost thousands of dollars to his gambling addiction, Dostoevsky was penniless (and longing for another trip to the casino). Ironically, he was so poor that he wrote *The Gambler* at the same time, rushing to finish it for another publisher who threatened to take over all of Dostoevsky's copyrights if he did not settle his debts.

READY, AIM, SNICKER

In 1849, Russian writer Fyodor Dostoevsky was sentenced to death for anti-government revolts against Tsar Nikolai I. However, his captors mocked the execution and left him standing blindfolded in the snow, anticipating the sting of bullets from a firing squad. After their cruel joke came to a close, they instead sentenced him to manual labor.

OTHER AUTHORS WITH GAMBLING DEBTS

- Leo Tolstoy
- Edgar Allan Poe

★ ★ ★ ★ ★

My Lips Are Sealed: Stephen King

His Big Secret: He's more like his characters than you think he is.

The Juicy Details Unveiled: King is known around the world for his suspenseful, chilling reads, but few fans know that his own life once reflected the unstable antagonists of his novels. For years King refused to admit his transgressions, that is, until his buddies stole one of his trashcans and dumped it on the floor in front of him. A soiled confession of King's secrets—the pile of beer cans, Valium, NyQuil, and Xanax—forced him to come clean about his addictions. It was then that he finally admitted the crazed father

DID YOU KNOW

Although he believed the conflict was unconstitutional, Stephen King was nearly drafted into the Vietnam War, but a doctor determined he had high blood pressure, flat feet, poor vision, and a punctured eardrum.

he wrote about in *The Shining* was not based on his own father, as he had once claimed, but on himself. He cleaned up his act and was sober by the late 1980s.

★ ★ ★ ★ ★

MY LIPS ARE SEALED: LEWIS PAGE MERCIER

His Big Secret: He screwed up several historic Jules Verne books.

The Juicy Details Unveiled: Although English-speaking countries have long criticized Frenchman Jules Verne's writing, his misunderstood literature can only be blamed on the Brits. One man in particular, a book translator named Lewis Page Mercier, allegedly took it upon himself to change the author's manuscripts without permission from the publisher. Feeling that some of Verne's content was a bit too critical of the British Empire, Mercier cut out the details of Captain Nemo's political ties in the 1870 sci-fi novel *Twenty Thousand*

Leagues Under the Sea. He also hated the metric system and made a mess of Verne's numbers in an attempt to convert them to something more understandable—sometimes he converted the figures to Imperial, sometimes he kept them in metric but changed the units to Imperial, and sometimes he accidentally dropped the numbers altogether. The laziness made Verne look like a babbling fool in great need of a calculator (if not a math tutor). In 1965, some of his works were re-translated in their original form, but many copies full of errors still exist.

Jules Verne's publishers often told him his anti-Semitism and pessimistic views of human progress were too dark for his readers. Publisher Pierre-Jules Hetzel changed the endings of several of Verne's books to lighten the mood:

- *Mysterious Island* (1874)—A tale of Americans stranded in the South Pacific, Verne's original ending described survivors as living the rest of their lives nostalgically, missing the island. Hetzel rewrote them as heroes who build a replica of the island so they can live happily ever after.

- *Twenty Thousand Leagues Under the Sea* (1870)—In Verne's first draft, the valiant Captain Nemo was introduced as a Polish noble, bitter that his family had been murdered under Russian oppression from 1863–1864. Hetzel feared Russia would ban the book and upset its ally, France, and instead described Nemo as a Hindu who resents the British for their conquest of India.

★ ★ ★ ★ ★

My Lips Are Sealed: Henry David Thoreau

His Big Secret: He never got a diploma because he was too cheap.

The Juicy Details Unveiled: Thoreau graduated from Harvard University in 1837, but because of his own frugalness (and stubbornness), he never received an official diploma. Legend holds that the college required a $5 payment before graduation, but Thoreau refused to shell out that kind of money for a "piece of paper." Unfortunately, the college rules stated that the Master of Arts degree held no academic merit unless the fee was paid in full.

★ ★ ★ ★ ★

MY LIPS ARE SEALED: JD. SALINGER

His Big Secret: He freaked out when his publisher put his face on his book.

The Juicy Details Unveiled: Salinger was not happy with the first edition of *The Catcher in the Rye* because it had a big picture of his face on the dust jacket. Although he reveled in the success of big sales, he was annoyed by everyone who began to recognize him.

After flunking out of one private high school as a young man, author J.D. Salinger studied at Valley Forge Military Academy in Pennsylvania. One year he got an 88 in English, 88 in French, 76 in German, 79 in History, and 88 in Dramatics. His IQ was tested as 115, and he was a member of the glee club, aviation club, and French club, as well as the literary editor of the yearbook. He began writing short stories by flashlight under the covers after "lights out" and dreamed of one day selling them to Hollywood.

Salinger quickly got tired of dodging autograph and advice-seeking fans. He called the attention "demoralizing." As a result, very little is known about his personal life, particularly his childhood and teenage years. He says he won't talk about "that David Copperfield kind of crap." Years ago, he wouldn't even tell interviewers what contemporary writers he preferred. He always seemed nervous about publicity.

★ ★ ★ ★ ★

My Lips Are Sealed: Shel Silverstein

His Big Secret: He was a pal of Playboy bunnies.

The Juicy Details Unveiled: Famed for the ever-popular *The Giving Tree* and *Where the Sidewalk Ends*, children's author Shel Silverstein, who died in 1999, wasn't the innocent rhyming writer most parents thought he was. In fact, he began his career as a photographer, writer, and cartoonist for *Playboy* magazine. He ended up living in the Playboy Mansion and continued to write occasional pieces for the raunchy publication up until a year before his death. When he wasn't babbling with blondes, Silverstein was also dreaming up songs—he wrote the lyrics for "A Boy Named Sue" for Johnny Cash and "One's On the Way" for Loretta Lynn.

★ ★ ★ ★ ★

My Lips Are Sealed: KINGSLEY AMIS

His Big Secret: He was bored while "fighting" for his country.

The Juicy Details Unveiled: *Lucky Jim* (1954) author Kingsley Amis is a veteran of the Second World War, but don't let the heroic label fool you—he spent his entire  tour in a car. After training for months doing cross-country runs, shooting muskets, and making smoke bombs, Amis never used his skills once. His unit spent its time "at war" driving across Europe, nowhere near the front lines. He never fired a shot, and he never marched a step.

DID YOU KNOW

When Kingsley Amis first joined the army, another recruit told him his name was too hard to pronounce. Amis told him his middle name was actually William, but the recruit didn't like that either. Instead everyone called him Bill.

★ ★ ★ ★ ★

MY LIPS ARE SEALED: ALEXANDRE DUMAS

His Big Secret: He didn't write most of his own books.

The Juicy Details Unveiled: Although he publicly receives full credit for the creepy *The Count of Monte Cristo*, writer Alexandre Dumas actually did not pen much of the manuscript himself. To save time, he liked to use ghostwriters such as the famed Auguste Maquet, a history teacher who originally wrote the outline for *Monte Cristo* and much of *The Three Musketeers*. Dumas would take the rough draft from him and fill in the holes with quotes, details, and the last few chapters. All told, Dumas used seventy-three assistants to publish 250 books.

FROM RICHES TO RAGS

Although his writing earned him riches—he once brought in more than 200,000 francs per year—Alexandre Dumas spent much of his life in debt, due to his lavish lifestyle.

★ ★ ★ ★ ★

THEIR LIPS ARE SEALED: ROBERT AND ELIZABETH BARRETT BROWNING

Her Big Secret:
After secretly eloping,
she continued living with her parents.

The Juicy Details Unveiled: Because she suffered injuries from a riding accident and the grief of her young brother's drowning, Elizabeth Barrett had spent most of her life locked up in her room, devoid of social interaction. She would spend entire days doing nothing but reading books and plays on her father's sofa. When Robert first wrote her a letter to say that he admired one of her pieces of writing, she did what any woman would do—she sat around and waited for more love letters. The two became pen pals (she often edited his work) and finally met in May of 1845. Although

LOVE'S LITTLE SURPRISES

The Brownings weren't the only poets to try and hide a secret marriage. In 1601, John Donne married Ann More, the niece of his boss, Sir Thomas Egerton. Egerton was so angry that he had him fired and put in jail for the lie. He even tried to have their marriage annulled.

she rarely even got up off the sofa to greet him when he visited her, the two were married the following year. Afraid to tell her parents of her

> The first book a young Robert Browning ever purchased was *Oassian*.

marriage, she continued to live at home and took off her wedding ring so they wouldn't know of her secret marriage.

★ ★ ★ ★ ★

My Lips Are Sealed: Dr. Seuss

His Big Secret: He was a grinch.

The Juicy Details Unveiled: Although remembered as a lyrical, fun-rhyming poet who entertained children of all ages with his tales of Whoville and green eggs and ham, Seuss actually has been accused of writing about his own bad attitudes in *The Grinch Who Stole Christmas*. The author's license plate read GRINCH, and in the book the Grinch complains of putting up with the Whos' Christmas cheer for the past 53 years—which was Seuss's age when he wrote the book. Seuss was never fond of noise and public celebrations. In fact,

---

TALES OF THE RUDE AND CRUDE

During World War I, Theodore Seuss Geisel (or as most know him, Dr. Seuss) was not ashamed of his German heritage. However, the other kids in school nicknamed him The Kaiser and threw rocks at him as he walked home from school. This ostracizing may be why he avoided crowds for most of his life.

he reportedly complained about having to answer the door on his birthday when children would come by to sing to him. He would have preferred to be in Las Vegas alone.

★ ★ ★ ★ ★

My Lips Are Sealed: David McCullough

His Big Secret: He thought he had one, but the beans were spilled years ago.

The Juicy Details Unveiled: After years of secrecy, *1776* author David McCullough has admitted to the public that while in college, he was a member of Yale University's elite Skull and Bones secret society. However, for years he was unaware that the club published membership lists up until 1971. McCullough isn't alone—other famous faces from the Skull and Bones listing include Presidents Howard Taft and George W. Bush, FedEx founder Frederick Smith, *New York Times* general manager Amory Howe Bradford, and a number of U.S. Senators.

★ ★ ★ ★ ★

My Lips Are Sealed: William Blake

His Big Secret: He was a part of the Gordon Riots.

The Juicy Details Unveiled:
While studying at London's Royal Academy in 1780, William Blake was a professional engraver eager to rebel against anything politically correct. In fact, in July he gathered together his favorite troublemaking pals and ran the unruly mob through Newgate Prison. They kept blue ribbons in their caps to symbolize their support of the American colonies. In response, King George III set up the city's first police force to help prevent such riots from happening again.

LOVE'S LITTLE SURPRISES
Both a poet and a professional engraver, William Blake married a poverty-stricken young girl named Catherine Boucher in 1782. She was so illiterate that she could only sign their wedding contract with an X.

★ ★ ★ ★ ★

MY LIPS ARE SEALED: IAN FLEMING

His Big Secret: He kept a diary.

The Juicy Details Unveiled: *James Bond* writer Ian Fleming kept a "book of golden words," a diary with phrases, character names, and quotes he wanted to save for future book ideas. For example, he kept note of a Bulgar proverb that read, "My enemy's enemy is my friend" and good villain names such as Mr. Szasz. He got the name James Bond from a book called *Birds of the West Indies*, written by an ornithologist named James Bond. After Fleming's famous books were published, Bond's wife wrote him a letter to thank him for using her husband's name.

★ ★ ★ ★ ★

MY LIPS ARE SEALED: WILKIE COLLINS

His Big Secret: He took opium to relieve pain ... then he took it again ... and again.

The Juicy Details Unveiled: A longtime pal of Charles Dickens, this old author had a heck of a case of arthritis, then known as "rheumatic gout." His joints needed some serious relief, but Collins popped his pain pills way too often. As a result, he became delusional, paranoid, and in the company of an invisible friend named Ghost Wilkie. Whether this new pal was an original or simply a version of his pesky alter ego, we may never know. Collins was so high on opium while he was writing the novel *The Moonstone* that when he finished, he had no recollection of coming up with large chunks of the book.

Chapter 2

A Few of Their Favorite Things

A Few of Their Favorite Things

If you ran into **J.K. Rowling** or **Woody Allen** tomorrow, how would you steal another minute of their time? Sure, you could wave and hold out something for them to sign like all the other annoying fans—or you could use some inside information to tap into what makes them tick when they're off the clock. Run into **Stephen King?** Grab a catcher's mitt. **Isaac Asimov?** Maybe a Dr. Spock figurine. Here's the skinny on your favorite authors—what they value, where they chill, and whom they adore.

Mark Twain loved the grace and independence of cats. He named his pet kittens Sin, Sourmash, Satan, Blatherskite, and Beelzebub. In *Puddn'head Wilson*, he wrote, "A house without a cat—a well-fed, petted and properly revered cat—may be a home, but how can it prove its title?"

377

★ ★ ★ ★ ★

CHEAP CIGARS

Mark Twain once estimated that he went through three hundred cheap, strong cigars every month. His peers actually believed that was an understatement. If he was on vacation and needed to get some work done, he would allow himself fifteen cigars every five hours. As he smoked, he would play billiards for hours on end. His billiard room was a true man's sanctuary, decorated with pool cues, wine bottles, and pipes. When he first married, he promised his wife that he would cut back and light up only once a week. The resolution didn't last long. The combination of writer's block and publisher deadlines drove him back to his old habits. Ignorant of the damage he was doing to his lungs, Twain thought it was a harmless pastime.

THE LAZY DAYS OF SUMMER ... AND FALL ... AND WINTER

In 1907, Mark Twain said that for several decades he had spent only three months writing each year. He spent the rest of his time on vacation.

★ ★ ★ ★ ★

A Plaster Dinosaur Footprint

In his home in La Jolla, California, **Dr. Seuss kept a rather unusual memento** on display for years—a plaster cast of a huge dinosaur track once found in his hometown, Springville, Massachusetts. It didn't add much to the décor of the home, but the footprint was a gift from his father. It reminded him that even after death, anyone could leave a mark on the world, something he strove to do for the rest of his life.

LOVE'S LITTLE SURPRISES (OR LACK THEREOF)

Dr. Seuss and his wife, Helen, never had children. When asked about his empty nest, he often replied, "You have 'em, I'll amuse 'em."

★ ★ ★ ★ ★

The Clarinet

The king of all things creative and quirky, **writer Woody Allen has played the clarinet since he was a teenager**. Born Allen Stewart Königsberg, he even came up with his own stage name at age sixteen as a tribute to famous clarinetist Woody Herman. Allen has performed multiple times since the 1960s. He even tooted his woodwind with the Preservation Hall Jazz Band on the Sleepers soundtrack. His band, Woody Allen and His New Orleans Jazz Band, plays every Monday at The Carlyle Hotel in Manhattan.

★ ★ ★ ★ ★

SPORTS INJURIES

Although injuries often serve as devastating, career-ending moments for athletes, **a track-and-field injury prompted author Nicholas Sparks to write**. He first picked up a pen while benched from the University of Notre Dame track team, and he hasn't put it down since.

★ ★ ★ ★ ★

BASEBALL

Stephen King loves the Boston Red Sox and often includes the team in his writing. One of his books, *The Girl Who Loved Tom Gordon* (1999), features the team's famous pitcher as the main character. He also co-wrote *Faithful: Two Diehard Boston Red Sox Fans Chronicle the Historic 2004 Season* after the team won the 2004 American League Championship Series and World Series. King frequently attends both home and away games.

DID YOU KNOW

Woody Allen was only nineteen years old when he started writing for *The Ed Sullivan Show* and *The Tonight Show*.

An avid baseball fan, Stephen King coached his son's team to the Little League championship game in 1989.

★ ★ ★ ★ ★

TALL POLITICIANS

Known for his reclusiveness and his manicured white beard, **Walt Whitman had a bit of a man-crush on the tall, top-hatted sixteenth President Abraham Lincoln**. During the Civil War, Whitman took a job taking care of wounded soldiers in Washington, D.C., and often saw the president around the city. One of his most famous poems, "O Captain! My Captain!"—made famous by the film Dead Poets Society—was Whitman's way of expressing his grief after Lincoln's assassination in 1865.

★ ★ ★ ★ ★

COMMUNISM (SORT OF)

Born to a white shoe keeper and a black schoolteacher in the early 1900s, **poet Langston Hughes had a thing for the Commies**. The battle between segregation and civil rights was at its peak in the South, and the party's promises of fair fortunes tickled his ears. Hughes already had an in with the CPUSA—they often published his poems in their newspaper. His interest turned out to be more of an infatuation than a full-fledged political affair, however. While Hughes was occasionally involved in Communist-led groups, he quickly backed off when the House of Representative's investigating committee paid him a visit in 1953. He never officially joined the Communist party, and he passionately denied ever being a Communist at heart.

★ ★ ★ ★ ★

GREEN THUMBS

U.S. poet Thedore Roethke may have won the Pulitzer Prize for his book *The Waking* in 1954, but putting pen to paper wasn't always his most passionate hobby. For much of his life, Roethke had a thing for gardening. His father had owned a greenhouse, and during his childhood Roethke spent endless hours poking around the garden. The skills stuck with him as much of his poetry reflected on nature.

Theodore Roethke died of a heart attack while swimming in a pool in 1963. The pool was later filled in and today stands as a moss garden on Bainbridge Island, Washington—but there is no sign labeling it as the writer's place of passing.

Scotland's Sir Walter Scott also had a thing for working the land. His friends sent him acorns by the cartful, enough to plant his own forest, some said. He became so busy digging and leveling out his land for the plants that he had to hire a tutor to care for his son during the day.

TALES OF THE RUDE AND CRUDE

Although Sir Walter Scott's son's tutor, George Thomson, had an amputated leg, he had to walk to the Scott home every day until he was eventually invited to move in.

★ ★ ★ ★ ★

SLAPSTICK COMEDY

Best known for his poem "The Love Song of J. Alfred Prufrock," which he wrote at just twenty-two years old, American-born poet T.S. Eliot had one true love late in life— Groucho Marx. Eliot exchanged friendly letters with the comedian and even hung Marx's portrait in his home next to the likes of writers William Yeats and Paul Valery.

MODERN REFERENCES TO MR. PRUFROCK

Written from the perspective of an old man who regretted never taking a risk for love, T.S. Eliot's "The Love Song of J. Alfred Prufrock" has been hailed as an icon in American pop culture:

- Simon and Garfunkel's song "The Dangling Conversation" (made famous by Joan Baez) was written as a parallel to the poem.

- Musicians the Crash Test Dummies released a single called "Afternoons and Coffee Spoons" in the 1990s that mentioned the poem.

- In the film *Apocalypse Now,* Dennis Hopper plays a photojournalist who quotes the poem.

★ ★ ★ ★ ★

CUTE QUAIL

John Steinbeck, author of *Of Mice and Men* and *The Grapes of Wrath*, **took to boating and fishing on San Francisco Bay**, which helped trim down the grocery bill on his $25-a-month budget. He had always wanted to hunt quail for dinner but told a reporter from the *New York World Telegraph* in 1937 that "every time I see one around the house I dash in and get a gun, and get it to my shoulder, and then I can't shoot." The birds just looked so cute that he couldn't pull the trigger. Embarrassed that he had just told such a silly story about himself, Steinbeck admitted to the reporter that it was the first time he had ever been interviewed— "and be damned sure that it's the last," he said. It wasn't.

DID YOU KNOW

Steinbeck was terrible with punctuation, but his wife proofread all of his writing and caught the errors before they went to his editor.

When Steinbeck had friends over to his California home, he would keep the beer cold by putting it on the bottom of his swimming pool.

★ ★ ★ ★ ★

SCI-FI STUFF

Long before the cult-classic jargon of *Star Trek*, one of history's greatest writers had a secret guilty pleasure—he was a sci-fi junkie. The penman of the famed *Foundation Trilogy*, Isaac Asimov loved science-fiction magazines. The obsession began in his early teenage years when he reveled in the excitement of his favorite heroes—Shadow and Doc Savage—and dreamed about outer space, time travel, and the mysterious unknown. He wrote letters to the editors of his favorite magazines, trying to get his own sci-fi short stories printed. Asimov even offered the magazines advice, asking the staff to smooth out the rough edges of the paper they printed on and

> Isaac Asimov's fascination with science fiction as a boy led him to write his first story, *Cosmic Corkscrew*, at just seventeen years old.

giving them his opinion on his favorite stories. Although he rarely received a response, Asimov did become pen pals with the other science-fiction junkies who had their letters published in the magazines. They frequently exchanged issues and stories through the mail.

★ ★ ★ ★ ★

PARTIAL BIOGRAPHERS

Robert Frost couldn't have been more upset with his choice of a biographer. Lawrance Thompson, a curator of rare books at the Princeton University Library, was an acclaimed writer who spent thirty-five years working on the book. Frost was furious with his honesty. The men's relationship was often strained, as Frost believed Thompson wrote too much about the negative side of his character, describing him as psychotic, jealous, resentful, and vindictive. However, ultimately Frost believed Thompson had simply tired of the project and was describing his own attitude.

★ ★ ★ ★ ★

LAWSUITS

Most authors wouldn't be pleased to find out that their highly anticipated work was prematurely put on the shelves, but *Harry Potter* mogul **J.K. Rowling made millions on the mishap.** On June 19, 2003, Rowling found out that the *New York Daily News* had picked up a copy of *Harry Potter and the Order of the Phoenix* at a local health store and printed information about the plotline before its true release-date two days later. The article also included a photo of an inside spread of the book, with two pages perfectly readable. Her fans may have had the secrets spoiled, but Rowling raked in $100 million.

> J.K. Rowling is a fan of actor Aaron Sorkin from the American television show *The West Wing*.

★ ★ ★ ★ ★

HANGING OUT WITH HENRY

Ralph Waldo Emerson and Henry David Thoreau were great pals. The land where Thoreau built his cabin on Walden Pond belonged to Emerson, and Emerson hired Thoreau to perform odd jobs at his house for extra money. In fact, after leaving Walden, Thoreau lived in Emerson's house while he was away on tour. However, the friendship soured after Emerson gave his buddy some bad business advice (he told him to publish his first book without many edits and advised him to use a publisher who made him take responsibility for much of the losses). The book bombed, and Thoreau was in debt.

★ ★ ★ ★ ★

MAGIC

Convinced that his hero Harry Houdini was possessed by supernatural powers, author Arthur Conan Doyle was amazed. The two men were friends for a time—until Houdini tried to convince him that the tricks were simply magic. Bitterly disagreeing on the issue of just how "real" the tricks were, the two butted heads until they had a very public falling out.

★ ★ ★ ★ ★

DEATH ROW INMATES

While working on his final research for the novel *In Cold Blood*, **Truman Capote desperately needed access to real, hardened criminals** at the state penitentiary in

DID YOU KNOW

While researching for *In Cold Blood*, Truman Capote became pen pals with two convicted criminals on death row who requested two things from him—a dictionary and a thesaurus. They wanted their descriptions of prison life to be accurate and sound smart, but their verbage was superfluous. One wrote that he had "many diverse subjects I am desirous to discuss."

Kansas. He found his men on death row, living with nothing more than a cot and a toilet. They showered once a week. However, to convince authorities to let him have at-will contact and mail privileges with two criminals (he was neither a relative or a lawyer) he bribed prison authorities with $10,000. The inmates, Perry and Dick, wrote him letters by the hundreds describing life behind bars—and the book was a hit.

★ ★ ★ ★ ★

Making Opinions Known

Novelist Iain Banks loves to heckle the editors of *New Scientist* magazine for their notes on creationism. If that weren't enough, he is also a

> While a college student at Stirling University, Banks was an extra in the filming of the final scene of Monty Python and the Holy Grail at Doune Castle in Scotland.

member of a left-wing British political group that has campaigned to have Prime Minister Tony Blair impeached for his support of the invasion of Iraq. To protest the Brits having joined the war, Banks publicly ripped up his passport and threw it down on Downing Street.

★ ★ ★ ★ ★

New Husbands

Romance novelist Danielle Steel has always been known for her ability to describe lovers in bliss... but, unfortunately, she was rarely putting her own love life on paper. In fact, Steel has been married a total of five times. Her first wedding, at age eighteen, was to Claude-Eric Lazard. The couple had one daughter before she moved onto her second beau—a convicted rapist named Danny Zugelder. It wasn't long before they separated and Steel found herself pregnant—out of wedlock—by a druggie named William Toth. To give their son a daddy (for a short while), the couple got married. Her fourth husband, John Traina, had two sons of his own. The couple also had four daughters and a son… but, as usual, Steel moved on when Tom Perkins came around.

★ ★ ★ ★ ★

Shots of Caffeine

Honore de Balzac was a maniac when it came to his work. He would stay up writing for fifteen hours at a time, throwing back as many cups of black coffee as he could. It's a wonder he kept up the social life he needed in order to complete the research for his books. In fact, many of his stories were based on conversations he overheard at parties. As he sucked down the caffeine, Balzac would edit his work over and over, annoying his printers with obscure last-minute changes.

★ ★ ★ ★ ★

DONATING TO CHARITY

MGM Studios often turns to secondhand clothes at garage sales around Hollywood, so while preparing for the 1939 film *The Wizard of Oz*, based on the book by L. Frank Baum, they hit the sales for some costumes. Ironically, when *Wizard* actor Frank Morgan put on his wardrobe for filming one day, he noticed a label on his overcoat. It read "Property of L. Frank Baum." Morgan got a laugh out of it, but after filming, Baum's wife looked at the costume and confirmed that it had been the author's. They had donated the jacket to charity several months before.

Chapter 3

Worst Week Ever:
The Bizarre (& Sometimes
Scary) Lives of
Thriller Writers

Worst Week Ever: The Bizarre (& Sometimes Scary) Lives of Thriller Writers

There are a number of circumstances that qualify a person officially having a horrible day. Some people have writer's block while all of their buddies come up with terrifying original tales. Some are smashed to pieces by an out-of-control driver while taking a Sunday stroll. Others wind up in jail, in an embarrassing costume, or in a shark's mouth. These authors take the cake in terms of the wacky predicaments in which they so often found themselves.

Agatha Christie learned much of what she knew about poison and pain while working as a pharmacist during World War I. She did not begin writing until her sister, who had always loved mysteries, challenged her to write a detective story.

★ ★ ★ ★ ★

AND THEN THERE WAS ONE

Whodunit writer Agatha Christie and her husband, Archie, once lived a rather posh life of travel and golf—that is, until he told her he was in love with another woman. When Christie freaked out and disappeared for ten days, the country panicked. Press, police, and detectives combed the neighborhood and eventually found her in a small-town hotel staying under an unusual pseudonym—the name of her husband's mistress. Now, decades later, only her daughter knows what she did during those mysterious ten days.

★ ★ ★ ★ ★

KING'S BIG BREAK

In the late 1990s, Stephen King was taking a stroll before joining his family for a screening of *The General's Daughter* when a van suddenly sped over a hill and threw him fourteen feet into the air. Medics airlifted him to a nearby hospital, but his lung collapsed—and doctors realized his leg was shattered, his hip and ribs were broken, and his spine was chipped in eight different places. After weeks in the hospital and even longer in physical therapy, King finally sat down to finish *On Writing*, but he was in such terrible pain after only thirty minutes of sitting down that he was forced to take lengthy breaks. One good thing did come out of his extensive time in the hospital—the experience inspired him to write the pilot episode of ABC's *Kingdom Hospital*.

PAYBACK'S A CINCH

Shortly after his recovery, Stephen King plotted revenge on the vehicle that crushed him in 1999—he bought it for $1,500 and then had it destroyed to prevent it from ever showing up on eBay.

THREE THINGS YOU NEVER KNEW ABOUT ... STEPHEN KING

- His mom worked in the kitchen of a mental institution when he was a child.

- Although he usually types on an Apple computer, he wrote the first draft of *Dreamcatcher* with a notepad and a fountain pen.

- He reads for four hours a day and writes for four hours a day. It is the only way to become a good writer, he says.

★ ★ ★ ★ ★

Nightmare on Name Street

Famous for works such as *The Mummy*, *The Witching Hour,* and *Interview with the Vampire,* **Anne Rice had no scarier day than the day her birth certificate was formally engraved**—with the name Howard Allen. Her parents wanted desperately to preserve their legacy in their daughter by incorporating both of their names—Katherine Allen and Howard O'Brien—in hers. However, Rice was mortified and tried out a series of new pseudonyms at school until she finally settled on Anne.

★ ★ ★ ★ ★

Super Fans Go Overboard

Infatuation may be one form of flattery, but when it comes to obsessed readers, this tale of super-literate enthusiasts takes the cake. Giddy about their chance to see their names in print, nineteen lucky readers paid to become part of a permanent piece of literary history. The bidding was a fundraiser for the First Amendment Project, a nonprofit group that protects freedom of information and self-expression. Participants pulled out their checkbooks in hopes of being named as a person or place in upcoming works by authors Stephen

DID YOU KNOW

Much of author Anne Rice's fictional writing reflects her real life struggles. For example:

When the vampire Louis grieves the loss of young Claudia in *Interview with the Vampire*, Rice is really conveying her own sorrow over the death of her own daughter, Michele.

When Tonio struggles with an alcoholic mother in *Cry to Heaven*, it reflects the problems Rice had with her own mother.

King, John Grisham, and Lemony Snicket. Super fan Pam Anderson of Fort Lauderdale, Florida, shelled out a whopping $25,100 so her brother, Ray Huizenga, could find his name in Stephen King's *Cell*. However, the "honor" was not guaranteed to be flattering—the novel is about a trouble-making mob of zombies. Only John Grisham promised his winning bidder would be cast as a "good guy."

SUPER FAN AUCTION

- David Brin—Winner can choose for their name to represent either a moon about to collide with a planet, a mystifying new disease, or a species of aliens. **Final Bid – $2,250**

- Lemony Snicket—Winner gets his/her name uttered (not necessarily correctly pronounced) in the thirteenth book in his Unfortunate Events series. **Final Bid – $6,300**

- Nora Roberts—Winner gets a character named after him/her in a book released in the spring of 2006. **Final Bid – $6,844.69**

★ ★ ★ ★ ★

THE YELLOW BADGE OF COURAGE

After pledging Delta Upsilon fraternity in 1890 as a freshman at Lafayette University, Stephen Crane had no clue what was coming next. When a group of older brothers ripe for hazing came pounding on his door the following week, he was terrified and refused to let them in. All in good fun, they kicked down the door—but then stopped in their tracks. Crane was standing in the corner of his room, in his nightgown, with a revolver pointed straight at them. Crane may have thought he was getting robbed, but when the evening was settled he was hazed no more. No brother would mess with him again, but it didn't really matter. He had flunked out of school by Christmas break.

★ ★ ★ ★ ★

KIPLING'S GREAT DEPRESSION

When the apostle Paul said that the love of money was the root of all evil, author **Rudyard Kipling should have taken the warning a little more seriously.** While honeymooning with his new bride, Caroline Balestier, in 1892, the unthinkable happened—his bank failed. Unable to finish the romantic vacation, the couple had to cash out their travel tickets to get back home. Unfortunately, the money only got them as far as Vermont, the home state of most of Caroline's family. Instead of trying to continue on their way, they made the most of the situation and settled down in a dark green house Kipling nicknamed his "ship."

TALES OF THE RUDE AND CRUDE

A native of Bombay, India, Rudyard Kipling was only six years old when his parents took him to England and abandoned him at a foster home.

★ ★ ★ ★ ★

THE BROTHERS GRIMACE

The year 1812 was a bad year for Jakob and Wilhelm Grimm. They were so poor that they ate a single meal a day, which explains why so many of the characters in their famous tales suffered from hunger (think Hansel and Gretel). If that weren't enough, the Brothers Grimm were not comfortable with going down in history as children's authors. They viewed themselves as folklorists preserving German oral tradition. In fact, original versions of their stories were much darker than after Disney turned them into feel-good animated films. For example:

- In *Snow White*, the evil stepmother dies after being forced to dance around in red-hot iron shoes.

DID YOU KNOW

Grimms' Fairy Tales have been translated into more than 160 languages and are most popular in Japan, where there are two theme parks inspired by the literature.

- In *The Goose Maid*, one of the servants is stripped down, shoved into a barrel of sharp nails, and then rolled down the street.

- In *The Frog King*, the princess does not kiss the frog—she throws him at the wall because it was so ugly. Once it bounced to the floor, it awoke as a prince.

★ ★ ★ ★ ★

PLAGIARISM OF JURASSIC PROPORTIONS

A Chicago native, Michael Crichton graduated summa cum laude from Harvard University and later received an M.D. from Harvard Medical School. So why would a man with such an esteemed education have the originality of his work questioned in court? Crichton was once summoned to trial to deny accusations that he plagiarized the film *Twister* (another screenwriter claimed that Crichton had stolen it from his version, entitled *Catch the Wind*). Although he defended that specific film while on the stand, Crichton did own up to the fact that he had plagiarized in the past—while a student at Harvard. One of his professors had been giving him unusually low grades, and to prove to another school authority that there was bias, Crichton submitted a paper by *1984* author George Orwell with his own name on it. He actually received a B- and told the jury that he never intended to give the school a bad name.

CHEESY MOMENTS OF CONTROVERSY

In 2003, Michael Crichton gave the unusual and controversial lecture "Aliens Cause Global Warming" while a guest of honor at the California Institute of Technology. He explained to students his theory of "junk science," which he believes is propaganda such as nuclear winters, global warming, and the dangers of secondhand smoke. He asserted that the belief in these theories, like the belief in aliens, is not proven scientific fact but a matter of faith.

★ ★ ★ ★ ★

SUCKING UP IN THE SLAMMER

The Call Of The Wild author **Jack London found himself in trouble with the law a few times in his life.** He had stolen things from orchards and hopped trains in the past—but when he was arrested for vagrancy in Buffalo, New York, at just eighteen years old, he couldn't believe it. Just visiting as a tourist, London was sentenced thirty days in jail. He wasn't even allowed to speak up for himself and claim his rights as an American citizen. Later, when he wrote *The Road*, he made public all the bizarre things that happened to him behind bars. He actually befriended a prison hand who, in exchange for small talk, got him a posh job as a hall monitor of sorts. Because he was on the warden's good side, London made

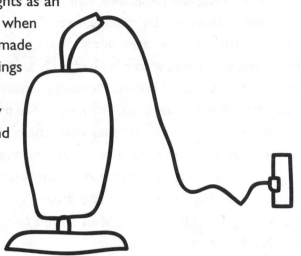

other friends who expected him to use his connections to help them organize crime upon their release—but London wouldn't have anything to do with it. He ran from the other ex-cons by hopping a freight train and never looked back.

★ ★ ★ ★ ★

HOMETOWN HORROR

The controversial author of *American Psycho*, **Bret Easton Ellis is from a hometown with a reputation nearly as scary as his movie.** In

In April 1991, *Rolling Thunder Magazine* published an interview with Bret Easton Ellis titled "Mamas, Don't Let Your Babies Grow Up to be Literary Rock Stars."

December 2004, a ten-year-old boy named Ashton Allen disappeared from Midland, Texas. Just one month prior, Ellis' nine-year-old son

Robby had disappeared, as well. The two families were neighbors, and authorities expected the disappearances to be related to a string of other vanishings in the area. In an attempt to figure out what had happened to his son, whom he had with actress Jayne Dennis, Ellis uncovered a series of Instant Message conversations Allen had had with the other missing boys. However, once a variety of websites got a hold of the conversations, they used them to make it look like all of the boys were unhappy at home and planned to run away together. Ellis was also derided as an unfit source because of his history with illegal substances and dreaming up "horrific scenarios" for a living. The case has not been solved to this day.

★ ★ ★ ★ ★

FIRED FOR BEING FRANK

Deliverance author **James Dickey marked his worst day ever in 1955**, while serving as a creative writing teacher at the University of Florida. Dickey had tired of his job and decided he would really rather focus on poetry. He didn't intend to quit right away, but he soon embarrassed the school enough to earn himself a pink slip. While speaking in front of faculty wives and influential women from around Gainesville, he read a poem he had written titled "The Father's Body," which describes how a young boy begins to notice the differences in sexual maturity between himself and his father. The women were appalled, and when Dickey refused to issue an apology, he was sent packing.

James Dickey played wingback during Clemson College's fall game against rival University of Carolina in 1942. The sport distracted him so much from his studies that when he was drafted into World War II, he was failing all but one class. When he returned from war a poet, his teachers were shocked and impressed.

DID YOU KNOW

In the mid-1950s, James Dickey wrote advertising copy for Coca-Cola and Lays Potato Chips.

★ ★ ★ ★ ★

TALL TALES AND NECK NAILS

Along with a group of friends who were also young writers, *Frankenstein's* **Mary Shelley set out to organize a ghost-story writing contest** in the 1800s. They were all so captivated by the frightening tales they had read in the book *Fantasmagoriana* that they wanted to create similar stories. Although one of Shelley's friends, Dr. John Polidori, came up with *The Vampyre*—which would later influence Bram Stoker as he wrote *Dracula*—Shelley couldn't come up with a thing. However, the following night she had a terrifying dream that inspired one of the most famous pieces of science-fiction literature in history. Shelley saw an image of a

LOVE'S LITTLE SURPRISES
Mary Shelley's husband, Percy, believed in free love and tried to "share" her with his friend, Thomas Hogg. She, like Percy's first wife, refused the offer.

student kneeling beside some creature he had made. When she woke up, she put the story on paper. It would later evolve into *Frankenstein*—a piece that lasted long after her friends' silly tales.

★ ★ ★ ★ ★

A WRECK MADE HIM A WRECK

He may be famous for writing about space travel, but *Fahrenheit 451* author **Ray Bradbury's imaginative courage was challenged forever when he witnessed a gruesome car accident** as a boy. He may have grown up to write about travel, but thanks to the fear the image instilled in his life, he has never once driven a car. Not only automobiles scare him either—he did not set foot on an airplane until he was sixty-two, with the exception of a ride in the Goodyear Blimp two decades before.

★ ★ ★ ★ ★

A FASHION POLICE NIGHTMARE

Oscar Wilde had one thing in life more frightening than anything else—his hideous floral wallpaper. Author of the famed 1891 *The Picture of Dorian Gray*, Wilde joked to a friend while on his deathbed: "My wallpaper and I are fighting a duel to the death. One or the other of us has to go." The witty statement became so famous that the Paris hotel where he was staying at the time left that same wallpaper up in the first-floor room for the next one hundred years. It wasn't replaced until 2000, when it was covered with blue-green frescos to match the rest of the hotel.

★ ★ ★ ★ ★

SNORED STIFF

Some people say there's nothing a good night's sleep can't cure. J.R.R. Tolkien hated those people—**he spent most of his marriage sleeping in a different room than his wife**, because she couldn't stand his snoring. Mrs. Tolkien called dibs on the bedroom, while he had to settle for snoozing in the bathroom/dressing room. Each morning he could wake up and hop into the bathtub without even leaving the room. Not much of a morning person, Tolkien was known to stumble around the house at an ungodly hour to get his two youngest boys up for mass. His greatest feat each day—trying not to trip over their toy trains.

Like most boys, his sons were train fanatics—but Tolkien just didn't get it. To him, trains represented everything noisy and dirty, but he put up with the toys and tried not to stub his toe while wiping the sleep out of his eyes.

★ ★ ★ ★ ★

A TIME (NOT) TO KILL

Although he was as much of a womanizer as his classy protagonist James Bond, author Ian Fleming lacked courage. While working for the Naval Intelligence Division during the war, Fleming volunteered to go through espionage training. While learning how to assassinate someone, however, he lost his nerve and failed for not being able to pull the trigger.

Ian Flemming wrote *Casino Royale* and his other famed James Bond books in Jamaica, in a house he called Goldeneye, where he wouldn't be distracted by busy London life. He awoke at 7:30 a.m., went skinny-dipping in the ocean, ate scrambled eggs, laid in the sun, and then got to work.

★ ★ ★ ★ ★

DEATH BE NOT PROUD (OR QUICK)

Famous for his pessimistic tale *Heart of Darkness*, author **Joseph Conrad had a fear of imminent death after marrying his wife**, Jessie George, in 1896. Before he proposed to her, he even explained that he didn't think he had long to live and that he had "no intention of having children." His anxiety was needless—he lived 28 more years, to the ripe old age of 67.

★ ★ ★ ★ ★

A SHARK'S SWEET REVENGE

The original author of *Jaws*, **Peter Benchley had a fearful realization as he swam about in a shark cage** off the coast of Australia in 2000— "What if the sharks got back at me for giving them such a bad reputation?" The comment was only a half-fear of his, he said, adding that if he had started the book later than he did, he wouldn't have been able to write it. Why? Because in the 1970s, sharks were known as ruthless killers who stalked the oceans for human feasts. Today some scientists maintain that Great White shark aggression is simply curiosity, not vengeance.

Peter Benchley was nearly killed by a shark when he got caught in a fisherman's line while swimming in the Bahamas after writing Jaws. He was filming a television program about ocean life. A shark grabbed the stick that was attached to his wrist and dragged him through the water.

Regardless, Benchley's book caused a lot of people to panic and go out hunting for their own sharks to kill. Laughing that he could never have predicted how his fans would react to Jaws, Benchley compared the situation to a date he had in 1961—"When I went to see Psycho ... my date wet her pants. I cannot be responsible for how people react."

★ ★ ★ ★ ★

ALONG CAME A FAILURE

The brainchild of American writer James Patterson, *Along Came A Spider* should have been a hugely successful thriller when it was made into a movie in 2001. However, when the film opened at the box office, and movie critics at CNN put their fingers to their keyboards, the day proved a bad one for the story's original author. Although billed as a "psychological suspense thriller" with big name actors such as Morgan Freeman, the film flopped. Critics noted that the villain's motive was foolish, several of Patterson's plot lines had been cut out, and the script was completely illogical. Patterson spent the rest of the week hoping his fans picked up *his* version—the book—and stayed away from the theatres. He could finally relate to best-selling author John LeCarré, who once said, "Having your book turned into a movie is like seeing your oxen turned into bouillon cubes."

★ ★ ★ ★ ★

HALLOWEEN HUMILIATION

The writer of such creative sci-fi works as *The Whores of Babylon,* Ian Watson's jaw hit the floor when he arrived at the British National Science Fiction Convention in 2005. The staff had decided to

have a little fun with each attendee by assigning them secret identities. Watson's costume was a tall, curly wig, tight pants, and a silver sword. His character? Inigo Montoya from *The Princess Bride.* Despite looking strikingly similar to Captain Hook, Watson spent the entire evening faking a laugh to cheesy lines such as, "You killed my father. Prepare to die!" At least he won the award for best costume.

CLEAR AND PRESENT DANGER (ON YOUR LAWN)

Tom Clancy lives in a fifteen thousand-square-foot mansion with a half-mile driveway, basketball courts, tennis courts, and a football field. His home has twenty-four rooms, sixteen-foot ceilings, four computers, seven TVs, an indoor swimming pool, and a pistol range. So what could his wife possibly get him for Christmas as a surprise? A yard ornament that would scare him and then make him wet his pants with excitement—his very own World War II tank. Clancy may have thought he was living one of his own plotlines for a brief second, but after he realized the tank was all his, he jumped for joy.

★ ★ ★ ★ ★

GONE WITHOUT A TRACE

Ambrose Bierce wrote a lot about war,  but he never envisioned he would get caught up in one himself. In October 1913, the seventy-something writer decided to take a leisurely trip visiting old Civil War battlefields. A few months later, he had been through both Louisiana and Texas—but to get there he had to drive through warn-torn El Paso, which was teeming with revolutionaries at the time. Curious as always, he joined a small

villa's army to scope out the situation. However, he must have gotten more caught up in the action than intended, because once the group got to Chihuahua, Bierce was nowhere to be found. The last recorded proof of his existence was a letter he wrote to a friend on December 26. His disappearance remains a mystery to this day. Could Bierce have known of his imminent fate? Maybe. Not long before he vanished, Bierce wrote in a letter, "Good-by—if you hear of my being stood up against a Mexican stone wall and shot to rags please know that I think that a pretty good way to depart this life. It beats old age, disease, or falling down the cellar stairs. To be a Gringo in Mexico—ah, that is euthanasia."

★ ★ ★ ★ ★

PANIC AND PRACTICAL JOKES

While Robert Bloch was working on _Psycho_ in the 1950s, he was inspired by how spooked he was of his own hometown of Weyauwega, Wisconsin. Serial killer Ed Gein was on the prowl, and many people in the city feared that any neighbor could be the monster they had heard so much about. Bloch always had the killer in the back of his mind, and after he wrote the book he realized that his own antagonist greatly resembled Gein's crimes and motivation.

Bloch may have been freaked out, but he wasn't so scared he couldn't have a little fun on set. One day, he took the prop he was using for the mother's corpse and put it in actress Janet Leigh's dressing room. He judged how scary it was by the loudness of her scream.

THREE THINGS YOU NEVER KNEW ABOUT... PSYCHO

- When the book was made into a movie, it was the first film to kill off its only main character halfway into the plotline. Viewers had no clue where the story would go from there.

- It was the first movie to show a toilet flushed onscreen.

- It was rumored that Alfred Hitchcock made the water in the shower ice cold so his actress' scream would be genuine. However this was denied on several occasions. In fact, the water was so warm that the coverings used to hide her body accidentally started peeling off during filming.

Chapter 4

✯

Off Their Rockers: Famous Poets Gone Loony

Off Their Rockers: Famous Poets Gone Loony

Crazy can manifest itself in a number of ways. There's the babbling fool who talks himself into the grave. There's the impatient idiot who destroys a world-class poem after one bad critique. There's the arrogant loser who turns down the Nobel Prize because his feelings got hurt. Whether they were loony enough to be institutionalized or simply had a screw loose, when it came to making judgment calls, these writers led lives just as odd and unpredictable as their poetry.

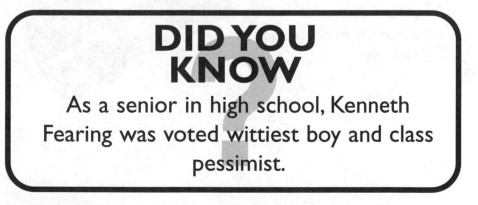

DID YOU KNOW

As a senior in high school, Kenneth Fearing was voted wittiest boy and class pessimist.

★ ★ ★ ★ ★

THE MYSTERIOUS MUMBLER: EDGAR ALLAN POE

If marrying your thirteen-year-old cousin isn't enough of a red flag to prove you are nuts, then running around the streets of Baltimore in a panic attack—while wearing another man's clothes—should be. Edgar Allan Poe did both. On October 3, 1849, he was found wandering, delirious and incoherent. He spent the next several days in and out of consciousness at Washington College Hospital and never got the chance to explain the episode before he died four days later. Unfortunately, Poe's physicians and acquaintances from that night never agreed on a cause of death. Some said he had gotten miserably drunk, while others argued that they never smelled liquor on his breath. Every possible condition— from brain disease and diabetes to rabies and syphilis—was considered, but the true tale of his demise may never be known.

> # DID YOU KNOW
>
> At age forty, Edgar Allan Poe was one of the youngest American writers to die during the nineteenth century. Only Sidney Lanier and Stephen Crane died younger.

★ ★ ★ ★ ★

THE TEASING TEACHER: ANNE SEXTON

Anne Sexton loved to get her crowd a little anxious before she did poetry readings. She would purposefully show up ten minutes late. When she arrived, she would mosey over to the microphone, light a cigarette, and greet them with a pithy line—"I am going to read a poem that tells you what kind of poet I am, what kind of woman I am, so if you don't like it, you can leave." However, the kind of woman Sexton was was anything but graceful—she suffered from suicidal thoughts and often admitted to hating herself. Even as a child she had thoughts about death. When her boyfriend was late for a date one winter morning, he found her motionless in the snow with what looked like blood on her head. He panicked, but she thought it was a good joke.

Addicted to sleeping pills, Sexton spent some time in mental institutions before committing suicide in 1974. Her female fans could relate to her dissatisfaction with being a housewife and a woman in the 1960s.

★ ★ ★ ★ ★

THE SILLY DRUNK: DYLAN THOMAS

Twentieth-century Welsh poet **Dylan Thomas had a little love affair with liquor**. Known as one of the most exciting, theatrical writers of his day, he would often tour the country to visit his admirers. After one rowdy night in a New York City bar called the White Horse Tavern, however, Thomas suddenly collapsed and died. Although many believed the man drank himself to death, official records claimed it was actually pneumonia that did him in. Regardless, Thomas's last words were recorded as "I've had 18 straight whiskeys; I think this is a record!"

MYSTERIOUS MYTHS
Some music buffs report that songwriter Bob Dylan, born Robert Allen Zimmerman, changed his name as a tribute to writer Dylan Thomas. However, the musician has always insisted the claim is not true.

★ ★ ★ ★ ★

THE ANXIOUS BRIDE: SARA TEASDALE

After ignoring a sudden bout of cold feet before walking down the aisle, poet Sara Teasdale decided that her marriage to Ernst Filsinger was nothing like she imagined. Although she never told him, just moments after she accepted his proposal she sat alone, terrified that she had given him the wrong answer. What would this mean for her poetry? She also had an old lover from a summer fling who wrote letters to her, begging her not to marry another. If that weren't enough, once they were married Sara insisted she and her young husband have separate bedrooms. She had always had her privacy, she said, and feared she could not rest with someone else lingering about. The couple divorced shortly after their fifteenth anniversary.

★ ★ ★ ★ ★

THE PRIDEFUL PIMP: LORD BYRON

In the early 1800s, Lord Byron was living large in the luxurious four-floor Palazzo Mocenigo in Venice, Italy. He had fourteen servants and dedicated an entire floor of his home to his pets, which included a variety of dogs and monkeys. His affection for women was even greater, though, and the rest of his spacious home accommodated a long list of Venetian lovers. Byron was so promiscuous that rumors of his relationships spread as far as England. His daily routine: sleep late, take an afternoon ride on one of his horses, sleep with his women, and then write late into the night.

> ### LOVE'S LITTLE SURPRISES
> Lord Byron once boasted that he had sex with more than 250 women in Venice in only one year.

★ ★ ★ ★ ★

THE OVERREACTOR: SIR WALTER SCOTT

Paranoid about whether or not his work was up to par, Sir Walter Scott was a little misled when he received criticisms of his first serious poems. After reading a few stanzas to some friends who gave him very few compliments in return, he threw a fit and tossed the manuscript into a fire. Once he realized that he had overreacted and his buddies

were actually interested in his continuing the piece for publication, he panicked and had to write it over again. Six weeks (and many late nights) later, "The Lay of the Last Minstrel" was complete.

★ ★ ★ ★ ★

DOOMED BY HIMSELF: JOHN DONNE

Long known for his beautiful stanzas and Christian sermons, John Donne was a charmer. However, not many people know that he may have predicted his own death. While ill in 1631, his thoughts constantly turned to the grave. In what ended up being his last speech from the pulpit, Donne delivered what sounded like his own eulogy. During that time, merely weeks before his death, Donne even had his portrait made while wearing the shroud in which he wanted to be buried.

TALES OF THE RUDE AND CRUDE

John Donne's brother was imprisoned, where he died of a fever, for protecting a priest. His uncle, a Jesuit, was hanged, drawn, and quartered for his faith.

★ ★ ★ ★ ★

THE DATE WHO WAS DUMPED: ROBERT FROST

While a college student, Robert Frost published a short book of poems called _Twilight_ for his girlfriend, Elinor White, who was studying at Saint Lawrence University in New York. He printed only two copies and made a special trip to New York to present her with the special gift. However, Elinor took the book and said goodbye

SLUGGISH IN SCHOOL

Robert Frost received more than forty honorary degrees in his lifetime, but he never bothered to actually earn one. He dropped out of Dartmouth College after only one semester and quit Harvard after less than two years. He never trusted what he called "academic knowledge."

without sticking around to talk about it. It upset Frost so much that he destroyed his own copy. The one remaining copy of *Twilight* is one of the most valuable collectibles in the publishing industry.

★ ★ ★ ★ ★

THE THIRD WHEEL: EZRA POUND

American poet and critic Ezra Pound may have been a dazzling influence to classic writers such as Ernest Hemingway and Robert Frost, but his reputation for being a little nutty only increased with age. In 1922, Pound and his wife, Dorothy Shakespeare, added a third-party to their relationship—violinist Olga Rudge. The three of them remained "committed" until the end of Pound's life. After World War I, he faced charges of treason but was dismissed for being insane, so instead of jail time he was simply moved to St.

Elizabeth's Hospital in Washington, D.C. For the next twelve years, Pound passed the time in his padded, white-wall rooms writing books, enjoying conjugal visits with a number of female visitors, and communicating with the States' Rights Democratic Party about his strategies to continue racial segregation in the South.

★ ★ ★ ★ ★

THE PAINFUL PRESCRIPTION: LORD TENNYSON

The master behind "Sir Launcelot and Queen Guinevere," **Lord Tennyson came down with what he called a bad cold in 1845**—but he didn't go to a regular doctor. Instead, he put himself up in a mental institution that promised to cure his "symptoms." There he was denied reading, sitting near a fire, and sipping tea and coffee. He had to lie on wet sheets all day long and get up only to alternate between icy baths and steaming showers. Tennyson's

TALES OF THE RUDE AND CRUDE

Lord Tennyson once wrote a poem about Poland that was hundreds of lines long, but one of his maids accidentally used it as fodder for a fire.

429

caretakers promised that "severe cold water treatment" combined with avoiding alcohol and rich foods would cause his body to expel whatever toxins were making him sick. Of course, this was through vomiting and diarrhea.

★ ★ ★ ★ ★

THE ANNOYING ACQUAINTANCE: WALT WHITMAN

Accustomed to the flexible life he led in the woods while writing *Leaves of Grass*, **poet Walt Whitman was a bit of a nuisance later in life** when it came to being a houseguest. Partially crippled from a stroke, he was cared for by his brother (George Washington Whitman) and his wife, Louisa, in Camden. However, when Louisa would ring the dinner bell, Whitman would ignore it. Instead of coming down for the meal, she would find him splashing around in the bathtub singing "The Star Spangled Banner," "When Johnny Comes Marching Home," or an array of Italian operas. She would find him leashing his yellow and white dog, Tip, for a walk. She would find him asleep in his room. There was no way to get

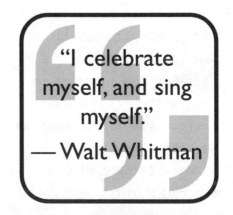

"I celebrate myself, and sing myself."
— Walt Whitman

Whitman to comply with a firm schedule. In fact, he was so stubborn that he even refused book offers simply because they hadn't been his idea or they wouldn't work well with his lazy daily life.

★ ★ ★ ★ ★

THE GRUDGE MATCH MASTER: BORIS PASTERNAK

When authors are awarded the Nobel Prize for Literature, they are rarely crazy enough to say "no thanks" and return the checks. However, Boris Pasternak did just that. He was proud of his work on *Doctor Zhivago*— the main character, whose surname means "live" in Russian, was supposed to represent the author's love for life. But Pasternak turned bitter when he couldn't find a single publisher to accept the work in his home country. He had to smuggle it to Italy for its 1957 release, and even then the Soviet Union waged a wide-scale campaign against it. When he was awarded the Nobel Prize in 1958, he declined to accept it. Not until 1987 was *Doctor Zhivago* finally published in the USSR.

THREE THINGS YOU NEVER KNEW ABOUT ... BORIS PASTERNAK

- He worked at a chemical factory during World War I.

- He wrote a poetry collection titled *My Sister Life* after falling in love with a young Jewish girl, but he was too embarrassed to have it published for four years.

- After he wrote a collection of poems titled *The Second Birth*, his colleagues described him as "Emily Dickinson in trousers."

★ ★ ★ ★ ★

THE THREE-RING CIRCUS: W.H. AUDEN

While working on a book of poems for a publishing company in the early 1940s, W.H. Auden paid $25 a month to rent a bedroom and living room in the top floor of a boarding house. He had high hopes for intelligent, highbrow roommates with whom he could share deep discussions and lines from his poetry.

One roomie did turn out to be *The Heart is a Lonely Hunter* novelist Carson McCullers—however, the rest of them belonged in the loony bin. The circus-like atmosphere included a chimpanzee and a man who could puff a cigarette with his rear end. However, Auden was happy living there and eventually deemed himself "House Pop." He insisted that everyone arrive for meals on time, dismiss their guests before 1:00 a.m., and stick to just a few squares of toilet paper when they used the bathroom. He may have been a little pushy—especially when he found out the other boarders were stealing his cigarettes—but he sincerely cared about each and every one of them.

★ ★ ★ ★ ★

PANICKED AND PARANOID: ROBERT BURNS

When Scottish poet Robert Burns was a boy, his mother had a maid named Betty Davis who would fill his imagination with tall tales of witches, fairies, ghosts, giants, and dragons. While Davis probably thought the bedtime stories were all in good fun, Burns was actually paranoid for years, peeking around corners and over his shoulders for the monsters he had heard about so many years earlier. In addition to his preoccupation with fear, by the time he was a teenager, Burns was a hypochondriac.

★ ★ ★ ★ ★

THE SECRET BRIDE: ELIZABETH BARRETT BROWNING

Elizabeth Barrett Browning, poet and lover of writer Robert Browning, **counted down the days until she and her fiancé were wed.** Though the seriousness of their relationship was a secret, she kept detailed notes about their love. Elizabeth was so careful to keep the truth about their "friendship" from her family that her ninety-first meeting with Robert (recorded in her diary as such) was the first time they saw each other outside of her father's house. It was also their wedding day. As she made up a tale to her parents and snuck away to elope, she was so nervous that she fainted and had to be dragged into a chemist's shop to be revived. Not long after Elizabeth said her "I do's," she had to head back to her father's home. It was weeks before anyone found out they had married.

★ ★ ★ ★ ★

Trouble with Twins: Katherine Mansfield

When short-story-writer-turned-poet Katherine Mansfield moved to Europe for the first time as an adult (at twenty years old) in 1908, she was a rebellious, crazy wreck. Within ten months of living there, she had already borne an illegitimate child, divorced a lover after less than twenty-four hours of marriage, dappled with drugs, and suffered a miscarriage. She was so wild that when her childhood love, Arnold, wrote her a letter saying that they no longer had a future together, she reacted like any crazed woman would do and moved on to a new love— Arnold's twin brother, Garnet.

★ ★ ★ ★ ★

Mama's Boy Mayhem: Kenneth Fearing

"Angel Arm" (1929) poet Kenneth Fearing was too stubborn to develop a good work ethic. He couldn't keep a nine-to-five job for more than a few months until after his fiftieth birthday. His work history is rumored to have included short spurts as a journalist, a mill hand, a pants salesman, and a lumberjack. When his wife, Rachel, had a baby in the 1930s, however, Kenneth's mother forced his non-committal attitude to an end. She stopped giving him his $15/month allowance and insisted he start accepting his responsibilities as a father. From then on, he did his best to put bread on the table.

★ ★ ★ ★ ★

Inspired by Visions: Vachel Lindsay

Made most famous by his poem "Euclid," **Vachel Lindsay started a habit of writing in a diary when he was just seven years old.** While the hobby isn't much to write home about, what was odd was that Lindsay labeled each notebook with the phrase "This Book Belongs to Christ." He claimed to have had visions of the Old Testament prophets twice and saw his poems as a way to spread "the gospel of beauty." He may have taken

his religious vows a little too far, though. He was so naïve (and so afraid of what his father threatened to do to him if he ever had sex) that he never formed serious relationships with women beyond idealized infatuations.

★ ★ ★ ★ ★

FOLLOWING IN LOONY FOOTSTEPS: CHARLOTTE MEW

English poet Charlotte Mew was doomed to a life of bad, crazy luck. Born in London to an architect who died early in his career, Mew had two siblings institutionalized for mental illness. Fearing a similar fate, Charlotte and her sister Anne vowed never to get married—they couldn't bear the thought of possibly passing on a recessive gene to children. Unfortunately, Anne died. Mew became severely depressed and was admitted into a nursing home, where she killed herself by swallowing disinfectant.

Chapter 5

✩

Authors' Hall of Shame: Most Embarrassing Moments

Authors' Hall of Shame: Most Embarrassing Moments

Everyone has moments of incredible shame—those defining incidents when all eyes are on you ... and you'd give anything to take back the silly thing you just said or did. You thought tripping down the stairs in high school was bad enough, but wait until you hear these tales of blushing blunders from across the literary globe.

CHEESY MOMENTS OF CONTROVERSY

When he was just fifteen years old, Leo Tolstoy's brothers took him to a brothel for his first sexual experience with a woman. Although initially plagued with guilt, he eventually became promiscuous and contracted gonorrhea.

★ ★ ★ ★ ★

I DRINK YOU'VE HAD TOO MUCH TO THINK

The Culprit: William Faulkner

Why He's Blushing:
He got tipsy before giving one of the most important speeches of his life.

The Rest of the Story: Faulkner has long been known for his challenging works, but when he got drunk before giving an acceptance speech at the 1949 Nobel Prize awards, his words were more confusing than ever. His nephew knew he was prone to binging before big events and tried to trick him into staying sober, but as soon as Faulkner found out he was setting sail for Stockholm, he tipped up the bottle and didn't look back. He mumbled his inebriated speech, and stood way too far away from the microphone for anyone to hear what he had to say. Not until the public read the printed version of the speech could they decide whether it was even worthy of applause.

DID YOU KNOW

Although his true motives are unknown, some suspect that William Faulkner changed the spelling of his name from Falkner to Faulkner to make him sound like more of a British aristocrat when he entered the Royal Air Force as a young man. Others believe it was simply to make it easier to spell.

★ ★ ★ ★ ★

PRETTY IN PINK

The Culprit: Ernest Hemingway's parents

Why He's Blushing: His mother tried to pass him off as a girl.

The Rest of the Story: You know it's going to be a hard life when you spend your childhood dressed as the opposite sex. Ernest Hemingway's mother wanted twin girls so

THREE THINGS YOU NEVER KNEW ABOUT... ERNEST HEMINGWAY

- He began his career as a seventeen-year-old reporter for *The Kansas City Star* in 1916.

- He wrote *The Sun Also Rises* (1926) in around six weeks from his favorite Paris restaurant, La Closerie des Lilas.

- Several members of his family committed suicide including his father, both of his siblings, and himself.

much that when he was born in 1899, she tricked the town by dressing him just like his sister, who was eighteen months older. She paraded them around with similar haircuts and identical clothing, hoping her peers would believe the children to be twins. In public, she even referred to Hemingway as Ernestine instead of Ernest.

★ ★ ★ ★ ★

FAME AND FROSTBITE

The Culprit: Francis Bacon

Why He's Blushing: He killed himself with his best idea yet.

The Rest of the Story: One would assume that Francis Bacon, one of the most famous philosophers of the seventeenth century, would have enough street smarts not to freeze to death. However, while driving home one winter day he had a brilliant idea— why not preserve his groceries with snow? As he rushed off to stuff his chickens with icy slush, Bacon got a little over zealous. By the time he was

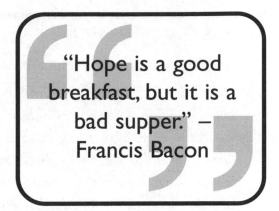

"Hope is a good breakfast, but it is a bad supper." – Francis Bacon

finished, he had contracted a severe case of pneumonia. He died less than a month later. The one thing he got out of the deal—he didn't have to pay his £22,000 debt.

★ ★ ★ ★ ★

SONNETS AND SHOTGUN WEDDINGS

The Culprit: William Shakespeare

Why He's Blushing: Bullies spread rumors that he hinted at homosexuality in his writing.

The Rest of the Story: Shakespeare was an easy target for jokes when it came to his love life. He was

OTHER AUTHORS WITH A THING FOR THE SAME SEX

William Shakespeare wasn't the only writer to be accused of being bisexual or homosexual. HERE'S A LIST ...

- Emily Dickinson—Although often portrayed as a recluse, she frequently wrote letters to a schoolteacher named Susan Gilbert. Dickinson's family threw most of Gilbert's old letters to their daughter into the fireplace once they discovered the collection after her death, but Dickinson's letters to Gilbert still remain. In one letter she wrote: "Sweet Hour, blessed Hour, to carry me to you ... long enough to snatch one kiss, and whisper Good bye, again."

- Bret Easton Ellis—Born in Los Angeles, this *Rules of Attraction* novelist was bisexual for most of his life but refused to publicly admit it until 2005, when he told *The New York Times* that his partner had died at the age of thirty.

- Oscar Wilde
- Tennessee Williams
- A.E. Housman
- Allen Ginsberg
- Willa Cather
- Carson McCullers
- Adrienne Rich
- Fannie Flagg

- Gore Vidal
- Edward Albee
- Marcel Proust
- Andre Gide
- Amy Lowell
- Edna St. Vincent Millay
- Sara Teasdale
- Virginia Woolf

rumored to have married Anne Hathaway when she was already three months pregnant, and his reputation among both women and men forever changed once critics read his works. Twenty-six of his sonnets appeared to be love poems to a married woman, referred to as the Dark Lady, and another 126 are addressed to a man, Fair Lord. Although Elizabethans commonly referred to their friendships as more aggressive types of love in poetry, critics believed Shakespeare was actually referring to sexual rendezvous. Some argue that the "speaker" in the poems does not necessarily have to be Shakespeare; he could have been writing in third person. Others disagree and insist he was indeed bisexual.

★ ★ ★ ★ ★

A Great Gets His Hopes Up

The Culprit: Truman Capote

Why He's Blushing: He promised buddies his latest story would be printed in one of the country's most popular magazines—but it never was.

The Rest of the Story: *Breakfast at Tiffany's* was originally supposed to be printed as a fictional article in *Harper's Bazaar* magazine in the 1950s—but at the last minute, *after* the magazine requested some of Capote's raffish language be changed and had it laid out to be printed, the editors changed their minds. Embarrassed and outraged at the broken contract, Capote announced that the magazine had stopped running "quality fiction" for their readers. He later sold the manuscript to *Esquire* and Random House Publishing.

DID YOU KNOW

Truman Capote got the title *Breakfast at Tiffany's* from a story he once heard about a young Marine in World War II. The man's friend offered to take him to breakfast, but it was Sunday and the shops were closed. "Where would you like to go? Pick the fanciest, most expensive place in town," he said. The Marine's reply, "Let's have breakfast at Tiffany's."

★ ★ ★ ★ ★

Dreaming Up Dirt

The Culprit: Mitch Albom

Why He's Blushing: He "used his imagination" in what should have been hard news.

The Rest of the Story: Author of the popular *Tuesdays with Morrie* and *The Five People You'll Meet in Heaven*, Mitch Albom hasn't always been the reflective literary giant most believe him to be. A graduate of Brandeis and Columbia Universities, he was disciplined while working as a journalist at the *Detroit Free Press* for allegedly fabricating information in one of his stories. He assured readers that two former Spartan basketball players would attend a Final Four game – but they never showed up. Albom's harshest critics called for him to be fired, and he has been trying to live the scandal down ever since.

★ ★ ★ ★ ★

OH SALLY ... I MEAN SONYA

The Culprit: Leo Tolstoy

Why He's Blushing: He bragged about past lovers on his wedding night.

The Rest of the Story: Lonely and in desperate need of a bride, Leo Tolstoy broke down one New Year's Day and vowed that if he did not get married by the end of 1859, he would count himself a bachelor forever. It didn't happen, but he did eventually marry three years later. However, Tolstoy put a damper on their marital bliss with an odd request on the wedding night—he insisted his new bride, Sonya, read all of his old diaries, which included details about his past relationships with other women. Tolstoy may have simply wanted to dispel all secrets, but Sonya was disgusted. The day after the wedding, she wrote in her own diary about her jealousy and the "filth" to which she had been subjected.

> "I clearly realized that my biography, if it suppressed all the nastiness and criminality of my life—as they customarily write biographies—would be a lie, and that if one is going to write my biography, one must write the whole truth."—Leo Tolstoy

★ ★ ★ ★ ★

PINING FOR A PRENUP

The Culprit: Tom Clancy

Why He's Blushing: His ex-wife took him for all he was worth.

The Rest of the Story: Espionage thrillers such as *Clear and Present Danger* may have put Tom Clancy on the literary map, but his trip up the corporate ladder came to a shrieking halt when his ex-wife got her share of

the divorce settlement in 1998. Clancy was making offers to purchase the Minnesota Vikings when the settlement came through and caused his net worth to plummet. Stories of an alleged affair with an assistant district attorney Clancy had met online reached the wrong ears, and the author could no longer afford the team.

★ ★ ★ ★ ★

A PRIEST WITH A PROBLEM

The Culprit: Horatio Alger

Why He's Blushing: He got caught "making friends" with little boys.

The Rest of the Story: Horatio Alger was one of the best-known nineteenth century American authors. He wrote more than 130 rags-to-riches dime novels such as *Ragged Dick* and *Luck and Pluck*. After being rejected from service during the Civil War because of his pesky asthma attacks, Alger decided to become a minister. Instead of preaching the word of God, however, he got personal with people way below the legal age limit. In 1866 he suddenly left his position at First Parish Unitarian Church of Brewster. It was later uncovered that he had been kicked out for initiating sexual relationships with several boys.

★ ★ ★ ★ ★

THE IMPORTANCE OF BEING BULLIED

The Culprit: Oscar Wilde

Why He's Blushing: He was beat up for being a sissy, then teased by his boyfriend's dad.

The Rest of the Story: Clues about Oscar Wilde's sexual orientation came early in life. In college, he rebelled against trends and wore his hair long; made fun of masculine sports; and decorated his room with china, sunflowers, and peacock feathers. He was not easily accepted by other students (he frequently had his room trashed and was dunked in a nearby river for being so odd), but he was not ashamed of his homosexual tendencies. Not yet, at least. His true embarrassment regarding his reputation would come later in life, when his boyfriend's father went to great lengths to break up the relationship. The 9th Marquess of Queensbury, he made shameless plans to throw

LOVE'S LITTLE SURPRISES

While in prison, Oscar Wilde wrote a 50,000-word letter to his boyfriend, Lord Alfred Douglas, which he wasn't allowed to send until he was released.

vegetables at Wilde while he was on stage and leave him calling cards referring to him as a sodomite. Wilde tried accusing him of criminal libel, but in court things just got worse. He actually admitted to lying while on the stand and ended up in court for "committing acts of gross indecency with other male persons."

★ ★ ★ ★ ★

Shocked Stupid

The Culprit: Paulo Coelho

Why He's Blushing: His parents gave him electro-shock therapy for misbehaving.

The Rest of the Story: Brazilian author Paulo Coelho, best known for his work on *The Alchemist*, had big plans for his future—that is, until his parents started bugging him about how much money he could make as an engineer. They strongly discouraged him from a literary life, but Coelho soon became rebellious and made a habit out of breaking the family rules. His plan backfired,

however, and his father decided that the only way to fix his son's attitude was to put him in a psych ward. At just seventeen years old, Coelho was locked up for what his dad called "signs of mental illness." The treatment—a few rounds of painful electroconvulsive therapy.

After he was released, the author became independent, joined a theater group, and got a job as a journalist. However, his peers had such a reputation of immorality that his parents, once again, threatened to send him back to the "hospital." He eventually was taken back, and when he got out, he became intensely withdrawn and depressed. On a hunch, his parents called for a second opinion from a different doctor who urged them to leave their son alone.

★ ★ ★ ★ ★

FAMILY CONTROVERSY

The Culprit: Gertrude Franklin Horn Atherton

Why She's Blushing: Her book brought shame to her family.

The Rest of the Story: Born in San Fransisco, Atherton eloped at age nineteen and quickly had two children. However, her new hubby discouraged her love

for writing. The publication of her first novel, *The Randolphs of Redwoods* (1882), scandalized her family because of its feminism and sexual content. From then on she published other controversial works, such as *What Dreams May Come*, under a pseudonym.

★ ★ ★ ★ ★

THE PICKY EATER

The Culprit: Sherwood Anderson

Why He's Blushing: He died from swallowing a toothpick.

The Rest of the Story: Anderson was chewing on a toothpick after a meal in the early 1940s when suddenly—gulp—it slid right down his throat. At first he was probably amused, surprised that it actually made its way down to his stomach. But before long, the little sliver of wood took its revenge. As it passed through Anderson's intestines, the toothpick punctured the organ, causing an often fatal condition called peritonitis.

> **DID YOU KNOW**
> As a boy, Sherwood Anderson was nicknamed "Jobby" for working so many odd jobs to raise money for his family.

★ ★ ★ ★ ★

WE'RE OFF TO SEE THE UNEMPLOYMENT OFFICE ...

The Culprit: L. Frank Baum

Why He's Blushing: He did a crappy favor in hopes of a big break that never worked out.

The Rest of the Story:
He may be famous for his children's story *The Wonderful Wizard of Oz*, but L. Frank Baum had quite an embarrassing start to his theatrical career at age eighteen. A performing arts center duped him into revamping their stock of costumes in exchange for lead roles in their plays. However, the theater never came through on their end of the deal, and Baum never appeared front and center. Disappointed, he quit working there and instead took on a series of odd jobs, including breeding chickens and working as a clerk in his brother's-in-law dry goods company.

★ ★ ★ ★ ★

THE FASHION OF THE CHRIST

The Culprit: James Kirkup

Why He's Blushing: He was sued for dishonoring Jesus Christ.

The Rest of the Story: James Kirkup thought he was being ingenious when he first wrote the famous poem "The Love That Dares To Speak Its Name"—especially when he got it published in the June 3, 1976, issue of *Gay News*. However, reader Mary Whitehouse wouldn't have such "filthy" rhymes pass by her eyes a second time. She was so offended, calling the poem "a blasphemous libel concerning the Christian religion," that she sued both the magazine and its publisher for allowing it to print. She wanted £7,763—paid by Gay News Ltd and the publisher. Kirkup was never involved in the settlement, but he was horrified that his piece would receive such a public flogging. *Gay News* couldn't care less about the fine, however—they raised a whopping £26,435 from the homosexual community to pay their dues, protect their right to free speech, and still have money leftover for pizza. Only one question remained—why was a pious Ms. Whitehouse flipping through the latest issue of *Gay News*?

★ ★ ★ ★ ★

HIGH SCHOOL HERESY

The Culprit: John Ashbery

Why He's Blushing: He was accused of plagiarizing his first serious poetry submission.

The Rest of the Story: As a high school student, twentieth century American poet John Ashbery hoped to have his poems published in a local journal. However, when he mailed in a piece, he received a simple reply of "Sorry." The rejection wasn't because Ashbery lacked talent—the editors thought he had plagiarized the poem. One of Ashbery's classmates had been so impressed with his work that he had already submitted the same poem, thinking Ashbery would be too humble to do it himself.

★ ★ ★ ★ ★

LIAR, LIAR DIPLOMA ON FIRE

The Culprit: L. Ron Hubbard

Why He's Blushing: He got caught lying on his résumé.

The Rest of the Story: For years psychological-thriller writer L. Ron Hubbard bragged about his prestigious education. He said he graduated from George Washington University as a nuclear physicist, but school records show that he dropped out after two years—

456

during which he failed physics and was on probation for poor grades. He also claimed to have received a Ph.D from California's Sequoia University. It was exposed as a mail-order diploma.

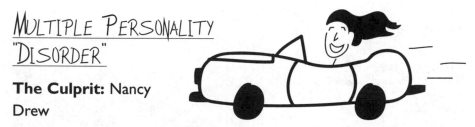

Unfortunately, academics wasn't the only area of life that Hubbard felt the need to embellish. While in the Navy, Hubbard claimed his crew detected Japanese submarines approaching California and spent seventy-two hours bombing (depth charges) the area and celebrating that they had sunk at least one of the enemy ships. However, later investigations revealed that there were never any foreign subs— Hubbard had simply been firing at a "magnetic deposit" in the ocean.

★ ★ ★ ★ ★

MULTIPLE PERSONALITY "DISORDER"

The Culprit: Nancy Drew

Why She's Blushing: The authors who wrote about her couldn't keep their stories straight.

The Rest of the Story: One of the most popular mystery series of the twentieth century, *Nancy Drew* featured a strong protagonist.

However, among the multiple authors who wrote under the pen name Carolyn Keene, Nancy's story just couldn't stay straight. Some of the books briefly mention that Nancy's mother died when Nancy was just ten years old—others claim she was three. In some of the books, Nancy's snooping counterpart is named Buck Rodman—others call him Burt Eddleton. Originally a blonde, the sleuth is referred to as "titian-haired" (or strawberry blonde) in later books. She also has an incredible number of cars for such a young girl. Her blue roadster suddenly turns maroon, then green, then black. In later books she instead has a coupe and a blue convertible.

If changes in appearance and sidekicks weren't enough, Nancy also becomes more politically correct as the authors change hands and revised reprints are made of the original stories. For example, the early first edition manuscripts contained a handful of negative stereotypes about Asians and Hispanics. Nancy also used to be sneakier. She carried a revolver, trespassed on private property, and "stole" her evidence. More recent versions describe her as a more passive, law-abiding sleuth.

★ ★ ★ ★ ★

MAVERICK'S BIG MISTAKE

The Culprit: Roald Dahl

Why He's Blushing: He tried to land at an airport that didn't exist.

The Rest of the Story: While serving in the Royal Air Force in the fall of 1940, Dahl received an assignment to fly his Gladiator from Egypt to Libya. The trip was so long that it required multiple stops to refuel. However, while attempting to land for the final time, Dahl fumbled and couldn't see the airstrip below. Running out of fuel quickly, he had to navigate in the dark and make an emergency landing in the middle of the desert. The undercarriage of the plane smacked a boulder as it skidded in the sand, resulting in a horrific crash. Dahl cracked his skull, smashed his nose, and was suddenly blinded. After being rescued, he received word that there was no airstrip in that part of the desert—he had been looking for a plot of land that didn't even exist. His sight finally returned after eight weeks of hospital care.

★ ★ ★ ★ ★

THE BLUSHING BIOGRAPHY

The Culprit: Christina Rosetti

Why She's Blushing: Her biographer told the world that a dead mouse caused all of her problems.

The Rest of the Story: Born in London in 1830, Christina Rosetti was a beautiful little girl who spoke Italian and won the

When poet Christina Rosetti was a young adult, she shunned the theater because the actors had a lazy "moral tone," quit playing chess because she noticed that she was "too eager to win," and regularly fasted. She even refused to go into the Mummy Room of the British Museum because she feared the world would come to an end and the corpses would come to life before her eyes.

hearts of many. However, she was a little odd when it came to animals. Once, while visiting her grandpa in Buckinghamshire, she came across a dead mouse. Feeling sorry for the vermin, she buried it. A few days later, she returned to see how it was doing. When she dug it up, a big beetle scurried out. Rosetti ran away screaming and never went back—but her biographer, Virginia Moore, read a little further into the situation. It may be a stretch, but Moore believes Rosetti was affected by her encounter with the beetle for the rest of her life. In a chapter she wrote in *Distinguished Women Writers* (E.P. Dutton & Co., Inc., 1903), Moore attributes Rosetti's heart trouble, cancer, chronic cough, and "disease of the eyes" to the fear that resulted from the event, a fear her brother referred to as "skeletons in Christina's various closets."

★ ★ ★ ★ ★

THE NUDIE CONTROVERSY

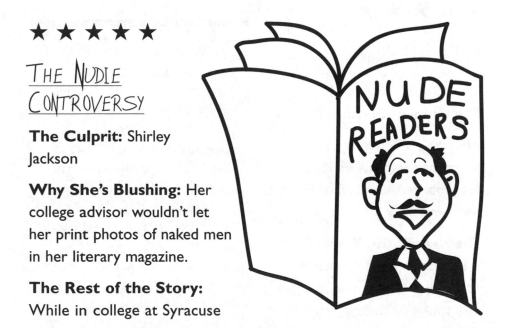

The Culprit: Shirley Jackson

Why She's Blushing: Her college advisor wouldn't let her print photos of naked men in her literary magazine.

The Rest of the Story: While in college at Syracuse

University, short-story guru Shirley Jackson lost her job working for *The Syracusan* humor magazine when the decision was made that it would no longer include fiction. For a new job, she decided to start her own on-campus literary publication, *The Spectre*, named after a line from a William Blake poem. Thanks to campus censorship, however, her first issue didn't come out as intended. With fifty mimeographed pages ready to be bound and distributed, she was stopped by an advisor who told her the unthinkable: she wasn't allowed to print naked photos! In an editorial in the following issue, Jackson explained to her readers:

> Here we are, already a magazine with a lurid past. Just before our first issue was bound ... the English department (working through our faculty advisor) tapped us on the shoulder gently and informed us that we were a menace to public morals. It seems we had two pictures of nude male bodies, and if you want to have nude bodies in a campus publication, without corrupting morals, they have to be female bodies.

Needless to say the images came out, but after the rag's distribution other people spoke up and wrote letters of complaint that there was plenty more "dirty" content in the form of stories that would make anyone blush in mixed company.

Chapter 6

And Then They Were Young: Cheesy Childhood Anecdotes

And Then They Were Young: Cheesy Childhood Anecdotes

• •

Whether they were seriously spoiled, touted as geniuses or punished for bending the rules at school, these creative youngsters give a whole new meaning to the term "kidding around."

DID YOU KNOW

Tennessee Williams birth name was Tom Williams, but he changed it. His ancestors were "Indian-fighting Tennesseans," and his friends gave him the nickname because of his soft Southern drawl.

★ ★ ★ ★ ★

LIVIN' IN THE SPOOK HOUSE

The Call of the Wild author **Jack London was desperate for attention as a boy.** With a mother too busy planning séances and get-rich-quick schemes, he was stuck being toted around by his stepsister, Eliza. At just four years old, he would join nine-year-old Eliza at school because he had nowhere else to go. He would flip through picture books while the other children practiced writing in cursive. At

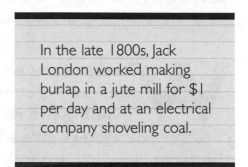

In the late 1800s, Jack London worked making burlap in a jute mill for $1 per day and at an electrical company shoveling coal.

home, he often got wrapped up in his mother's wacky experiments. He claims that when he was six, his mother set him on a table during a séance, and the table levitated off of the floor. London's friends called his home "the spook house" and were afraid of his mother's whooping and hollering when she claimed to be "possessed" by a spirit.

★ ★ ★ ★ ★

CHICKEN RUN BACKWARDS

One of Savannah, Georgia's claims to fame is being the hometown of acclaimed author Flannery O'Connor. It wasn't the most exciting place to grow up, however. The most interesting thing that ever happened to her as a child? **She owned a pet chicken**

that walked backwards. Later, she lived on a farm and took care of hundreds of birds, including peacocks, ducks, and hens.

★ ★ ★ ★ ★

Take an Antibiotic and Call Me in the Morning

While in medical school in the early 1940s, Lancelot author **Walker Percy was conducting autopsies on patients with tuberculosis** at Bellevue Hospital when he and a band of fellow interns failed to follow sanitation procedures and contracted the disease. Combined with the results of a Freudian psychoanalysis he had to undergo, Percy was so frustrated by the mistake that he quit medicine and began pursuing literature instead.

★ ★ ★ ★ ★

Dusty Treasures

When Southern-born writer Rick Bragg was a young boy, his estranged father gave him two gifts—a 22-caliber rifle and three boxes of old books, including everything from William Shakespeare and Mark Twain to Sir Arthur Conan Doyle and Ernest Hemingway. His father, of course, didn't really know who any of those writers were. He just knew that the books looked pretty with their faded, leather-wrapped covers. They looked like something rich people would own, he said. Bragg's father warned him that if there were any pornographic books in there, he should toss them out before his mother caught sight of them. Luckily, they were all classics.

★ ★ ★ ★ ★

IT'S ALL IN THE GENES

Seeking a "normal" reputation, **Lord Byron spent much of his life desperately trying to live down the rowdy, rakish ways** of his ancestors—especially his grand uncle, the fifth Lord Byron, who was notorious for causing a ruckus. He attempted to kidnap a famous actress, killed his cousin in a duel, and built a miniature castle and fort on a lake for no reason at all. Regardless of Byron's efforts to escape his grand uncle's actions, however, he was often mocked. He was born with a club foot, and for some time his mother couldn't afford to buy him a corrective shoe and brace.

CHEESY MOMENTS OF CONTROVERSY

Lord Byron's nurse, May Gray, was fired for being drunk, violent, and sexually precocious with him before he was even a teenager.

★ ★ ★ ★ ★

THE TEA TIME TROUBLEMAKER

A rebel at heart, J.R.R. Tolkien liked to cause trouble while students at King Edward's School in Birmingham, England, kept their noses in the books. He and three friends formed a secret society they called the Tea Club and Barrovian Society, or T.C.B.S. They would buy tea in Barrow's Stores and sneak it into the school library (which was prohibited). What rebels.

★ ★ ★ ★ ★

AN ENCOUNTER WITH ICKY INSECTS

As a boy, Christian writer **Clives Staples (C.S.) Lewis had an unusual fear of insects**. Its origin? A pop-up children's book. Lewis had

once seen a photo of a giant stag beetle towering over a tiny Tom Thumb-like character. Made from cardboard, the bug's horns came off

DID YOU KNOW?

C.S. Lewis' parents often called him by one of his many nicknames—Jack, Jacko, Kricks, and Klicks.

the page at Lewis as if they were going to pinch his little fingers. It was his earliest memory of fear, and from that day on Lewis never overcame his disdain for insects. His mother felt guilty and called the book an "abomination," something she never should have allowed in a nursery.

★ ★ ★ ★ ★

THE GLOATING GENIUS

Call him a savant or not, but Robert Browning was a whiz. At just twelve years old he had written his first book of poetry. Like a true hormone-ridden pre-teen, however, he destroyed it when it was turned down by a handful of publishing companies. A bit of a snob when it came to getting along with the other kids at school, Browning ended up being taught by a private tutor most of his life. By age fourteen, he was fluent in five different languages and by age sixteen he enrolled as a freshman in London's University College. Continuing his childhood disdain for the organized classroom, however, he dropped out after just two semesters.

★ ★ ★ ★ ★

A TALE OF SIX SHILLINGS

Charles Dickens was a regular at his hometown boot-blacking factory, and while most children his age were playing cops and robbers, he worked ten hours a day gluing labels on jars of shoe polish in a room overrun with rats. His family was stuck in a debtor's prison, and Dickens took his father his earnings, six shillings a week, to support them as they paid off their debts. Once a socialite, Dickens' father had gone broke entertaining the public and desperately trying to maintain his status as a bigwig. The writer never forgave his family for making him work in such harsh, crowded factory conditions—and until his death in 1870, he made the plight of the working class a focus of his literature.

★ ★ ★ ★ ★

PAYBACK'S A SNITCH

Poet turned-playwright Tennessee Williams never had much interest in masculine things. A lengthy illness during his childhood had made him both passive and sensitive. Williams' father, Cornelius, was embarrassed by his effeminate ways and often teased him about how he needed to be more of a man. He even called him "Miss Nancy" to get on his nerves. But Williams ultimately got his revenge—he wrote his father's personality into many of his scripts. Big Daddy, the overbearing and overly masculine (even abusive) protagonist from *Cat on a Hot Tin Roof*, was one way Williams released his anger over the way his father ridiculed him as a child.

★ ★ ★ ★ ★

THE SPOILED SON

The youngest of six children, *Charlotte's Web's* **E.B. White garnered all the pampering that a little brother can expect**. Being the youngest—and being born just before his father started making big bucks—White was the talk of the town. He was the first child on his block to own a bicycle and bragged about a sixteen-foot green canoe his father got him when he was just eleven. Daddy didn't just give him material things, though. For his twelfth birthday, White's father wrote him a note on Park Avenue Hotel stationery reminding him, "You have been born in the greatest and best land on the face of the globe under the best government known to men. Be thankful then that you are an American."

When E.B. White, born Elwyn Brooks White, was a child, he believed that his birthday—July 11—was a lucky day because the numbers seven and eleven were lucky numbers.

★ ★ ★ ★ ★

PRETENDING TO PREACH

As a boy, Thomas Hardy was quite the do-gooder. On rainy days, he would wrap himself in his mother's tablecloth, stand on a chair, and read the family's morning prayer aloud. His cousin would shout the "Amens," and his grandmother, acting as the mock congregation, would clap while eating breakfast. Hardy would give a short sermon, piecing together things he remembered from the priest's most recent speeches. It was all in good fun, but Hardy was actually afraid of growing up. He didn't like hearing people talk about becoming a man. He liked his jokes and his lazy childhood ways. Despite Hardy's liking to act like a child, it hurt his mother's feelings when he told her of his wish to stay a boy forever.

★ ★ ★ ★ ★

PUPPY LOVE GOES KA-PUT

Like most adolescents, F. Scott Fitzgerald was obsessed with girls during his late teenage years. Despite many college crushes, one in particular stayed with him much of his life. He met Ginevra King on one of the last days before Christmas break in 1915. She was from a wealthy Chicago family, and the two instantly became pen pals, writing their passionate feelings for each other back and forth. By the end of the year, however, Fitzgerald had dropped out of Princeton because of illness and poor grades. He wrote in his diary about being crushed that the romance had fizzled and he subsequently rarely heard from King.

F. Scott Fitzgerald eventually earned the riches he once admired in his college crush. Although he made plenty of cash off the books he published, he spent thousands keeping up his socialite status.

★ ★ ★ ★ ★

THE [ABBREVIATED] BIRDS AND BEES

Daphne du Maurier came from a family that was extremely shy about sexual matters. When she turned twelve years old, du Maurier's mother gave her a speech about her impending menstrual cycle: "You mustn't be surprised if something not very nice happens to you in a few weeks … it can't be stopped … it goes on happening, every month, until [you] are middle aged, and then it stops." That was all the counseling she received, and she was even forced to swear that she would not blab about the "occasion" to her little sister, Jeanne. Du Maurier dreaded the day, even holding tight to a dream that maybe she would turn into a boy before her first menstruation.

★ ★ ★ ★ ★

Dancing King

Although his father protested because of the family's devout religious beliefs, **Ernest Hemingway's mother enrolled him and his siblings in dance lessons.** A former opera singer, Grace Hall Hemingway loved the arts and encouraged her children to do so as well. Despite the artsy façade, Hemingway grew up to join his father as an avid sportsman with a love for hunting and fishing.

★ ★ ★ ★ ★

Tossing Out the Carbs

As a boy, playwright Arthur Miller had a part-time job at a New York bakery delivering fresh bread and rolls every morning before he went to school. They expected their bread to be on time. Unfortunately, while riding his bicycle through town one sleepy morning, Miller

hit a patch of ice, and rye bread, onion rolls, and pumpernickel flew in every direction. Panicked, he gathered them up as quickly as he could. Unfortunately, it wasn't long before he realized he could never repack the bags accurately. Instead of returning to the bakery, he decided to make it fair. Every bag got an equal amount of bread—and he ate the leftovers.

★ ★ ★ ★ ★

AN UNLIKELY CRITIQUE

When he was barely thirteen years old, Henry Wadsworth Longfellow had one of his very first poems, "The Battle of Lovell's Pond," published in the Portland *Gazette*. When his father picked up the paper the morning it was delivered, Longfellow waited eagerly for a compliment, but no one seemed to notice. Later that evening, he hoped that at least his father's friends had seen his work of genius. They had, but their response wasn't exactly complimentary. Not

DID YOU KNOW

Henry Wadsworth Longfellow's poems often reflected his strong aversion to war, which may have been influenced by the early death of his uncle, a Navy lieutenant, who was his namesake.

knowing who was the author of the poem, one friend commented that what he had read that morning was "very stiff. It is all borrowed, every word of it." Too embarrassed to tell them the poem had been his, Longfellow kept his mouth shut and cried himself to sleep.

★ ★ ★ ★ ★

Poor but Prudent

Born the son of a tweny-two-year-old shoemaker in Denmark, **Hans Christian Andersen lived in a one-bedroom shack.** Regardless of his cramped quarters, Andersen's imagination took off at a young age. He memorized entire Shakespeare plays and recited them, using wooden dolls as actors on a toy stage he built.

At one point, Andersen's father believed the family was related to nobility. The Father Hans Christian Andersen Center has records that Andersen's grandmother spilled the beans and told him he was secretly upper-class. However, there is no official historical proof of the

TALES OF THE RUDE AND CRUDE

In his free time, Hans Christian Andersen worked in a cigarette factory with co-workers so crude that they would place bets on whether or not he was actually a girl.

matter. The Andersens did have some connections to Danish royalty, but they were simply part of a business relationship.

★ ★ ★ ★ ★

A TALE OF TWO PERSONALITIES

Joseph Conrad showed signs of a slightly bi-polar personality as a teenager. He flip-flopped between being extremely reserved and organized to impulsive and dangerously wanton. When he was seventeen, his romantic notions of life on the sea led him to a career onboard a boat. In 1874, he joined the Spanish Carlists. After years as a gun runner, he wrecked the ship that his uncle had helped him finance and gambled away the rest of his savings.

★ ★ ★ ★ ★

THE FREUDIAN FAKER

A whiny little daydreamer, Jewish author **Elie Wiesel caused his parents to panic when they noticed he had lost weight** and became suddenly picky about what foods he wanted to eat. They spent hundreds of dollars going from doctor to doctor to ask about his weight loss and his headaches. However, Wiesel had no plans for getting better; he used his complaints as an excuse to skip school even when he was well. It wasn't because he hated school—it was because he was addicted to being around his mother. Wiesel loved staying at home in bed where he could hear her working around the house. When she would leave to help at the family store, he would suddenly feel abandoned and afraid. Even when Wiesel was at school, he counted down the minutes until they would be reunited.

★ ★ ★ ★ ★

A Story of Stump Babies

The author of *The Color Purple: A Novel*, **Alice Walker was always playing jokes on her siblings**—even while in the womb! In fact, when she was born, her older sister had wanted another child around the house so bad that she was fooled by African-American folklore. Based on a Southern myth that babies came from stumps, Ruth had spent several years looking around the yard for a new sister. She even nearly drowned once while peeking into a tree that was next to a creek to see if there was a little baby inside. When her mother went into labor with Alice, Ruth hid in the closet to see how the stump would be brought in. She later realized that Alice had come from her mother's belly.

★ ★ ★ ★ ★

GIRL OF GOTH

Amelia Atwater-Rhodes is well known among modern writers of young-adult fiction. She finished her first vampire novel at just thirteen years old, and even then she had a handful of other incomplete stories sitting at home just waiting to be finished. Amelia's family and friends didn't always believe that she was a natural with a pen, however. While touring a local high school as an eighth grader, one of her friends bragged to a teacher that Amelia had already written a book. He took a look at her work and was so blown away by the maturity in her writing that he became her literary agent. Since then, Amelia has been featured in *The New Yorker*, *Entertainment Weekly*, *Seventeen Magazine*, *USA Today*, and on a variety of national morning shows.

★ ★ ★ ★ ★

DO AS I SAY, NOT AS I DO

In the 1900s, thriller-writer Eric Ambler's parents performed in troupes as the incredible "Reg and Amy Ambrose," but they wouldn't let their eager teenage son join in the fun. They wanted him to do something more respectable with his life—to get as far away from the stage as possible. He got an engineering scholarship to London University, but it wasn't long before he was writing song lyrics and plays.

★ ★ ★ ★ ★

THE SHOE-IN STORY

When acclaimed fiction writer Josephine Haxton began writing, she would often send early versions of her manuscripts to friends for their edits and opinions. One was so impressed that he showed it to his boss at Houghton Mifflin, and the editor called Haxton personally to tell her that he would like to submit the novel for an upcoming fellowship competition. Haxton was hesitant, afraid that the book would not be complete in time. However, he talked her into it, saying, "If you want me to help you make up your mind … if you will enter the competition, your novel has won."

★ ★ ★ ★ ★

TEA-TIME TYPING

Herman Melville's heritage always pointed him to the sea. His grandfather, Major Thomas Melville, partied hard during the

Boston Tea Party in 1773. For years, Herman's eyes were glued to a piece of memorabilia on his grandfather's mantel—a bottle of tea that he had squeezed from his wet clothes after the event.

Chapter 7

★

Fun Facts About Your Favorite Children's Authors

Fun Facts About Your Favorite Children's Authors

They say good writers write what they know, but these children's book authors didn't always enjoy the idyllic lives presented in their stories. In real life, they suffered from writer's block and were afraid of being kidnapped. They were accused of being serial killers and had their books censored. Here's some other wacky stuff you never knew.

S.E. Hinton loves horseback riding and reading, but her true love may be taking classes at local colleges (not for credit). When she has time to sit down and write, Hinton says she first writes on paper in longhand, then types into a computer later.

S.E. HINTON, THE OUTSIDERS

The Outsiders gave novelist S.E. Hinton a quick dose of fame, but with the fanfare came a lot of pressure. Being nicknamed "The Voice of the Youth" was just too much for Hinton, and she quickly became overwhelmed. The pressure resulted in three years of writer's block. Luckily for Hinton, her boyfriend wouldn't put up with the slump and began insisting that she write two pages every day if she wanted to leave the house. The ploy worked, and her career has been strong ever since.

★ ★ ★ ★ ★

PHILIP PULLMAN, DARK MATERIALS

Young-adult author Philip Pullman has found himself in hot water in the past, accused of actively denouncing Christianity. He has, in fact, denounced C.S. Lewis's classic *Chronicles of Narnia* as faith-based propaganda. In response he wrote his own series that remarkably resembled Lewis's. His *Dark Materials* and *The Chronicles of Narnia* both tell the story of talking animals and children entering parallel worlds at odds with each other. Like *The Lion, the Witch and the Wardrobe*, the first book in the *Dark Materials* series features a girl hiding in an old wardrobe. Despite the similarities, there is still a difference—critics have accused Pullman of actively rejecting some of Lewis's themes. For example, Pullman believed Lewis created false hope for children with cancer or children whose parents have cancer when he penned a fictional cure for the disease in one of the Narnia books.

★ ★ ★ ★ ★

LOIS LOWRY, THE GIVER

Born in Hawaii, Lowry was originally named "Sena" after her Norwegian grandmother. However, once the grandmother got word of the baby's new name, she quickly sent a telegraph to try and change Lowry's parents' minds. Why shouldn't the girl have an American name? she asked. After a bit of coaxing from grandma, who obviously didn't care about serving as the child's namesake, Lowry's father changed her name to Lois, after one of his sisters.

Lowry's most controversial book, *The Giver*, has received both rave reviews and harsh criticism across the United States. In 2005, the Associated Press reported that a group of disgruntled parents were picketing to remove the book from their children's eighth grade reading list. They argued that it was "sexually explicit" and "violent." Regardless of the group's insistence that nothing should enter a child's mind that is not positive and uplifting, the school board voted to keep the book in school as planned.

★ ★ ★ ★ ★

ALEKSEY NIKOLAYEVICH TOLSTOY, NIKITA'S CHILDHOOD

A writer from Soviet Russia, Tolstoy started out a rich man. In 1900, his father died, leaving him thirty thousand roubles and a family name worth even more. He was proud of his heritage, but he also mocked it while playing dirty tricks on his friends. Tolstoy bought a truckload of random antique portraits and hung them around his fancy home. When he had visitors, he would take them from portrait to portrait, talking about the legacy of the "family members" in each one. When they would leave, however, Tolstoy would laugh with friends about how he had no idea who was in the portraits and had completely fabricated the stories about his family's respectable past.

★ ★ ★ ★ ★

ERIC CARLE, THE VERY HUNGRY CATERPILLAR

Few children know that one of their favorite interactive picture books, *The Very Hungry Caterpillar*, was originally titled *A Week with Willi*

Worm. The star of the original plot? A bookworm. However, Carle's editor was concerned that children wouldn't be huge fans of a big green worm. In the end, the story was translated into more than fifty different languages worldwide. In 2005, a copy of the book was sold every fifty-seven seconds.

★ ★ ★ ★ ★

FRANCES HODGSON BURNETT, THE SECRET GARDEN

As an adult, Frances Hodgson Burnett was so good at storytelling and pretending that she often found it difficult to get along with fellow grown-ups. Bored around people her own age, Burnett would light up when children begged her to tell them stories. Even when she was

At just seven years old, Frances Hodgson Burnett was obsessed with the fiction she found in magazines such as *Young Ladies' Halfpenny Journal*, *London Society*, and *Godey's Lady's Book*. Mimicking the tales she was used to reading, Burnett spun her own stories for peers and family. It wasn't long before she was submitting stories to *Godey's* editor Sara Lucretia Hale, who didn't believe such a young girl could have written such good British fiction. She made Burnett write a second story to prove the legitimacy of the first.

at parties with friends, she would find excuses to run off with the kids. She loved to surprise them by playing fairy godmother. On one occasion, she waved her opera glasses about and pulled a toy boat from behind her back—a toy she had known one of the little boys wanted. He was so enthused by the trick that he didn't care about the boat—he asked her for the "wand" instead.

★ ★ ★ ★ ★

BEATRIX POTTER, THE TALE OF PETER RABBIT

The creator of the classic mischievous bunny who sneaks under the fence into Mr. McGregor's garden, Beatrix Potter grew up with parents who lived solely off of their inheritances— neither of them worked. Potter was raised by nannies, and when she was old enough to go to school, they banned her from intellectual development and instead made her a housekeeper. She became so lonely that she often snuck little animals into the home to keep her company—something that is reflected in the stories she wrote as an adult. Potter's parents were so strict that they even refused to approve her engagement to publisher Norman Warne because he worked for a living. They would rather their daughter lead a life of lazy luxury just like them.

★ ★ ★ ★ ★

ROALD DAHL, JAMES AND THE GIANT PEACH

At just eight years old, Roald Dahl was joking around with four of his best friends at school when he came up with a brilliant game—what if they put a dead mouse in a jar of candy at the local sweet shop? Dahl didn't like the owner anyways; he described her as a "mean and loathsome" old woman named Mrs. Pratchett. Like most children concocting sneaky plans against adults, Dahl was caught in the act and was whipped by the headmaster at his school. From then on, Dahl's parents sent him to a long list of boarding schools.

As much as Dahl hated boarding schools, however, it was while he was studying at Repton School that the Cadbury chocolate company began sending boxes of new recipes to be taste-tested by students. For years he

In 1920, when Roald Dahl was only three years old, his older sister died of appendicitis and his father died of pneumonia.

dreamed of inventing his own chocolate bar that would wow Mr. Cadbury himself. The experience served as his inspiration for the book *Charlie and the Chocolate Factory*.

★ ★ ★ ★ ★

DAV PILKEY, CAPTAIN UNDERPANTS

Born in 1966 in Cleveland, Ohio, Dav Pilkey was quite the disruptive student in elementary school. Later diagnosed with Attention Deficit Disorder, he was often forced to move his desk out into the hallway, where he would work on writing the comic book stories he hid in his desk. Pilkey was called David until he worked in a pizza parlor, where his boss accidentally spelled his name "Dav" on a nametag. His friends got a kick out of the mishap, and though he may not have worked in the restaurant business for long (he published his first book at nineteen years old), the nickname stuck.

★ ★ ★ ★ ★

BRIAN JACQUES, TRIBES OF REDWALL SERIES

When Brian Jacques' teacher told him to go home and write a story about animals for homework one day, he came up with a cute little tale about a

Before he became a full-time writer, Brian Jacques worked as a policeman, truck driver, boxer, bus driver, comic, sailor, and folksinger. Today he enjoys reading but says he avoids reading other children's-book authors' work to avoid unintentional plagiarism.

bird whose job was to clean a crocodile's teeth. The story was so impressive that his teacher had him caned by the principal for plagiarism. Regardless, Jacques loved the topic and spent the rest of his life writing about animals. However, some critics believe Jacques endorses social class systems by suggesting that the "good" and "bad" characters in his book are based on particular species. For example, squirrels, hedgehogs, and mice are usually praised, while foxes and rats are portrayed as stupid and greedy.

★ ★ ★ ★ ★

LEWIS CARROLL, ALICE IN WONDERLAND

With a story as bizarre as *Alice in Wonderland*, it's no wonder Lewis Carroll's life is surrounded by wild rumors. In 1996, a fellow author named Richard Wallace published a book called *Jack the Ripper, Light-Hearted Friend* that directly accused Carroll of being one of two men involved in the infamous Jack the Ripper serial killings. However, both Carroll and Thomas Vere Bayne, the other man accused, had come up with perfect alibis for the nights of each murder. Carroll had expressed vague interest in the cases, but there was never any substantial evidence connecting him to the crimes.

★ ★ ★ ★ ★

SELMA LAGERLÖF, JERUSALEM

A Swedish children's author, Selma Lagerlöf became a part of the Swedish Academy, a group that nominates people for and awards the Nobel Prize in literature. She was such a generous woman that when World War II began, she sent her own Nobel Prize medal to Finland to help the government finance its battle against the Soviet Union. The group was so honored by the gesture that they couldn't possibly sell it or melt it down, so they said thank you and returned it promptly.

★ ★ ★ ★ ★

ASTRID LINDGREN, PIPPI LONGSTOCKING

When Swedish author Astrid Lindgren began dreaming of her concept for the funky, impulsive Pippi Longstocking, she was greatly inspired by Lucy Maud Montgomery's *Anne of Green Gables*. Like protagonist Anne, Pippi has red hair, freckles, and

As of 1995, Astrid Lindgren's *Pippi Longstocking* books had been translated into fifty-six languages and sold four million copies in Germany alone.

an assertive attitude. The name of Pippi's home, Villa Villekulla, is even a lighthearted reference to the Swedish name of Anne's home—Grönkulla. Unfortunately, when translated to English some of Lindgren's humor is lost. For example, in Swedish "pippi" means crazy.

★ ★ ★ ★ ★

VERNA AARDEMA, WHY MOSQUITOES BUZZ IN PEOPLE'S EARS

This famous author had never considered writing for children until she got frustrated with her own daughter, who refused to eat dinner until she got a bedtime story first. The little girl was brilliant at the bribes, and Verna often came up with tales related to communities and countries she had recently read about.

★ ★ ★ ★ ★

A.A. MILNE, WINNIE-THE-POOH

Few people know that author A.A. Milne was most inspired by his son's collection of stuffed animals, which included a bear named Winnie-the-Pooh. As for the one human character in Milne's popular series, Christopher Robin was named after his son.

★ ★ ★ ★ ★

HANS AUGUSTO REY, CURIOUS GEORGE

While living in Paris one year, Hans was recognized as such a talented artist that a French publisher practically begged him to write a children's book about animals. It wasn't long before *Rafi and the Nine Monkeys* hit the shelves, but they weren't much of a hit. However, one of the book's characters, Curious George, was so loved by children that Hans made him the star of his own story. The writer's new work was interrupted by the beginning of World War II, when he fled Paris on a bicycle with his wife before the Nazis intervened. One of the few things he chose to take with him—the manuscript for *Curious George*.

★ ★ ★ ★ ★

LOUIS SACHAR, SIDEWAYS STORIES FROM WAYSIDE SCHOOL

Sachar's first book for children, *Sideways Stories From Wayside School*, was accepted for publication during his first week as a law school student. A few years earlier, Sachar had signed up as a volunteer at a local elementary school. He was asked to be the Noon Time Supervisor, who keeps an eye on the children while they eat lunch. Instead of being an authority figure, however, Sachar played games with them, earning him the nickname "Louis the Yard Teacher." Memories of those times stuck with him the all through law school, and after he passed the bar exam he decided to be a full-time writer.

★ ★ ★ ★ ★

BEVERLY CLEARY, RAMONA QUIMBY SERIES

At four years old, Cleary's first experience with a book was a frightening one. Living on an Oregon farm, she was invited by a neighbor to borrow a picture book any time she wished. However, the woman's son loved to tease Cleary, convincing her that he had sold her for a nickel to another neighbor, Quong Hop, who would soon be moving back to China. Falling for the joke, Cleary had to walk past the Hop home every time she wanted to borrow the book. She would slither through the grass like a snake so no one would see her and snatch her off to Asia.

★ ★ ★ ★ ★

E.B. WHITE, CHARLOTTE'S WEB

When his publisher first accepted the manuscript for *Charlotte's Web* in 1952, **E.B. White could only receive payments up to $7,500 a year in royalties,** allowing him to collect money from the book's success over a longer period of time. Twenty-seven years later, when he decided it was time to liquidate all assets due him, he collected a lump sum of more than half a million dollars. Needless to say, a large chunk of that check went to taxes.

> Beverly Cleary has never tried out her book manuscripts on children because they are "conditioned to please adults" and never answer honestly.

> While in school, E.B. White developed a paralyzing fear of public speaking and has declined every invitation to speak in public since then.

★ ★ ★ ★ ★

MICHAEL BOND, PADDINGTON BEAR

When Michael Bond first wrote the Paddington Bear series, **many people assumed Paddington was drawn after a bear native to Peru,** the spectacled bear. However, no one has ever proven a resemblance between the bear in the books and the photos from the wild.

Chapter 8

Cocktail Party Conversation: Useless Trivia

Cocktail Party Conversation: Useless Trivia

Do you know **Pippi Longstocking's** full name? **What author gave his birth date to a friend? Who really wrote the Little House books? What did many historic authors use as "inspiration" for writing? Use these juicy tidbits about your favorite authors to spice up your next cocktail party and stump your friends.**

★ ★ ★ ★ ★

- Author Robert May wrote "Rudolph, the Red-nosed Reindeer" in 1939. While brainstorming the story, he initially considered naming the famed reindeer Rollo or Reginald.

- At the age of fourteen, Anna Sewell fell while walking home from school in the rain, injuring both her ankles. The injury was likely not treated correctly, and she became lame for the rest of her life, unable

to stand or walk for any length of time. For greater mobility, she frequently used horse-drawn carriages, which contributed to her love of horses and concern for the humane treatment of animals. As she wrote *Black Beauty*, she dictated the text to her mother or wrote on slips of paper that her mother later compiled.

- Ralph Ellison's favorite books as a child were *Wuthering Heights*, *The Last of the Mohicans,* and *Jude the Obscure.*

- "Tintern Abbey" was one of the only poems William Wordsworth ever wrote that he didn't completely change through revisions and editing.

- *Pride and Prejudice* author Jane Austen was so humble and shy about her writing that no one ever caught her with a pen in hand. "No matter how suddenly one arrives, she has heard the door close … and hidden the white sheets," writes biographer Virginia Moore.

- *Pride and Prejudice* was originally titled *First Impressions.*

- Pippi Longstocking's full name is Pippilotta Provisionia Gaberdina Dandeliona Ephraimsdaughter Longstocking.

- When *Treasure Island* author Robert Louis Stevenson died in 1894, he put in his will that his November 13 birthday be gifted to a friend who hated her Christmas birthday.

- Born around 635 BC, Sappho was considered one of the first poets—she is remembered as "The Poetess"—while Homer, who was one of the only other poets to precede her, is remembered as "The Poet." Sappho's poems were first written on waxed wooden blocks before papyrus was discovered. Her works have survived through being quoted in Greek, Roman, and Egyptian documents. Only one of her poems exists in completion—"Hymn to Aphrodite"—which was quoted by Dionysius of Halicarnassus in 25 BC.

- When she was forty years old, Emily Dickinson said of Shakespeare's writings, "Why is any other book needed?"

- Critics of the Little House books often question just how involved Laura Ingalls Wilder's daughter, Rose, was in penning the series. Some argue that she was simply an encourager who helped her mother get in touch

with publishers and agents. However, others believe that Rose took the rough drafts and transformed them into the magical stories they are known as today.

- When short-story writer Eudora Welty was twenty-six years old, she offered her first story, "The Death of a Traveling Salesman," to be published in a little magazine that could not pay her for it. Until that point, she had never studied writing in college, nor had she ever belonged to a literary group.

- Washington Irving wrote *Rip van Winkle* overnight while staying with his sister in Birmingham, England.

- Some historic authors may have gotten their "inspiration" from fungi that feed on old papers. A British medical journal once reported that they can be hallucinogenic and can cause "enhancement of enlightenment" in readers.

- John Grisham is a distant cousin of former president Bill Clinton.

- Irish writer John Banville's wife described him as "a murderer who's just come back from a particularly bloody killing" when he sat down to write.

- Most famous for writing the play *Rozencrantz and Guildenstern Are Dead* and the screenplay for *Shakespeare in Love*, Tom Stoppard also edited scripts for *Indiana Jones and the Last Crusade* (1989), *Sleepy Hollow* (1999), and *The Widowmaker* (2002).

- Like most widowers, poet Sylvia Plath's husband took over her personal and literary estates when she committed suicide in 1963. He had overseen the publication of many of her manuscripts for years, but to protect her privacy he destroyed the journal encompassing three years of their relationship.

- Considered the father of the African novel, Chinua Achebe has received more than thirty honorary degrees from universities around Canada, South Africa, Scotland, England, Nigeria, and the United States. The schools include Dartmouth, Harvard, Brown, Cape Town, and Southampton.

- The original stage version of *The Wonderful Wizard of Oz* was quite different from L. Frank Baum's book. In fact, it was aimed at adults instead of children. Toto was replaced by a new character named Imogene the Cow, and included a waitress and a streetcar operator, among Dorothy's gang of fellow victims. On stage, Baum even had actors make critical references to Theodore Roosevelt, Senator Mark Hanna, and oil tycoon John D. Rockefeller.

- Isaac Asimov once said, "If my doctor told me I had only six minutes to live, I wouldn't brood. I'd type a little faster."

- At least twenty-one publishers rejected Golding's *Lord of the Flies* before Faber and Faber printed it in 1954.

- Rudyard Kipling died of a brain hemorrhage in 1936. He was seventy years old. However, it wasn't the first time his death was publicly announced. Several years earlier it was incorrectly printed as fact in a magazine. When he read the statement, he wrote, "I've just read that I am dead. Don't forget to delete me from your list of subscribers."

- While helping develop the James Bond films in 1962, writer Ian Fleming asked directors to let his cousin, actor Christopher Lee, play villain Dr. Julius No.

- Some believe that naturally left-handed *Alice's Adventures in Wonderland* author Lewis Carroll suffered psychologically by being forced to use his right hand.

- A treasure map with an X marking the location of the buried treasure is one of the most familiar pirate props, yet it is entirely a fictional invention which owes its origin to *Treasure Island* author Robert Louis Stevenson's original map.

- As a college student, poet Paul Blackburn became pen pals with the famed Ezra Pound. He even hitchhiked to Washington, D.C., a few times to pay his friend a visit in the hospital.

- Once when *Inferno* author Dante Alighieri was walking down the street in Verona—where his work was well known—he overheard a couple of women gossiping about him. One of the women, obviously commenting loudly enough for the author to overhear, crossed herself, then said, "Do you not see how his beard is crisped and his colour darkened by the heat and some down there?" She was referring to hell, of course.

- When poet Bob Kaufman heard about the assassination of John F. Kennedy, he was inspired by Buddhism to take a vow of silence. He didn't speak again until the end of the Vietnam War in 1975. His first words after several long years? He recited the poem "All Those Ships that Never Sailed."

- To please his father, William Golding enrolled in Oxford's Brasnose College as a science major before finally switching to his true love—English and poetry—after his junior year.

- Best known for his Church of Scientology self-help books, L. Ron Hubbard is an Eagle Scout.

- British science-fiction writer John Wyndham's real name is John Wyndham Parkes Lucas Beynon Harris.

- Belgian writer Georges Joseph Christian Simenon was able to write sixty to eighty pages a day and published 450 novels and short stories during his career.

- Children's author Gary Paulsen was a regular competitor at the Iditarod. He had to give up sledding and sold his dogs in 1990 because of heart problems. However, after more  than a decade in retirement sailing throughout the Pacific Ocean, he returned to the sport in 2003. He was supposed to compete in the 2005 Iditarod tournament but withdrew shortly before the race began.

- When Birmingham, Alabama, native and nationally acclaimed poet Sonia Sanchez was born in September 1934, her parents couldn't agree on a name for their second daughter and instead let relatives decide. They chose Wilsonia Benita. Her mother died during childbirth, and Wilsonia spent the next nine years going from relative to relative.

- Geoffrey Chaucer's father was kidnapped in 1324 by one of his aunts, who hoped he would force his son to marry her daughter. She was arrested and fined £250.

- Ralph Ellison's father, who died in a car accident when Ralph was just three years old, named his son after Ralph Waldo Emerson and had dreams that he would one day be a poet.

- Romance-novelist-turned-mystery-writer Janet Evanovich admits on her web site that at one point in her career, she collected rejection letters sent to her by publishers. When the box started overflowing, she would "burn the whole damn thing," put on some pantyhose, and head out to find some temp work.

- In 1932, *Death of a Salesman* author Arthur Miller couldn't afford to go to college so he worked as a truck driver, a waiter, and in an auto-parts warehouse for $15 per week.

- When poet Audre Geraldine was born, she didn't cry. She was so nearsighted that doctors thought she was legally blind. She didn't start talking until she learned how to read at four years old. It was at this point that she changed the spelling of her name, Audrey, because she did not like how the "y" hung down below the other letters. She opted to leave the "y" off, and she has spelled it that way ever since.

- In high school, Audre Geraldine became literary editor of the school arts magazine and had her first love poem published in *Seventeen*.

- The poet Lord Tennyson loved "tavern food" including stead, cheese, and new potatoes.

Real Cheesy Facts About: U.S. Presidents

Chapter 1

✦

Young and Restless: Presidents Before They Were Stars

TRUMAN

Young and Restless: Presidents Before They Were Stars

★ ★ ★ ★ ★ ★ ★ ★ ★ ★ ★ ★ ★ ★ ★ ★ ★

Not yet in the political limelight, the presidents filled their younger days with penny-pushing, romance, liquor, and a bit of mischief. From arguing with Mom over the family budget to nearly marrying the daughter of a famous Ku Klux Klan leader, these boys had a lot to learn before taking their pre-politician baggage to the White House.

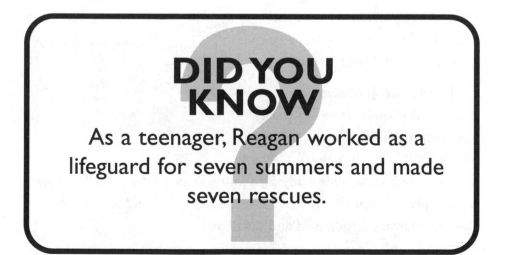

DID YOU KNOW

As a teenager, Reagan worked as a lifeguard for seven summers and made seven rescues.

★ ★ ★ ★ ★

WHAT'S IN A NAME?

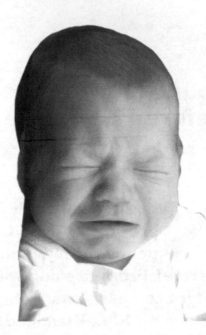

Thirty-third President Harry S. Truman's middle name is just that—"S." After a family feud about whether the new baby should be named after his paternal grandfather, Shippe, or his maternal grandfather, Solomon, Truman's mother threw up her hands and settled with what would please both sides.

Truman wasn't the only president with nominal issues. **President Eisenhower was initially named after his father**, David Dwight Eisenhower. However, the two men tired of being confused with the other, so Eisenhower decided to call himself Dwight David instead.

George Washington often carried a portable sundial in his pocket.

Lyndon B. Johnson's household didn't strive for clarity between their identities either—the entire family's initials are L.B.J. When Johnson realized his wife, Lady Bird Johnson, bore the same initials, the couple decided to stick with the cheesy trend and name their children likewise: Lynda Bird and Luci Baines.

★ ★ ★ ★ ★

DOLLARS AND SENSE

Not a very trusting woman, Mama Sara Roosevelt never allowed her son (Franklin Delano, that is) to manage the family money. Apparently, she didn't think he was capable of keeping track of the bills. She must have been waiting for his training—years spent presiding over one of the largest fiscal annual budgets on Earth while serving as president from 1933–1945.

As a young man, President James Buchanan was a stickler for a tight budget. His account books included nearly every penny he gave and received throughout his entire life. Even when he was worth more than $200,000 while serving as American Minister to Great Britain, Buchanan kept a careful list of everything he purchased—down to the buttons on his suspenders. In fact, he once refused a $15,000 check from friend Jeremiah Black because it was miswritten by ten cents.

> # DID YOU KNOW
> Eisenhower played football in college and was injured trying to tackle Jim Thorpe.

★ ★ ★ ★ ★

AILMENTS AND MALADIES

Possibly the sickliest president in U.S. history, James Madison suffered a nasty array of medical problems, from hemorrhoids and headaches to bouts of the flu, throughout his life. During the Revolution, Madison's health problems kept him from serving in the Continental Army.

Some early physicians suggested that staying indoors too much would weaken a man's health, so Madison's doctors pleaded with him to spend less time reading and more time strolling about outdoors. However, Madison wasn't one to listen. He often shut himself in a dark room as early as 9:00 a.m. to ward off the bothersome sunlight that provoked his migraines.

The son of a Presbyterian minister, Woodrow Wilson also seemed too plagued by ailments to have any future in politics. He struggled with dyslexia as a child. He also suffered from such severe heartburn that he often pumped water into his stomach to equalize the acid build-up.

However, by the time he was in his late forties, Wilson covered the sickly façade with charm, and he became a shoe-in for the presidency. He had received a Ph.D. from Johns Hopkins University and had authored several acclaimed history books on American politics. He went on to become famous for powerful legislative acts—the Federal Trade Commission Act and the Federal Reserve Act—that helped stabilize the country's desperate financial situation.

fabulous firsts
First left-handed president: James Garfield

★ ★ ★ ★ ★

LAST CALL FOR ALCOHOL

Rumors of Franklin Pierce's excessive drinking darkened his reputation as a senator in the 1830s. His wittiest opponents called him "a hero of many a well-fought bottle." At one point, he seemed to have gotten the problem under control, leaving his Senate seat for a career as a lawyer and joining the Temperance League in New Hampshire.

However, when Pierce became president, he fell off the wagon when a string of bad luck (and wild company) drove him back to the bottle. His son died in a train accident, his marriage fell apart, and he was surrounded by party-animal congressmen who just couldn't wait for a night (or two) on the town.

As a result, Pierce's years as president were plagued with loneliness and criticism. In 1869, he died of stomach inflammation, probably as a result of excessive alcohol consumption.

General Ulysses S. Grant was also known for his love of whiskey, but his heaviest drinking days were on the battlefield. A temperance committee once visited Lincoln and asked him to fire the general because of his nasty rumored addiction.

Noting Grant's widespread fame for winning battles, however, on November 26, 1863, the *New York Herald* reported Lincoln's reply as "I wish some of you would tell me the brand of whiskey that Grant drinks. I would like to send a barrel of it to every one of my other generals." Lincoln claimed the *Herald's* report was anything but accurate and denied ever making the comment.

Zachary Taylor did not vote at all until he was sixty-two years old. Because he was a soldier and moved so frequently, he couldn't establish legal residency and therefore could not even vote for himself when he ran for office.

★ ★ ★ ★ ★

THE FUGITIVE

The son of a laborer and a weaver, a poor couple who owned no land in their home state of North Carolina, **Andrew Johnson was by far the president most praised for turning rags into riches**.

But Johnson nearly ruined his chances of escaping poverty. When he became an apprentice to a tailor, he fled town without finishing the job (apparently he and some friends had thrown rocks at a neighbor's house and were afraid of being arrested).

Fourteen-year-old Johnson eventually begged for his job back, but his pitiful pleas were denied. Johnson honed his skills and moved his family to the

As a teenager, James K. Polk had a gallstone operation without any anesthesia.

Tennessee mountains to open a tailor's shop. Luckily, the business succeeded, and Johnson was able to marry his sixteen-year-old sweetheart, Eliza McCardle, before accepting the pressures of politics and running for governor.

★ ★ ★ ★ ★

HANGMAN HEAVEN

Born in New Jersey, Grover Cleveland made his fame and fortune while serving as the sheriff of Erie County and the mayor of Buffalo, New York, before running for president in 1893. During his tenure as sheriff, however, he did something no other American president had ever done before (and no future president would ever do)—he personally noosed the necks of a few of Erie County's most infamous criminals.

★ ★ ★ ★ ★

MEET THE PRESS

Warren Gamaliel Harding edited a blossoming small-town newspaper in Ohio called the *Star*. He loved his job so much that he actually had to be convinced to run for a Senate seat in the early 1900s. Compared to the hustle and

When nineteen-year-old Warren Harding and a few of his friends purchased the *Marion Star* in 1884, the paper was scarcely more than a flyer and had just a few hundred subscribers. Five years later, it had become the most popular newspaper in the county and one of the most successful newspapers in the state.

bustle of daily deadlines, however, politics seemed like a breeze.

Harding once said the only reason he stayed in the Senate for four whole years was that he had become a somewhat famous, respectable "gentleman" overnight and could pay the bills while under less stress than at the *Star*.

A man with very little confidence, Harding acclimated to the lazy days of socialite schmoozing and never dreamt of taking complete responsibility for the U.S. government. His wife, whom he called Duchess, disagreed. She wanted the prestige of living in the White House so badly that she eventually convinced him to campaign. Mrs. Harding thought she knew what was best, but she may have been wrong—while in office, her husband had two quite scandalous affairs with other women.

★ ★ ★ ★ ★

I CAN'T GET NO RESPECT

The only twentieth-century president not to have a college degree, Harry S. Truman received little respect from his political colleagues. He grew up working as a mail clerk, a bookkeeper, and a farmer. After fighting in World War I, he moved home and opened a men's clothing store in Kansas City, with little success.

Truman took a stab at politics, serving as a judge and a senator for a few years before his party talked him into running for vice president. However, Truman never had the tenacity and confidence to win over his political opponents. In fact, when he arrived at his predecessor's funeral in 1945, no one even stood to acknowledge that he had just become the new commander in chief.

Wary of filling FDR's shoes, Truman worked to earn clout, authorizing the use of atomic bombs against Japan to win World War II. Regardless, no one thought Truman would win reelection because of the country's drastic post-war economic slump.

On Election Day, the _Chicago Daily Tribune_ had already printed "DEWEY DEFEATS TRUMAN" on the front page of the following day's paper. Truman won, but he hardly had time to celebrate before the Cold War exploded, a communist dictatorship overtook China, and the Soviet Union started openly constructing atomic bombs.

Unfortunately, the bad luck of Truman's boyhood carried over into his second term—he just couldn't get a break.

★ ★ ★ ★ ★

SIX DEGREES OF PRESIDENTIAL SEPARATION

Some presidents may have been genetically set up for success—many of them were related to each other and to some of the brightest characters in history.

- **George Washington** was James Madison's half cousin twice removed, Queen Elizabeth II's second cousin seven times removed, Robert E. Lee's third cousin twice removed, and Winston Churchill's very distant cousin.

- **James K. Polk** was a great-grandnephew of John Knox, the founder of the Scottish Presbyterian Church.

- **Theodore Roosevelt** was Martin Van Buren's third cousin twice removed.

- **Grover Cleveland** was Ulysses S. Grant's sixth cousin once removed.

- **Franklin D. Roosevelt** was related to Winston Churchill and to his own wife, Eleanor (a second cousin). He was also related by either blood or marriage to eleven other presidents: John Adams, John Quincy Adams, Ulysses S. Grant, William Henry Harrison, Benjamin Harrison, James Madison, Theodore Roosevelt, William Taft, Zachary Taylor, Martin Van Buren, and George Washington.

- **George W. Bush** is distantly related to Benedict Arnold and Marilyn Monroe. He is also Franklin Pierce's fifth cousin four times removed, Theodore Roosevelt's seventh cousin three times removed, and Abraham Lincoln's seventh cousin four times removed.

  > George W. Bush and John Kerry have several cousins in common: Walt Disney, Michael Douglas, Clint Eastwood, the Wright Brothers, Hugh Hefner, Clara Barton, Princess Diana, and Howard Dean.

★ ★ ★ ★ ★

REDSKIN REBELLION

As a young captain serving under General "Mad Anthony" Wayne in the Northwest Territories, **William Henry Harrison proved stalwart against Native Americans** trying to stop white men from pushing west. In fact, he was so ruthless that President Adams made him governor of the Indian Territory (now Indiana and Illinois) to "negotiate" treaties with locals.

However, Harrison's idea of negotiation was a bit askew. He first defeated the tribes in battle, and then forced them to give up their land for pennies on the dollar. He paid one tribe a single cent for each 200 acres of a fifty-one million-acre deal.

Shawnee Chief Tecumseh did everything he could to organize a resistance and prevent the taking of his land by force, but he was killed after teaming up with the British in the War of 1812. As a result of his efforts to squash Native American resistance, Harrison became a national hero.

TAYLOR

Years later, **twelfth President Zachary Taylor was also famed as an "Indian fighter,"** but his motives as a soldier were for peace rather than prosperity. Taylor married Margaret Mackall Smith in 1810 and moved his family from military post to post before finally settling in Baton Rouge, Louisiana.

He often protected Native American lands from violent white settlers looking to invade. Taylor longed for peaceful coexistence between the two groups and relied on military involvement to keep both sides at bay. In the end, he was nicknamed "Old Rough and Ready" for his willingness to get his hands dirty and join his troops in battle for the sake of justice.

★ ★ ★ ★ ★

Win One for the Gipper

Young Ronald Wilson Reagan got his start in the acting world when his mother, a devout follower of the Disciples of Christ, made him take part in short skits at church. The audience's applause was intoxicating, and Reagan couldn't get enough of being the center of attention.

Graduating from college in the height of the Depression, Reagan lucked out with a part-time job as a sports announcer. He was officially discovered by Warner Brothers studios in 1937. His ability to memorize lines with ease made him a director's dream, and Reagan went on to make more than fifty-five films during a span of four decades. Most famous for his role as inspirational Notre Dame football player George Gipp in *Knute Rockne: All American*, Reagan made B-list film audiences swoon for many years.

Despite his romantic roles on the big screen, Reagan surrendered his dreamy ways when it came to his first wife, actress Jane Wyman. The two twisted lovebirds planned their marriage ceremony in Forest Lawn Cemetery in Glendale, California. (It's no wonder he became the first divorced president.)

★ ★ ★ ★ ★

SCHOOL'S OUT FOREVER

Whether as a short-time gig for some extra cash or a term as a university president, more than fourteen American presidents served as educators before or after their time at the White House. But dealing with restless children and belligerent parents weren't their most shining moments in history.

John Adams was the first president to become a teacher when he graduated from Harvard University in 1755 and became Latin master at a grammar school in Worcester, Massachusetts. It didn't take long before Adams was describing his students as "little runtlings, just capable of lisping A, B, C and troubling the master." After only two years of teaching, he fled education and became a lawyer.

Adams wasn't the only president-to-be who sprinted from the classroom to the courtroom. Andrew Jackson taught near his South Carolina hometown but hated it so much that he quit after less than a year to study law. Woodrow Wilson did the opposite—he quit his Atlanta law practice, earned a Ph.D., and went on to serve as a professor for nearly a decade. He taught history and coached football at Bryn Mawr College in Pennsylvania and taught political economy at Princeton University before being elected as president of the university and then president of the United States.

★ ★ ★ ★ ★

EXPULSION 101

> Ulysses S. Grant was nicknamed "Useless" as a child. His birth name was actually Hiram Ulysses Grant, but he changed it to Ulysses S. after fearing his classmates at West Point would tease him for having the initials H.U.G.

It's hard to believe that, after being expelled from his undergrad program as a young college boy in the early 1800s, **James Buchanan wormed his way back into college** and went on to become the fifteenth president.

Hoping his son would one day work alongside him, Buchanan's father sent him to study law at Dickinson College. But after one year, Buchanan senior received a letter saying his son had been kicked out due to "disorderly conduct." The school's president admitted that he would have dismissed Buchanan even sooner if his father weren't so darn respectable. Despite his reputation for drinking, smoking cigars, and taking part in a long list of other rowdy college-boy behaviors, Buchanan cajoled a family friend, who had just become president of the Board of Trustees, into reconsidering. He was granted his wish to re-enroll, and in September 1809, he graduated with a bachelor's degree.

★ ★ ★ ★ ★

SCHOOL OF SPANGLISH

When he was only twelve years old, **James Madison diligently studied both Spanish and Japanese**. But his language skills later proved painfully inadequate and led to paralyzing embarrassment. While a student at Princeton University, Madison was asked to serve as an interpreter for a French visitor. Madison soon realized he could barely understand what the man was saying. Ultimately, Madison passed the buck, blaming his old Scottish schoolmaster for teaching him a worthless dialect of "Scotch French."

★ ★ ★ ★ ★

WHITE SUPREMACY STUPIDITY

Once engaged to the daughter of a Texas Ku Klux Klan leader, Lyndon B. Johnson called off the wedding when he found out that his future father-in-law called his family a bunch of "shiftless dirt farmers and grubby politicians." "None of them will ever amount to a damn," he said, unaware that Johnson would one day become vice president under John F. Kennedy and later the thirty-sixth president of the United States.

★ ★ ★ ★ ★

SMALL-TOWN TINKERING

William McKinley was a simple man with simple beginnings. When he was born in 1843, his small Ohio hometown had "3 churches, 3 stores, 1 blast furnace, rolling mill, nail factory, forge, and about 300 inhabitants," the *Niles-Tribune Chronicle* wrote in 1999.

Several biographers have attributed McKinley's good manners, love of hymns and poetry, and dedication to his often-ill wife to his strong, small-town Methodist upbringing. Originally Scot-Irish Presbyterians, McKinley's parents were often caught up in fiery religious revivals and became Methodists when they moved to Ohio in the early 1800s. After a week of Methodist camp meetings in 1859, young McKinley asked to be baptized.

Although his mother prayed fervently for him to become a minister, the Civil War called him to battle instead. His regiment was devoutly religious and became known as "the psalm singers of the Western Reserve" for their fervent commitment to prayer and preaching. As president, McKinley wrote speeches that often reflected his religious commitments, as they were sprinkled with Christian phrases such as "the Lord most high" and "Him who is sovereign of land and sea."

Aaron Morton, one of McKinley's pastors from back home, said he "was not what you would call a 'shouting Methodist' but rather one who is careful of his acts and words."

★ ★ ★ ★ ★

POP GOES THE PISTOL

Before spending twenty-three years as a soldier, two-year-old Ulysses S. Grant was immune to the loud pop of gunfire. In fact, when a neighbor suggested playing a joke on the young child by firing a pistol nearby, Ulysses's father, Jesse, challenged the man to try it. He even bet that his son would not flinch at the noise. Though the pistol was fired close to the child's head, young Ulysses sang out in amusement, "Fire it again!"

★ ★ ★ ★ ★

SWORN INTO THE SKULLS

Born in 1924 to a wealthy banker named Prescott Bush, **George H.W. Bush went on to become the youngest pilot in the Navy** when he was just eighteen years old. After his plane was shot down during a WWII bombing mission in 1944, Bush returned home to Connecticut and married sweetheart Barbara Pierce, who once said Bush was the first man she ever kissed. The couple had six children (one died of leukemia at just three years old), and Bush enrolled at Yale University. There, he played baseball and became a member of an elite secret society known as Skull and Bones.

★ ★ ★ ★ ★

DITCHIN'

Reflecting on his rebellious childhood, **John Adams once told friends he hated studying Latin grammar** so much that he told his father he would rather do something else. In turn, his father suggested he try "ditching," and made him start digging a ditch in the family meadow. Though sweaty and exhausted by the manual labor, stubborn Adams stuck to his work for two days before laying down his pride and admitting he would, indeed, rather study Latin. For the rest of his life, Adams said the ditching experience played an important role in forming his character.

DID YOU KNOW

James A. Garfield weighed ten pounds when he was born and was the last president born in a log cabin.

★ ★ ★ ★ ★

RIGHT TO BITE

In the early 1900s, while president of Princeton University, **Woodrow Wilson ran into some roadblocks** when trying to promote intellectual growth among the country's most promising students. He conceived a system of "quadrangles" where students would live, eat, and study with faculty members on campus. Other highbrow institutions, such as Oxford and Cambridge, had been modeling similar programs, but Princeton's existing "fraternity-like eating clubs" refused to be replaced with the new concept. Eventually, the clubs' alumni rebelled, intimidating the school's trustees into dropping the idea.

★ ★ ★ ★ ★

MR. INDEPENDENT

Mature beyond his years, **John Quincy Adams did not feel the need to receive much schooling** before jumping into an early career in diplomatic affairs. At just fourteen years old, he became the private secretary of Francis Dana, the Chief Justice of Massachusetts. He then spent six months traveling in Europe before joining his father's political efforts in Paris. Adams ultimately ditched his daddy's dollars to live in the United States on his own. In his diary, he wrote, "I am determined that so long as I shall be able to get my own living in an honorable manner, I will depend upon no one."

★ ★ ★ ★ ★

HE'S GOT THE BLUES

After graduating from college in the mid-1700s, **James Madison fell into a surprisingly religious funk**. He immersed himself in biblical studies and turned from a lover of poetry and romance to a hard-nosed theologian, reasoning endlessly on the issue of free will. While other Virginia boys were romancing women, racing horses, and wrestling outdoors, Madison delved into the Scriptures, trying to find solutions to the obsessions that plagued him.

Chapter 2

Shaking Hands and Kissing Babies: Moments in Campaign History

JACKSON

Shaking Hands and Kissing Babies: Moments in Campaign History

★ ★ ★ ★ ★ ★ ★ ★ ★ ★ ★ ★ ★ ★ ★ ★ ★

With their lyrical "Tippecanoe and Tyler Too," William Henry Harrison's remarkably cheesy campaign strategy during the 1840 presidential election, the Whigs set the pace with the first campaign slogan ever. Since then, the desperate race to serve as the next commander in chief has led to everything from silly sing-song slogans and ridiculous rhymes to candidates' faces and poetic jingles on flasks and packs of cigarettes. Whether official jargon or simply products loosely associated with the campaign, these strategies are the worst of the worst.

When Andrew Jackson beat out John Quincy Adams in the election of 1828, the town of Adams, New Hampshire, originally named after the latter, changed its name to Jackson.

★ ★ ★ ★ ★

THE KNOW NOTHINGS

In 1849, New York's patriotic partisans formed a **secret society called The Order of the Star Spangled Banner**, which became so popular that just five years later, they had enough members to hold a national convention and nominate a candidate for presidency. However, the group did little to convince Americans that they had the know-how to run the country. Its members were strictly instructed to keep The Order's decisions and happenings secret, so they quickly became known as the "Know Nothing Party."

When asked for details on the party's political plans, members would reply, "I know nothing," and walk away. As ignorant and silly as the pact may have seemed, the appeal of the mystery worked until the group divided on the issue of slavery, and their candidate, former President Millard Fillmore, lost the election miserably.

When John Adams moved his family to Washington to live in the White House, they got lost in the woods for several hours. As they circled, they had no idea that they were just barely north of the city.

★ ★ ★ ★ ★

TIPPECANOE AND TYLER TOO

JACKSON

The first "modern" presidential campaign—one with rallies, slogans, and a slew of advertising—was organized in 1840 by the Whigs, an anti-General Jackson party that adopted its name from the British group opposing the monarchy. The Whigs were desperate to beat Jackson's incumbent, Martin Van Buren, and pulled out all the stops to woo voters. They held public barbecues and bonfires where they passed out cider in log-cabin-shaped bottles to support their candidate, William Henry Harrison.

An acclaimed war hero of the Battle of Tippecanoe in 1840, Harrison and his running mate, John Tyler, wanted to remind America who the bravest candidate on the ballot was with the slogan "Tippecanoe and Tyler Too." "Tippecanoe" referred to the battle in which Harrison and his forces slaughtered Native Americans resisting the western movement of white settlers in the early 1800s.

DID YOU KNOW?
Warren G. Harding coined the word "normalcy."

Regardless of the disrespect to the deceased, Old Tippecanoe managed to win the race. However, his victory was short-lived, as he died just thirty days after he took office. His grandson, Benjamin, would later carry on his legacy as president in 1889.

★ ★ ★ ★ ★

WHO IS JAMES K. POLK?

With his slogan—**"Who is James K. Polk?"**—Henry Clay tried to assert that no one had ever heard of (and therefore should never vote for) his opponent, the Democratic Party's nominee for president. But Clay's strategy backfired and may have actually imprinted Polk's name into voters' minds. The Democrats had deadlocked on other options for the candidacy and probably expected their "dark horse" to lose miserably, but Polk surprised them with a win.

★ ★ ★ ★ ★

THE CONTINENTAL LIAR FROM THE STATE OF MAINE

Grover Cleveland also thought he would slander his political opponent with a catchy slogan leading up to his 1884 election. Aware of some unethical investments and business deals Republican James G. Blaine had allegedly made during his career in the railroad industry, he came up with the sing-song "Blaine, Blaine, James G. Blaine—The Continental Liar from the State of Maine." While it sounds like a childish rhyme a group of six-year-old girls might sing while skipping rope, the slogan worked, and Cleveland sailed into office.

"Sensible and responsible women do not want to vote."
—Grover Cleveland

Blaine may have lost miserably, but he wasn't going down without a fight. He retaliated with his own jingle, taunting Cleveland for the out-of-wedlock child he was accused of having fathered before the election: "Ma, Ma, Where's My Pa ... Gone to the White House, Ha, Ha, Ha." Apparently America saw right through the raw rivalry and opted for a womanizer over a cheating businessman.

The turning point in this dirty mudslinging contest came when a Blaine supporter, Protestant minister Samuel Burchard, announced that Democrats were a party of "rum, Romanism, and rebellion." While Blaine could have stepped up and disassociated himself with the comments, he chose to stay out of the rumor mill. However, he was quickly tied to the minister's tirade, as the public assumed he, too, thought urban immigrants were "drunkards, followers of the pope, and the cause of the Civil War." Of course, Blaine lost his appeal to Irish voters, and Cleveland won by twenty thousand votes.

★ ★ ★ ★ ★

COX AND COCKTAILS

When James Cox announced his opposition to Prohibition just before he ran for president in the early 1920s, his opponent, Warren G. Harding, made up a catchphrase to paint him as a dark drunk with the slogan "Cox and Cocktails." Rather than conjuring up fond memories of college keg parties, the slogan worked, and Harding eased into his first term.

Cox wasn't the only presidential candidate to suffer from an anti-Prohibition stance. In 1928, New York Governor Alfred E. Smith was running against Herbert Hoover when it came down to influential Josiah William Bailey and Methodist Bishop James Cannon to influence voters nationwide. Bailey supported Democratic candidate Smith, while Cannon—an ardent Prohibitionist—was an energetic leader in the fight against him.

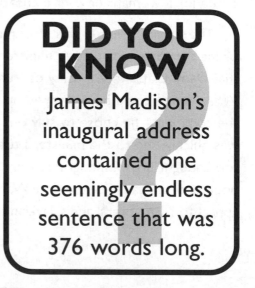

DID YOU KNOW

James Madison's inaugural address contained one seemingly endless sentence that was 376 words long.

★ ★ ★ ★ ★

ANYONE BUT PIERCE

It's one thing to be jeered at and slandered by your opponent's campaign, but **when your own party turns against you** and begs America not to vote for you, you know the strategy has gone south. In 1857, Democrat Franklin Pierce experienced this unfortunate scenario firsthand. His own party unofficially changed its slogan to "Anyone But Pierce." Understandably, the fourteenth president abandoned all hope for reelection.

★ ★ ★ ★ ★

PUT YOUR MONEY WHERE YOUR FAITH IS

When Republican Barry Goldwater and running mate William Miller campaigned for the presidency in 1964, they thought they would tug on the heartstrings of Christians nationwide with their request to **"Put Your Money Where Your Faith Is."** The couple claimed to have what "money can't buy"—their dedication, determination, and strong religious faith.

After they convinced America they were trustworthy men of God, they started pleading for pocket change to go not into the collection plate but toward their campaign, so they could fund what money can buy—television time, billboards, and newspaper ads.

> "I just won't get into a pissing contest with that skunk."
> —Dwight Eisenhower, referring to Senator Joe McCarthy

★ ★ ★ ★ ★

VOTE YOURSELF A FARM

In 1860, the **Republican Party and its shoe-in presidential candidate, Abraham Lincoln**, decided to play on the sympathies of a country thirsty for the quick money of the American Dream. In hopes that their "Vote Yourself A Farm" campaign paid off (literally), Lincoln and his associates promised to pass a law granting free land to anyone who moved their family out west.

But Lincoln didn't pioneer the concept. One widely distributed handbill from 1848, twelve years before Lincoln ran for president, read:

"Are you an American citizen? Then you are a joint owner of the public lands. Why not take enough of your property to provide yourself a home? Why not vote yourself a farm?

"Are you a party follower? Then you have long enough employed your vote to benefit scheming office seekers. Use it for once to benefit yourself: Vote yourself a farm.

"Are you tired of slavery? Of drudging for others? Of poverty and its attendant miseries? Then vote yourself a farm."

THE BULL MOOSE BLUES

"I want to be a Bull Moose
And with the Bull Moose stand
With Antlers on my forehead
And a Big Stick in my hand."
—Bull Moose Party jingle

★ ★ ★ ★ ★

YANKEE DOODLE WENT TO VOTE

Most of the cheesy (yet effective) campaign songs were parodies of popular American favorites, such as "Battle Cry of Freedom" and "John Brown's Body." Alfred Wheeler wrote the following tune for Zachary Taylor's 1848 campaign:

(sung to the tune of "Yankee Doodle")

We'll sing a song to suit the times,
With voices bold and steady,
And cheerily we'll tell in rhymes
Of good old Rough and Ready.
His foes may slander as they can,
And bluster at his manners,
Who cares a fig? He's just the man
To lead the Yankee banners.

Chorus:
Then Rough and Ready let it ring,
And set the bells a chiming,
Where'er we go we're bound to sing
His praises in our rhyming.

In Florida he gained a name
That won our admiration,
And loudly has his gallant fame
Been echoed thro' the nation.

There's not a heart in all the land,
That beats not firm and steady,
For the hero of the Rio Grande,
Old gallant Rough and Ready.

★ ★ ★ ★ ★

A FULL DINNER PAIL

When William McKinley campaigned for the presidency in 1900, he hoped **to win the hearts of the American public by passing out stamped metal dinner pails.** The hokey, but brilliant, scheme reminded voters of the country's prosperity during McKinley's first term as president. He won, but his second term came to an early, tragic end when he was assassinated at the Buffalo Pan-American Exposition in September 1901.

FDR served hot dogs to the King and Queen of England when they came to the White House for a visit

★ ★ ★ ★ ★

A CHICKEN IN EVERY POT AND A CAR IN EVERY GARAGE

Talking his fellow countrymen into the notion that they would be economically sound and secure if he were president in 1928, Herbert Hoover told voters that they would have **"a chicken in every pot and a car in every garage."** Little did he know that his staff would face the worst depression the country had ever seen.

★ ★ ★ ★ ★

NOT JUST PEANUTS

Jimmy Carter may have made a fortune working on the family peanut farm in Georgia, but he had other qualifications, too. During his campaign, Carter felt the need to plead with America (inconspicuously, of course) to consider the fact that he did have talents other than the ones related to his homegrown farmer-boy image. He passed out a T-shirt featuring his face and the line "Not Just Peanuts" to prove his point.

★ ★ ★ ★ ★

CHEESY MEMORABILIA: THE EARLY YEARS

Political campaigns have always meant freebie trinkets for those willing to stock their closets and put old items on eBay. Some historians say Andrew Jackson was the first presidential candidate to organize and distribute campaign memorabilia. However, most associate the diversity of mass-produced junk with William Henry Harrison's "Log Cabin" crusade. Aside from the ever-present lapel button, which made its appearance in the 1896 McKinley/Bryan election, tacky collectibles have included everything from paperweights and potholders to coffee mugs and pocket combs.

In 1945, the nonprofit organization American Political Items Collectors was founded "to encourage the collection, preservation, and study of political Americana." Today, the group has three thousand dedicated members (with too much time on their hands), including former Presidents Bill Clinton and Jimmy Carter. In honor of history buffs and trinket geeks alike, it is important to pay tribute to some of the strange, often desperate, attempts to win over the American public with stickers, beer mugs, and more.

★ ★ ★ ★ ★

SMOKIN' SAMUEL TILDEN

In the 1870s, Democratic candidate (and Governor) **Samuel Jones Tilden of New York teamed with Blackwell Durham Bull Tobacco Company** to print a round of advertisements pushing what would be his failed run for the presidency. On the front of the card was Tilden's face. As the card opened, it transformed into President Ulysses S. Grant, a Republican from Ohio who had served the term before and did not run in 1876. Tilden hoped to appeal to both political parties with the card, but his choice to campaign on a cigarette box just didn't pay off. The Republicans barely won the election, and Rutherford B. Hayes took office.

The card read:

> Come all you true born Democrats,
> You hardy hearts of oak,
> Who know a thing when it is good
> And Blackwell's Durham smoke.
> Gaze on this face and you will see
> Your presidential nominee
> The sage and statesman S.J.T.
> And all you good Republicans
> Will surely be enchanted
> When you behold the visage here
> And take the fact for granted
> That he will win if he will be
> Your presidential nominee
> The soldier, hero, U.S.G.
>
> But though you differ in your views
> Political, we hope
> You coincide when we remark
> The choicest brand to smoke
> Is Blackwell's Genuine Durham that
> Suits every taste no matter what,
> Republican or Democrat.

★ ★ ★ ★ ★

DRINKING DAYS ARE HERE AGAIN

Before smoking and drinking became today's health taboo, many candidates chose to win voters' hearts with tobacco and alcohol. Some passed out whiskey bottles. After Prohibition was repealed, FDR passed out shot glasses that read, "Happy Days Are Here Again." Tobacco-related campaign giveaways originated with free snuffboxes during early nineteenth-century elections. In the 1950s, Ike passed around cigarettes by the dozen, and in the 1950s, candidate Adlai Stevenson actually pasted his own face on a pack of cigarettes. In 1972, Nixon campaigned with bubblegum cigars.

Although George Washington was one of the wealthiest men in America, he had to borrow money to attend his own inauguration. His wealth was attributed to his vast amounts of property, but he had very little cash.

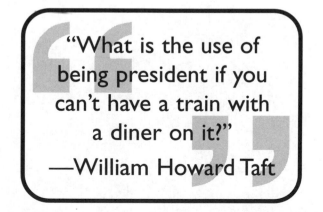

"What is the use of being president if you can't have a train with a diner on it?"
—William Howard Taft

Chapter 3

Fact and Fiction: Debunking Myths and Legends

Fact and Fiction: Debunking Myths and Legends

★ ★ ★ ★ ★ ★ ★ ★ ★ ★ ★ ★ ★ ★ ★ ★

Elvis was abducted by aliens, and the scary man with the hook knows what you did last summer. Well, not quite. American history is sprinkled with a ridiculous list of mind-boggling myths. From the origin of the seventh-inning stretch to the humble log-cabin beginnings of some of our favorite commanders in chief, one wonders if the history books ever get it right. The lavish, trend-setting lives of the American presidents are no different, yet so many history buffs tell tales that, well, never actually happened.

> William Taft was the tubbiest commander in chief to ever hold office. Maybe he should have cut back on the cheese.

★ ★ ★ ★ ★

MYTH 1 • THE SEVENTH-INNING STRETCH

Taft is credited with accidentally instigating a major baseball tradition—the seventh-inning stretch. Apparently, as a game between the Washington Senators and the Philadelphia Athletics dragged on, he became quite restless in his small, wooden stadium chair and got up to stretch his legs in the middle of the seventh inning. Seeing their president rise to his feet, the crowd stood to show its respect. When Taft sat down a few minutes

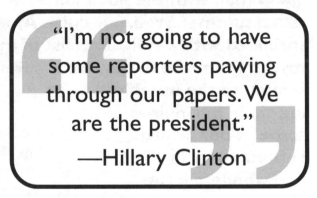

"I'm not going to have some reporters pawing through our papers. We are the president."
—Hillary Clinton

later, everyone else in the stadium followed his lead and the game continued. Unfortunately, the tale is nothing more than folklore.

On April 14, 1910, Taft did become the first president to throw the first pitch commemorating the baseball season's opening day. The Senators and the Athletics were warming up at Griffith Stadium when, at the last minute, umpire Billy Evans tossed Taft the game ball and asked him to give it a throw toward home plate. Every president since—except Jimmy Carter—has opened at least one season.

Taft is not the only man credited with having inspired this baseball tradition. Some say Brother Jasper of Manhattan College invented it in the late 1800s. Others credit Harry Wright of the Cincinnati Red Stockings. Historians claim to have uncovered an 1869 letter in which Wright observed that baseball fans naturally tend to mill about during the seventh inning. Ultimately, very little evidence remains that Taft was the first to practice it.

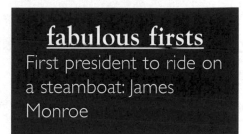

fabulous firsts
First president to ride on a steamboat: James Monroe

★ ★ ★ ★ ★

MYTH 2 • WRITING ON RUBBISH

Most children learn that **Abraham Lincoln penned his famous Gettysburg Address on the back of an envelope** while traveling on a train. While the story is inspiring (and impressive, considering how bumpy railroads were in the 1860s), records at The Lincoln Museum in Fort Wayne, Indiana, suggest otherwise. They show that

Lincoln worked on the address both before and after his train ride from Washington, D.C., to Gettysburg. And he used official stationery, not an old scrap of envelope, for the first handwritten draft.

★ ★ ★ ★ ★

MYTH 3 • IT'S A FARMER'S LIFE FOR THEE

American history hails the tale of the heartless liberals who once told Native Americans to **join the culture of white men and learn how to farm or die**. In 1808, Thomas Jefferson did tell the Delewares to "begin every man a farm, let him enclose it, cultivate it, build a warm house on it, and when he dies let it belong to his wife and children after him."

However, author James W. Loewen says legislation had been passed in at least one state that would punish anyone who taught Native Americans how to read and write. And as for teaching them how to farm, Native Americans in many states already lived a life of agriculture. Regardless of what the history books may say, Loewen believes conflict was inevitable.

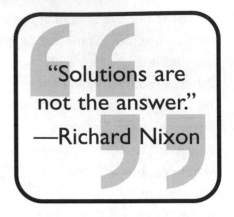

"Solutions are not the answer."
—Richard Nixon

★ ★ ★ ★ ★

MYTH 4 • THE WHOLE TOOTH AND NOTHING BUT THE TOOTH

While it is true that at his inauguration President George Washington only had one natural tooth, **his dentures were never actually made**

of wood. Nor were they made by Paul Revere, as many legends proclaim. Washington did go through several pairs of choppers, but they were made out of lead and human or animal teeth. In fact, his inauguration speech— only 183 words long—took a whole ninety seconds to read because the dentures were so cumbersome.

Elementary-school lessons aside, Washington also never chopped down a cherry tree. And he never threw a dollar across the Potomac River. Where did all these myths originate? They most likely made their first appearance in the book *A History of the Life and Death, Virtues, and Exploits of General George Washington*, which was published by a parson named Mason Locke Weems just after Washington's death. Washington was larger than life to his admirers, and that's just how Weems wanted to portray him.

fabulous firsts

First president to ride in an automobile to his own inauguration: Warren G. Harding

One of Weems's fabrications about George Washington's life, however, still persists at Valley Forge National Historic Park. In the popular, beautiful Washington Memorial Chapel, a stunning stained glass window portrays General Washington kneeling in prayer. A National Historic

Park pamphlet explains that the image commemorates a moment of humility as Washington sought God's guidance at a desperate time of war. The same image of the kneeling general is displayed in bronze statues at the Pennsylvania Freedom Foundation and in a painting at the Valley Forge Historical Society museum. In a magazine article in 1804, Weems wrote, "while Washington ... lay encamped at Valley Forge, a certain good old friend, of the respectable family name of Potts ... had occasion to pass through the woods near headquarters. Treading his way along the venerable grove, suddenly he heard the sound of a human voice ... [it was] the commander in chief of the American armies on his knees in prayer!"

Despite the story's romanticism, historian Paul F. Boller Jr. insists the fable is completely false. The man by the name of Potts who Weems claimed saw Washington was certainly not near the forge in that winter of 1777. Regardless, the myth lives on—in 1928, the United States Postal Service issued a two-cent stamp, displaying Washington on his knees, in honor of the battle at Valley Forge's 150th anniversary.

"If it takes the entire army and navy of the United States to deliver a postcard in Chicago, that card will be delivered."
—Grover Cleveland

THE LINCOLN-KENNEDY COINCIDENCES

While some think the strange-but-true links between Abraham Lincoln and John F. Kennedy are incredible, others are skeptical. Freaky but historically true, is this timeline a twilight-zone trick or simply a coincidence? You be the judge.

- Lincoln was elected to Congress in 1846.

- Kennedy was elected to Congress in 1946.

- Lincoln was elected president in 1860.

- Kennedy was elected president in 1960.

- The names Lincoln and Kennedy both contain seven letters.

- Both lost their children while living in the White House.

- Both were shot with one bullet, in the head, on a Friday.

- Lincoln was shot in Ford Theatre.

- Kennedy was shot in a Ford Lincoln vehicle.

- Lincoln's secretary was named Kennedy.

- Kennedy's secretary was named Lincoln.

- Both men's successors were named Johnson. Andrew Johnson was born in 1808. Lyndon Johnson was born in 1908.

- John Wilkes Booth, who assassinated Lincoln, was born in 1839.

- Lee Harvey Oswald, who assassinated Kennedy, was born in 1939.

- Booth ran from the theater and was caught in a warehouse. Oswald ran from a warehouse and was caught in a theater.

- Both assassins were assassinated before their trials.

★ ★ ★ ★ ★

MYTH 5 • BATHTUB HISTORY BLUFF

In 1917, a writer named **H.L. Mencken published a startling account of America's love affair with the bathtub** in the *New York Evening Mail.* An obvious crock, his tale was written off the top of his creative little journalistic head—but the public believed every word. In the article, Mencken notes that physicians across the nation believed bathtubs to be a serious health danger. At one point, he writes that legislators in Boston and Philadelphia tried to pass laws against owning them, but he writes that opposition to bathing sitting down ended in 1851, when Millard Fillmore had a tub installed in the White House. If the president could have one, then the people could too.

Shocked (and amused) that his lie had become a part of American history, Mencken remained silent for ten years while his story grew roots and became household trivia. In May 1926, he finally publicly admitted that his article was fabricated and that he never expected such widespread acceptance (and so little fact checking). Regardless, the article was published again, just a few months after his confession, in *Scribner's Magazine.* In the 1930s, a book was written on his theory. The madness doesn't stop there—in the 1970s, Mencken's spoof was even published in the *Dictionary of American History.*

★ ★ ★ ★ ★

MYTH 6 • DEAF MAN WALKING

If you've ever seen the Lincoln Memorial, it's hard to deny that the hands on **the giant stone statue seem to be posed in the American Sign Language symbols for the letters "A" and "L."** However, the daughter of sculptor Daniel Chester French insists that molding the president's initials was not her father's intent. French claimed to have modeled his work after casts of both Lincoln's hands and his own hands. Thus, there is no secret message communicated through the memorial. Some suspicious history buffs claim that the face of Lincoln's greatest nemesis, Confederate leader Robert E. Lee, was secretly carved into the back of the statue. That, too, is a myth.

★ ★ ★ ★ ★

MYTH 7 • THE PILFERED CADAVER

Panic-stricken Lincoln fanatics can breathe a sigh of relief: His corpse was never stolen by a band of thrill-seeking thieves. Between 1865 and 1871, Lincoln's body was kept in a receiving vault, then in a vault at Springfield's Oak Ridge Cemetery, before being transferred to the official Lincoln Tomb in 1871. There was a plot to steal the body eleven years after Lincoln's death, but the 1876 attempt to steal it and hold it for ransom was thwarted by officials before the theft could be pulled off. When the tomb was rebuilt three decades later, it was covered with several feet of concrete to prevent bandits from dreaming of a burglary.

★ ★ ★ ★ ★

MYTH 8 • THE FLATULENT STEED

In November 2003, the Internet was rife with e-mails circulating the story of **President George W. Bush and his stinky carriage ride** from an airport in Great Britain to Buckingham Palace with Queen Elizabeth II. After riding in a 1934 Bentley to Central London, Bush and Her Majesty boarded a magnificent seventeenth-century coach pulled by six stunning white horses, the e-mail read. "Suddenly the scene was shattered when the right rear horse let rip the most horrendous, earth-shattering, eye-smarting blast of flatulence, and the coach filled with noxious fumes." Apparently, the two managed to keep their cool until the Queen apologized for the incident. Bush, confused, thought she was admitting to being the source of the dizzying stench.

While Bush did make a formal visit to England and dine with Queen Elizabeth II in November 2003, the story about the carriage ride is mere imaginative Internet banter. The joke, writes a reporter for a popular urban legend website, is an old one. Through the years,

---

SLANG OF THE UNION

While some doubt that the phrase "It's OK." originated with Martin Van Buren, the legend is true. Van Buren grew up in Kinderhook, New York, and became known as "Old Kinderhook" when he first got involved in politics. When asking for him, his associates would say, "Is it O.K.?" The phrase stuck and has been carried through more than 150 years of slang ever since.

variations of the story have been told, placing the Prime Minister of Canada, the Archbishop of Canterbury, and a slew of other bigwigs in the protagonist's smelly seat. One Internet version even makes Ronald Reagan and Bush's forerunner Bill Clinton the subject of the tall tale. The earliest version, however, may have been in the 1972 novel *Post Cabin*, by Patrick O'Brian.

★ ★ ★ ★ ★

MYTH 9 • THE REAL FIRST PRESIDENT

While the most widely accepted historical accounts name George Washington as the first official president of the United States, it is not exactly true. Some say **John Hanson, Maryland's representative at the Continental Congress, was the first true leader of the nation**. On November 5, 1781, he was elected by his associates as the "President of the United States in Congress Assembled" and served for one year. Two other men served before him, but he was the first to use the title. Seven other leaders succeeded him before Washington was elected.

★ ★ ★ ★ ★

MYTH 10 • JEFFERSON MIS-REMEMBERED

The Jefferson Memorial in Washington, D.C., presents the writings of Thomas Jefferson so that sightseers can reflect on the third president's infinite wisdom. Most visitors don't know, however, that the Jefferson Memorial rearranges several quotes and therefore (according to some historians) misrepresents Jefferson's original message and ideals.

For example, one panel leaves out five words of the preamble and conclusion of the Declaration of Independence. The fantastic fumble was purposeful, as the architect who built the memorial thought it would make the carefully etched phrases fit better on the display.

On another panel, which displays Jefferson's thoughts on religious freedom, the memorial first presents three quotations from Jefferson's "Act for Religious Freedom" and then adds to the end a random fourth sentence that was not a part of the Act at all—it is from a letter he wrote to James Madison ten years later. The sentence reads, "I know but one code of morality for men whether acting singly or collectively." However, in this sentence, Jefferson was not talking about religion at all—he and Madison were corresponding about the economy.

★ ★ ★ ★ ★

Myth 11 • Rough Riders Redeemed

Teddy Roosevelt has long been famous for leading his Rough Riders up San Juan Hill during the Spanish-American

War's Battle of San Juan. However, they actually charged up nearby Kettle Hill—a smaller mound of land to the right of famous San Juan. By the time Teddy and gang ascended and descended Kettle Hill and followed the rest of the American troops up San Juan Hill, the Spanish fleet was long gone, having fled in surrender. Regardless, the Rough Riders were so popular with the American public that when Roosevelt ran for governor of New York in 1898, he had several former soldiers dress in their military garb and campaign alongside the president-to-be.

★ ★ ★ ★ ★

Myth 12 • Log Cabin Lies: Part 1

William Henry Harrison did not live up to the rumors of his log-cabin birth. Instead, he was born in a brick mansion on a wealthy plantation along the James River. The log-cabin myth actually came about during Harrison's 1840 campaign for presidency, when a newspaper accused him of wanting nothing more out of life than a "pension, plenty of hard cider, and a log cabin." Instead of taking the comment as an insult, the Whigs took advantage of the mockery and presented their candidate as a humble, simple man with a small-town background to which any man could relate. Harrison never validated the rumor that he was born in a log cabin, but to uphold his image, he never denied it, either.

★ ★ ★ ★ ★

Myth 13 • Log Cabin Lies: Part 2

Lincoln is rumored to have been born in a small cabin on Sinking Spring Farm near Hodgenville, Kentucky, in February 1809. However, by the time Lincoln was assassinated, the cabin seemed to have disappeared. It may have burned down, or neighbors could have torn it apart to use the wood for their own construction efforts.

In 1895, two men, Alfred Dennett and Rev. James Bigham, bought the Lincoln family's farmland, built their own cabin on the property, and tried to pass it off to tourists as the actual building in which Lincoln was born. Fortunately, few passersby made the trip to tour their "historic" hoax, but Bigham wasn't through with his scheming. If the tourists wouldn't come to them, they would go to the tourists. They took the cabin apart and reassembled it at the 1897 Tennessee Centennial Exposition in Nashville and the 1901 Pan-American Exposition in Buffalo.

Eventually, magazine publisher Robert Collier bought the Hodgenville farm and the logs from the so-called Lincoln Cabin (for a whopping $1,000) and shipped them back to Kentucky—stopping the train in a few cities along the way so people could pay to touch them for good luck.

Although it was honest about the building's true beginnings for a time, today the Park Service in Hodgenville claims the "Traditional Lincoln Birthplace Cabin" is real (and even prohibits visitors from using flash photography for fear it could damage the sacred logs). In his book *Lies Across America*, myth-buster James W. Loewen reports that the National Park Service brochure "Abraham Lincoln Birthplace" does say, "because its early history is obscure, there is lack of documentation to support to authenticity of the cabin," but many other sources cite its absolute validity.

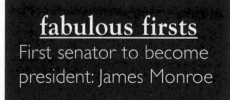

fabulous firsts
First senator to become president: James Monroe

★ ★ ★ ★ ★

MYTH 14 • THE NAKED TRUTH

A typo in The Washington Post made Woodrow Wilson the object of America's gruesome gossip mill when a reporter described his evening out at the theater with new fiancée Edith Galt in 1915. Despite the article's report that "the president spent most of his time entering Mrs. Galt" that evening, rumors that the two lovebirds were getting it on in the back row were completely untrue. The reporter meant to write that "the president spent most of his time entertaining Mrs. Galt."

That press error wasn't the only terrible mix-up suffered by a president, however. After his inauguration in 1901, Teddy Roosevelt suffered the fallout from a similar spell-check mistake when a New York reporter writing on the occasion accidentally misspelled the word "oath" in the article. Instead of an "o," he printed a "b," and his report read, "For sheer democratic dignity, nothing could exceed the moment when, surrounded by the cabinet and a few distinguished citizens, Mr. Roosevelt took his simple bath, as President of the United States." Talk about a revealing mix-up.

Chapter 4

Red-handed and Pants Down: White House Bad Boys on Their Worst Behavior

HOOVER

Red-handed and Pants Down: White House Bad Boys on Their Worst Behavior

★ ★ ★ ★ ★ ★ ★ ★ ★ ★ ★ ★ ★ ★ ★ ★

Kissing babies and decreasing the country's deficit are all well and good when it comes to improving the future (and the image) of America, but the tantalizing secrets of the presidents' private lives are much more interesting. While busy charming voters, each man had a few skeletons in his closet. Some commanders in chief were abhorrent whiners, while others dodged rumors of adultery. Some cursed the press, while others skirted nasty run-ins with the law. From spitting on the White House carpets to embarrassing America abroad, these moments of presidential misbehavior made for some of the White House's greatest public relations nightmares.

John Tyler became the only former president named a sworn enemy of the United States when he joined the Confederacy twenty years after his term ended in 1845.

575

★ ★ ★ ★ ★

SEXUAL HEALING

Bill Clinton may have been the most recent U.S. president to shame his family name with a romp around the White House, but sex scandals are not new to the Oval Office.

In 1802, rumors of Thomas Jefferson's alleged rendezvous with slave Sally Hemings were widely published in capital newspapers, but historians tend to dismiss the accusations as nothing more than rumors.

Ten years before Grover Cleveland became president in 1885, a store clerk named Maria publicly named him as the father of her illegitimate son. Cleveland did not deny the claim, but he kept quiet until the press dug up the truth during his campaign years later. Cleveland's opponents used his dirty little secret against him, taunting him with the rhyme "Ma, ma, where's my pa? Gone to the White House, ha, ha, ha!"

Twenty-ninth President Warren G. Harding was also no stranger to paternity problems. Known as quite the ladies' man, he fathered a child out of wedlock in 1919 while he served in the Senate. Despite public knowledge of the relationship, it continued throughout his presidency. After Harding's death in 1923, his mistress got rich off the juicy details printed in her best-selling book, *The President's Daughter*.

★ ★ ★ ★ ★

STRAIGHT FROM THE AP (ANNOYING PRESS, THAT IS)

Lyndon B. Johnson wasn't going to put up with any crap from nosy members of the press looking to pry into his personal life and political agenda. When a reporter once asked a question Johnson didn't feel like answering, he replied, "Why do you come and ask me, the leader of the Western world, a chicken-shit question like that?"

DID YOU KNOW

At twenty-four, Warren G. Harding suffered a nervous breakdown and spent several weeks in a sanitarium in Battle Creek, Michigan.

Johnson was known to be crass in all areas of his life, however—not just with the media. He would belch, curse, and throw back whiskey in front of guests at his ranch in Texas. He also was known for his way with words and often remarked, "I never trust a man unless I've got his pecker in my pocket."

Ronald Reagan may not have used such colorful language at home or at press conferences, but he did have his own tactics for avoiding nosy reporters. He would often take their questions on the White House lawn with his helicopter roaring in the background, which distorted his voice and left interviewers straining to hear his replies.

★ ★ ★ ★ ★

DUELING DUDES

Although famed as a gentle, self-controlled leader, Abraham Lincoln accepted Democrat James Shields's challenge to a duel in 1842. Angry that Lincoln had written a series of anonymous letters mocking him in the *Sangamo Journal*, Shields wanted his revenge. Lincoln proposed they fight in a 10-by-12-foot square with "cavalry broad swords of the largest size." Being much shorter than Lincoln, the standards put Shields at quite a disadvantage, but he was prepared to fight to the death. Luckily, the two men stalled long enough for friends to arrange a peaceful settlement before the duel ever took place. Both men walked away with nothing more than hurt pride.

★ ★ ★ ★ ★

SLAVE-HATER HYPOCRITE

Thomas Jefferson's original version of the Declaration of Independence actually incorporated a clause to abolish slavery, condemning it as abhorrent, but the Continental Congress disagreed and removed the phrasing from the final draft. While Jefferson was an outspoken opponent of slavery all of his life, no one really understood his passionate (and hypocritical) stance—Jefferson's personal estate housed and was run by more slaves than nearly any other estate in the nation.

Historians can only speculate as to why Jefferson thought he needed hundreds of slaves. Even with so much help, Jefferson had serious financial problems most of his life. He was more than $100,000 in debt by the time he died in 1826.

★ ★ ★ ★ ★

BOYS WILL BE BOYS

Andrew Jackson was quite the man's man when it came to bad habits. In an attempt to make his love for chewing tobacco less revolting, he bought a handful of spittoons for the East Room of the White House. While some complained Jackson was wasting government money, others acknowledged that the

president's nasty spitting could ruin the expensive carpets (and gross out guests). And Jackson wasn't the only president to have a tantalizing taste for tobacco.

John F. Kennedy loved the smell and taste of Cuban cigars so much that he commissioned a friend to buy and stockpile 1,500 premium Havanas just before the signing of the Cuban Trade Embargo, legislation that would have prevented him from buying his beloved stogies in the future.

Franklin Delano Roosevelt was also a sucker for a smoke. Although his doctors urged him to quit smoking, a long cigarette dangling from his lips became his trademark look.

All stories of White House smoking and spitting aside, **no president lit up more than Ulysses S. Grant**. While some thought his horrible drinking habit would lead to his death, the more likely cause was his love affair with the cigar. Grant rarely was seen without one in his mouth, and his adoring public contributed to his addiction. After Grant's victory at Fort Donelson on February 16, 1862, admirers sent him more than ten thousand boxes of cigars. Perhaps the attempt to smoke them all led to his death from throat cancer in 1885.

> "You know, if I were a single man, I might ask that mummy out. That's a good-looking mummy."
> —Bill Clinton, admiring an Inca mummy named Juanita

★ ★ ★ ★ ★

Do As I Say, Not As I Do

For a president serving at the peak of Prohibition in the 1930s, Herbert Hoover was a pro at finding the legislation's loopholes (and the nearest watering holes). He would often visit the Belgian Embassy in Washington, D.C., for cocktails. Because the building was considered foreign soil, all libations served there were perfectly legal.

HOOVER

★ ★ ★ ★ ★

PRAYING PLAYBOY

Jimmy Carter was open about his religious duties during his presidency, often juggling cabinet meetings with Bible studies and teaching Sunday School at First Baptist Church in Washington, D.C. For some reason, however, the evangelical Christian agreed to an interview with *Playboy* in 1976.

In his discussion with the reporter, Carter admitted that he had lust in his heart and, from time to time, felt attracted to other women. "I've looked at a lot of women with lust," he said. "This is something that God recognizes I will do … and God forgives me for it." His confession was shocking to some but amusing to others, who were happy to see the human side of their president. Carter was quick to tell his interviewer that he was shamed by this fatal attraction and felt it was as bad as if he actually had cheated on his poor wife, Rosalynn.

★ ★ ★ ★ ★

SILENCE OF THE MAN

Not a man of many words, Calvin Coolidge was nicknamed "Silent Cal" by some. He was once so rudely quiet at his own White House dinner party that a female guest made a bet that she could get him to say more than two words. Upon hearing about the wager, the president looked her in the eyes and said, "You lose." Coolidge and his family were often so discreet about the conversations they did have in public that they would use sign language so as not to be overheard. "If you don't say anything, you won't be called on to repeat it," Coolidge said.

★ ★ ★ ★ ★

HANKY PANKY

Republican President William McKinley wasn't much help when it came to his wife's medical woes. Though journalists tried to protect her integrity by rarely writing about her health, First Lady Ida was an epileptic. She often had untimely seizures at public political gatherings, speeches,

Some say the term "the big cheese" originated when Thomas Jefferson was given a 1,235-pound chunk of cheese.

and dinners—in the middle of which her not-so-charming husband would simply place his handkerchief over her face until the embarrassing episode subsided. McKinley claimed the darkness of his hanky helped calm his wife's episodes.

★ ★ ★ ★ ★

PR FOR THE POTTY MOUTHS

While dishing out moral codes as a general, George Washington decided to clean up the dirty language raging on the battlefield to create a more honorable image for the U.S. army. To that end, he issued an order that forbade soldiers from swearing.

★ ★ ★ ★ ★

EPICUREAN ETIQUETTE

As America came into its own and the country's etiquette shifted away from prim and proper English traditions, **Thomas Jefferson became the first president to shake hands rather than bow** to his respected visitors. His patience was tested, however, after he was sworn into the presidency in 1801. When he returned to his boarding house for dinner, he found the place packed. Every seat was filled, and no one rose to offer a seat to the nation's newest leader. Eventually, a Kentucky senator's wife stood up for him, but Jefferson—never one to dethrone a lady—politely declined.

Jefferson's table manners, on the other hand, were often hardly up to par. He was known to let his pet mockingbird, Dick, perch on his shoulder throughout the day and eat bits of food directly out of his mouth at the dinner table.

★ ★ ★ ★ ★

VULGAR VEGGIES

Regardless of any charm President George H.W. Bush may have communicated on camera, he was less polite while dining, both at home and in public. He refused to eat broccoli, pitching a little fit and saying, "I am the President of the United States, and I don't have to eat it!" Southern vegetable farmers were so upset at his pronouncement that they delivered truckloads of broccoli to the White House in protest.

★ ★ ★ ★ ★

CULTURE SHOCK

Bush's faux pas extended beyond the dinner table. In January 1992, he drove through Australia holding up to the crow what he thought was a universal symbol for "victory." Unfortunately, no one bothered to tell the president, who had just told the press that he was an expert at global hand gestures, that the "V" he was forming with his fingers was tantamount to flashing the middle finger in the United States. By the time Aussie demonstrators returned the symbol to Bush and chanted their disdain for American leadership, it was simply too late for apologies.

DID YOU KNOW? McKinley could shake hands at the rate of 2,500 per hour.

The following term, **Bill Clinton suffered similar cross-cultural woes** when he wrote a letter to the Romanian government, thanking them for the lovely poncho they had given him after his most recent trip to their country. Confused, government officials had to explain to Clinton that what they had given him was not a poncho but a Romanian flag. The center of the flag, which used to bear the symbol of communism, had been cut out after the country overthrew the previous communist regime. Clinton assumed the hole was for his head.

CLINTON

> "Our enemies are innovative and resourceful, and so are we. They never stop thinking about new ways to harm our country and our people, and neither do we."
> —George W. Bush

★ ★ ★ ★ ★

Unanimity

In an act of bitter history-making during the 1820 election, one New Hampshire delegate cast his electoral college vote for an unknown candidate rather than for favorite James Monroe. Why? Because he wanted George Washington to remain the only president in history to be elected unanimously.

★ ★ ★ ★ ★

Sacred Sabbath Services

When Zachary Taylor was inaugurated in May of 1849, he inconvenienced the entire country by refusing to take the Oath of Office on a Sunday. This left the offices of president and vice president vacant for the day, so David Rice Atchison, the president pro tempore of the Senate, had to be sworn in. When asked what he did on his one day as president, Atchison said, "I went to bed. There had been two or three busy nights finishing up the work of the Senate, and I slept most of Sunday."

★ ★ ★ ★ ★

POMP AND HONORARY CIRCUMSTANCE

When thirteenth **President Millard Fillmore was offered an honorary Doctor of Civil Law degree** from Oxford University, he refused. "No man should accept a degree that he cannot read," he said. Eighteen years later, however, Herbert Hoover couldn't have disagreed more. The youngest member of Stanford University's first graduating class, he received more than eighty honorary degrees in his lifetime.

★ ★ ★ ★ ★

WHITE HOUSE WHINERS

Moving into the White House proved quite a drag for twenty-third President Benjamin Harrison. The five-bedroom mansion suddenly seemed small, as he struggled to find space for his daughter's family and several of his wife's relatives who were dying to move in.

After building extra living quarters on 16th Street, the Harrisons found something else to complain about: the food. Apparently French cook Madame Pelouard's pastries just couldn't please the president. According to the *New York Sun*, "the new cook's dishes laid him out," and Harrison let her go in exchange for an African-American chef from Kentucky whose plain-Jane dishes were more pleasing to the Harrison family's picky palate.

If his hollerin' about housing and food weren't enough, Harrison may have suffered from a bit of jealousy as well. His grandchildren, cute little Benjamin and Mary Lodge McKee, were the joys of his life—but they were also a hot topic in the press. Truckloads of toys were delivered to the White House in their name. In fact, the babies received so much attention that Secretary Halford requested that reporters lay off the children and focus on the real political bigwigs. He would have hated, he said, for people to "believe the tales about this child's having more influence than the members of the Cabinet."

> Warren G. Harding once lost all of the White House china gambling on one hand of cards.

★ ★ ★ ★ ★

CELEBRITY STUDY BUDDIES

During his second year at Bowdoin College in Maine, Franklin Pierce attended class with the likes of Nathaniel Hawthorne and Henry Wadsworth Longfellow. Pierce, though, had the worst study habits and the lowest grades of anyone in his class. All first impressions aside, Pierce changed his slacker ways before graduation and ended up placing third in his class.

★ ★ ★ ★ ★

READY TO RUN

Despite how rude his ranting may have sounded, James Buchanan may have had good reason to complain about how tired he was of running the country. The nation was becoming increasingly divided over the issue of slavery, and the Whigs were destroyed, giving birth to the Republican Party. Buchanan's excitement for leaving office was so extreme that he actually slipped a note to his successor, Abraham Lincoln, wishing him better luck. "If you are as happy on entering the White House as I on leaving," the note read, "you are a happy man indeed."

> Theodore Roosevelt's lifelong interest in zoology began when, at seven years old, he saw a dead seal at a local market.

★ ★ ★ ★ ★

DIRTY DRAFT-DODGERS

When Grover Cleveland was drafted as a young man, he was so scared that he paid someone else to enter the armed forces in his place. During Cleveland's campaign for presidency, his opponent, James Blaine, ridiculed him for his yellow-belly ways, but the public soon discovered Blaine was guilty of the same deception.

Lincoln had a substitute fight for him during the Civil War, but he was no draft dodger. He actually felt strongly that a president should fight alongside his brave countrymen, but his presidential duties precluded his service. J. Summerfield Staples, the son of an army chaplain from Pennsylvania, heard of Lincoln's heartache and volunteered to fight in his place. He survived the war, and today his headstone reads:

> J. Summerfield Staples
> A private of
> Co. C176 Reg. P.V.
> Also a member of the
> 2, Reg. D.C. Vol.
> A substitute for
> Abraham Lincoln
> Died
> Jan. 11, 1888
> Age 43 yrs, 4 mos. & 27 days

★ ★ ★ ★ ★

TAKE ME DRUNK, I'M HOME

After coming down with typhoid fever just days before his vice presidential inauguration, Andrew Johnson found comfort in whiskey. The night before his big day he attended a party with a friend. The next morning a hung over and weak Johnson asked for more whiskey. He was a little tipsy upon arriving at the inauguration ceremony. Obviously feeling ill, he would have preferred to skip the proceedings altogether, but newly elected Lincoln suggested he reconsider. So Johnson showed up and delivered one of the most incoherent, slurred speeches in history.

★ ★ ★ ★ ★

Do the Bush Thing

In 1992, President George H.W. Bush visited Japan for a state dinner with dignitaries including Japanese Prime Minister Kiichi Miyazawa. After turning white as a sheet and nearly sliding out of his seat in pain, he threw up in Miyazawa's lap. Ever since, the Japanese have honored Bush with the word *bushusuru*, which literally means "to do the Bush thing," or to vomit.

★ ★ ★ ★ ★

Indecent Book Proposal

Martin Van Buren was not all that dedicated to treating his wife and family with respect. His home life always took a back seat to his political aspirations. Although he married a young Dutch woman who bore him five sons (it was rumored that the couple spoke Dutch at home), his wife died after twelve years of marriage. Later, when Van Buren penned his autobiography, politics continued to take precedent—he fails to mention his late wife a single time.

★ ★ ★ ★ ★

Driving Miss Crazy

Ulysses S. Grant was once arrested for driving his horse too fast on the streets of Washington, D.C. The president was fined $20, until the officer at the scene realized he had just pulled over the leader of the country. Grant, however, insisted he comply like any other law-abiding citizen and pay up.

The first president born in the nineteenth century, **Franklin Pierce also had his share of trouble with the law**. He was once charged with running over a woman with his horse, but the charges were dropped in 1853 when a judge decided there was insufficient evidence against him.

★ ★ ★ ★ ★

Road-Rage Reprimand

Woodrow Wilson was a stickler for conscientious driving and refused to accommodate people who even appeared to be traveling faster than he. In fact, he ordered his driver never to exceed twenty miles per hour and believed that anyone going fast enough to pass him was a reckless driver worthy of arrest. He ordered the Secret Service to pull over and question anyone who passed his limousine. However, his agents realized the ridiculous nature of Wilson's request and always returned empty-handed, claiming they simply could not catch the speeders. But the president continued his stubborn road-rage ways, even asking the attorney general to grant him the power to arrest speeding drivers. However, he was denied his request, and the Secret Service persuaded the president that it would be fruitless to go about policing the roadways himself.

★ ★ ★ ★ ★

RAGING RACIST

Richard Nixon was impeached after the government subpoenaed his library of taped conversations. In the process, America gained a whole new insight into the president's sharp personal opinions on an array of topics.

- On Italians: "Difference is … they smell different, look different, act different. … The trouble is, you can't find one that's honest."

- On affirmative action: "With blacks you can usually settle for an incompetent because there are just not enough competent ones."

- On reporters: "I wouldn't give them the sweat off my balls."

- On leadership: "You're never going to make it in politics. You just don't know how to lie."

★ ★ ★ ★ ★

I Cannot Tell A Lie

Telling a tall tale for the sake of political protection, Grover Cleveland once announced he was going on a fishing trip in July 1893. In truth, he was having surgery to remove a strange growth from inside his mouth. Most of his upper-left jaw had to be removed and replaced with an artificial jaw made of vulcanized rubber. He kept the condition under wraps because he feared rumors of his health might darken the country's bleak economic landscape further. The secret was safe with his surgeon, though. The truth didn't surface until twenty-four years later.

★ ★ ★ ★ ★

Million-Dollar Crybaby

Theodore Roosevelt was blind in his left eye. To compensate for the poor physique he inherited in the wake of a sickly childhood, he began working out at the gym and took up boxing lessons. While a student at Harvard University, he lost the boxing championship  during an infamous fight with C.S. Hanks. Most people believe Roosevelt was blinded after a punch in a friendly White House boxing match during his term.

★ ★ ★ ★ ★

ROB THE CRADLE OF LOVE

After unexpectedly becoming president when William Henry Harrison died in April of 1841, John Tyler got straight to work (wooing his son's girlfriend, that is). Tyler's son, John Jr., was in love with a young girl named Julia Garner from New York. Julia had probably come to town simply to find herself a husband, and the two met while mingling among society's richest bigwigs. However, before John Jr. could make his move, his father stepped in. While Julia was captivated by the president's power, she refused his proposal of marriage. But when her father was killed in an accident, Julia fainted in despair like a true Southern belle. Tyler came to her rescue and carried her off—the ultimate romantic gesture. She married him June 26, 1844.

★ ★ ★ ★ ★

MEN APART

John Adams and Thomas Jefferson couldn't have had less in common. Adams was a Northerner and a lawyer determined to abolish slavery. Jefferson, on the other hand, was a Virginia man who depended on slavery to maintain his extravagant lifestyle. Regardless, the two men mutually respected each other—until arguments over tactics during the French Revolution and the limits of the president's power tore them apart. Eventually, the two men stopped talking altogether. Publicly expressing his disdain for Adams, Jefferson once said, "He is vain, irritable, and a bad calculator of the force and probable effect of the motives which govern men." Ironically, both men died on the same day: July 4, 1826.

★ ★ ★ ★ ★

RETURN TO SENDER

Quite thrifty when it came to his snail mail, Zachary Taylor refused to cover any postage due on correspondence sent to the White House. After the Postal Service issued its first official stamp (one year before Taylor's nomination), mail was paid for by the recipient rather than the sender. A great war hero from the Mexican War, Taylor was a popular pen pal, but was unwilling to pay the ten-cent charge and, as a result, refused most of his mail. Because of this stingy stance, he didn't receive notification of his nomination as the Whig party's candidate for presidency until several days after the fact.

★ ★ ★ ★ ★

DINNER IS SERVED

Twenty-second **President Grover Cleveland was used to the bachelor life** when he moved into the White House for the first time in 1885. (He served two nonconsecutive terms and returned as the twenty-fourth president in 1893.) He certainly was not accustomed to ornate china,

CLEVELAND

exquisite living quarters, or fine foods. "I must go to dinner," he once wrote in a letter, "but I wish it was to eat a pickled herring, a Swiss cheese, and a chop at Louis' instead of the French stuff I shall find [here]."

★ ★ ★ ★ ★

WHO'S YOUR DADDY

While he may have been a tightwad at the dinner table, Cleveland was even worse when it came to appropriating government money. He once denied desperate farmers in drought-stricken Texas $10,000 worth of seed grain. He also vetoed a bill proposing private pension plans for Civil War veterans who incurred disabilities from somewhere other than the battlefield. Cleveland explained that passing out funds and "running to the financial rescue every time a countryman cried for help would only establish the government as a Daddy to bail everyone out in times of trouble."

★ ★ ★ ★ ★

PRESIDENTIAL POINT-OF-VIEWS

While you may not want to do business with someone who is stubborn and disagreeable, research presented at the American Psychological Association's (APA) annual convention in August 2000 revealed these two character traits are often associated with America's greatest presidents. The report also indicated that "good" presidents were extroverted and assertive, but not straightforward, organized, or vulnerable. In the end, each American president was put in one of eight categories (some fell into more than one group):

- **The Dominators**—Nixon, Andrew Johnson, Lyndon Johnson, Jackson, Polk, Theodore Roosevelt, and Arthur

- **The Introverts**—John Adams, John Quincy Adams, Nixon, Hoover, Coolidge, Buchanan, Wilson, and Benjamin Harrison

- **The Good Guys**—Hayes, Taylor, Eisenhower, Tyler, Fillmore, Cleveland, Ford, and Washington

- **The Innocents**—Taft, Harding, and Grant

- **The Actors**—Reagan, Harding, William Henry Harrison, Clinton, and Pierce

- **The Maintainers**—McKinley, George H.W. Bush, Ford, and Truman

- **The Philosophers**—Garfield, Lincoln, Jefferson, Madison, Carter, and Hayes

- **The Extroverts**—F.D.R., Kennedy, Clinton, Theodore Roosevelt, Reagan, William Henry Harrison, Harding, Jackson, and Lyndon Johnson

Chapter 5

Fads and Fetishes: Presidential Pastimes

CARTER

Fads and Fetishes:
Presidential Pastimes

★ ★ ★ ★ ★ ★ ★ ★ ★ ★ ★ ★ ★ ★ ★ ★ ★

The presidents and their adoring fans get a little out of control when it comes to the things they loved. Whether it's outrageous hobbies, preposterous pets, crazy collections, or the ridiculous gifts they both gave and received, these presidents' personal obsessions were legendary.

DID YOU KNOW

Warren G. Harding had an Airedale dog that sat in his own chair at Cabinet meetings. His dog, Laddie Boy, delivered his newspaper each day. It even had a birthday party, including a cake made of dog biscuits.

★ ★ ★ ★ ★

EARLY ENTREPRENEUR

Jimmy Carter may have been nuts about nuts, but he sometimes took the passion a bit too far. Sure, he became a millionaire when he improved production at the family peanut farm in Georgia, but who would have a giant peanut-shaped balloon at his own inauguration? Well, Carter did … but those who mocked his wacky escapade could learn a thing or two from the country-boy politician with a knack for making a buck. Before his peanut fame, at just nine years old, Carter bought a few bales of cotton for just five cents per pound and stored them until inflation caused the price to more than triple.

★ ★ ★ ★ ★

THE BREAKFAST OF CHAMPIONS

A kid at heart, Lyndon B. Johnson loved Fresca soda so much that he had the fountain drink installed in the White House. With the push of a button, he

Quite curious of psychic phenomena, Abraham Lincoln and his wife held regular séances on the White House grounds.

could have a cold one anytime—even first thing in the morning. Johnson wasn't the only president with wacky mid-morning cravings:

- **Ulysses S. Grant** regularly ate a cucumber soaked in vinegar for breakfast.

- **Calvin Coolidge** loved to have someone rub Vaseline on his head while he ate breakfast in bed each morning.

- **Franklin Delano Roosevelt's** wife, Eleanor, ate three chocolate-covered garlic balls every morning to improve her memory.

> **DID YOU KNOW?**
> John Quincy Adams owned a pet alligator and pet silkworms.

- **Theodore Roosevelt's** love affair with coffee made Maxwell House a huge success. One cold morning, while visiting Andrew Jackson's home in Nashville in 1912, he inspired their famed motto when after a warm gulp he said, "That coffee tastes good, even to the last drop!"

★ ★ ★ ★ ★

MARIJUANA MAN

George Washington and Benjamin Franklin may not have been potheads, but while in France raising money for the Revolution, Franklin

took over negotiations with the king so Washington could get home to his marijuana plants in Virginia. He was once quoted as saying, "I wouldn't miss the hemp harvest at Mount Vernon for all the tea in China." However, Washington never planned on getting high off his weed. Hemp, or marijuana, was the number one cash crop at the time and was used to make clothes and paper.

★ ★ ★ ★ ★

CARD SHARKS AND LINK LOVERS

During their two-term stay at the White House, Dwight and Mamie Eisenhower were obsessed with playing cards. In fact, they would regularly fly friends in to Washington, D.C., to make sure they had enough gamers for bridge night. Their addiction, however, never matched Old Ike's obsession with hitting the links. During his two-term presidency, he spent an incredible 150 days a year playing golf and even had a putting green built on the White House lawn.

Eisenhower was also quite picky about his help. Years serving as the most powerful man in the nation must have gone to his head, because he eventually demanded that someone help dress him daily. Assistant John Moaney was known to put the president's watch and even his underpants on Eisenhower. Once he left the

fabulous firsts
First president to host Thanksgiving Dinner at the White House: James Polk

White House, Eisenhower was completely unable to take care of himself. He had to learn how to turn on the television and even dial a phone for the first time in years.

THESE ARE A FEW OF MY FAVORITE THINGS

The oldest man to ever serve as president, Ronald Reagan caused quite a stir when he announced both his guilty pleasures and his medical provisions. When he purchased a hearing aid during his White House reign, sales for the product went up a whopping 40 percent in the United States. When he joked with the press about his sweet tooth and obsession with the bowl of jelly beans in the Oval Office, sales of jelly beans also skyrocketed (some records say the White House purchased twelve tons of the candy during his term).

LESS (CLOTHING) IS MORE

An avid skinny-dipper, John Quincy Adams was committed to taking nude baths in the Potomac River nearly every morning at dawn (when the weather agreed, of course). Anne Royall, a curious national journalist desperate for an interview, went to the river one morning to try and catch him at one of his most … vulnerable moments. Refusing to leave without a decent quote, Royall sat on the president's change of

> "If you have a job in your department that can't be done by a Democrat, then abolish the job."
> —Andrew Jackson

clothes until he bashfully agreed to talk to her from the water. Before then, no woman had ever interviewed a president.

★ ★ ★ ★ ★

PARDON ME

Most people know that Abraham Lincoln was a man of great mercy—when it came to pardons, he loved to rescue indigents on death row. All it took was an influential letter from an admiring fan (or an influential politician), and he would let a criminal off the hook. Lincoln's lenient ways were tested in 1862, when he was asked to authorize the largest mass hanging in American history.

A group of Sioux Indians had murdered more than eight hundred men, women, and children in a Minnesota settlement in an attempt to take over the town and eat their food (they were literally starving to death). A total of 307 Native Americans had been sentenced to death. Afraid that they had been tried unjustly and therefore would be punished unjustly, Lincoln reviewed all 307 convictions. True to form, he pardoned all but thirty-eight of them. It still qualified as the largest mass hanging in the nation's history, and thousands of spectators showed up to watch the executions.

★ ★ ★ ★ ★

The Unlikely Inventor

Thomas Jefferson was a man of many talents, but few people know that his home, Monticello, is sprinkled with an array of peculiar creations. When historians first toured the building, they found inventions including a homemade copy machine, dumbwaiters, a hideaway bed, a calendar clock, and a rotating closet shelf so that—with the turn of a stick—his hanging clothes could spin on display.

★ ★ ★ ★ ★

Life, Liberty, and the Pursuit of Fish

Herbert Hoover was most content in the woods, hiking through rugged trails and fishing for trout. At a meeting for the Izaak Walton League of America, an organization that works to preserve and protect the nation's woods and wildlife, he once said of his favorite pastime, "Man and boy, the American is a fisherman. That comprehensive list of human rights, the Declaration of Independence, is firm that all men (and boys) are endowed with certain inalienable rights, including life, liberty, and the pursuit of happiness—which obviously includes the pursuit of fish."

Just before his death, Hoover published a book on the topic called *Fishing for Fun and To Wash Your Soul*, reminding his readers of the joy and peace that comes from life in the outdoors.

In fact, Hoover was such an advocate for outdoor exercise that he had White House physician Admiral Joel T. Boone invent a game called Hoover-Ball to keep him fit. A combination of tennis, volleyball, and medicine ball, the game was given its name by a clever *New York Times* reporter in a 1931 article titled "At the White House at 7 a.m." Early each morning, a group of four to eighteen friends known as the Medicine Ball Cabinet would show up for the Hoover-Ball games on the White House lawn.

★ ★ ★ ★ ★

FOR LOVE OF THE GAME

Herbert Hoover wasn't the only sports fan to grace the White House. **Grace Coolidge, wife of thirtieth President Calvin**

RULES OF HOOVER-BALL

- Teams of 2-4 players play on a 66-by-30-foot court

- Equipment: Six-pound medicine ball and an 8-foot volleyball net

- Scoring is modeled after tennis, and teams play best-of-five or best-of-seven games.

- The ball is served from the back line, and points are scored when a team fails to catch a return, fails to return the ball across the net, or returns the ball out of bounds.

- There is no running with the ball or passing to teammates before throwing the ball back over the net.

- A ball returned from the front half of the court must be returned to the back half of the opponent's court.

- A ball that hits the out-of-bounds line is counted as in.

- A ball that hits the net on its way over is a live ball.

- Women's rules differ. They may serve from the mid-court line, pass once before a return, and return the ball to any area of the opponent's court.

- Good sportsmanship is required. Points in dispute are played over.

Coolidge, was known as "the greatest White House baseball enthusiast of all time." She called the sport "her very life" and would often implore her husband to make sure they were in town for all the big games at Fenway Park. It is rumored that she would curl up in a chair in the sitting room and knit while she listened to radio play by plays of all the games she could not attend.

Grace also used baseball to fuel her other passion—encouraging children with disabilities. A lip-reading teacher at the Clarke School for the Deaf in Massachusetts, she and Red Sox manager Joe Cronin once organized a special day for local deaf children to attend a Boston game. Her love for the game was so intense that her *Boston Globe* obituary on July 9, 1957, was headlined, "Long Active Red Sox Fan."

★ ★ ★ ★ ★

GOD BLESS US EVERYONE

A loyal reader of the works of Charles Dickens, James A. Garfield attended Dickens's lectures every time he visited the United States. In fact, during one visit, Dickens was doing a formal reading of *A Christmas Carol* when an unruly dog in the building barked obnoxiously just as he read the words "Bless his heart: It's Fezziwig again!" Garfield thought the event was so hilarious that every time he met someone who had attended one of Dickens's readings he greeted them with "Bow wow!"

President Zachary Taylor used to ride his horse in the womanly sidesaddle position as he rode into battle. After the glory days, he kept his old warhorse grazing on the White House lawn for years. Little did he know that visitors would pluck hairs from it for souvenirs.

★ ★ ★ ★ ★

Light 'Em Up

A thorough prankster,
George H.W. Bush loves his own
sense of humor and often
cracks himself up. He made a
hobby of messing with the stiff
politicians who passed
through the White House
from time to time.
Sometimes he greeted
Oval Office visitors with
a windup bumblebee
that would spin around

the floor as they entered the room. He was also known to carry
around a voice-activated monkey toy that would bop itself on the
head whenever someone started talking. His favorite game, though,
was something he called "Light 'em Up." He would roll down the
windows in his limousine, pick people out in a crowd, and make them
smile. He would look at them until they noticed his goofy stare and
realized that the president of the United States was looking right at
them. When his target's face lit up in joy, Bush would win the game.
"Did I get her? Did I light her up?" he would say.

★ ★ ★ ★ ★

SILLY SUPERSTITIONS

Abraham Lincoln's mother, Nancy, passed on a lifetime worth of obsessions and superstitions to her presidential son. H. Donald Winkler, author of *Lincoln's Ladies*, writes that "a bird flying in the window, a horse's breath on a child's head, a dog crossing a hunter's path—all meant bad luck to Nancy Lincoln and her frontier neighbors."

Woodrow Wilson loved golf so much that he would even play in the winter and use black golf balls so he could spot them in the snow.

The Lincoln family also believed that the brightness of the moon played a huge role in daily decision making. One could only make soap or plant certain trees and vegetables when the moon shone brightly. Above all, Nancy insisted that adversity would plague a project started on a Friday. Abe would spend the rest of his life a bit confused by all the suspicions his mother had taught him at such a young, influential age.

But Lincoln was not the only president to be distracted by superstitions. Dwight Eisenhower carried three coins with him at all times for good luck—a silver dollar, a five-guinea gold piece, and a French franc. Franklin Roosevelt would never light three cigarettes off of the same match, and he hated the number thirteen. He refused to sit at a table set for thirteen guests.

★ ★ ★ ★ ★

JESUS IS MY HOMEBOY

Touting one's religious affiliation has long been a fad among politicians. Theodore Roosevelt announced some of his most passionate stances as a Christian. At the same time, he strongly opposed the engraving of "In God We Trust" on the nation's new $20 gold coin in 1907. He felt it was blasphemous to put God's name on money so often used to buy "worldly" things, and he pressed for the motto to be removed. Sinful spending aside, the public disagreed with Roosevelt and the motto remains.

Thomas Jefferson was also not afraid to flaunt his fascination with all things religious. It has been argued that his writings communicate a confusing conundrum of beliefs that bounce among Deism, Episcopalianism, and Unitarianism. Jefferson was never an official member of a congregation or denomination, and in some of his works he even rejected the divinity of Jesus Christ.

fabulous firsts
First president to own a radio: Warren G. Harding

According to a report by the Public Broadcasting Service, "Jefferson was convinced that the authentic words of Jesus written in the New Testament had been contaminated. Early Christians, overly eager to make their religion appealing to the pagans, had obscured the words of Jesus with the philosophy of ancient Greeks and the teachings of Plato."

Jefferson wrote several books based on what he believed to be the true message of Jesus in Christian texts. In 1820 he completed *The Life and Morals of Jesus of Nazareth Extracted Textually from the Gospels in Greek, Latin, French, and English.* In the book, printed after his death and typically referred to as the "Jefferson Bible," Jefferson

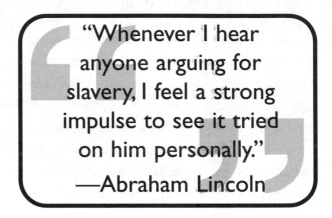

"Whenever I hear anyone arguing for slavery, I feel a strong impulse to see it tried on him personally."
—Abraham Lincoln

translated the New Testament in four different languages, omitting any words he thought were "inauthentic." His critics, however, argue that all he did was rearrange passages that either sounded supernatural or simply rubbed him the wrong way.

Finally, **William McKinley also referenced God when making political decisions.** In 1899, when trying to decide whether to annex the Philippines, he told a group of Methodist clergymen that God told him to go ahead with the deal. Apparently, he had prayed about the issue while pacing around the White House and God finally told him just to consider the islands "a gift from heaven."

★ ★ ★ ★ ★

FURNITURE FASHION POLICE

Chester Arthur may not have planned on taking up the hobby of decorating the White House when he was inaugurated in 1881, but when he first swung open the doors to the famed mansion, he was so appalled at the mismatched furniture that he ordered every piece removed. After a whopping twenty-four wagonloads took the furniture to auction, Arthur had the entire White House remodeled in late Victorian style. When William McKinley moved into the White House in 1897, his wife, Ida, was similarly disgusted with one particular color—yellow. She hated the color so much she forbade its use on the grounds. She even had the gardeners pull every yellow flower out of the garden.

★ ★ ★ ★ ★

PRESIDENTIAL PETS

When it comes to presidential pets, the nation's greatest leaders had some of the most interesting pets to ever grace the country. Check out the following fun facts on the coolest animals to ever lift a leg on the White House lawn:

- **Lyndon B. Johnson** had two pet beagles named Him and Her. Him's paw prints are actually imprinted in the sidewalk leading up to the White House pressroom. Later, J. Edgar Hoover gave Johnson a third beagle named Edgar.

- **Jimmy Carter** had a dog named Grits.

- **George Washington** had six white horses. He had their teeth brushed every morning.

- **William Henry Harrison** had a pet goat named His Whiskers.

A sucker for weird morning rituals, Thomas Jefferson claims to have soaked his feet in cold bath water every day for sixty years. He said it was what led to his unusually long lifespan of eighty-three years.

- **Martin Van Buren** was given two tiger cubs by the Sultan of Oman in 1837, but Congress decided they were a gift to the American people—not just the president—and the animals went to the zoo.

- **William McKinley's** pet parrot could whistle "Yankee Doodle."

- **Woodrow Wilson** kept a flock of sheep on the White House lawn. He often used their wool to raise money for the Red Cross during World War I. One of the sheep, named Old Ike, was rumored to chew tobacco.

- **Calvin Coolidge** had a number of dogs and cats, as well as a donkey named Ebenezer, a raccoon named Rebecca, and a goose that was once cast in a Broadway play.

- At the height of the Cold War, Russian Premiere Khrushchev sent **John F. Kennedy's daughter, Caroline**, a dog named Pushinka.

It was the puppy of the first dog in space, Strelka. Before Kennedy allowed his daughter to take the pooch, he had the army x-ray it for bugging devices.

- Explorers Lewis and Clark gave **Thomas Jefferson** two grizzly bear cubs. He was so fascinated by them that he had a cage built on the White House lawn so all visitors could marvel at the beasts from the West.

- **George H.W. Bush's** wife, Barbara, had a spaniel named Millie that was once referred to as "the ugliest dog in the capital." Ignoring the comment, the First Lady went on to write the bestselling *Millie's Book*, a look at life in the White House through her dog's eyes.

> ### fabulous firsts
> First president to use loudspeakers at his inauguration: Warren G. Harding

Less than twenty miles from the White House, The Presidential Pet Museum in Lothian, Maryland, is a mecca for presidential-pet fanatics. Founded in 1999 as a means to "preserve information, artifacts, and items" related to all the animals who have ever scratched or sniffed their way around the presidential mansion, the museum displays more than 1,500 "items of interest," including a portrait of Reagan's Bouvier des Flandres and photos of George Washington's pony. A little too highbrow for walk-ins, the museum can be toured only by appointment.

★ ★ ★ ★ ★

PRESENTS FOR THE PRESIDENTS

Presidents have had both friends and enemies among the American public. Many of them make a hobby out of collecting cheesy, handmade creations from their adoring fans. Some of the most unsightly gifts have been put on display across the country.

An exhibition in the Circular Gallery of the National Archives put some of these thoughtful, yet sometimes hideous, collections on display in March 1996. And while the gifts are unusual (for lack of a better word), museum officials' overzealous descriptions were even worse. "Although most of the artists represented are not well known, their works are no less striking," a commemoration on a government website reads. "Often expertly crafted, these gifts are heartfelt expressions of admiration and affection for the president." You be the judge.

★ ★ ★ ★ ★

RIDE 'EM COWBOY

This wooden image of a cowboy lassoing Adolf Hitler was given to Franklin D. Roosevelt by Secretary of Commerce Jesse Jones during the first few months of World War II.

Image provided by White House Historical Association

★ ★ ★ ★ ★

THESE BOOTS WERE MADE FOR WALKING

These hand-painted, steel-toe shoes were customized for President Eisenhower.
Complete with symbols of the U.S. Capitol, the Great

Image provided by White House Historical Association

Seal of the United States, and sunflowers from his home state of Kansas, they're some patriotic footwear.

★ ★ ★ ★ ★

CARICATURES GONE WRONG

When Lyndon B. Johnson was recovering from gallbladder surgery in the middle of his six-year term, Texan Gene Zesch thought he would brighten the president's day with a painted wooden figure representing his great progress. Although Johnson had certainly made political strides, signing more than two hundred bills into law

Image provided by White House Historical Association

during his term, he was probably a little alarmed by the not-so-flattering depiction of his persona.

Image provided by White House Historical Association

Like a laughable marionette, this **Richard Nixon** look-alike doll was given to the president as a symbol of America's victory in World War II.

Finally, **Gerald Ford** received this painted Pennsylvania river stone from Michael Manning of Pennsylvania in 1976. At a whopping seventy pounds, the rendering makes the president look quite round.

Image provided by White House Historical Association

★ ★ ★ ★ ★

OPERATION CHESS

During Operation Desert Storm in the early 1990s, E. Howard Kellogg's nephew was held hostage in Iraq. Kellogg found comfort in recreating the battlefield at home with a handmade chess set. After America's victory and his nephew's safe return, Kellogg mailed the game set to President George H.W. Bush for safekeeping.

Image provided by White House Historical Association

★ ★ ★ ★ ★

HALF-ASSED

When Harry S. Truman enacted his Fair Deal domestic program, calling for increased funding for education, a tax cut, an end to discrimination, and new economic support for farmers, Secretary of Agriculture Charles F.

Image provided by White House Historical Association

Brannon was so thrilled that he sent Truman this giant papier mâché donkey for a job well done.

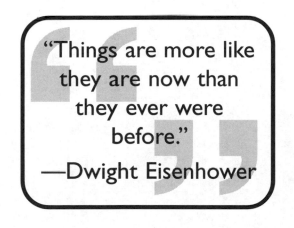

"Things are more like they are now than they ever were before."
—Dwight Eisenhower

Chapter 6

Fast Times and First Ladies: Women Behind the White House

MADISON

Fast Times and First Ladies: Women Behind the White House

★ ★ ★ ★ ★ ★ ★ ★ ★ ★ ★ ★ ★ ★ ★

Over the past 250 years, the first ladies have sported a wide range of perky (and parched) personalities. Among all their quirky habits and hobbies, they left a long list of legacies. Lou Henry Hoover helped found the Girl Scouts of America. Eleanor Roosevelt tried to take up shooting but couldn't hit a target with her gun if she wanted to. Julia Dent Grant was cross-eyed. Some were hot-tempered, antisocial, and overzealous. Others were bookworms, some were accused of adultery, and many more were groundbreaking fashionistas. Regardless of their differences, each first lady left a lasting impact as she stood by her husband during his years in office.

During his first three years as president, Hoover and his wife dined alone only on their wedding anniversary.

★ ★ ★ ★ ★

I'M SORRY, MRS. JACKSON

When Rachel Donelson and Andrew Jackson married in 1791, they had no idea that Rachel's former husband, Lewis Robards, had never actually filed their divorce papers. Though it was an honest mix-up, a cloud of rumored adultery hung over Rachel's head.

> "Mrs. Monroe hath added a daughter to our society who, tho' noisy, contributes greatly to its amusement."
> —James Monroe

Jackson stood by Rachel's reputation and was extremely sensitive to accusations anyone made regarding the legal mistake. His reactions often resulted in violent outbursts. In 1806, Charles Dickinson made the mistake of muttering something crude, which resulted in a heated exchange between the two men. During the subsequent argument, Dickinson shot Jackson in the chest, just a few inches from his heart. But Jackson was too enraged to collapse in pain. Instead, he shot and killed Dickinson and then walked away. The bullet lodged so close to Jackson's vital organs that doctors opted not to operate, so he bore the consequence of his famous duel for the rest of his life.

Jackson also threatened to cut off the ears of a man who accused him of infidelity, and he later challenged Tennessee Governor John

Sevier to a duel after he made comments about Mrs. Jackson. After offering a long apology, Sevier was pardoned, and Jackson withdrew his plans for revenge. Ultimately, Rachel died before Jackson ever took office, but he defended her purity and innocence on her tombstone in the garden at The Hermitage just outside

According to some records, John Tyler was so poor that just five years after leaving office, he was unable to pay a bill for $1.25.

Nashville, Tennessee. Her epitaph reads, "A being so gentle and so virtuous slander might wound, but could not dishonor."

★ ★ ★ ★ ★

Good Golly, Mrs. Dolley

Political socialites were shocked when shy, taciturn James Madison announced his engagement to the vibrant and animated political party girl Dolley Payne Todd, who had occasionally hosted soirees for the Jefferson administration. Raised in Quaker-influenced Philadelphia, Dolley grew up under strict

discipline. But once Philadelphia became the capital city and cute, young politicians came to town, she let down her dark curls and soaked up the attention. By the time she married Madison, then a U.S. Representative, she had become a local trendsetter and quite the entertainer. Often criticized for gambling, wearing excessive makeup, and using tobacco, Dolley seemed like an unlikely match for Madison, but she went on to become one of the most popular First Ladies to grace the White House. Her fame and fortune outlived her husband's, and she continued to enjoy the city's social life long after his term was over.

★ ★ ★ ★ ★

BE OUR GUEST

After Dolley Madison's exciting escapades, American gossip queens were not so pleased with shy newcomer Elizabeth Monroe. Regardless of the sophistication she acquired while living abroad in Great Britain and France, where she was known as *la belle Americaine,* Elizabeth immediately abandoned Dolley's traditions of holding regular open houses and entertaining diplomats' wives at lavish dinner parties. When she did try out a new social schedule, the press balked at the guests present at the formal affairs. One journalist for *Munsey's Magazine* wrote, "The secretaries, senators ... farmers, merchants, parsons, priests, lawyers, judges, auctioneers, and

> "Forget that I'm president of the United States. I'm Warren Harding, playing poker with friends, and I'm going to beat the hell out of them."
> —Warren G. Harding

nothingarians—all with their wives and some of their gawky offspring—crowd to the president's house every Wednesday evening; some in shoes, most in boots, and many in spurs; some snuffing, others chewing, and many longing for their cigars and whiskey punch left at home; some with powdered heads, some frizzled and oiled; some whose heads a comb has never touched, half hid by dirty collars."

★ ★ ★ ★ ★

EVERY PARTY HAS A POOPER

The first woman to ever be called "First Lady of the Land," Rutherford B. Hayes's wife, Lucy, took her reformed White House duties to the extreme. Likely as a direct result of her family's strict religious beliefs, she banned smoking and card playing from

government grounds during her husband's term. She was nicknamed Lemonade Lucy by her more worldly cohorts angered by her passionate stance against alcohol.

James K. Polk's administration was also a dud when it came to partying. His wife, Sarah, banned dancing at the White House (she didn't even dance at the Inaugural Ball) and refused to attend the theater or local horse races. To make matters worse, Polk considered it a waste of money to provide refreshments to his (probably bored) guests. With so many rules to remember, it is no wonder he died of exhaustion just after his term ended.

★ ★ ★ ★ ★

READY, AIM, MISFIRE

When it came to protecting Franklin Roosevelt's wife, Eleanor, from any harm, he simply was not able to overcome her stubborn independence. Eleanor refused to be escorted by Secret Service agents, so government officials gave her lessons on how to use a personal handgun. But after a trip with her to the FBI firing range, then-FBI Chief J. Edgar Hoover had his doubts. "Mr. President," he said, "if there is one person in the U.S. who should not carry a gun, it's your wife. She cannot hit a barn door."

★ ★ ★ ★ ★

TOMBOY TURNED GIRL SCOUT

"The independent girl is truly of quite modern origin, and usually is a most bewitching little piece of humanity," wrote fifteen-year-old Lou Henry. Later the eccentric wife of outdoorsman President Herbert Hoover, Lou was a revolutionary during a time when most women were confined to the home. Known for her history of fishing and camping with her father, Lou was recruited by Juliette Low to serve as a founding member of the Girl Scouts. She is credited with initiating the Girl Scout cookie sale during her second term as president of the organization.

Lou's involvement in the Girl Scouts was a reflection of her inner tomboy. She loved camping in the Sierra Mountains, studied at the London School of Mines, and became the first woman in the United States to earn a degree in geology. The day after her wedding, in February 1899, she left on a series of world travels that would eventually take her to China, Belgium, France, Russia, New Zealand, Australia, Burma, and Egypt.

During Hoover's term as president, the couple built Camp Rapidan, a rustic fishing resort in Virginia's Shenandoah Mountains. There, they threw horseshoes with Charles Lindbergh and sat on a log brainstorming with other world

> The only president never to be married, James Buchanan had his niece act as first lady.

leaders about upcoming issues and conferences. "The joyous rush of the brook, the contemplation of the eternal flow of the stream, the stretch of forest and mountain all reduce our egotism, smooth our troubles, and shame our wickedness," Lou wrote.

★ ★ ★ ★ ★

ANYTHING YOU CAN DO I CAN DO BETTER

All of the first ladies who have passed through the White House differ in talents and tastes. In 1980, editors at *Good Housekeeping* magazine decided to rank the presidential hostesses based on their role as hostess, campaigner, leader in causes, feminist, and traditionalist. The editors also considered their interest in politics, improvements made to the White House, influence on the president, helpfulness to the president, outspokenness, charisma, and inspiration to other women.

> "I think the American public wants a solemn ass as president, and I think I'll go along with them."—Calvin Coolidge

SUBSIDIZING SON

Tad Lincoln, son of Abraham and Mary Todd, was born with a cleft palate that caused him to have a frustrating lisp and a hard time eating. However, Tad put his sob story aside and spent much of his boyhood as an advocate for the Sanitary Commission—a Civil War organization similar to today's Red Cross or Salvation Army. At just eleven years old, he was one of their most eager fundraisers, and his moneymaking schemes were both elaborate and conniving.

The assessment wasn't exactly scientific, but the results were as follows:

1. Lady Bird Johnson

2. Eleanor Roosevelt

3. Rosalynn Carter

4. Lou Hoover

5. Jackie Kennedy

6. Betty Ford

7. Helen Taft

8. Pat Nixon

9. Bess Truman

10. Florence Harding

11. Edith Roosevelt

John Tyler was playing marbles when he learned he was to become president.

12. Edith Wilson

13. Grace Coolidge

14. Mamie Eisenhower

15. Ellen Wilson

★ ★ ★ ★ ★

MUSICAL INTERLUDE

President John Tyler's wife, Julia, was the first person to initiate the tradition of playing "Hail to the Chief" whenever the president appeared in public. The piece was originally written for the stage version of *The Lady of the Lake,* a poem by Sir Walter Scott. The tune was retitled "Wreaths for the Chieftain" and given new lyrics for the late George Washington's 1815 birthday celebration in Boston. It was first performed by the Marine Band on July 4, 1828, at a ceremony attended by President John Quincy Adams. Julia Tyler made the band's performance a regular affair, and Sarah Polk (of the next administration) followed her lead. The song has been associated with the commander in chief's presence ever since.

★ ★ ★ ★ ★

JOKING WITH THE JESUS FREAK

When James K. Polk asked Andrew Jackson for dating advice in 1823, Jackson replied that he should marry "the one who will never give you no trouble." With that, Polk pursued Sarah

Childress, the daughter of a well-to-do merchant from Murfreesboro, Tennessee. He may have thought she was tame at first, but Sarah could be anything but reserved. During her husband's 1844 campaign, she was taunted by a supporter of opponent Henry Clay who said that Mrs. Clay would make a better first lady because she made a dang tasty batch of butter and was a very "economical housekeeper." With a bitter look, Sarah replied that she could run the family budget so well that she would never *have* to make her own butter.

From time to time, however, Sarah was quite prudish and was often teased for her devout religious commitments. She was famous for insisting on taking to church any of Polk's associates who visited the White House on a Sunday. Aware of her tradition, one particular politician decided to play a joke on her when she told him there was a new preacher in the pulpit that day. "I would like to go with you, Madam, for I have played cards with him many a time!" Of course he was kidding, aware that Sarah disapproved of the sinful practice of card playing and dancing.

When Abigail Powers Fillmore saw the scarcity of books in the White House, she immediately had her husband ask Congress to appropriate money for a new presidential library on the second floor of the mansion. Many of the books she acquired remain there today.

Another night, over dinner at the White House, a friend from South Carolina said, "Madam, I have long wished to see the lady upon whom the Bible pronounces a woe!" Shocked at the apparent insult, everyone at the table waited for his explanation. "Does not the Bible say, 'Woe unto you when all men shall speak well of you?'" Relieved that the comment was actually a compliment, Sarah and her guests burst into laughter.

★ ★ ★ ★ ★

MISERY LOVES COMPANY

Although Martha Washington burned most of the letters exchanged between George, herself, and their beloved family and friends after his death, a few surviving pieces of correspondence reveal that she was miserable in her role as first lady. "I think I am more like a state prisoner than anything else, there is certain bounds set for me which I must not depart from," she once wrote. However, Martha did her best to remain cheerful both in private and public, for "the greater part of our happiness or misery," she wrote, "depends upon our dispositions, not upon our circumstances."

★ ★ ★ ★ ★

DEAR JOHN

During his lengthy relationship with Ann Rutledge, Abraham Lincoln had to put up quite a fight to win her from previous suitor John McNeil, who had once wooed Ann while Lincoln was running for the

legislature. Although considered quite a catch in their New Salem hometown, McNeil dropped a bomb on Rutledge after their engagement—he had a double life. His real name was McNamar, and he was going to New York to bring his underprivileged family back to Illinois to enjoy the fortune he had worked so hard to acquire. He had allegedly changed his name for fear that they would find and move in with him before he had time to "accumulate any property." Many people believed Ann was a fool for believing such a tale and ostracized her for being ditched by the town's most eligible bachelor.

After being romanced by Lincoln, Ann was in better spirits and wrote her former fiancé, whom she had not heard from in a year, that she would soon marry another. He sent no reply, but months later Ann received a letter in which McNamar expressed his excitement to finally be home and married to her. Either he had not received her Dear John letter, or he wanted to guilt her back into his arms. With the help of girlfriends at home, Ann stood her ground and planned to tell him about her relationship with Lincoln and dump him for good as soon as he returned. Unfortunately, she fell ill with what the local doctor called "brain fever" and died before she had the chance.

★ ★ ★ ★ ★

The Doghouse Blues

Lincoln may have suffered a bout of depression after his first love died in her early twenties, but he soon married Mary Todd, who would take him to new levels of frustration. A hotheaded woman with a flaring temper, she threw tantrums that would earn their home the nickname "suburb of Hades." She chased Abe out of the house with broomsticks, threw books across the room, and tossed a servant boy's suitcase out of a second-floor window. When political friend Jesse K. Dubois walked Lincoln home after work one day, Mary met them at the door and screamed, "You brought the wrong kind of meat! I can't use this!" and slapped him in the face. Needless to say, Abe frequently slept on the couch in his office.

★ ★ ★ ★ ★

INQUIRING PHOTOGRAPHERS WANT TO KNOW

Jacqueline Lee Bouvier, future wife of President John F. Kennedy, once won first place in a *Vogue* magazine Prix de Paris contest, in which she submitted a composition and was quizzed in an interview with the publication's editors. However, instead of accepting their offer to work for the magazine, she accepted a job at the *Washington Times Herald*, where she put together the "Inquiring Photographer" column for $42.50 per week.

Jackie's articles were anything but hard news—she would feature a local person's photograph next to their answer to simple questions such as "Have you done your

Christmas shopping?" or "Do women marry because they are too lazy to go to work?" On November 7, 1952, her column featured Richard Nixon's six-year-old daughter, who commented on whether her father was fit to take over

the presidency. Her quote read, "He's always away. If he's famous, why can't he stay home?"

★ ★ ★ ★ ★

Singing Sorority Girl

Long before she married Calvin Coolidge in 1905, Grace Anna Goodhue founded a chapter of

> The candy bar Baby Ruth was named after Grover Cleveland's daughter, Ruth.

the Phi Beta Phi women's fraternity at the University of Vermont. A "sister" through and through, she maintained close ties with the chapter even after she moved to the White House in 1923. In April 1924, 1,300 fraternity members assembled in the East Room of the White House to present a portrait of Grace with her collie to the White House Collection. If the crowded celebration weren't enough, the girls formed a semicircle around the room and sang the Phi Beta Phi anthem to their beloved alumna.

★ ★ ★ ★ ★

SNEAKIN' OUT

While this ex-schoolteacher never really spoke up about women's rights, when Abigail Powers Fillmore's husband became president, she occasionally broke the mold and rebelled against the proscribed roles of a wealthy politician's wife. When Jenny Lind, the "Swedish nightingale," visited Washington, Abigail spent a night on the town without her hubby on her arm. On another occasion, she took her daughter Mary Abigail to a public banquet in honor of a famous Hungarian liberator. During a time when first ladies were expected to never leave the White House grounds without their husbands, she was an exception.

★ ★ ★ ★ ★

OPPOSITES ATTRACT

Franklin and Jane Pierce were an unlikely pair from the beginning. He was an outgoing Democrat who loved mingling with loud, boisterous politicians. Her family members were Whigs, she was shy and socially awkward, and she was often annoyed by her husband's devotion to politics. Although they could appreciate his ambition, Jane's relatives warned her that her husband-to-be was rumored to drink a little too much.

The story of how the couple met, however, is quite romantic. While studying in the Bowdoin College library, Jane saw dark clouds accumulating outside the window and rushed out the door so she could make it home before the storm broke. As she ran, the rain burst from the sky and a clap of thunder sent her huddling under an old oak tree. Franklin Pierce, another student at Bowdoin, ran to her rescue, explaining that she was likely to get struck by lightning when holding a tree so tightly. He took her in his arms and escorted her home—the rest is history.

★ ★ ★ ★ ★

THOSE LYIN' EYES

Julia Dent Grant was cross-eyed and often toyed with the idea of having corrective surgery while her husband was president. However, as she was verifying the appointment, her husband talked her out of it, saying, "I don't want you to have your eyes fooled with. ... They look just as they did the very first time I ever saw them—the same eyes I looked into when I fell in love with you." Julia had only scheduled the surgery because she thought it would please her husband, so she canceled the appointment and was cross-eyed until the day she died in December 1902.

★ ★ ★ ★ ★

ARSENIC EXFOLIANT

Frances Cleveland never gave advertisers permission to use her name and photograph in their print advertisements for medicine and soap. However, one ascribed Frances's attractiveness to her use of arsenic as a facial cleanser. "Mrs. Cleveland's Remarkable and Beautiful Complexion," it read. "The secret of her beautiful complexion … is simply the use of arsenic, which can safely be taken and which can be procured from the New York doctor whose name is signed to this advertisement." Frances received a large stack of letters from Americans who could not believe she would sell her likeness to promote such a product, and the event prompted the National Women's Temperance Convention to prohibit "the immoral exhibition of the faces and forms of noted women."

★ ★ ★ ★ ★

THE WRITE STUFF

While previous presidential wives may have been a little half-hearted when it came to keeping up with pen pals, Eleanor Roosevelt seriously considered responding to all of the 300,000 letters she received in 1933. She threw away the hate mail, passed the rest on to the appropriate departments, and personally replied to the more important letters.

Amid the gaggle of fans, there was sure to be a nutcase or two. One woman wrote asking Eleanor to help her adopt a baby. A second letter said that once she got the baby, she would need a cow

… and then an icebox in which to put the milk. Other women wrote to complain about hemorrhoids, hernias, and "female troubles." No matter how off-color the requests, Eleanor managed to reply with grace and love.

As if replying to ridiculous fan mail didn't cramp her hand enough, Eleanor took up journalism in the 1920s and 1930s. She was a monthly columnist for *Woman's Home Companion*, writing on a variety of topics from education to gardening and old age to traditional morals. In 1941, she committed to another monthly column called "If You Ask Me" in *Ladies' Home Journal* (the column later moved to *McCall's*). Each month, she gave inquisitive readers her honest opinions and anecdotes about life as the first lady.

★ ★ ★ ★ ★

THE PRESIDENT'S WIVES PASS AWAY

Unfortunately for their husbands, a few first ladies died in the midst of their rise to political immorality.

- **Martha Wayles Skelton Jefferson**—The wife of third President Thomas Jefferson, Martha and four of Jefferson's six children died nineteen years before he became president. He kept his promise to never remarry and had socialite Dolley Payne, who would later marry James Madison, serve as the "unofficial hostess" of White House social affairs.

- **Letitia Christian Tyler**—The wife of tenth President John Tyler, Letitia moved into the White House in 1841 paralyzed from a stroke. She only appeared in public once while her husband was president—at her daughter Elizabeth's wedding. She and Tyler had eight children, and within a few months of Elizabeth's wedding, she had a second stroke and died.

- **Ellen Lewis Herndon Arthur**—The wife of twenty-first President Chester Arthur, Ellen died just a few months before her husband moved into the White House. Because the couple's only child was just ten years old at the time, Arthur appointed his sister to act as hostess. To honor his wife's memory, he was known to put a vase of fresh flowers under Ellen's portrait every day.

- **Caroline Scott Harrison**—The wife of twenty-third President Benjamin Harrison, Caroline was bedridden by a bout of tuberculosis while serving as first lady. She died less than one month before her husband lost his bid for reelection in 1893.

- **Ellen Axson Wilson**—The wife of twenty-eighth President Woodrow Wilson, Ellen suffered from a kidney disorder called Bright's disease and died at the White House during her husband's first term. Until Wilson remarried in 1915, Ellen's daughter, Margaret, handled all the womanly duties at the executive mansion.

- **Rachel Donelson Jackson**—The wife of seventeenth President Andrew Jackson, Rachel died of a heart attack not long after her husband was elected president. Because the Jacksons had no children, Rachel's niece Emily took over as chief entertainer

Chapter 7

Hot and Not: Political Highs and Lows

KENNEDY

Hot and Not:
Political Highs and Lows

★ ★ ★ ★ ★ ★ ★ ★ ★ ★ ★ ★ ★ ★ ★ ★

Not all of the United States' presidents posed as nude models for their college classmates in their younger days, but many of them had their own ways of adapting to (or rebelling against) the latest fashions of their time. Some had unusual biological challenges in terms of their appearance (such as Kennedy's stubby leg and Carter's missing testicle), while others effortlessly captivated the ladies. Love them or hate them, here is the skinny on the high-maintenance studs and their charming ways.

DID YOU KNOW?

James Madison was the shortest and slightest president at 5 feet, 4 inches and only one hundred pounds.

★ ★ ★ ★ ★

RATS TAIL REBELLION

Not a fan of the high-society fashions of the late 1700s, George Washington refused to wear a powdered wig like the rest of the aristocrats of his time. As a compromise, he instead rubbed white powder through his reddish brown hair and tied it in a short braid down his back.

Andrew Johnson was the only president to sew his own clothes.

Thomas Jefferson wasn't a fan of the elaborate British fashion trends either. To him, the Revolution had done away with England's tyranny and anything that suggested it. He just wanted to be another "voting member of the public" and couldn't wait to ditch the ridiculous attire and start acting like an average Joe.

★ ★ ★ ★ ★

REAGAN'S FULL MONTY

While in college in 1940, Ronald Reagan was voted "Most Nearly Perfect Male Figure" by his classmates at the University of California. His prize? The opportunity to pose nude for university art students learning how to sculpt the human body.

fabulous firsts

First president sworn in wearing long trousers: John Quincy Adams

★ ★ ★ ★ ★

MODEL ATHLETE

Gerald Ford was a stud long before he took office and long after, some would say. A member of the University of Michigan football team from 1931-1934, he was offered professional tryouts with the Green Bay Packers and the Chicago Bears. But instead he went on to coach at Yale while studying law. In 1939, he and his girlfriend tried their hand at modeling and were pictured in a *Look* magazine article about the lives of the country's most beautiful people. Three years later, he got his next big break on the cover of *Cosmopolitan*.

But was Ford all brawn and no brains? It could seem that way. His history in front of the camera may have made him a little hard to take seriously, and his countless clumsy conundrums made his reputation even worse. Whether he was accidentally locking himself out of the White House or tumbling down the steps of Air Force One, Ford couldn't deny being a klutz. He quickly became the joke of news reports and late-night comedy skits around the world.

DID YOU KNOW

Abraham Lincoln was the tallest president at 6 feet, 4 inches.

★ ★ ★ ★ ★

MAN IN UNIFORM

In December 2004, George W. Bush became the first U.S. president to wear a uniform when he sported a traditional military jacket while addressing the troops in Marine Corps base Camp Pendleton. Even former Presidents Eisenhower and Grant never donned military garb when they ceased to be generals and switched to civilian clothes (as would be expected from Bush). Traditionally, only dictatorial national leaders wear uniforms.

Often depicted wearing a tall black stovepipe hat, sixteenth President Abraham Lincoln was rumored to carry letters, bills, and notes in his hat.

★ ★ ★ ★ ★

THERE WAS A CROOKED MAN...

President John F. Kennedy, a Democrat from Brookline, Massachusetts, had one leg significantly longer than the other. To correct his crooked stance, he had to wear corrective shoes to make up the 3/4-inch difference.

★ ★ ★ ★ ★

Smokin' Shoulders

Woodrow Wilson once described Franklin Delano Roosevelt as "the handsomest young giant I have ever seen." The quote was a friendly tease. Although FDR was 6 feet, 2 inches tall and weighed 190 pounds, he lost the use of his legs to polio. Soon after he was confined to a wheelchair, he buffed up his upper body to build some impressive muscle. "Maybe my legs aren't so good, but look at these shoulders! Jack Dempsey would be green with envy," he once said.

The president was known to make light of his disability. When Madame Chiang Kai-shek visited the White House during his term, she politely asked him not to bother with standing out of respect as she rose to leave the room. "My dear child," he laughed, "I couldn't stand up if I had to!"

★ ★ ★ ★ ★

Bathtub Blues

Historically remembered as the tubbiest commander in chief to hold office, William H. Taft tipped the scales at more than three hundred pounds. Most accounts of his presidency are quick to point out his troubles fitting into the White House bathtub. To accommodate his mass, Taft had a new tub installed that could easily have held four average-sized men.

★ ★ ★ ★ ★

A FACE FOR RADIO

Although not a big fan of his own appearance, Woodrow Wilson was a good sport about his awkward reflection. He once made up a limerick about himself that read:

> For beauty I am not a star
> There are others more handsome by far
> But my face I don't mind it
> For I am behind it
> It's the people in front that I jar.

Abraham Lincoln may have had charm, wit and wisdom, but he was shy about his looks and was often lighthearted about his appearance. During a debate in 1858, Stephen Douglas called him two-faced. Lincoln replied, "If I had another face, do you think I would wear this one?" And finally, Lyndon B. Johnson was so disgusted with the way he looked in his official presidential portrait that he would not allow it to hang anywhere in the White House. He said the painting was "the ugliest thing I ever saw."

> Franklin Delano Roosevelt's mother forced him to wear dresses until he was five years old.

DID YOU KNOW

McKinley liked to wear a white vest and a lucky red carnation in his buttonhole.

★ ★ ★ ★ ★

CLOTHES HORSE

Charming, sweet-talking Chester Arthur never would have become president if his predecessor, James A. Garfield, hadn't died in office. Arthur was a heck of a dresser and was rumored to have owned as many as eighty pairs of pants. With a love for all things lavish, he spent much of his time dressed to the nines and riding in his laughably extravagant carriage—complete with gold lace curtains and the Arthur family coat of arms emblazoned on the side.

Chester Arthur, who changed clothes often was, nicknamed "Elegant Arthur."

★ ★ ★ ★ ★

HAIR TODAY, GONE TOMORROW

CNN Washington Bureau writer Bruce Morton wasn't kidding when he reported on the effectiveness of Former Vice President Al Gore's "salt-and-pepper" speckled beard in 2002. In his online article, Morton suggested that Gore follow the lead of past presidents and give his face a clean shave. No president has sported

DID YOU KNOW

Washington wore size 13 shoes, was 6 feet, 2 inches tall, and weighed about 175 pounds (until he put on about twenty-five more pounds later in life).

facial hair in the last century, he wrote, and only five presidents had a beard or mustache before then. Abraham Lincoln may have struck gold when he followed the advice of an

fabulous firsts
First president to set up a Christmas tree in the White House: Franklin Pierce

eleven-year-old girl who told him he should grow out his whiskers for the 1860 election—but he was a rare exception. Some speculate that Thomas Dewey was the last presidential candidate with facial hair to run for office. He and his dashing mustache just couldn't seem to swing the votes his way in 1944 or 1948. After his two miserable losses, candidates took

Jimmy Carter had only one testicle.

note of Dewey's grubby, hobo-like looks, and nothing but a five o'clock shadow has been sported since.

★ ★ ★ ★ ★

HARRISON LETS HIMSELF GO

After his term ended in 1893, Benjamin Harrison lost his edge as a bachelor. He enjoyed the lazy days of early retirement and took up the hobby of ... doing nothing. He moved home to Indianapolis and took a long, lethargic break from anything that required too much brain power. Some say he took an entire day to unpack one box of china, then crawled back into bed. His one commitment, however, was turning down offers for jobs as a lawyer or the president of a bank. Instead, he charged *Ladies' Home Journal* $5,000 for a handful of freelance articles.

DID YOU KNOW

Besides being known for his bulging shoulder muscles, FDR was also quite the trendsetter when it came to clothes that were easy for his personal assistants to dress him in. Because putting on a heavy overcoat was so difficult, he became known for his trademark navy cape, which kept him warm during the winter.

While most would assume Harrison's break from the social scene (and the working world) would serve as a turnoff to most women, Harrison's charm and social standing were revamped when, at sixty-two years old, he remarried. In fact, the new bride was his former wife's

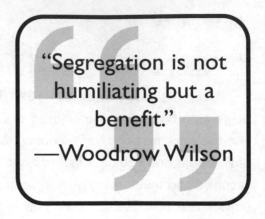

"Segregation is not humiliating but a benefit."
—Woodrow Wilson

niece. The two married in a spring wedding at St. Thomas's Episcopal Church in New York City. In no time, Harrison and the Mrs. were back at local parties and concerts, rubbing elbows with the nation's most popular political leaders.

★ ★ ★ ★ ★

EXTREME HOME MAKEOVER

As the presidents have come and gone through its doors, the White House has undergone an impressive array of facelifts and upgrades:

- **George Washington** surveyed the country's new capital and picked out the site for the first president's home during the late

1700s. On October 13, 1792, the cornerstone was laid and construction began.

- **Known by a variety of friendly nicknames**, including President's House and Executive Mansion, the first "First Family" home had no name until 1798,

Buchanan cocked his head to the left because he was nearsighted in one eye and farsighted in the other.

when the original sandstone exterior was whitewashed. The facelift prompted the nick name "White House," but the term was initially more popular in England than in America. One hundred years after the residence's construction, Theodore Roosevelt officially proclaimed White House as the mansion's title and the nickname finally stuck.

- Although **French Minister Louis Barbe Serurier encouraged him to leave the White House untouched** during the War of 1812 because of its significance as a national landmark, British

DID YOU KNOW Martin Van Buren had large mutton-chop sideburns.

General Robert Ross burned the building to the ground when his army stormed Washington, D.C. Dolley Payne Madison was able to save a few keepsakes from the fire, however, including a priceless painting of George Washington.

- **As the White House was rebuilt,** President and Mrs. James Monroe sold their personal furniture to the government to permanently outfit the place when he moved in. The charred remains of what used to decorate the interior were used to fill a pit so Monroe could plant a vegetable garden. The remains were found years later by archaeologists when President Ford decided to dig a swimming pool in that very spot.

The teddy bear was named after Theodore Roosevelt. While hunting in the South in 1902, Roosevelt's dogs cornered a bear, but he refused to kill it. His mercy was praised in a newspaper cartoon, and friend Morris Michtom asked Teddy for permission to use his name for the creation of a new toy bear.

DID YOU KNOW

John Adams was not very interested in clothes and was rumored to have worn the same hat for ten years.

Chapter 8

Dead and Gone:
Taken Too Soon

LINCOLN

Dead and Gone:
Taken Too Soon

★ ★ ★ ★ ★ ★ ★ ★ ★ ★ ★ ★ ★ ★ ★ ★ ★

On her hit show *Roseanne*, actress **Roseanne Barr** once said, "If you spend all your time worrying about dying, living isn't going to be much fun." The leaders of America may not have spent much time stressing about when their time would come, but maybe they should have— six escaped assassination attempts and eight died in office. Some barely survived childhood, while others experienced the death of coworkers and family members. From slipping off a log, suffering a serious case of indigestion, or navigating the ridiculous home remedies of their days, they made their deaths (and near deaths) darn inspiring.

> Just as Coolidge entered the presidency in 1924, his son, sixteen-year-old Calvin Jr., got a blister on his toe while playing tennis that caused a fatal blood infection.

★ ★ ★ ★ ★

(ALMOST) SAVED BY THE BELL

The second president to be shot while in office, James A. Garfield might have survived if it weren't for the stupidity of those trying to save his life. Treated for his gunshot wound in the White House for two whole months, Garfield was visited by more than fifteen doctors who wanted to nurse him to health and find the missing bullet lodged somewhere in his body. Probing him with medical instruments and their curious, stubby fingers, the doctors actually worsened the situation by accidentally puncturing the president's liver. Oblivious to their

> After being shot, Ronald Reagan said jokingly, "I forgot to duck."

mistake, the group continued their worthless search and called on an old inventor friend—Alexander Graham Bell— to help find the pesky bullet.

Bringing his new metal detector to Garfield's room, Bell and his associates scanned the president for any signs of metal in his chest. The thing went haywire, and nobody quite knew why. No one had thought to move Garfield off his bed, which was made of metal springs. When he died on September 19, 1881, an autopsy showed the bullet's true location. Doctors concluded that Garfield could have survived had he simply been left alone.

DID YOU KNOW

Truman escaped assassination on November 1, 1950 when Oscaar Collazo and Griselio Torresola tried to shoot their way into Blair House where Truman and his family were staying while the White House was being renovated. A White House guard was killed, and two others were wounded.

★ ★ ★ ★ ★

SHIVER ME TIMBERS

William Henry Harrison was asking for trouble when he gave the longest inauguration speech in history, outdoors, on one of the coldest days the city had ever seen. In order to appear more prestigious, Harrison refused to wear a jacket and gloves. After an hour and forty-five minutes of shivering through the dissertation-like speech, he fell terribly ill. Although he

BRR

665

DID YOU KNOW

Eight presidents died in office: William Henry Harrison (after having served only one month), Zachary Taylor, Abraham Lincoln, James Garfield, William McKinley, Warren G. Harding, Franklin D. Roosevelt, and John F. Kennedy.

recovered just a few days later, he was back in bed with the chills in no time. Rounds of home remedies—spoonfuls of castor oil, ipecac, opium, brandy, and camphor—were little help and likely worsened his condition. Harrison passed away on April 4, 1841, making him the first president to ever die in office.

★ ★ ★ ★ ★

THE SHOW MUST GO ON

While the length of William Henry Harrison's speech made him the first president to die in office, the length of one of **Teddy Roosevelt's speeches actually saved his life**. As he was preparing to address the crowd at the Hotel Gilpatrick in Milwaukee, Wisconsin, in October 1912, an assassin ran out of the crowd and fired a shot at him. However, the bullet slowed down significantly when it ripped through Roosevelt's thick speech manuscript.

DID YOU KNOW?

Franklin D. Roosevelt contracted polio at thirty-nine. Through rigorous exercise, he learned to stand with braces.

Surprisingly, stubborn Roosevelt insisted on delivering part of his speech with the bullet still in him. Blood soaked the front of his shirt, until he finally collapsed and was rushed to the hospital. The shooter, John Schrank, later said that "any man looking for a third term ought to be shot." Roosevelt later held up the torn, bloody manuscript and said, "You see—it takes more than that to kill a Bull Moose."

An edition of the *Detroit Free Press* described the unlikely event as follows:

> Milwaukee, Wis., October 14—A desperate attempt to kill Col. Theodore Roosevelt tonight failed when a .32-caliber bullet aimed directly at the heart of the former president and fired at short range by the crazed assailant, spent part of its force in a bundle of manuscript containing the address which Col. Roosevelt was to deliver tonight, and wounded the Progressive candidate for President. Col. Roosevelt delivered part of his scheduled address with the bullet in his body, his blood staining his white vest as he spoke to a huge throng at the auditorium. Later, he collapsed, weakened by the wound, and was rushed to Emergency Hospital.

★ ★ ★ ★ ★

YOU ARE WHAT YOU EAT

After pigging out on cherries and milk at a Fourth of July ceremony at the Washington Monument **in 1850, Zachary Taylor had a bout of severe stomach problems**, got sick from the heat, and—despite efforts to treat him with leeches and opium—died five days later. Years later, Taylor's body was exhumed because of rumors that his death seemed too unusual to be natural. Was it a result of foul play rather than a terribly embarrassing case of diarrhea? Accusations that Taylor's wife, Peggy, had poisoned him aside, all tests for traces came back negative. Today, most historians say that Taylor likely died of cholera.

★ ★ ★ ★ ★

(WOULD-BE) INDEPENDENCE DAY DEATH

An epileptic and the namesake of Madison, Wisconsin, James Madison was younger than both of his vice presidents—yet both George Clinton and Elbridge Gerry died while he was in office. When it was Madison's time to go, in 1836, White House officials had a brilliant

It took Garfield eleven weeks to die after being shot by assassin Charles Guiteau on July 2, 1881. He died on September 19, 1881 in Elberon, New Jersey. He was forty-nine years and 304 days old or 10 months.

DID YOU KNOW

Two months before his inauguration, the Franklin Pierce family was involved in a train wreck, and their eleven-year-old son, Benjamin, was thrown from the car and crushed to death before their eyes.

idea for how he could ride into the proverbial sunset. They offered him drugs to keep him alive until the Fourth of July so he could pass away on the anniversary of his nation's independence. Not interested in postponing the inevitable for the sake of symbolic romanticism, he refused treatment and died on June 28.

★ ★ ★ ★ ★

BLASPHEMOUS BIRD

At Andrew Jackson's funeral, in 1845, his pet parrot had to be escorted out of the service for interrupting the solemn event with excessive swearing.

Chester Arthur spent his last years in office knowing he could very well die of Bright's disease before his term ended. He knew that the more active he was, the greater his chance of succumbing to the disease, and yet he even made an attempt to gain his party's nomination for another term.

★ ★ ★ ★ ★

I VANT TO DRAIN YOUR BLOOD

After taking a long stroll to inspect his estate on December 12, 1799—a chilly day of snow, sleet, and rain on Mount Vernon—George Washington came down with a bit of a sore throat. Two days later his condition worsened, and doctors predicted that his lungs and his throat were "shutting down." To try and treat his aches and pains, Washington's physicians had a bright idea—draining blood out of the former president's body and placing a strip of flannel soaked in ammonium carbonate around his neck.

Not surprisingly, the remedy failed to prolong Washington's life, but it was something other than needles (and the stench of the flannel) that kept him from being able to simply die in peace. He had an intense fear of being buried alive and made his secretary promise multiple times not to put his body in the

DID YOU KNOW

As a boy, William McKinley nearly drowned in Mosquito Creek in Niles, Ohio.

ground less than three days after his death—just to be sure. (Apparently, Eleanor Roosevelt had a similar fear of being buried alive—she ordered that her veins be cut before her burial.) At sixty-seven years old, Washington died while taking his own pulse. One of the last things he said was, "I die hard, but I am not afraid to go."

★ ★ ★ ★ ★

TECUMSEH'S COY CURSE

Obviously not a fan of the war-mongering white men who continued to steal land from his fellow Native Americans, Shawnee Chief Tecumseh claimed to have placed a curse on William Henry Harrison when he was elected in 1840, proclaiming that Harrison (along with every other president elected in a year that ends with a "0") would be doomed to die in office. Harrison died of pneumonia after just weeks in office. Lincoln (elected in 1860), Garfield (1880), McKinley (1900), Harding (1920), Roosevelt (1940) and Kennedy (1960) also all died before their terms as president were up. The so-called curse was not broken until Reagan was elected to office in 1980, and he was nearly assassinated in 1981.

Reagan's would-be assassin, John Hinkley, wanted to kill the president to impress actress Jodie Foster. After the assassination attempt, he was put in a mental institution.

★ ★ ★ ★ ★

SLIPPIN' ON THE DOCK OF THE BAY

As a rowdy young boy, Abraham Lincoln had two close calls with death. At seven years old, he and best friend Austin Gollaher were romping in the woods when Lincoln slipped off a slimy log and fell into Knob Creek. Unfortunately, neither boy could swim. All Gollaher could do to help was hold out a pole for Lincoln to snag. After a few minutes of struggling, Lincoln finally grabbed on and was pulled out of the muddy water. Afraid of what their mothers might say about their dirty clothes, the boys stripped to their skivvies and let their garb bake dry in the sun. On another occasion, at just nine years old, Lincoln was working at a gristmill when he was kicked in the head by an angry mare. Bloody and confused, the boy appeared lifeless until he suddenly awoke shouting the same thing he had said to the mare just before being whacked unconscious: "You old hussy!"

DID YOU KNOW

Unsuccessful assassination attempts were made on the lives of Andrew Jackson, Theodore Roosevelt, Franklin D. Roosevelt, Harry Truman, Gerald Ford, and Ronald Reagan.

As president, Lincoln had a terrifyingly prophetic dream about his own death before the fall of Richmond during the Civil War. He envisioned that he was in the White House and heard crying from a room down the corridor. When he entered the room and asked who had died, he saw himself in the coffin across the room. Lincoln was assassinated one week later. His killer, John Wilkes Booth, had been plotting the attack for some time. Booth stalked the president from early in his political career and can be seen lingering close to Lincoln in photographs from his Inauguration Day.

★ ★ ★ ★ ★

KICK THE BUCKET BANDWAGON

During Benjamin Harrison's administration from 1889-1893, a whopping twenty of his friends, family members, and political associates kicked the bucket and left him to his lonesome. Former President Rutherford B. Hayes and Secretary of State James G. Blaine died. (Some physicians reported that the latter simply gave up on life because he "lacked the courage to live.") Harrison's wife also died, and his adorable granddaughter Marthena succumbed to scarlet fever. Despite his grief, Harrison moved on. In 1901, after remarrying and having another child in his early sixties, Harrison died of pneumonia like his grandfather William Henry Harrison, the ninth president of the United States.

★ ★ ★ ★ ★

LAST DANCE WITH ELLEN WILSON

Famous for his role in ending World War I and overseeing three popular amendments to the Constitution, Woodrow Wilson seemed unstoppable. But just a few months into his term, his beloved wife, Ellen, died and left a depression so deep that he sat stunned by her cold body for two straight days. His sullen demeanor would not heal until after he met and married his

Speaking to reporters about his health, Nixon once claimed that he had never had a headache during his whole life.

DID YOU KNOW

Lincoln's son Robert Todd Lincoln was seconds away from possibly being able to save his father's life, as well as the lives of two other assassinated presidents. He had arrived to meet his father at Ford's Theatre just seconds after John Wilkes Booth pulled the trigger. He was on the way to meet President Garfield and arrived just minutes after he was shot as well. Finally, Robert was en route to New York from Buffalo to meet President McKinley the same day he was assassinated at the Pan-American Exposition in 1901. Talk about being at the wrong place at the wrong time.

second wife, Edith Bolling Galt, the following year.

However, by that time, Wilson's health had deteriorated significantly. A stroke in 1906 had left him blind in one eye, and he had high blood pressure and frequent headaches. Another stroke in 1919 left him paralyzed on one side. With that, Edith decided it was her turn to step up to the political plate.

Eventually, she took over many of her husband's responsibilities, serving as a middleman between him and other government officials. She reviewed important documents and made decisions she didn't consider serious enough to bother her husband about. In fact, her leadership earned her the nickname the "Secret President" and the "first woman to run the government."

In 1921, the Wilsons returned to their comfortable Washington home, and in February 1924, the former president's body finally gave out.

★ ★ ★ ★ ★

TOMBSTONE TYPO

As death approached, **Thomas Jefferson wrote his own epitaph**

without mentioning that he served as president of the United States. The tombstone reads:

> There was buried
> Thomas Jefferson
> Author of the Declaration of American Independence
> Of the Statute of Virginia for Religious Freedom
> & Father of the University of Virginia

★ ★ ★ ★ ★

PEACHY KEEN

Although he did survive the common illnesses that often took the lives of young boys, **Ulysses S. Grant did nearly die twice as a youth**. Once, he fell off a log into a flooded creek. Another time, the unruly horse pulling his carriage nearly dragged him off a steep embankment. Although he survived his own near-tragedies, Grant unfortunately watched one of his friends die when his friend lost control of the horse he was riding and was crushed by the animal.

After leaving the White House in 1877, however, Grant's health began to fail and his financial situation looked even worse. (The Marine Bank had collapsed and left him with nothing. At one point, the Grants had only $180 to their name.) However, a ripe, juicy peach would ultimately predict Grant's painful end. One hot summer day, while taking a bite out of the delicious fruit, he felt a sharp pain in his esophagus. His handwriting suddenly turned from formal to a messy scraggle, and he started to suffer severe choking fits. His cigar smoking had caught up with him, and in June 1885, the general died of throat cancer. The one thing that kept him alive that long, doctors said, was his determined will to finish his book, *Personal Memoirs.*

★ ★ ★ ★ ★

SHOT IN A NEW YORK MINUTE

Excited about a scheduled appearance at the Pan-American Exposition in Buffalo, New York, in 1901, William McKinley could not wait to mingle among the public. Although his personal secretary, George Cortelyou, feared the trip would pose danger, the president disagreed and insisted on attending as scheduled. After crossing the Canadian border to visit Niagara Falls on September 6, McKinley returned to the New York fairgrounds to rub elbows with the common folk.

Although more than twenty-four guards were monitoring McKinley, a young man named Leon Czolgosz stepped forward to shake the president's hand with his bandaged right arm. A .32-caliber revolver was hidden among the bandages. The bullet penetrated McKinley's stomach, and he was rushed to the hospital.

DID YOU KNOW

Some people believe that a casual conversation in a Chicago tailor shop sealed McKinley's fate. There, Czolgosz announced to a friend that he was planning on killing a priest later that year. "Why kill a priest?" his friend inquired. "There are so many priests; they are like flies—a hundred will come to his funeral." Czolgosz must have heeded his friend's suggestion to be more creative and changed his mind, because a few months later he shot William McKinley at the Pan-American Exposition in Buffalo, New York.

Selfless until the end, McKinley worried about everyone else as people ran to his aid. He begged officials not to hurt the gunman and tried to warn his secretary of how his invalid wife might react to the news of his injury. At the hospital, he seemed in high spirits as he shared food and cigars with Pan-American Exposition President John Milburn. Unfortunately, McKinley succumbed to gangrene and died eight days after being shot.

★ ★ ★ ★ ★

THREAT ME BABY ONE MORE TIME

When it came to death threats, Rutherford B. Hayes had more than his fair share. At his inauguration, he was secretly sworn into office because local officials feared a riot would break out and his life would be in danger. Later, Hayes barely dodged a bullet that was fired into a window in his home.

But why was he such a target for assassination? Because he had actually lost the election to Democratic candidate Samuel Tilden. Before the presidential contest began, everyone knew the race would be close. Corruption ran rampant throughout the election—South Carolina, Louisiana, and Florida each submitted two conflicting sets of electoral votes when it came time to count the ballots. Though Tilden won the popular vote, Congress had to set up a special committee to sidestep the three states' screw-up and decide the fate. Unfortunately, eight members of the committee were Republicans and seven were Democrats, so Tilden never had a chance for a fair fight.

TV & MOVIES
WHERE WE GOT THIS STUFF

Bathroom Readers' Hysterical Institute. *Uncle John's Bathroom Reader Plunges Into Great Lives.* San Diego: Portable Press, 2003.

Beasley, Jake. *Celebrity Aliases Unmasked.* USA: Sweetwater Press, 2004.

Clarke, John. *The Greatest Rock and Pop Miscellany Ever!* Italy: Sanctuary Publishing, 2004.

Cox, Stephen. *The Beverly Hillbillies.* Nashville: Cumberland House, 2003.

DiFranco, JoAnn and Anthony DiFranco. *Mister Rogers: Good Neighbor to America's Children.* Minneapolis: Dillon Press, 1983.

Epting, Chris. *James Dean Died Here: The Locations of American Pop Culture Landmarks.* Los Angeles: Santa Monica Press, 2003.

Fingeroth, Danny. *Reese Witherspoon.* New York: Rosen Book Works, 2003.

———. *Liv Tyler.* New York: Rosen Book Works, 2003.

———. *Elijah Wood.* New York: Rosen Book Works, 2003.

Grossberg, Josh. "'Bachelor Bob' Sings Lawsuit Blues." December 22, 2003, www.cnn.com.

Hamrick, Craig. "TV Guide's Ultimate Trivia Quiz!" *TV Guide,* August 7, 2005.

Kamm, Jim and Matteo Molinari. *Oops! Movie Mistakes That Made The Cut.* New York: Citadel Press Books, 2002.

Keller, Julie. "Leo Gets a Date… And Lawsuit." November 1, 1999, www.cnn.com.

McCracken, Kristin. *James Van Der Beek.* New York: Rosen Book Works, 2001.

People Magazine, ed. *100 Greatest TV Stars of Our Time.* New York: People Books, 2003.

Petras, Kathryn and Ross. *Unusually Stupid Americans.* New York: Villard Books, 2003.

Roeper, Richard. *Schlock Values: Hollywood at Its Worst.* New York: Hyperion Books, 2004.

Sandys, Jon. *Movie Mistakes.* London: Virgin Books, 2005.

Snipes, Stephanie. "The little dog that could." www.cnn.com, August 20, 2004.

Sova, Dawn B. *Forbidden Films: Censorship Histories of 125 Motion Pictures.* New York: Checkmark Books, 2001.

Stone, Tanya Lee. *Success with an Open Heart: Oprah Winfrey.* Connecticut: The Millbrook Press, 2001.

Stuart, Mel and Josh Young. *Pure Imagination: The Making of Willy Wonka and the Chocolate Factory.* New York: St. Martin's Press, 2002.

Sweetingham, Lisa. "Robert Blake denies plotting to kill his wife." Court TV, October 3, 2005, http://www.courttv.com/trials/blake/100305_ctv.html

Tonks, Douglas. *TV's Most Wanted.* Virginia: Brassey's Inc., 2003.

Vaz, Mark Cotta. *The Lost Chronicles.* New York: Touchstone Television, 2005.

Wheeler, Jill C. *Jessica Simpson.* Minnesota: ABDO Publishing Company, 2005.

Wild, David. *The One With All Ten Years: FRIENDS 'Til the End.* New York: Time, Inc, 2004.

WE ALSO USED THESE SOURCES:

www.hollywood.com
www.eonline.com
www.imdb.com
www.cagenews.com
www.wikipedia.org
http://lindablairworldheart.com
www.Munsters.com
Former Child Star Central, http://members.tripod.com/~former_child_star/where.html
www.geocities.com/Hollywood/Academy/5228/ddlgbv.html
www.inthe80s.com
www.inthe90s.com
www.cagefactor.com
http://news.bbc.co.uk/1/hi/entertainment/showbiz/1710311.stm

ROCK 'N' ROLL
WHERE WE GOT THIS STUFF:

Associated Press, "Rock and Roll hall sues Jewish rock hall." *MSNBC*, February 8, 2005, http://msnbc.msn.com/id/6936995/

Bathroom Readers' Hysterical Institute. *Uncle John's Bathroom Reader Plunges Into Great Lives.* San Diego: Portable Press, 2003.

Bathroom Reader's Institute. *Uncle John's 4-Ply Bathroom Reader.* New York: Barnes & Noble Books, 1991.

Beasley, Jake. *Celebrity Aliases Unmasked.* USA: Sweetwater Press, 2004.

Bordowitz, Hank. *Turning Points in Rock and Roll.* New York: Kensington Publishing Corporation, 2004.

Clarke, John. *The Greatest Rock and Pop Miscellany Ever!* Italy: Sanctuary Publishing, 2004.

Cloud, David W. "The Religious Affiliation of Rock and Roll Star Buddy Holly." *Adherents.com*, July 19, 2005, http://www.adherents.com/people/ph/Buddy_Holly.html

———. "The Religious Affiliation of Rock and Roll Star Roy Orbison." *Adherents.com*, July 19, 2005, http://www.adherents.com/people/po/Roy_Orbison.html

D'Angelo, Joe. "Dave Matthews Buys Grass for University of Virginia." *VH1.com*, www.vh1.com/artists/az/dave_matthews_band/news.jhtml?p=76&q=25

Joseph, Mark. *The Rock and Roll Rebellion*. Nashville: Broadman & Holman Publishers, 1999.

Joseph, Mark. *Faith, God and Rock and Roll*. Grand Rapids: Baker Books, 2003.

Kitts, Jeff, and Brad Tolinski, eds. *Guitar World Presents: Greatest Guitarists of All Time!* Milwaukee: Hal Leonard Corporation, 2002.

Melloan, Maryanne. *Rock and Roll Revealed: The Outrageous Lives of Rock's Biggest Stars*. New York: Smithmark, 1993.

Morse, Tim. *Classic Rock Stories*. New York: St. Martin's Griffin, 1998.

Moser, Margaret, and Bill Crawford. *Rock Stars Do the Dumbest Things*. New York: St. Martin's Griffin, 1998.

Palmer, Robert. "Copyright Nightmare Haunts Bee Gees," *New York Times*, April 6, 1983.

Patel, Joseph. "P. Diddy Cleared In Lawsuit Brought by TV Interviewer." *MTV.com*, February 24, 2004, http://www.mtv.com/news/articles/1485297/20040224/p_diddy.jhtml?headlines=true

Patterson, R. Gary. *Take A Walk on the Dark Side: Rock and Roll Myths, Legends, and Curses*. New York: Simon & Schuster, 2004.

Petras, Kathryn and Ross. *Unusually Stupid Americans*. New York: Villard Books, 2003.

Reid, Shaheem. "Impulse Shopper Nelly Nearly Purchases a Small Town." *VH1.com*, March 19, 2002, www.vh1.com/artists/az/nelly/news.jhtml?p=126&q=25

Shea, Stuart. *Rock and Roll's Most Wanted*. Washington D.C.: Brassey's, Inc, 2002.

Sullivan, James. "Rock's 10 Wildest Myths." *Rolling Stone*, October 12, 2004, http://www.rollingstone.com/rsmyth

Thompson, Graeme. "The 10 Greatest Rock'n'Roll Myths." *The Observer*, February 20, 2005, http://observer.guardian.co.uk

Turner, Steve. *Hungry for Heaven: Rock 'n' Roll and the Search for Redemption*. Illinois: InterVarsity Press, 1995.

Zappa, Frank. *The Real Frank Zappa Book*. New York: Touchstone Books, 1989.

WE ALSO USED THESE SOURCES:

www.beliefnet.com
www.cbsnews.com
www.chartattack.com
www.classicbands.com
www.corsinet.com
www.cnn.com
www.digitaldreamdoor.com
www.eonline.com
www.fiftiesweb.com
www.foxnews.com
www.hinduismtoday.com
www.history-of-rock.com

www.jewsrock.org
www.jokesnjokes.net
www.leftlion.co.uk
www.legalzoom.com
www.memphisrocknsoul.org
www.news.com
www.rockhall.com
www.vh1.com
www.wikipedia.org
mental_floss magazine

FAMOUS AUTHORS
WHERE WE GOT THIS STUFF

Abraham, Gerald. *Tolstoy*. New York: Haskell House Publishers, 1974.

Allen, William Rodney. *Walker Percy: A Southern Wayfarer*. Jackson: University Press of Mississippi, 1986.

Ambrosetti, Ronald J. *Eric Ambler*. New York: Twayne Publishers, 1994.

Angelou, Maya. *Hallelujah! The Welcome Table*. New York: Random House, 2004.

——. *All God's Children Need Traveling Shoes*. New York: Random House, 1997.

Auslander, Joseph and Frank Ernest Hill. *The Winged Horse: The Story of the Poets and their Poetry*. New York: Doubleday, Doran & Company, 1930.

Barker, Juliet. *A Life: Wordsworth*. New York: Harper Collins, 2000.

Barry, Elaine. *Robert Frost*. New York: Continuum Publishing, 1988.

Bauder, David. "Benchley Wouldn't Write Same 'Jaws' Today." *The Trentonian*, April 5, 2000.

Bixler, Phyllis. *Frances Hodgson Burnett*. Boston: Twayne Publishers, 1984.

Bragg, Rick. *All Over But The Shoutin'*. New York: Vintage Books, 1997.

Busby, Mark. *Ralph Ellison*. Boston: Twayne Publishers, 1991.

Cady, Edwin H. *Stephen Crane*. Boston: Twayne Publishers, 1980.

Calhoun, Richard J. and Robert W. Hill. *James Dickey*. Boston: Twayne Publishers, 1983.

Carpenter, Humphrey. *JRR Tolkien: A Biography*. Boston: Houghton Mifflin Company, 2000.

——. *W.H. Auden: A Biography*. Boston: Houghton Mifflin Company, 1981.

Clarke, Gerald. *Capote: A Biography*. New York: Avalon Publishing Group, 1988.

Clinton, Paul. "Along Came a Spider spins tangled, dull tale." April 6, 2001. http://archives.cnn.com/2001/SHOWBIZ/Movies/04/06/review.spider/index.html

Dowden, Edward. *Robert Browning*. London: J.M. Dent & Co., 1904.

Eble, Kenneth. *F. Scott Fitzgerald*. Boston: Twayne Publishers, 1963.

Elledge, Scott. *E.B. White: A Biography*. New York: W.W. North & Company, 1984.

Evans, I.O. *Jules Verne and his work*. Boston: Twayne Publishers, 1966.

Fensch, Thomas, ed. *Coversations with John Steinbeck*. Jackson: University Press of Mississippi, 1988.

French, Warren. *J.D. Salinger*. Boston: Twayne Publishers, 1963.

Friedman, Lawrence S. *Wiliam Golding*. New York: The Continuum Publishing Company, 1993.

Friedman, Lenemaja. *Shirley Jackson*. Boston, Twayne Publishers, 1975.

Garson, Helen S. *Tom Clancy: A Critical Companion*. Connecticut: Greenwood Press, 1996.

Gillespie, Stephenie Miller. "Police Confirm Disappearance of Local Boy, Age 10." *The Midland Star*, December 15, 2004.

Hardy, Florence Emily. *The Life of Thomas Hardy*. Connecticut: Archon Books, 1970.

Hayman, Ronald. *Arthur Miller*. New York: Frederick Ungar Publishing, 1972.

Hays, Peter L. *Ernest Hemingway*. New York: Continuum Publishing, 1992.

Hewlett, Dorothy. *Elizabeth Barrett Browning: A Life*. New York: Alfred A. Knopf, 1952.

Higginson, Thomas Wentworth. *Henry Wadsworth Longfellow*. Boston & New York: Houghton Mifflin Company, 1902.

Hillway, Tyrus. *Herman Melville*. Boston: Twayne Publishers, 1979.

Inge, Tonette Bond. *Southern Women Writers: The New Generation*. Tuscaloosa: The University of Alabama Press, 1990.

Jacobs, Eric. *Kinglsey Amis: A Biography*. New York: St. Martin's Press, 1995.

Jeppson, Janet, ed. *Isaac Asimov: It's Been a Good Life*. New York: Prometheus Books, 2002.

Kaplan, Justin. *Walt Whitman: A Life*. New York: Simon and Schuster, 1980.

Kelly, Richard. *Daphne du Maurier*. Boston: Twayne Publishers, 1987.

Kermode, Frank. *John Donne*. London: Longmans, Green & Co Ltd., 1957.

Lauber, John. *The Inventions of Mark Twain: A Biography*. New York: Hill and Wang, 1990.

Levi, Peter. *Tennyson*. New York: Charles Scribner's Sons, 1993.

Kronick, Joseph G. "Vachel Lindsay's Life." *Modern American Poetry*. http://www.english.uiuc.edu/maps/poets/g_l/lindsay/lindsay_life.htm

Kulii, Beverly Threatt and Ann E. Reuman and Ann Trapasso. "Audre Lorde's Life and Career." *Modern American Poetry*. http://www.english.uiuc.edu/maps/poets/g_l/lorde/life.htm

MacDonald, Ruth K. *Dr. Seuss*. Boston: Twayne Publishers, 1988.

McIntyre, Ian. *Robert Burns: A Life*. New York: Welcome Rain Publishers, 2001.

Metcalf, Eva-Maria. *Astrid Lindgren*. New York: Twayne Publishers, 1995.

Meyers, Jeffrey. *Robert Frost: A Biography*. London: Constable and Company, 1996.

——. *Katherine Mansfield: A Biography*. New York: New Directions Books, 1978.

Middlebrook, Diane Wood. *Anne Sexton: A Biography*. Boston: Houghton Mifflin Company, 1991.

Moore, Virginia. *Distinguished Women Writers*. New York: E.P. Dutton & Co., Inc, 1903.

Morgan, Janet. *Agatha Christie*. New York: Alfred A. Knopf, 1985.

Murray, Brian. *Charles Dickens*. Continuum Publishing: New York, 1994.

Nelson, Benjamin. *Arthur Miller: Portrait of a Playwright*. New York:
    David McKay Company, 1970.

Parker, Jamie. "Who Is Buried in Edgar Poe's Grave?" United States Naval Academy
    Website. http://www.usna.edu/EnglishDept/poeperplex/gravep.htm

Pearson, Hesketh. *Sir Walter Scott: His Life and Personality*. New York:
    Harper & Brothers Publishers, 1954.

Pflieger, Pat. *Beverly Cleary*. Boston: Twayne Publishers, 1991.

Porter, Katherine Anne. "A Curtain of Green." *Eudora Welty*. Chelsea House
    Publishers: New York, 1986.

Roberts, Bette B. *Anne Rice*. New York: Twayne Publishers, 1994.

Rosenburg, Bruce A. *Ian Fleming*. Boston: Twayne Publishers, 1989.

Ryley Robert M. "Kenneth Fearing's Life." *Modern American Poetry*.
    http://www.english.uiuc.edu/maps/poets/a_f/fearing/life.htm

Sinclair, Andrew. *Jack: A Biography of Jack London*. New York: Pocket Books, 1977.

Tischler, Nancy M. *Tennessee Williams*. Austin: Steck-Vaughn Company, 1969.

Trueblood, Paul G. *Lord Byron*. Boston: Twayne Publishers, 1977.

Tucker, Martin. *Joseph Conrad*. New York: Frederick Ungar Publishing, 1976.

Warnke, Frank J. *John Donne*. Boston: Twayne Publishers, 1987.

White, Evelyn C. *Alice Walker: A Life*. New York: W.W. Norton & Company, 2004.

Wiesel, Elie. *All Rivers Run to the Sea: Memoirs*. New York: Schocken Books, 1995.

Wilson, A.N. *C.S. Lewis: A Biography*. New York: WW Norton & Company, 1990.

Zeiger, Henry A. *Ian Fleming: The Spy Who Came In with the Gold*. New York:
    Duell, Sloan and Pearce, 1965.

WE ALSO USED THESE SOURCES:

www.evanovich.com

www.wikipedia.org

The Thomas Hardy Association, www.yale.edu/hardysoc

African American Literature Book Club, http://aalbc.com/authors/maya.htm

www.litencyc.com/php/speople.php?rec=true&UID=5876

James Thurber's Comic Vision, www.todayinliterature.com/stories

The Edgar Allan Poe Society of Baltimore, www.eapoe.org

www.fyodordostoevsky.com

www.woodyallenband.com

www.stephenking.com

www.online-literature.com/dumas

www.cnn.com

www.online-literature.com/kipling/

www.nationalgeographic.com/grimm/article.html

www.randomhouse.com/kvpa/eastonellis

www.peterbenchley.com.

www.uselessknowledge.com
www.ianwatson.info/news.html
www.ltolstoy.com
www.online-literature.com/gertrude-atherton
www.sehinton.com

U.S. PRESIDENTS
WHERE WE GOT THIS STUFF

Beschloss, Michael. *The Presidents*. New York: Ibooks, 2000.

Boller, Paul F. *Presidential Anecdotes*. New York: Oxford University Press, 1996.

Boller, Paul F. *Presidential Wives: An Anecdotal History*. New York: Oxford University Press, 1988.

Caroli, Betty Boyd. "Jacqueline Kennedy." In *American First Ladies*, ed. Lewis L. Gould. New York & London: Garland Publishing, 1996.

Furman, Bess. *White House Profile: A Social History of the White House, Its Occupants and Its Festivities*. Indianapolis: Bobs-Merrill, 1951.

Hunt, Gaillard. *The Life of James Madison*. New York: Russell & Russell, 1968.

Johnson, Paul. A History of the American People. HarperPerennial: New York, 1997.

Lamb, Brian. *Who's Buried in Grant's Tomb? A Tour of Presidential Gravesites*. New York: PublicAffairs, 2000.

Loewen, James W. *Lies Across America*. New York: Touchstone Books, 1999.

——. *Lies My Teacher Told Me*. New York: Touchstone Books, 1999.

Morse, John T. Jr. *John Quincy Adams*. New York & London: Chelsea House, 1980.

O'Brian, Cormac. *Secret Lives of the U.S. Presidents*. Philadelphia: Quirk Books, 2004.

Perret, Geoffrey. *Ulysses S. Grant: Soldier and President*. New York: Random House, 1997.

Pessen, Edward. *The Log Cabin Myth*. New Haven: Yale University Press, 1984.

Phillips, Kevin. *William McKinley*. New York: Times Books, 2003.

Reiger, Kurt and Richard Shenkman. *One-Night Stands with American History*. New York: Perennial Press, 2003.

Roosevelt, James. *My Parents*. Chicago: Playboy Press, 1976.

Sievers, Harry J. *Benjamin Harrison: Hoosier President*. New York: The Bobbs-Merril Company, Inc, 1968.

Winkler, H. Donald. *Lincoln's Ladies*. Nashville: Cumberland House Press, 2004.

WE ALSO USED THESE SOURCES:

www.allpresidents.org
www.americanpresident.org/history
www.historybuff.com/presidents
www.presidentsusa.net

http://urbanlegends.about.com
www.suite101.com
www.thelincolnmuseum.org
www.civil-liberties.com/factoids
www.apa.org/releases/presidents.html
www.hoover.nara.gov
www.whitehouse.gov/history
www.calvin-coolidge.org
www.archives.gov/exhibit_hall/tokens_and_treasures/tokens_and_treasures
    _home.html
http://archives.cnn.com
www.u-s-history.com
www.acfnewsource.org/art/poli_memorabilia.html
www.pbs.org
http://statelibrary.dcr.state.nc.us/nc/bio/public/johnson.htm
www.apgrolier.com
www.geocities.com/presfacts/bush.html
http://en.wikipedia.org/wiki/Gesture
www.geocities.com/presfacts/clinton.html
http://encarta.msn.com/list_uspresidents/10_Things_You_Didnt_Know_About_U_S_Presiden
    ts.html
www.cyberbee.com/campaign/music.html
http://www.mackwhite.com/dictator.html
http://www.geocities.com/ultrastupidneal/Knowledge-Fact-President.html
http://www.divasthesite.com/Political_Divas/Trivia/Trivia_Eleanor_Roosevelt.htm

ABOUT THE AUTHOR

Camille Smith Platt is a freelance writer and the editor of *Chattanooga Christian Family* magazine. A graduate of the Samford University Department of Journalism and Mass Communication, she has also done research and writing for national trivia magazine *mental_floss* and Birmingham lifestyle magazine *PORTICO*. Her love-hate relationship with trivia stems from a fascination of quirky knowledge and a lifetime of always being stumped. She and her husband, Daniel, live in Chattanooga, Tennessee.